Miraculous Response

Doing Popular Religion in
Contemporary China

Miraculous Response

Doing Popular Religion in
Contemporary China

Adam Yuet Chau

STANFORD UNIVERSITY PRESS

Stanford, California 2006

Stanford University Press
Stanford, California
© 2006 by the Board of Trustees of the
Leland Stanford Junior University

Library of Congress Cataloging-in-Publication Data

Chau, Adam Yuet.
    Miraculous response : doing popular religion in
contemporary China / Adam Yuet Chau.
        p. cm.
    Includes bibliographical references and index.
    ISBN 0-8047-5160-9 (cloth : alk. paper)
    1. Shaanxi Sheng (China)—Religion. 2. Shaanxi Sheng
(China)—Social conditions. 3. Religion and culture—
China—Shaanxi Sheng. I. Title.
BL1945.S52C43 2005
299.5'1'095143—dc22

                                        2005009492

Printed in the United States of America
Original Printing 2005
Last figure below indicates year of this printing:
15   14   13   12   11   10   09   08   07   06

Typeset at Stanford University Press in 10/13 Sabon

TO MY PARENTS

Contents

Maps, Table, and Figure

Photographs

Acknowledgments

First and foremost, I thank the people of Shaanbei for their warm hospitality. The members of the Shenmu and Zizhou county opera troupes were wonderful. The people of Longwanggou and surrounding villages (especially Batawan) are the best informants and friends an ethnographer can hope for. A few individuals in Shaanbei deserve special acknowledgments. Gao Changtian, Professor of History at the Yan'an University (Yanda), was my first host in Shaanbei in the summer of 1995. During each of my research trips to Shaanbei, Professor Gao went out of his way to assist me. Many doors were opened thanks to Professor Gao's introductions. Zhang Junyi of Zizhou County, writer and local historian, helped me in innumerable ways. Mandur (Driver Zhang of Longwanggou) and Feifei (Zhang Zhifei), both of Batawan Village, and their families provided warm *kang*, bowls of delicious millet and bean gruel, and cozy sociability. Feifei served as my language tutor and informal research assistant; he and his grandmother, my "second aunt," taught me many earthy Shaanbeihua expressions. Temple boss Wang Kehua (Lao Wang, or "Old" Wang) at Longwanggou (the Dragon King Valley) welcomed and hosted me at the Black Dragon King Temple during my yearlong dissertation research. He kindly provided me with not only a room in the temple dormitory building but also the most favorable research environment at Longwanggou. Without Lao Wang's kindness and generosity this project would not have been possible.

I thank Professor Yang Shengmin of the Central Nationalities University in Beijing for having pointed my way to Shaanbei. He hosted me on numerous occasions when I passed through Beijing, for which I am grate-

ful. I am indebted to Dr. Luo Hongguang of the Chinese Academy of Social Sciences for being a host, adviser, and trusted friend. Dr. Luo introduced me to Longwanggou's temple boss Lao Wang. Because the people
of Longwanggou believed that "Hongguang's friend is our friend," they
received me with open arms. Dr. Luo served as my academic adviser in
China, generously shared his work on Shaanbei with me, and provided
invaluable guidance concerning my project from its inception. Many
ideas in this book resulted from discussions with Dr. Luo over the years.
He and other members of his family, Dr. Jiang Yan and Lulu, provided
me with a home away from home whenever I went through Beijing. Even
though I did not officially affiliate with either the Institute of Ethnology
of the Central Nationalities University or the Institute of Sociology of the
Chinese Academy of Social Sciences, both institutions provided needed
logistic help. For this help I thank Professor Yang and Dr. Luo again.
Other *qianbei*, colleagues, and friends in Beijing who welcomed me and
listened to my ideas include Guo Yuhua, Pan Jiao, and Zhang Haiyang,
among others. I also want to thank the few former sent-down youths I interviewed in Beijing.

I owe my greatest gratitude to my graduate school principal advisers
and mentors Arthur P. Wolf (Chair of my dissertation committee) and
Hill Gates. In the beginning of my graduate career they opened my eyes
to the exciting and expansive worlds of China studies and anthropology,
and over the years they have provided me with both intellectual and personal nurturance. As the third member of my dissertation committee, Andrew G. Walder was a wonderful critic and supporter. All three have
served as models of high standards in scholarship.

Many other people at Stanford deserve my sincere thanks for having
contributed to my learning and well-being. Bernard Faure helped me see
the link between anthropological and religious studies approaches to the
study of popular religion. I also learned from many other teachers: Ha-
rumi Befu, George Collier, Jane Collier, Carol Delaney, Joan Fujimura,
Akhil Gupta, Purnima Mankekar, Donald Moore, Hayden White, and
Sylvia Yanagisako, among others. The staff of the Department of Anthropology, especially Ellen Christensen, Beth Bashore, and Shelly Coughlan,
steered me through the graduate program with timely assistance and wise
counsel. The staff of the Center for East Asian Studies, especially Connie
Chin and Shen Xiaohong, and the librarians of the Hoover East Asian
Collection, especially Alberta Wang and Mark Tam, helped me in countless ways. People in my cohort were always there to support and help me;

Erich Fox Tree and Jen Roth-Gordon deserve special mention. The first drafts of a number of chapters of the book were attempted at a dissertation seminar. I thank members of the seminar for their valuable critique. I want to thank my undergraduate teachers at Williams College, especially my adviser David Edwards, Carol Benedict, Jeanne Bergman, Jonathan von Kowallis, and Angela Zito, who encouraged me to pursue an academic career in China anthropology. Other teachers from whom I learned much include Michael F. Brown, George T. Crane, Robert Jackall, Peter Just, and Philip Kasinitz.

Thanks are also due to the following scholars for having discussed ideas with me and shown interest in my project: Catherine Bell, Uradyn Bulag, Ursula-Angelika Cedzich, Kenneth Dean, Arif Dirlik, Stevan Harrell, Jun Jing, David Jordan, Xin Liu, Richard Madsen, Jean Oi, Ellen Oxfeld, Elizabeth J. Perry, Frank Pieke, P. Steven Sangren, Gary Seaman, James L. Watson, Rubie S. Watson, Robert P. Weller, Yunxiang Yan, and Yu Kuang-hung, among others.

I thank the friends who in one way or another sustained me over the years: Au Kin-cheung, Genevieve Bell, Chan Kai-tai, Magnus Fiskesjö, Ho Kwok-keung, Norman Lui, Arzoo Osanloo, Nikolai Ssorin-Chaikov, Mark Swislocki, Phoenix Wang, Scott Wilson, Mei Zhan, Zhen Zhang, and many others.

Some ideas that appear in this book were presented at the Center for East Asian Studies at Stanford University, panels at annual meetings of the American Anthropological Association, a CHIME conference in Prague, the Center for Chinese Studies at UC Berkeley, the University of Oregon in Eugene, and the International Conference on the Politics of Religion in China organized by Yoshiko Ashiwa and David Wank. I thank the people who invited me, the organizers, fellow participants, and audience members.

I gratefully acknowledge the following agencies and organizations for having funded my research and writing. The Mellon Foundation's Summer Research Grant, administered by the Department of Anthropology, allowed me to conduct preliminary research in Shaanbei in the summer of 1995. The Center for East Asian Studies' Women in Asia Research Grant brought me back to Shaanbei for another summer's preliminary research in 1996. The Mellon Foundation's Bridge Grant, administered also by the Department of Anthropology, enabled me to begin my dissertation research in early summer of 1997. The yearlong (1997–98) dissertation research was supported by a Small Grant for Dissertation Research from the Wenner-Gren Foundation for Anthropological Research and a Graduate Fellowship from the Committee on Scholarly Communications with China (CSCC), with funds from the United States Information Agency, administered by the American Council of Learned Societies. The first year of dissertation write-up was supported by a Mellon Foundation dissertation write-up grant, administered by the Department of Anthropology. A Young Scholars Award from the China Times Cultural Foundation sustained me during the second year of write-up. The final revisions of this book were done when I was an An Wang Postdoctoral Fellow at the Fairbank Center for East Asian Research, Harvard University.

Some portions of this book have first appeared as articles in *The Journal of Chinese Religions* (Chau 2003), *Asian Anthropology* (Chau 2004), and *Modern China* (Chau 2005). I thank the editors and reviewers of these journals and the publishers for permission to use materials for this book.

Robert Weller and the other reviewer (anonymous) of the book manuscript gave many invaluable comments and suggestions. Most appreciated was their encouraging me to deepen the theoretical engagements in the book to make it useful not only for readers interested in China Studies but also for those with comparativist interests. Paul Katz gave several chapters of the book a critical reading during the last stage of revision. The book is much stronger thanks to his detailed and learned comments and suggestions. Christina Gilmartin lent a much appreciated helping hand when I prepared the index.

Thanks are due to members of the Stanford University Press for bringing this book to publication: senior editor Muriel Bell, associate editor Carmen Borbon-Wu, production editor John Feneron, and others. Muriel's encouragement and support were particularly crucial. I thank Louise Herndon for copyediting and Bill Nelson for making the maps.

I thank my family members for their nurturance and encouragement: my parents, who are in Hong Kong, my sister, who is in Australia, my paternal grandparents, who are in Shanghai, and my parents-in-law, who are in Kyoto. I especially want to thank my grandfather Zhou Tuimi, calligrapher and poet. His erudition in matters of Classical Chinese has always been an inspiration. Last but not least, I thank Hideko Mitsui for her good humor and good sense, and her intellectual companionship.

None of the above-mentioned people or institutions are responsible for the interpretations or any shortcomings in the book.

A Note on Units of Measurement, Romanization, and Dates

All monetary units in this book appear as Chinese dollars (*yuan*) unless otherwise indicated. In 1997 and 1998 the official renminbi—U.S. dollar exchange rate was about 8.10 yuan = 1 U.S. dollar. One Chinese mile (*li*) = ½ kilometer (distances in this book are described either in kilometers or *li*, depending on the context); one Chinese *jin* = ½ kilogram.

The *pinyin* system of romanization of Mandarin Chinese is used for most Chinese expressions, e.g. (*miaohui*). Specifically Shaanbei dialect expressions are transliterated into pinyin and are indicated with an "S," e.g. (S. *shouku*). When the Shaanbei expression is the same as that in Mandarin but with only slight difference in pronunciation, I romanize the expression in standard Mandarin.

Most dates in this book are in the lunar calendar count, following the customary usage of most Shaanbei people, especially when the dates of temple festivals are concerned. Instead of writing "the third of the third month" or "the thirteenth of the sixth month" I have chosen to represent the dates as "Third Month Third" and "Sixth Month Thirteenth" to try to capture the flavor of the Chinese original, i.e., *sanyue san* and *liuyue shisan*. Dates that stand for special occasions such as temple festivals and traditional calendrical festivals are capitalized.

Miraculous Response

Doing Popular Religion in
Contemporary China

Introduction

> The gods were erected by peasants. When the right time comes, the
> peasants themselves will throw away these gods with their own
> hands.
> —Mao Zedong

Research Questions and Overview of Main Themes

The reform era (from the early 1980s onward) of the People's Republic of China has witnessed a massive reemergence of ostensibly traditional
Chinese folk beliefs and practices. For more than thirty years the Communist state had tried to eradicate cultural expressions of the old, pre-
Communist China, stigmatizing them as superstitious or "feudalistic,"
while building a new, socialist culture. Then Mao died, and the economic
reforms began, accompanied by significant ideological relaxation. It is in
this historical context that the folk cultural revivalism phenomenon is
happening: all of a sudden people are busy rebuilding or renovating temples, ancestral halls, and graves that were torn down during the Cultural
Revolution, reconstructing family genealogies that were burnt by the Red
Guards, reenacting long suppressed rituals around births, weddings, and
deaths, going to temple festivals, reading ritual handbooks and consulting fortune-tellers and geomancers, praying for male babies, or simply
thinking feudalistic thoughts (see Wolf 1996). It is clearly not yet the time
for the peasants to throw away the gods with their own hands, as Mao
had hoped. What if the peasants want to keep the gods?

If many Chinese peasants today are engaged in popular religious practices that are traditional in appearance, one would like to know: *What
makes this repertoire of traditional beliefs and practices compelling for
people today? How have various factors combined to enable the revival
of religious expressions that are often still prohibited by law?* This study
attempts to answer these questions by providing an ethnography of the
revival and social organization of one particular temple in rural Shaan-

bei, north-central China (see map 1). Through this case study it explores the more general and widespread cultural logics and sociopolitical processes underlying the revival of popular religion in reform-era China.[1]

One of the many simplistic explanations of the religious boom in reform-era China is that, disenchanted with the bankruptcy of Communist ideologies, the Chinese people feel "spiritually empty" and therefore want to return to traditional religious practices (or to seek new spiritual solace, as evidenced by the rapid growth of the number of Christian converts). This study emphatically argues against this kind of monocausal explanation for a phenomenon as complex as popular religious revival. My research shows that popular religious revivalism is the result of many factors. At the core of Chinese popular religion is the concept of magical efficacy (*ling*), which is conceived of as a particular deity's miraculous response (*lingying*) to the worshiper's request for divine assistance (granting a son, granting magical medicine, bringing rain, resolving a dilemma through divination, granting prosperity, etc.). However, these miraculous responses are socially constructed: it is people and their actions that enable the establishment of human-deity relations and interactions. Shaanbei people "do" popular religion not only by praying and presenting offerings to the deities but by building temples, organizing and participating in temple festivals, sponsoring and watching local operas, making and buying incense and spirit paper money, bribing local state officials, networking with other temples and other institutions, fighting over temple leadership positions, and even planting trees and building schools. The revival of popular religious institutions and activities thus illustrates the coming together of many social forces: the political ambition of local activists, the regulatory and paternalistic interventions of local state agencies, the economic interests of temples, merchants, and related specialists (including folk musicians and opera performers), the collective religiosity and fun-seeking spirit of the worshipers, and the increasingly frequent translocal linkages between social actors in local communities and outside actors. An adequate interpretation of popular religious revival has to take into consideration all the different social actors' desires and actions.

Even though the revival of popular religion is a very complex phenomenon, temple-based religious activities are the most exciting and popular in Shaanbei. According to a recent survey conducted by Shaanbei local folklorists, the number of temples that have been revived in Shaanbei exceeds ten thousand. Because of the increasing prosperity of the area, the scale of temples and temple festivals is often many times larger than that in the past. Temples typically sponsor and "stage" a wide range of folk cultural activities such as performances by folk dance troupes (*yangge*), music bands and storytellers, folk opera, "offering presentation" processions, animal sacrifices, and temple festivals. It is not an exaggeration to characterize temples as the "motor" of popular religious revivals and a major carrier of folk cultural traditions. Therefore this book focuses on temple-based popular religious revivals in depth in order to bring to light the processes and mechanisms of the social organization of folk culture in reform-era Shaanbei.

By way of anticipating the arguments in this book, I will briefly lay out the many intertwined sociopolitical factors that enabled popular religious revivalism in Shaanbei. *First*, temple associations are a key folk social institution that is pivotal in producing and reproducing popular religion. *Second*, popular religious activities such as temple festivals provide the loci for expressing enduring peasant values and desires such as hosting and mutual help. The modes of "producing" popular religion entail replicating and extending the principles and mechanisms of the organization of peasant secular life, which enabled quick revitalization of popular religion even after severe suppression. *Third*, village-level local activists seize upon temples and temple associations as a valuable political, economic, and symbolic resource. The reappearance of temples as sites of power generation and contestation is accompanied by the emergence of a new kind of village- and township-level local elite. The story of a temple boss and his political strategies illustrates the shifting sociopolitical terrain in contemporary rural China. *Fourth*, shifting priorities compel the local state to regulate and even to profit from popular religion rather than suppress it, thus giving temples space to thrive. Different local state agencies interact with temple associations and temple bosses, and this interaction indicates a new kind of state-society relationship in the reform era.

Let me now provide a brief overview of the intertwined themes of the book: 1) popular religion and folk cultural revivalism; 2) agrarian political culture and agrarian public sphere; and 3) the local state and shifting state-society relations.

Popular Religion and Folk Cultural Revivalism

This book investigates the post-Mao revival and the social organization of a dragon king temple in a place called the Dragon King Valley

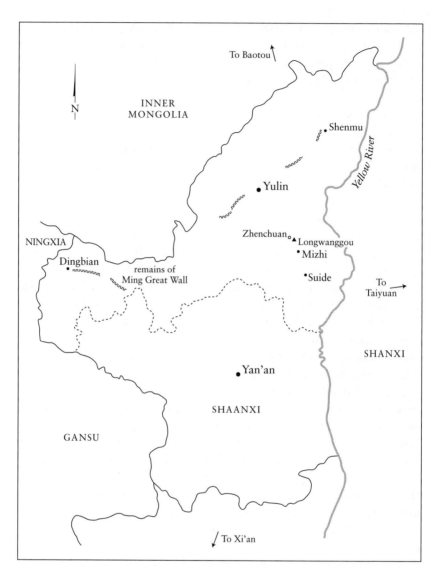

MAP 1. Shaanbei, Showing Yan'an and Yulin Prefectures and Location of Longwanggou

(Longwanggou) in the Shaanbei area (northern Shaanxi Province) of north-central China.[2] Since the early 1980s, the Heilongdawang (Black Dragon King) Temple has evolved into what I call the Longwanggou Complex, which includes, in addition to the main temple, two subsidiary halls, a primary school, and a large-scale reforestation project. The core of the book is a case study of the social organization of the Longwanggou Complex. Based on ethnographic materials gathered in one locale, this book follows the tradition of local studies in anthropology. However, it is neither a community study nor a study of a temple cult. Rather, it reveals the sociocultural processes that enable folk cultural revivalism in contemporary China and examines the impact these revivals have on the agrarian sociopolitical landscape.

Scholars of Chinese religion have customarily distinguished the localized, textually-light popular religious cults from the translocal, universalizing and textually-heavy elite traditions of Daoism, Buddhism, and Confucianism (Faure 1987; Yang 1961; see also Teiser 1995).[3] Like all dragon king cults in agrarian China, the cult of the Heilongdawang is a popular religious cult *par excellence*, despite its recent development into a regional pilgrimage center in Shaanbei and its even more recent inclusion into the officially recognized Daoist institutional structure.

Even though I will discuss the nature of Shaanbei people's religiosity and some of the religious activities that take place at Longwanggou, the emphasis of the book is on more than the *religious* aspects of popular religion. For example, I hope to highlight the temple organization that animates Longwanggou as a *folk social institution* that sprang back to life during the reform era. The temple association, though a structurally simple folk social institution, is nevertheless extremely versatile in its capacities. It enables the building and maintenance of the temple, staging the annual temple festivals, coordinating and interacting with other institutions such as other temple associations, opera troupes, folk music bands, local state bureaus, and even foreign NGOs. These different institutions all have different logics of operation, but somehow they have worked together to enable folk cultural revivalism. This study will show that the temple association plays a crucial role in staging Shaanbei "folk culture" (e.g., temple festivals), expanding folk cultural space, and affecting the local sociopolitical terrain.

Few China observers today would deny the fact of folk cultural revivals, i.e., the reappearance of a repertoire of traditional practices. However, some scholars point out that though many of these practices assume a traditional form, they carry meanings different from those of the past, and therefore we should not mistake the return of these practices as a revival of unadulterated tradition. For example, Helen Siu argues that Chinese local society has been so thoroughly transformed by the monopolization of state power that folk tradition has been irrevocably "diluted" and transformed, and that traditional practices we see today are "cultural fragments recycled under new circumstances" (Siu 1989b: 134). Using the example of a female shaman practicing in the reform era who employs many Maoist jargons and imageries in her exorcist ritual, Emily Chao expresses a similar view on the immense impact of the socialist era on tradition (Chao 2000). She argues that this kind of "ritual bricolage" and the audience's ambivalent reception of it only reveal that reform-era rural China (in her case among the Naxi minority people of Yunnan) no longer has "a singular all-encompassing belief system" (ibid.: 506).

This perspective points out the differences between "traditional practices" in the reform era and those before the Maoist era. It echoes the "invention of tradition" argument influential in recent anthropological studies (Hobsbawm and Ranger 1983) and warns us against taking cultural innovations as continuations of past traditions. However, this perspective might lead one to assume that what existed before Maoist suppressions was a tradition that was more coherent and authentic. Yet such an apparent coherence was equally a result of "inventions" and efforts of "recycling." Different cultural inventions slowly cohered into a "tradition" or "traditions" (e.g., Buddhism or Daoism or a particular deity cult) over hundreds of years, but the constituent parts can always be broken apart, recombined, and reformulated into new traditions (hence the simultaneous novelty and traditionalism of new religious movements such as Falungong). The "feudal tradition" that came to be suppressed or destroyed during anti-traditionalist campaigns during the Maoist period and reinvented in what appears to be a piecemeal or haphazard manner in the reform era is a complex, dynamic, ever-changing cluster of institutions, practitioners and consumers, knowledge and practices fully amenable to innovations, inventions, and reinventions all the time. Popular religion is "traditional" in precisely this sense. It allows for individual innovation, collective experimentation, and probably plenty of failures (e.g., Chao's female shaman). It can also endure suppressions, lie dormant for a long time, go underground, minimalize, and reemerge in new forms in response to new historical conditions. It is undeniable that religious traditions in China in general suffered enormously under the rationalist regimes of the twentieth century. Yet suppressions also cause the dispersal of religious personnel and knowledge and the disaggregation of coherent traditions that prepare the ground for the recombination of different elements and a freer space for innovation. The rapid growth of different qigong sects with innovative, syncretist teachings after Mao's death attests to the vitality of Chinese religious traditions.

The form (organizational framework) of temple-based popular religion is relatively simple: there are no elaborate and symbolically complicated rituals; there are no intricate theological maneuvers; there is typically no priesthood. One can even characterize popular religious temples as *minimalist religion.* However, even though the form is simple, the contents need not be. Under unfavorable conditions, popular religion survives in its minimalist, bare-bones state, almost hibernating. Elaborate temples and statues are replaced by secret home altars and small, carved statuettes; long chants accompanied by bells and drums are replaced by a few muffled murmurs (see DuBois 2005: 172). Under favorable conditions, however, popular religion expands, elaborates, and no degree of exuberance is unimaginable. The Heilongdawang Temple has developed from a small, makeshift shrine in the early 1980s to the multibuilding, multifunctional Longwanggou Complex of today. Many of Taiwan's temples and their festivals also attest to popular religion's expansiveness. Temples, temple oracles, temple associations, temple festivals, opera troupes, worship, and pilgrimage, all go together to form a cluster of mutually constituting and reinforcing popular religious cultural idioms or elements. Because of this close inter-connectedness, the revival of one cultural idiom necessarily sparked off a chain reaction of the revival of the other cultural idioms. Throughout Chinese history, popular religion has waned and waxed, minimalized and elaborated, and what we have witnessed in the past half century is simply one cycle in the long course of its changing fortunes.

Some scholars have argued that the return of popular religion during the reform era signals the strength of local communities to reassert their autonomy and to resist the state (see Feuchtwang 2000). The return of lineage power in many parts of southeastern China is the most obvious example; so is the return of village or community-wide festivals. Wang Mingming, who conducted fieldwork in southern Fujian, points out that the revival of community-wide ritual actions indicates a desire on the part of the villagers to rediscover the cultural and historical meanings of local communities, which had been neglected or attacked during the collectivist era. The rotation of responsibilities among villages to organize the annual temple festival renews villagers' sense of locality and communal solidarity and mutual cooperation (Wang 1996: 70, 76). Ann Anagnost argues that the rebuilding of temples and the procession of local tutelary deities are instances of local communities' symbolically reclaiming their own space from the homogenizing, totalizing party-state. The state in turn periodically repossesses these spaces during anti-superstition campaigns; thus the state and local communities are engaged in a protracted "politics of ritual displacement" (Anagnost 1994: 222–23). For the local communities to be negotiating with and resisting the state at all is proof of the resurgence of communal power during the reform era. Based on her fieldwork in rural Wenzhou in Zhejiang Province, Mayfair Yang (2000) argues that local ritual traditions operate on an "archaic" economic logic of ritual expenditure that not only resists the state's developmental economic regime but also the incursions of global capitalism. Yang also emphasizes the importance of spatial negotiations with the state and Capital in the revival of religious sites in the reform era (Yang 2004).

Perhaps the best example of treating popular religion as communal resistance is Jun Jing's study of the revival during the reform era of a Confucius lineage hall/temple in a village in Gansu Province (Jing 1996, 2000). The Kong-surnamed village was subjected to grave social suffering during the Maoist era. The villagers were politically persecuted because of their implication in regional interethnic violence and sectarian movements and their connection to the arch-symbol of the feudal era, Confucius. They were also forcibly relocated from their village because of the building of a large hydroelectric dam nearby and were poorly compensated. During the reform era, the villagers sought political and moral-cultural redress by rebuilding the village lineage temple as well as other deity temples. At the center of this revival movement was the politically charged process of retrieving memories of the community prior to its destruction.

My own study builds on the insights of these scholars. However, I have tried to focus even more on the state-society interface. Too much emphasis on communal resistance diverts attention from other important aspects of popular religious revivals such as the actions of the local state and the power claims of local elites, and the frequent mutual accommodation, negotiation, and collusion between local state agents and local elites. In the local world, state and society are complexly imbricated.

While popular religion does have the potential to serve, and sometimes does serve, as a vehicle of popular resistance against the state, I suggest the political implications of the revival of popular religion are often more complex than the resistance perspective can fully capture.

One aspect of popular religion often neglected by China anthropologists is that of temples as providers of magical efficacy as a symbolic good (but see Gates 1987; Moskowitz 2001). Scholars of Japanese religion have recently highlighted the service provider aspects of contemporary Japanese religion (Hardacre 1997; Reader and Tanabe Jr. 1998). Much of popular religion in China too involves the provision of spiritual services (e.g., exorcism, protective talismans, divination, spiritual counseling such as fortune-telling) and the payment for these services (on the spot or delayed, e.g., in the form of vow-fulfillment). This service provider perspective points to the undeniable fact that religion is business in addition to involving beliefs and sacred symbols. It also brings our attention to analyzing the *social organization* of popular religious enterprises. Of course, temples are not merely businesses; yet they can hardly survive without a "business model" (i.e., ways of generating income). Recognizing the economic aspects of popular religion should not be seen as economic reductionism or as cheapening the religious experience of my informants; rather, not recognizing them and limiting our understanding of religious activities as purely "religious" or "spiritual" would risk another kind of reductionism.

Agrarian Political Culture and Agrarian Public Sphere

Since the 1940s many anthropologists have studied both the characteristics of, and changes in, peasant societies.[4] Anthropologists who studied China confronted an agrarian empire whose large rural sector demanded scholarly attention. Even though the agrarian nature of mainland China has diminished significantly in the past century, it still looms large on the national sociopolitical landscape. Yet the Chinese agrarian society of today differs considerably from those of the Maoist era (1949–1980), the Republican era (1911–1949), and the late imperial era (Ming, Qing dynasties). A long list of scholars, including social historians, political scientists, anthropologists, and sociologists, have traced its various transformations: the nature of peasant rebellions, peasant support of the Communist Revolution, the Land Reform and its consequences, collectivization and Maoist rural politics, the peasants' role in de-collectivization, and reform-era rural politics. In a word, scholarly attention has been mainly trained on the thoroughly *political* nature of state-peasant relationships, especially during the post–1949 socialist era. The imagery is one in which the state attempted to capture the peasantry for its political purposes and the various peasant actors at various historical moments welcomed or resisted these state initiatives.

Even though my study is situated squarely within this tradition of scholarship on Chinese agrarian society, its focus on social aspects of popular religion also relies on another scholarly tradition, the anthropology of Taiwan, in which studies of popular religion occupy a place of honor. Among other concerns, studies of popular religion in Taiwan often highlight the *politics* of popular religious organizations and rituals (notably Ahern 1981a, 1981b; Bosco 1994; Gates 1996, 2000; Katz 2003; Rohsenow 1973; Sangren 2003; Seaman 1978; Weller 1985, 1987b, 1994). Political factors such as the state, ethnicity, class, and local factionalism are the mainstay of these analyses. As the PRC undergoes political economic "liberalization," its transformational trajectory in some ways resembles that of Taiwan in the past half century. Therefore it is important to see whether popular religion in the PRC plays a similar or different role in articulating, among other things, the interests and desires of various social actors in agrarian society. I argue that the revival of popular religious organizations does not denote simply "people power" reclaiming power from a previously hegemonic socialist state; rather, these folk social institutions contribute to the formation of a new power field in which the local state interacts with local society in new ways and with new rules.

Studying the revival of folk rituals and temple communities in southern Fujian, Kenneth Dean contends that the communities created by these ritual systems, e.g., the Three in One cult network, are "disruptive communities" because they are irreducibly local and multitudinous (Dean 1997: 177). Ritual actions induct individuals into communities of believer-practitioners, and these "multiple public spheres" not only challenge the state's cultural and ideological strictures but also provide a case against the Habermasian concept of a singular bourgeois public sphere which supposedly bridges the state and society (ibid.: 191). With rising popular appeal among the rural masses, popular religion is in the process of regaining its institutional significance within what might be called the *agrarian public sphere* in rural China. The contexts of popular religious activities such as temple festivals, spirit medium séances, and funeral and wedding banquets encourage and facilitate a kind of sociality radically different from that of the Maoist era, where political campaigns, militarized organizations, collectivist production drives, and class struggle dictated villagers' social lives (see Solomon 1971). Instead of responding to state-imposed political ideals and campaign goals, villagers today are engaged in social interactions based on kinship or community obligations and responsibilities, a desire to seek fun and excitement, or otherwise mostly personal and familial concerns.

As opposed to the bourgeois public sphere discussed by Jürgen Habermas in the context of Western European sociopolitical development in the 18th and 19th centuries, the agrarian public sphere in today's rural China is not characterized by a conscious and open engagement with issues of politics or government or the formation of a "public opinion" (even though it has such potentials); it is "public" in form and expression but is not "for the Public" in the sense of ideological orientation toward the greater good of the "imagined community" of nation, state, or some such larger collectivity. In the idealized world of the salon and the café, members of the Western bourgeoisie discussed and debated public issues and gradually formed a public (understood as a *political* public) between the state and the private individuals and families (see Keane 1998). In this model of civil society, "rational" communication is key: ideas were exchanged and debated. However, worshipers at temple festivals typically do not engage in political discussions (or any "reasoned discourse"), and the ephemeral nature of temple festivals prevents the worshipers from forming a viable public. There have been isolated instances of communal protests that have been reinforced by common membership in worship communities, but these tend to be locale-based protests that do not have the potential for wider development (see Jing 2000). Robert Weller (1999) expresses doubt that religious communities based on territorial cults could ever become the basis for forming a larger civil society. It is too early to say in which directions temple-based cultural forms might evolve in China. Given the significant role popular religion plays in Taiwanese politics today, similar developments might also occur in the PRC.

In the past decade or so the idea of "minjian" (civic, nongovernmental) gained salience in public discourses in the PRC. While the idea of "people" (*renmin*) still retains a lot of currency (as object to be acted upon by the state or to be served by "civil servants"), the idea of minjian points to an expanding public sphere where citizens act upon their own initiatives (see Yang 1994). Temple associations are minjian organizations that spring from the autochthonous needs of different sectors of society (see Brook 1997; Fukao 1998). A temple association is a condensed and visible form of communal power of a particular locale. This communal power is manifested in the grandeur of the temple and the scale of the temple festival. As one of the most vibrant folk social institutions, temple associations have played a crucial role in expanding the folk cultural space and agrarian public sphere in reform-era China (see Gates 2000).

China scholars have long recognized the crucial role the local elite play in mediating the larger polity (imperial state or modern state) and the local peasant communities (Duara 1988a; Esherick and Rankin 1990; Friedman et al. 1991; Hsiao 1960). Local elites occupy positions of prominence in local society because of their wealth, formal political position, political influence, social connections, moral authority, education, ritual knowledge, experience, leadership abilities, or a combination of these factors. Their strategies of maintaining an elite status across generations involve the conversion between symbolic capital (e.g., education, imperial degree titles) and other forms of capital (land, business, political connections, etc.) (see Bourdieu 1984). Local elites are usually the most aware of, and responsive to, outside forces. They tend to desire to occupy local leadership positions especially when these positions yield tangible or intangible dividends (e.g., extra income, prestige, opportunities to network with other local elites, etc.). For example, Gregory Ruf describes how the managing elites of the reform-era village enterprises in the Sichuan village he studied are comprised of the village Party secretary and his relatives and social intimates (Ruf 1998: 144). In my analysis, the local elite is comprised of village- and township-level local leaders who are often outside the formal state officialdom, even though they might be co-opted by the state in one way or another (e.g., being selected as a member of the county Political Consultative Conference).

One very interesting phenomenon in Shaanbei is that many temple leaders are current or former village Party secretaries. In many cases, Party secretaries are the most genuinely respected and knowledgeable members of the community, so their being elected to be temple bosses is not surprising. In other cases, they have become temple bosses because only they have the know-how and connections to the local state to negotiate with, for example, the local Religious Affairs Bureau. One may also speculate that during the reform period, the Party secretaries have lost a considerable amount of power and therefore they want to capture the popular religious sphere to compensate for their loss of power.

As soon as we understand popular religion as a local resource, similar to local enterprises, it becomes easier for us to see why certain members of a community are particularly enthusiastic about reviving and expanding local temples. These are people who are interested in reviving and capturing the popular religious sphere to build or augment their basis of local influence and authority. Such an interest is usually couched in terms of serving the deity or the community. For example, in Jun Jing's study of the revival of the Confucius Temple in the village in Gansu, the new temple managers (called vow-takers) are middle-aged or elderly male villagers most of whom had suffered political persecution and social discrimination during the Maoist era (Jing 1996: 21). Through the rebuilding of the temple and the reestablishment of rituals, these men reassert their authority as ritual specialists and the moral leadership roles denied to them in the previous era. In this book, I highlight the career of Lao Wang, the temple boss at Longwanggou, so as to delineate the changing character of the local elite, who build on and capture institutional resources in local society while reaching out to the state and other extra-local resources and sites to buttress their legitimacy and power.

Another category of social actors actively involved in popular religious revival is of course the many kinds of religious specialists (i.e., Daoist priests, geomancers, Buddhist monks, spirit mediums, fortune-tellers), who hire out their service for a fee. Because of their specialized training and higher literacy, these religious specialists are not so much local elites as local *cultural* elites. So instead of viewing the revival of popular religion as a common interest shared by an undifferentiated mass (peasant communities), we can unpack this mass and look at different social actors' different interests. Looking at the actions of local elite activists does not undermine the importance of popular religiosity, for without this latter element it would be impossible for the local elite to mobilize the support of the average villager.

The Local State and Shifting State-Society Relations

That popular religious institutions like Longwanggou can exist at all in the People's Republic of China today is not self-evident. The Chinese Communist Party that controls the state apparatuses is committed to an atheistic worldview. While for political purposes the party-state tolerates orthodox and "proper" Buddhism, Daoism, Islam, and Christianity as "recognized religions," cults for dragon kings and fertility goddesses are "feudal superstitions" and thus decidedly beyond the pale. Like hundreds of thousands of local temples throughout China, the Heilongdawang

Temple was destroyed during the early phase of the Cultural Revolution in 1966; yet, like countless other local temples, the Heilongdawang Temple was rebuilt almost as soon as the reform era began in the early 1980s. In 1998 the temple was even recognized by the local state as an official Daoist shrine, thus raising it to a new height of legitimacy, unthinkable a mere decade or so before.

Important to my account of the revival of folk social institutions such as Longwanggou is the analytical distinction between the two guises of the Chinese socialist state: the policy-making central state and the *local state* that implements and often bends the policies. In the reform era the local state has increased its administrative and fiscal autonomy considerably vis-à-vis the central state. Previous studies of the relationship between the state and popular religion have often stopped short of providing a picture of the behavior of the local state. The state does not act directly upon popular religion; rather, it is the local agents of the state who do. If left unpacked, "the state" tends to become reified. Similarly, "the people" (or "the community") might also risk being reified, especially when treated as "resisting," always presumably in a *collective* manner, the state's interference in their religious life. Neither the state nor the people are monolithic actors, and as far as popular religion is concerned, many different kinds of social actors and many different kinds of social actions and desires are involved. Recently some China scholars have tried to look beyond the central party-state and analyze the behavior of the local state (Blecher and Shue 1996; Esherick 1994; Oi 1989, 1999; Pieke 2004; Shue 1995; Siu 1990; Wank 1995, 1999), focusing on the realms of political actions and the economy. Because of its nested interest in the locale, the local state necessarily behaves differently than the central state. (I sometimes use "local state" as shorthand to refer to local state agents and agencies as a collectivity, but I do not intend to reify the local state. Just like the state, the local state is also an amalgam of administrative structures, political processes, policies, and crosscutting intentions and desires.)

In our story of Longwanggou the local state takes the forms of township (Zhenchuan), county (Yulin County), and prefecture (Yulin Prefecture) level government bureaus and bureaucrats. In this book I try to show, with the case of Longwanggou, that in Shaanbei the local state has entered into a new, more regulatory relationship with local society characterized by practical mutual dependence. I argue that the tolerance toward, and even encouragement of, popular religion by the local state is, among other things, an instance of local state protectionism, i.e., the local state's effort at providing an environment that fosters local social and economic welfare. In the eyes of the local state popular religious temples are also resources to be cherished and taken advantage of, e.g., taxing the merchants at temple festivals. One county government is necessarily going to protect its county's temples against those in other counties. My study thus contributes to the recent discussion of local state behavior and shifting state-peasant relations in reform-era China.

In order to survive and thrive, temple associations and temple bosses have to negotiate with different local state agencies and to accommodate official rent-seeking so as to secure different kinds of official endorsement and protection. In other words, as the agrarian public sphere expands, it necessarily has to accommodate local state penetration. Some scholars have argued that in China the growth of civil society is led and enabled as much as constrained by the state (Chamberlain 1993; Brook and Frolic 1997). Philip Huang (1993) has proposed the concept of "the third realm" to characterize the protean space that lies sandwiched between state and society and is subject to both processes of "state-ification" (i.e. state encroachment) from above and "societalization" (i.e. capture by societal forces) from below. Temple-based popular religious activities and the local state's involvement in endorsing these activities constitute an important part of this realm in today's Shaanbei (see also Dean 1998b; Katz 1995: 180–89).

Doing Fieldwork in Shaanbei

This book is based on materials collected during eighteen months of ethnographic fieldwork in Shaanbei between 1995 and 1998 (summers of 1995 and 1996 plus fourteen months in 1997 and 1998). I conducted the fieldwork on my own, without being accompanied by any officials. Being Chinese helped me avoid the bureaucratic red tape and official restrictions that often hinder foreign researchers. I deliberately did not seek out an official research or educational institution for formal affiliation because I knew the topic of my research, i.e. popular religion, could be quite sensitive and could bring unwanted trouble to my host institutions. I was extremely fortunate that the temple boss of Heilongdawang Temple, Lao Wang, took interest in my work and allowed me to use Longwanggou as my fieldwork base. The dormitory room at the temple became my home and workspace. The temple turned out to be an excellent base because things happened constantly. Given the Heilongdawang's popularity among Shaanbei people, I could literally sit at the temple and still be able to talk to people from all over Shaanbei and beyond. I could also visit neighboring villages and towns or go on extended trips to other Shaanbei locales whenever I wished. During the course of my fieldwork I ran into and talked to many local officials and police officers. I told them I was researching local folk customs and they were happy to leave me alone. As long as they were not told officially about my presence (e.g., through a letter of introduction from an official agency), they would not have to take responsibility for me if something went wrong. My affiliation with Longwanggou was often enough to guarantee that I could be safely accommodated (*meiwenti*, literally "no problem"). The legitimacy of Longwanggou and the status of Lao Wang provided the smooth acceptance of my prolonged presence in the local arena.

Even though the focus of my research was on the Heilongdawang Temple, I visited dozens more temples and their festivals. I traveled widely in multiple locales in Shaanbei, especially in the counties of Yulin, Shenmu, Mizhi, Zizhou, Hengshan, Suide, and Yan'an City. When speaking with informants I engaged them in casual conversations instead of conducting formal interviews. The thousands of Shaanbei people I encountered and talked with included temple officers, opera troupe members, cultural workers, educators, local officials, ritual specialists, and ordinary villagers and townspeople. For data collection, participant observation was as important as conversations with informants.

Even though I can call myself a "native anthropologist" because I am originally from China, rural China presented to me a world very different from the one I had known. Having grown up in Beijing and Hong Kong, I encountered rural China in a sustained manner for the first time during my fieldwork in Shaanbei. Shaanbei was very much culturally "Other" to me. I speak fluent Mandarin, the official language, which is comprehensible to most urban Shaanbei people but only partially comprehensible to Shaanbei peasants (thanks mostly to their increasing exposure to television programs). Shaanbei dialect (*Shaanbeihua*) belongs to the northern dialect group (from which Mandarin was derived), though it differs from Mandarin significantly. It required some effort to learn to understand Shaanbeihua, especially the rich repertoire of unique vocabulary.

Organization of the Book

Besides the introduction, this book has eleven chapters. In *Chapter Two* I present a survey of the history, society, and culture of Shaanbei as a region, emphasizing the social structure and organization of contemporary Shaanbei society (e.g., town and country, class and status groups, the village and the peasant family).

Chapter Three covers the general aspects of popular religion in Shaanbei. I first trace briefly the turbulent history of the fate of popular religion in Shaanbei in the 20th century. Then I outline the popular religious landscape in contemporary Shaanbei, including discussions of temples, temple associations, and religious specialists (e.g., spirit mediums and yinyang masters). In *Chapter Four* I analyze Shaanbei people's religiosity and examine the ways in which Shaanbei people construct the deities' magical efficacy. I examine the bureaucratic and personal models of conceiving and interacting with deities. By identifying different modalities of "doing" religion in China, I also provide a possible resolution to a well-known debate in the study of Chinese religions: is there one or more Chinese religions?

Chapter Five recounts the legends of the deity and presents snapshots of the history of the temple from the early Republican era, through the different phases of the Maoist era, and finally up to the present day. I introduce the concept of "text act" to characterize the extensive use of markers of textual and inscriptional legitimation at the temple.

In *Chapter Six* I describe the social organization of the temple complex and examine the ways the temple provisions the Black Dragon King's magical efficacy to worshipers. I examine the temple association as a folk social institution. I present the activities and organization of the temple complex in today's Longwanggou (e.g., temple finance, personnel). I look at the key to the rising popularity of the temple: the versatility and the efficient running of the temple association. I propose that we see temples as, among other things, providers of magical efficacy. In *Chapter Seven* I compare and contrast the organization of a funeral with that of a Longwanggou temple festival. I propose the concept of "event production" and argue that when Shaanbei people produce popular religious events such as funerals and temple festivals they mobilize a very basic set of principles and mechanisms. I suggest that the simplicity of the organizational structure underlies the ease with which popular religion is revived.

I also present "hosting" as a major cultural idiom in the organization of major peasant household events and temple festivals. *Chapter Eight* details the native concept of red-hot sociality (*honghuo*). I argue that temple festivals provide the ideal occasions for Shaanbei people to produce and share red-hot sociality, one of the most desirable states of being for social events. I also engage in a discussion of the political implications of peasants' desire for honghuo.

Chapter Nine tells the story of temple boss Lao Wang. I examine his rise to prominence in the local community as master craftsman, petty capitalist entrepreneur, peasant intellectual, and local elite. With the example of Lao Wang I try to elucidate the processes and mechanisms of the rise of a new kind of local elite in rural China. *Chapter Ten* deals with the ways in which popular religion is embedded in the larger agrarian political culture. I present examples of the articulation of temple politics and village politics in Longwanggou. I look at how the expansion of the temple has drastically changed the configuration of village power and authority structure and how village factionalism informs temple leadership struggles.

In *Chapter Eleven* I analyze the role the local state plays in the revival of popular religion in Shaanbei. I first discuss the dynamics between policy and practice in relation to "feudal superstitions." Then I outline the process through which Longwanggou interacted with, and gained approval from, different local state agencies, thus acquiring legitimacy and legality over time. I present and analyze two episodes of "rituals of legitimation" to show how temple boss Lao Wang harnessed power and legitimacy for both Longwanggou and himself. I end this chapter with a discussion of the interpenetration of politics and religion in the agrarian public sphere.

In *Chapter Twelve,* the concluding chapter, I revisit the central themes of the book and try to draw out some of the broader implications of the study.

Even though this is a study of China, I believe that many of the themes and concepts in the book will be of use to non-China specialists, especially those who work on the ethnography of the state, grassroots activism, the politics of legitimation, cultural production, civil society and the public sphere, popular religion, the role of religion in contemporary society, agrarian social change, post-socialism, and sociality. Particular conceptual and theoretical contributions that might interest comparatists include popular religion as idiom of communal hegemony (Chapter 4), text acts (Chapter 6), event productions (Chapter 7), red-hot sociality and rites of convergence (Chapter 8), agrarian public sphere (Chapters 8 and 11), local elites (Chapter 9), the local state and the politics of legitimation (Chapter 11).

CHAPTER TWO

Shaanbei History, Society, and Culture

Shaanbei as a Place and Shaanbei History

General Introduction

Shaanbei as a geographic area is not an official category in the PRC administrative hierarchy of nation, province, prefecture, county, township, and village. It is one of the three regions of Shaanxi Province customarily known as Shaanbei (northern Shaanxi), Guanzhong (middle Shaanxi), and Shaannan (southern Shaanxi), each characterized by distinct geographical and cultural features. Shaanbei lies on the northwest periphery of the so-called China proper. To the north it borders on the Ordos Desert, the alluvial plains of the Yellow River Loop (*hetao*), and the expansive steppes of Inner Mongolia. To the west it adjoins the Ningxia Hui Autonomous Region and Gansu Province with their many Chinese Muslim (*Hui*) communities. Toward the south the hilly loess plateau of Shaanbei flattens off into the densely populated Guanzhong Plain (Guanzhong literally meaning "within the pass"), the heartland of the so-called Qin culture, including the Shaanxi provincial capital Xi'an.[1] To the east Shaanbei is separated from Shanxi Province by the Yellow River. This has not prevented Shaanbei from being influenced profoundly by the so-called Jin culture of Shanxi, not least because most Shaanbei people are believed to be descendants of Shanxi immigrants.[2] In terms of customs and spoken language Shaanbei is largely an offshoot and peripheral part of the Shanxi/Jin cultural area with only modest influence from Qin culture and neighboring Muslims and Mongols. In terms of regional economic relations Shaanbei serves as an intermediary hinterland for the regional core of the northwest macroregion, centered on Xi'an of Shaanxi and Taiyuan of Shanxi, as formulated by G. William Skinner (1977: 214–15).

Today Shaanbei is administratively comprised of two prefectures (*diqu*): Yan'an Prefecture and Yulin Prefecture (see Map 1).[3] There are 13 counties in Yan'an Prefecture and 12 counties in Yulin; the prefectural capitals are Yan'an City and Yulin City respectively. The total territorial area of Shaanbei is 80,000 square kilometers, almost 40% of that of Shaanxi Province (Zhang and Pei 2000: 12). Shaanbei's population in 1998 was 5,090,000, or 14.5% of Shaanxi's population (ibid.). The population of Yan'an Prefecture was 1,916,000 and of Yulin Prefecture 3,147,000 (1997 figures, Shaanxi nianjian 1998: 387, 395).

Most parts of Shaanbei are covered with loess, a fine-grained, dusty, yellow soil. The "yellow earth plateau" (*huangtu gaoyuan*) is almost synonymous with Shaanbei. Though quite fertile, the loess land is extremely susceptible to erosion (see Hershkovitz 1993). As a result, its landscape is characterized by endless stretches of bun-like yellow hills broken up by precipitous and deep valleys. In a memorable passage, the American journalist Edgar Snow described Shaanbei's landscape:

> There are few genuine mountains, only endless broken hills, hills as interminable as a sentence by James Joyce, and even more tiresome. Yet the effect is often strikingly like Picasso, the sharp-angled shadowing and coloring changing miraculously with the sun's wheel, and towards dusk it becomes a magnificent sea of purpled hilltops with dark velvety folds running down, like the pleats on a mandarin skirt, to ravines that seem bottomless. (Snow, *Red Star Over China*; quoted in Selden 1971: 3)

This savage landscape has also been immortalized in the film *The Yellow Earth* (*Huangtudi*). Flatland is only found along major rivers. The major crops are wheat (winter and spring), maize, sorghum, millet, buckwheat, soybean, potatoes, black/green beans, peanuts, tobacco, and rice. The northern part of Shaanbei, however, runs into the Ordos Desert and the southern end of the Inner Mongolian grassland. There the land is flat, the soil infertile, and agriculture is supplemented with the herding of goats and sheep.

Traditionally, because of the lack of irrigation structures, there was not much difference in crop yield between the river plains and the hill slopes; rainfall was the limiting factor for agricultural production. In recent decades, however, thanks to the improvements in irrigation infrastructures and the spread of electric water pumps, "irrigable land" (*shuidi*) or

A typical Shaanbei landscape, with deep ravines caused by erosion. (All photographs are by the author)

"riverbank land" (*tandi*) has become much more productive than "land on the hills" (*shandi*). Even rice is grown to the south of Yulin City (centering on Yuhe Town) because of the ample water supply from irrigation canals. Frequent drought, however, is still the biggest problem in Shaanbei. I will return to a description of contemporary Shaanbei society in a later section in this chapter.

A Brief History of Shaanbei

Even though most parts of Shaanbei had been incorporated into Chinese territory since around 500 BC (Zhou Dynasty), it was repeatedly overrun by northern nomadic tribes or tribal confederacies and was occasionally made a part of ethnic rival kingdoms (e.g., the Great Xia Kingdom of the fourth century AD and the Western Xia of the eleventh century). Remains of the Great Wall, mostly dating to the Ming Dynasty, stretch through the six northern counties of Yulin Prefecture (from Fugu in the northeast through Shenmu, Yulin, Hengshan, and Jingbian to Dingbian in the southwest). It is known as the "border wall" (*bianqiang*), testifying to a bygone era of tumultuous military conflicts between the Chinese imperial state and the northern nomadic peoples. Yulin City (then known as Yansui) was one of the nine heavily militarized cities of the northern frontier (*jiubian zhongzhen*) during the Ming Dynasty. It was only during the Qing Dynasty that all of Shaanbei became firmly part of the interior of the Chinese empire (see Waldron 1990).

The land in Shaanbei, especially the northern part, was first developed for agriculture on a large scale in the 250s BPE by the last Qin king (later the first emperor of China). For centuries land development in Shaanbei was carried out by both soldiers stationed on the frontier and ordinary peasants who were recruited to move from the interior to the frontier so as to consolidate the border area.[4] Because of the frequent border warfare, raids by the nomadic tribes, natural disasters, and rebellions, the population in Shaanbei often went through dramatic fluctuations. During the Ming Dynasty, the state organized mass migrations to replenish the lost population to the north and northwest, using Hongdong (pronounced as Hongtong) County in southern Shanxi as a transfer station. Today, most of the people in Shaanbei claim that their ancestors came from the big locust tree in Shanxi (*shanxi dahuaishu*). Presumably their ancestors were the migrants who came from Shanxi and other overpopulated parts of China and who were stationed in Hongtong, known for its big locust trees (hence the legend), while waiting to go to their assigned destinations (see Huang, Gao, and Chu 1993; Xu 1982).

Despite the locust tree "origin story," however, one should not underestimate the volume of migrants to Shaanbei during the Qing Dynasty, the Republican era, and the People's Republic era. The physical proximity and the overpopulation of Shanxi has continued to make it a major source of migrants to Shaanbei. The biggest influx of migrants in recent Shaanbei history was in the 1930s and 1940s, when tens of thousands of war and famine refugees from northern China (especially Henan) flooded into the Communist-occupied areas in Shaanbei (see Keating 1997). It is also worth pointing out that Shaanbei has not only been a migrant-receiving region; Shaanbei people have migrated out of Shaanbei over the centuries because of war, famine, or simply to seek new opportunities elsewhere. A large number of Han migrants to the vast areas to the north, northwest, and west of Shaanbei are from Shaanbei. In fact, the big stretch of Shaanbei territory "beyond the pass (or the gates of the border walls)" (*kouwai*) resulted from agricultural colonization of former Mongol pastureland by Shaanbei peasants during Qing and Republican times.

As a result of the state-organized and -planned migrations, the extremely mixed origins of the migrants, and the wide availability of land in Shaanbei, intercommunity conflicts such as the ones that took place during the colonization of Taiwan and the recolonization of the sands of the Canton Delta during mid-Qing did not develop in the Shaanbei settlements (see Lamley 1981, 1990; Siu and Faure 1995). When violent conflicts did occur during the Ming and Qing dynasties, they were mostly in the form of peasant rebellions and Han and Mongol military expeditions into each other's territories. The greatest disturbances in Ming-Qing Shaanbei were the late-Ming peasant rebellions led by Li Zicheng and Zhang Xianzhong (see Parsons 1970), and the late-Qing Muslim rebellions that spread from Ningxia to Shaanbei (see Chu 1966; Fields 1978). In the late 19th century and the early 20th century there were also incidents of conflicts and violence related to Western missions.[5]

In the wake of the fall of the Qing dynasty in 1911 Shaanbei people suffered to varying degrees in the hands of bandits, warlords, landlords, and various agents of the state. Religious sectarianism (e.g., *Hunyuanjiao*), Boxer-like militias (*shentuan*) inspired by popular religion, and other forms of secret societies such as the powerful Elder Brothers Society (*Gelaohui*) thrived. The growth of opium poppies, and the trading in and smoking of opium became even more widespread. The de facto ruler of Shaanbei (especially Yulin Prefecture) from the mid-1910s until the mid-1930s was Jing Yuexiu, known in Shaanbei as His Highness Jing (*Jing daren*), who was stationed in Yulin City and maintained his power under many regimes during the volatile Republican era.

Communism first entered Shaanbei in the 1920s through some of the teaching staff at Shaanbei's new secondary and teachers' schools. In the 1920s and 30s many Communist guerrillas emerged, known as "red stirrings" (*naohong*), and numerous soviets were established. The Central Red Army led by Mao Zedong arrived in Shaanbei in 1935 after the tortuous Long March, absorbed and reorganized the local guerrillas, and made Shaanbei a base area to resist the many rounds of attack by the Nationalist army. The subsequent Shaan-Gan-Ning Border Region included large parts of Shaanbei, even though most of present-day Yulin Prefecture remained under the jurisdiction of the Nationalist Republican government. Soon after the Sino-Japanese War broke out, the Communists and the Nationalists entered into an uneasy partnership in fighting the invaders, the so-called Second United Front. Even though the Japanese army successfully occupied large parts of Shanxi and Suiyuan (a former province to the north of Shaanbei, now a part of Inner Mongolia), they never managed to cross the Yellow River and take Shaanbei. For a decade or so until the liberation of all of Shaanbei by the Communists in 1949, Shaanbei was divided into the so-called "soviet areas" (*suqu*) or "liberated areas" (*jiefangqu*) and "white areas" (*baiqu*), referring to areas controlled by the Communists and the Nationalists respectively.[6] During the Nationalist-Communist allied period against the Japanese invaders (1937–1945), a few counties in Shaanbei were under tension-filled joint jurisdiction. While Yan'an City served as the Red Capital, later to be elevated to the status of revolutionary Holy Land in post-Liberation Communist historiography (Apter and Saich 1994), the walled Yulin City was the administrative and military bastion of the "white areas," resisting numerous sieges by Communist forces during the Civil War (1945–1949), and was not liberated until May of 1949 when the stationing Nationalist army unit surrendered.

During the years of the "red-white" divide, Shaanbei was like two different societies. The "red areas," under the Communist regime, underwent land reforms and other quick-paced social transformations.[7] The Nationalists, on the other hand, reinstituted the traditional *baojia* system of mutual surveillance in the "white areas" and tried to resist Communist infiltration. Despite (or perhaps because of) the wartime turmoil, the economy in Shaanbei thrived. The trade between the Mongol herders in Inner Mongolia and the "border merchants" (*bianshang*) of Yulin City and other major trading towns along the Great Wall in particular continued to boom. Zhenchuan Town[8], the largest trading town in Shaanbei since the mid-Qing period and near which I conducted my fieldwork, benefited tremendously from wartime trade, especially the trafficking of opium (*dayantu*), much of which was grown locally in Shaanbei.

What happened after Liberation was a string of transformative events very familiar to historians of socialist China: the completion of land reforms, cooperatization, collectivization, de-privatization of commerce and industry, the Great Leap Forward, the institution of *hukou* policy, the Four Cleanups or Socialist Education Campaign, the Great Proletarian Cultural Revolution, the "Learn from Dazhai" Movement, de-collectivization with the introduction of the Household Contract System, and partial re-privatization in commerce and industry.[9] While going through these tumultuous decades of nationwide social transformations, Shaanbei, like any other locale, has had its own idiosyncrasies. The careful delineation of these historical details would call for another monograph.

However, some of the local color of these nationwide events will emerge in this book in the various interrelated accounts of popular religion in Shaanbei, the Heilongdawang Complex, and temple boss Lao Wang.

The Structure of Contemporary Shaanbei Society

Historically Shaanbei has been and still is one of the poorest regions of China proper due to its geographic isolation and unfavorable natural environment. Even though Shaanbei people contributed a lot to the Communist Revolution and despite the post-Liberation Communist party-state exaltation of Shaanbei as one of the virtuous revolutionary "old regions" (*laoqu*), Shaanbei was largely left behind during much of the Maoist period. Many Shaanbei people felt bitter that Mao never revisited Shaanbei during his reign, even though he had lived there for twelve years and had allegedly said, upon leaving in 1948, that Shaanbei was a nice place (*Shaanbei shige haodifang*). However, it is unfair to say that the central government has not done anything for Shaanbei people. Throughout the entire post-liberation five decades, the government of Shaanbei has depended on financial subsidies from the central government.[10] Yet compared to many other parts of China, there were very few large-scale, state-sponsored development projects in Shaanbei, and it has remained overwhelmingly agrarian/agricultural.[11]

It is only since the late 1980s that Shaanbei has picked up speed on the development and modernization path. Large reserves of oil, natural gas, and high-quality coal were discovered in Shaanbei,[12] and transportation and communications networks are quickly improving and expanding. Two small airports in Yan'an City and Yulin City service flights to and from Baotou in Inner Mongolia, Taiyuan in Shanxi, Lanzhou in Gansu, and the provincial capital Xi'an. In 1992 the railway reached Yan'an City from Xi'an, and it will continue onward following two paths, one to pass through Suide, Zhenchuan, cross the Yellow River, and eventually reach Datong and Taiyuan in Shanxi, and the other to pass through Yulin City, Shenmu, and eventually reach Baotou in Inner Mongolia. Major thoroughfares are being upgraded, and there is considerable "rural urbanization" as in most other parts of China, though far more modest in scale in comparison to coastal Guangdong, Fujian, and Zhejiang (see Guldin 1997a, 1997b).

The structure of Shaanbei society has been transformed greatly since the beginning of the 20th century. Yet one can also argue that it has not

been transformed that much after all. Within this paradox lies the perennial question in the study of any society, that of continuity and change.
By "structure of society," I mean the characteristics of social groupings
(e.g., class, occupational group), the relations among them, how different
social resources such as means of production, prestige, and power are distributed and employed, and the ways in which social life is institutionally
organized (e.g., family, village, *danwei*). What follows is a brief exposition of the structure of contemporary Shaanbei society in these terms.

Social Stratification (Class and Status Groups)

Ordinary Shaanbei peasants most readily distinguish between themselves, the "burden or bitterness sufferers" (*shoukuren*), and a number of
other broad categories of people: officials (*dangguerde*), state employees
(*zhigong* or *yougongzuode*), and private entrepreneurs. Officials and
state employees both belong to the category "state folks" (*gongjiaren*) because they work for, and receive salary from, the state (*gongjia*, literally
"collective household"). They belong to one of the two great "tributary
classes" (the other one being commoners) (Gates 1996: 21).

When talking about officials Shaanbei people are very conscious of
their rank, an indication of their relative position in the hierarchy of of-
fice-derived status and power. The highest-ranking officials in Shaanbei
are the Party secretaries and prefecture commissioners of Yan'an and
Yulin prefectures, who report to the Shaanxi provincial Party secretary
and governor. Their rank is that of a "prefecture division commander"
(*dishiji* or *tingji*). Their deputies' rank is that of a "deputy prefecture division commander" (*fudishiji* or *futingji*). At the next lower level are the
chief and deputy "county regiment commander" ranks (*xiantuanji* or
chuji), occupied by the chief and deputy county Party secretaries and
county administrators. Officials of the above-mentioned ranks all enjoy
the privilege, among many other things, of chauffeured sedans (*gongjia
xiaoche*).[13]

At the next lower level are the chief and deputy "section" ranks (*keji*),
occupied by the heads of different bureaus and offices of the county government as well as the top officials of township and *xiang* (rural district)
governments. There are normally about three or four dozen different bureaus (*ju*) and offices (*bangongshi*) in each county.[14] People who work
under the section heads in county governments and those subordinates in
sub-county governments are non-ranking "ordinary cadres" (*yiban
ganbu*) who are the modern equivalent of the *yamen* runners and clerks

of imperial times. These ordinary cadres are the most numerous and it is they who carry out most of the work of the local state.[15]

The majority of officials are CCP (Chinese Communist Party) members. All officials except those in the rural districts work in government office compounds, usually the most grandiose structures in a county or township seat. Large, vertical wooden plaques with black or red characters hang on each side of the courtyard gates of these compounds, indicating the nature of government agencies (*jiguan danwei*) inside: local branches of the CCP hang red-character plaques (S. *hongparpar*) while the government and other nonparty agencies hang black-character plaques (S. *heiparpar*). Like the yamen of dynastic times, these government office compounds are awe-inspiring, and ordinary people cannot easily gain access to them.

The total number of officials is close to 4% of the total working population (according to 1986 figures for Yulin Prefecture; see YLDQZ 127, 454). Because official status is accorded power, prestige, and economic security, officials are often recognized by ordinary Shaanbei people as "the people above people" (*renshangren*). In recent years, because of rampant corruption and official abuse of power, officials in Shaanbei as a group and as individuals are feared and often detested by ordinary people.

The other kind of "state folks" are the employees (*zhigong*) of state- or collectively owned enterprises (*qiye danwei*) and services (*shiye danwei*) such as factories, coal mines, oil and natural gas fields, shops and department stores, parks and museums, hotels and guest houses, hospitals, banks and insurance companies, communications and post offices, transport, roads and railroads, construction companies, restaurants, arts and sciences, broadcasting and television, or schools. Because Shaanbei people often perceive state employment as the only real employment, state employees are colloquially called "those who have jobs" (*yougongzuode*) or "those who work" (*gongzuoren*).

During the Maoist period these salaried people were in an enviable position because they held the so-called "iron rice bowl," enjoying regular income and many benefits such as housing, medical care, and even the opportunity to pass the jobs to their children.[16] During the reform era, however, a number of state and collective enterprises or services either "collapsed" (S. *daotale*) or were contracted out to private entrepreneurs. In the late 1990s, at the height of Premier Zhu Rongji's state sector structural reform, the threat of getting laid off, or "stepping down from duty" (*xiagang*), made even more state employees feel insecure. However, despite these destabilizing factors, state employment is still immensely attractive to ordinary Shaanbei people, who often crystallize their desire for state jobs with the image of "trying to crawl over the gate threshold of the state" (*pa gongjia menkar*). In this metaphor, the state sector is imagined as a house or a courtyard with a high gate threshold, which makes it difficult for ordinary people to climb in. Entering state sector employment also gives one the much-cherished opportunity to get to know officials, or people who know officials, who can be helpful when their help is needed.

Among the state sector employees, however, there are a large number of contract and temporary workers. They do not count as real state employees, and the struggle among them to become regular state employees (i.e., to "turn regular," *zhuanzheng*) is fierce and often involves competitive bribing of *danwei* (work unit) leaders (*danwei lingdao*). The differences in salary and benefits vary immensely from danwei to danwei, depending on the nature of the danwei. For example, banks, telecommunications companies, post offices, insurance companies, construction companies, and financially healthy factories are "hot" (*remer*) or "good" (*hao*), while schools, arts and sciences, and constantly in-the-red factories are bad. School teachers on government payroll always complain about how meager their salary is, and that they always receive their salary two, three, sometimes even four months late. Still, they are better off than those who are laid off because their danwei went bankrupt or "collapsed," e.g., the previously ubiquitous Supply and Distribution Cooperatives.

Like officials, an overwhelming majority of danwei employees live in cities and towns and have urban *hukou* (household registration), even though during the reform era hukou is becoming less and less relevant as a mechanism of social discrimination. The total number of employees working for state and collective enterprises and services is about 12% of the total working population (according to 1986 figures for Yulin Prefecture; see YLDQZ 127).[17]

The "state folks" make up 16% of the total work force[18], while the remaining 84% are non-state folks, i.e., people who do not hold the state's "iron rice bowls" (*tiefanwan*). The increasing privatization of the economy since the early 1980s has opened up a large terrain for private entrepreneurial activities in light industry, commerce, and service. The richest private entrepreneurs are civil engineering contractors (*baogongtou*), those who have contracted out lucrative factories and stores from the state, shareholders and managers of successful, privately owned oil or coal extraction companies, and businessmen and traders (*zuoshengyide* or *maimairen*) who have made it big through a combination of hard work, connections to the official world, and cunning. It is said that the personal assets of some of these super-rich private entrepreneurs exceed one million yuan. One village I visited in Mizhi County is famous for being the home village of a few big contractors. The richest among them had just spent more than two hundred thousand yuan expanding and renovating his home. My villager guide pointed to the one jeep, two bulldozers and three heavy-duty trucks, all parked awkwardly outside the rich man's home along the narrow, dirt country road, and said to me: "These are all his." One woman in Yulin City is said to be the richest woman in Shaanbei, owning a number of restaurants, factories, stores, hotels, and oil-drilling stations.

Below these super-rich people one finds the wide stratum of the relatively well-to-do, i.e., those private entrepreneurs whose assets are between ten thousand yuan and a few hundred thousand yuan. They are traders or owners of small factories, wholesale or retail shops, big or small buses, taxis, trucks, restaurants, dance and karaoke halls, automobile and motorcycle repair shops, gas stations, guest houses, clinics, and the like. They themselves sometimes take care of the day-to-day operations of their business but more often they rely on hired people (often relatives or co-villagers). It is very common for relatives and friends to enter into business partnership (*hehuo*). In this world of petty capitalists par excellence, hard work and good human relationships are paramount to good business, even though to get ahead one still needs frequent official patronage (and protection!) and occasional reliance on dishonest business dealings. Shaanbei small-time petty capitalists often complained to me about how hard business had become because so many people were doing the same thing; they said there were "too many hands" (S. *shouchou*) in any particular business for anyone to make much profit. For them, the hard work and the constant threat of losing money must have made state jobs look very desirable indeed. The number of private entrepreneurs (not including the non-partner employees) is difficult to estimate both because the number is increasing constantly and because of under-licensing. By my estimation they would make up no more than 5% of the total working population.

About 80% of the total working population in Shaanbei are peasants, who are at the bottom of a by now highly stratified society.[19] Traditionally, to do farm work is called "to endure hardship" (*shouku*, literally meaning receiving bitterness). It is a life of hard labor, "with your face toward the yellow earth and your back toward the sky" (*mian chao huang-tu bei chao tian*). The household contract system, instituted in the early 1980s, stipulated that agricultural land be distributed according to the number of persons in each household. The land belongs to the village collectivity, and ultimately to the state, and no one can sell or buy land. Thus the amount of agricultural land "owned" and farmed by each family is not a significant factor in intra-village socioeconomic differentiation in today's rural Shaanbei. No landlordism is developing out of the present-day system of landownership, even though it is common to find villagers farming for a friend or relative who choose not to farm by paying an agreed-upon rent.

A much more important factor in determining villagers' level of prosperity and social status is the geographic location of the village. There are in general three categories of villages: those in the "back valleys" (*hougou*) or "in the mountains" (*shanli*), those near or at the mouth of the valley that opens out to a big river (*chuankou*), and those that are on the plains along a big river (*chuanli*). Almost all county seats and large towns are found on the river plains along major rivers. The proximity to major urban centers offers river-plains villagers better opportunities to market their farm produce and to find sideline nonagricultural employment. Being along major roads also facilitates roadside businesses such as restaurants, motor vehicle repair shops, motels, or simply cold-drink stalls and watermelon stands.[20] The majority of the owner-operators and employees of these small enterprises, unlike those in larger towns such as county capitals, still farm their plots.

Shaanbei people's preference for river plains and aversion to the back valleys are best illustrated by the graduated flow of brides downward toward the plains from the hills, causing extremely high brideprice in the hills and negligible brideprice in the plains.[21] For example, the brideprice in county towns might be a symbolic sum of 240 yuan or 480 yuan, called one or two "portions" (*fen*) of brideprice (*caili*).[22] In the isolated back valleys, however, the brideprice can be as high as ten to fifteen hundred yuan, and one unit of brideprice there is called *yidun* (one bundle), which is 1,200 yuan. Consequently it is becoming more and more difficult for peasant men in the mountains to find wives. As Shaanbei peasant parents usually consider getting brides for their sons the most important thing in their lives, the difference of experience in securing (good) brides generated by a kind of "geographic fate" should not be overestimated. Once a mother of three sons—incidentally she has no daughters—from a prosperous plains village in Yulin County proudly told me that young male villagers in her village never have any problem getting good brides, and that the brides are all happy after they come to the village. Furthermore, she emphasized, the parents in her village never have to pay more than a modicum of brideprice (the symbolic 240 yuan) to secure daughters-in-law. Apparently she was very happy with her two daughters-in-law, and was not worried about her third son's marriage prospect. In fact, having no daughters was probably a blessing for her and her husband as parents because they did not have to "bleed" financially to furnish the ever-elaborate dowry befitting a bride from a prosperous plains village or a town. Had the same couple lived in a poor back-valley village, they most likely would have much suffering to endure to finance their three sons' marriages and no prospect of gaining financially through marrying off their daughters since they have none. In fact, worries of back-valley peasant parents about their sons' marriages and the hard work these worries induce constitute a major type of social suffering in contemporary Shaanbei.[23]

Differential geographic location of one's home village is of course an important but not all-determining factor affecting the life chances of peasant men and women. There are always exceptions to the plains/prosperous vs back-valley/poor dichotomy. The village in Mizhi County, which I mentioned earlier, has a number of big and rich civil engineering contractors but is by all standards a back-valley village with poor communications to the outside—it takes the minibus close to an hour to reach the county capital Mizhi Town along winding unpaved country roads that often become too muddy for any vehicle to maneuver after a heavy rainstorm. One of the main reasons why some individuals in back-valley villages have "made it" is that many peasants in these villages had been forced by circumstances to leave their natal villages to make a living outside and a few of them had managed to gain enough experience and important connections to not only secure a good living for themselves but also spread the benefits to some of their kin and co-villagers back home (e.g., by hiring them in the civil engineering teams as *mingong*, i.e., peasant laborers). Another example of the transcendence of geographic fate (or rather the overcoming of geographic fate by geological fate) is the discovery of rich reserves of natural gas, oil, and high-quality coal in many parts of Shaanbei in recent years. As state as well as private drilling and mining companies set up camps all over the Shaanbei landscape, peasants get compensated for their loss of farm and pastureland, and many bene-fit from being near the boomtowns induced by these extractive industries. For example, peasant villagers in the vicinity of Daliuta, a miraculously rapid-growing coal town in northern Shenmu County, have become much more prosperous than their neighbors to the south.

Many other factors come into play as well to shape the "fate" (*ming*) and "fortune" (*yun*) of peasant families and their individual members.[24] Individual capability (*benshi*) is one of the most important determinants of one's circumstances, and Shaanbei people frequently use it to judge themselves and others. One would say: "Maoer (a neighbor) has gotten rich these days, trading in Mongol land (*mengdi*). Look how capable he is (*you benshi*)!" On the other hand, the same person could self-depre-catingly say that he himself is not very capable (*mei benshi*), which ex-plains the less than prosperous circumstance of his family. When a fam-ily is prosperous, it is said to be "doing well" (*xingle*). When a family is just comfortable and financially in the black, it (or the head of the house-hold) is said to be "doing just fine" (S. *neng gudong*, i.e., able to make ends meet). A family struggling or in debt is said to be "not doing well" (*buxing*).

Because of the small plot of land for each household, no peasant fam-ily can become prosperous by farming and selling farm produce alone. Though trading and doing small business make some people rich, their risks are well-known and more often than not people lose money in these ventures and sometimes sink very low in their finances (e.g., spending years to pay off debts). Some peasant households are peasant in name only because they are specialist households of stone carvers, carpenters, traditional music performers, and even spirit mediums and itinerant beg-gars. Because of the special skills of their members, these households usu-ally do better financially.

Shaanbei people are usually very aware of the social stratification of their society (see Kuhn 1984; Luo 1995; Unger 1984; Yan 1992). They not only have a good sense of the entire structure of privilege and priva-tion, urbanity and rusticity, officials and commoners, but they typically know their respective place in the hierarchy and how they might be able to advance or at least preserve their standing. Though probably desiring to be rich and powerful, the typical Shaanbei peasant only hopes to make ends meet (S. *neng gudong*) or at most to do relatively well (S. *xingle*), knowing that a life of privilege is beyond their reach. Some might implore the deities to help them get rich or make their children into officials, but most simply ask for divine protection against life's many troubles.

The Village

In Shaanbei, the hierarchy of economic (and political) units roughly follows the nested central-place pattern described by G. William Skinner (Skinner 1964–65). Regional cities are only found outside of Shaanbei: Baotou in Inner Mongolia to the north, Yinchuan in Ningxia to the west, Taiyuan in Shanxi to the east, and the Shaanxi provincial capital Xi'an to the south. Yulin City and Yan'an City belong to the combined category of greater city and local city, whereas all the non-prefectural-seat county seats are central marketing towns. Zhenchuan Town, because of its regional economic importance, can also count as a central marketing town. Large towns along major highways are intermediate marketing towns, e.g., Sishilipu (Forty Miles Inn) and Yihe in Suide, Zhoujiajian and Matigou in Zizhou, Yuhe in Yulin, Boluo and Dianshi in Hengshan, Gaojiapu and Daliuta in Shenmu, Ningtiaoliang in Jingbian, Anbian in Dingbian, Taozhen and Longzhen in Mizhi, Tongzhen and Wuzhen in Jiaxian, and so forth. At the bottom of the marketing hierarchy are the rest of the rural district (*xiang*) seats, most of which are standard marketing towns that hold market days every five or ten days. Because of the institution of township and rural district governments, the political hierarchy follows almost exactly the marketing hierarchy.

The vast majority of Shaanbei's urban-hukou (*chengzhen hukou*, which means nonagricultural household registration) residents live in the two prefectural cities, Yulin and Yan'an, and the twenty-odd county seats. As close to 90% of Shaanbei's population is agricultural, the overwhelming majority of Shaanbei people live in villages and small towns (intermediate and standard marketing towns). As the focus of our story, the Dragon King Valley, is situated in village Shaanbei (albeit near an important marketing town), I will briefly introduce the characteristics of Shaanbei villages and the peasant households found therein in this and the next sections.

Shaanbei has a great many varieties of villages, one differing from another in terms of topography, location, settlement pattern, history, size, level of prosperity, and so on. Villages in major river plains tend to be larger and have mixed surnames (though usually with one or two much larger dominant surname descent groups), whereas most single-surname villages are small, of recent vintage, and are found in the valleys. Most large villages were founded in the Ming Dynasty, whereas those founded in the Qing Dynasty are the most numerous. According to a survey conducted in 1985 on villages in Zizhou County, out of the 1,222 natural villages, 47 were founded before the Ming, 307 during the Ming, 724 during the Qing, 102 during the Republican era, and 43 after Liberation (Zhang Junyi 1993: 110). In terms of village size, the same survey reveals that in 1985 in Zizhou County about two-thirds of Zizhou villagers lived in villages with 50 to 299 persons.[25] These figures, though representative of the Suide-Zizhou-Mizhi area, in no way apply to the flatter areas of north and northwest Yulin Prefecture or the relatively more recently redeveloped Yan'an Prefecture, which tend to have much smaller villages. Also, these figures represent the number of "natural" villages (*zirancun*), which refer to the villagers' own social and cognitive categories. Sometimes one or two households tucked away in the hills comprise one natural village. Superimposed onto the natural villages are the so-called administrative villages (*xingzhengcun*), which are the contemporary equivalent of the production brigade (*shengchandui*) of the collective era. For example, there are 1,620 natural villages in Yulin County but only 484 administrative villages (based on 1990 figures, YLDQZ: 819); in Jingbian County, 203 administrative villages are superimposed onto 1,694 natural villages (ibid.: 832); in Qingjian County there are 701 natural villages and 641 administrative villages (ibid.: 829).

The physical form of villages in Shaanbei can assume extremely different appearances. In the flat and semidesert areas of northern parts of Shaanbei village homes are dispersed, which makes it difficult for an observer to actually see "the village." In the hilly southern parts (which are more representative of Shaanbei topography), however, villages tend to be nucleated with homes clustered together.

To what extent do Shaanbei peasants identify themselves as members of the individual "village societies" in which they live? Are their social vision and personal networks more a function of the affairs they regularly attend in the standard marketing towns as G. William Skinner observed (Skinner 1964–65)? Or, as Wolf pointed out in reaction to Skinner's observation, are peasants situated at the bottom of the marketing hierarchy socially as well as culturally well integrated into the larger, region-wide body politic, as Skinner's model equally implies (Wolf 1989)? Or, to use another of Skinner's frameworks, are Shaanbei villagers' moral, political, economic, and sociocultural outlook and practice "open" or "shut," as their villages "open" or "shut" in accordance with changes in external circumstances (Skinner 1971)? Are perhaps all of these observations true to differing extents? These questions about the sociocultural significance of the village are important to our study of popular religion in Shaanbei because the overwhelming majority of Shaanbei temples are so-called "village temples" (*cunmiao*) and villages serve as an important space for the staging of folk cultural traditions such as funeral and wedding rituals (Liu 1996).

Today all Shaanbei administrative villages have an official (and officially endorsed) village leadership organization called the "villagers' committee" (*cunmin weiyuanhui*), which usually consists of a village head (*cunzhang*), the accountant (*kuaiji*), a women's leader (*funü zhuren*), and sometimes a village property custodian (*baoguan*).[26] These village officials are elected every three years, and they all receive a monthly salary from the village budget of amounts determined by the village assembly (normally in the vicinity of one hundred yuan). Each administrative village (former brigade) is subdivided into two, three, or more small groups (*xiaozu*), which are more or less the contemporary equivalent of production teams of the collective era. Each small group has a group leader (*xiaozuzhang*), elected by members of the group, even though they are not paid a salary. The village Party secretary (*cun shuji* or simply *shuji*) heads the village Party branch, which includes, depending on the size of the village, a dozen or so Party members. There is often considerable overlap in membership between the village Party branch and the villagers' committee. The Party branch is still supposed to "lead" the village, even though its symbolic and directive powers have largely evaporated in recent years. Members of the villagers' committee, the small group leaders, and the Party secretary are all considered to be and are called "village cadres" (*cungan*). In fact, they are still often called brigade/team cadres (*duigan*) as in the collective era.

Village officials are responsible for interacting with township officials and help accomplish government tasks such as collecting the agricultural tax, supervising birth control, and carrying out propaganda and educational work during campaigns.[27] They are also responsible for receiving the occasional visiting township officials who come to their village to stay for a short period (*dundiar*, literally "squat at one spot") or to "inspect work" (*jiancha gongzuo*), which often means little more than feasting and drinking at the village's expense.[28] Because of the general paucity of village-level collective enterprises, village officials in Shaanbei typically wield much less power than economically more developed areas better known through recent literature on rural China (e.g., Ruf 1998). In many villages few people want to be village officials for fear of the troubles entailed, while in some villages the posts fall into the hands of local strongmen or even local bullies.

Many villages support another important figure: the electricity overseer (*kandiande*). As the majority of Shaanbei villages now have electricity, someone must oversee and manage the electricity used for pumping drinking and irrigation water. The person is responsible for safeguarding the electric meter (usually in a locked box), making sure that nobody steals electricity, and interacting with employees of the County Electricity Bureau. The latter are commonly referred to as the "electricity tigers" (*dianlaohu*) because they can arbitrarily deny electrical supply to a particular village or a rural district during crucial moments (e.g., during temple festivals or peak irrigation days) if they are offended or not propitiated with the right number and "weight" of gifts. I once witnessed a sudden power outage in the middle of the opera performance at a temple festival in a village in Shenmu County. The festival organizers had a meeting and promptly dispatched a young man on a motorcycle to send the local electricity tiger half of a slaughtered goat and two cartons of cigarettes (200 cigarettes in each 10-pack carton). The electricity came back shortly afterwards. In another instance I witnessed, a local electricity tiger accused a village of having stolen electricity and subsequently cut off the electrical supply. Because it was the spring vegetable seedling-cultivating season with high water demand (hence electricity for pumping water from wells and rivers), the village could not afford to be without electricity for even more than a couple of days. There was an emergency Party members' meeting (*dangyuanhui*) where it was decided that a "cash gift" (i.e., bribe) should be taken immediately to the person concerned by the village Party secretary himself. My point in bringing up the problem of electricity is simply to illustrate one of the ways a village relates to the outside world as a unit.

Unlike what is commonly the case for villages in coastal Guangdong and Fujian, in Shaanbei tight social cohesion is not guaranteed in single-surname villages, nor is conflict necessarily common in mixed-surname villages. Social cohesion within a village depends on many other factors, such as the size of the village, the availability of charismatic village leaders, whether or not the village has rival villages nearby, past history of in-

tra-village animosities (e.g., during the various Maoist-era political campaigns), the presence or absence of contentious issues (e.g., how to fairly
contract out village land or enterprise to villagers, and so forth). One important reason why some single-surname villages might be internally divided is simply that, though of the same surname, there are descent
groups actually originating from completely unrelated focal ancestors.
Another reason is that a particular descent group, once having achieved
a certain size, usually divides into two, three, or several branches (S. *mer*
or *menzi*, usually called *fang* in South China), usually depending on the
number of brothers of the founding generation or the number of sons of
the founding ancestor. Villagers are not obligated to attend and help out
as kin at major rites such as funerals or weddings staged by villagers of a
different branch, though one representative from each non-branch-mem-
ber household usually has to attend and bring the appropriate contributions *as co-villager*. Intra-village conflicts conveniently, though not always, develop along branch lines. For example, one village I know has
three branches (S. *san menzi*), and one branch is considered by the other
two branches as the "bad" branch because it produced a few violent and
belligerent characters during the Cultural Revolution who organized attacks on the other two.[29] The ill feelings generated from that era have lingered on until today.

Usually in each village there are a couple of favorite spots where villagers gather to shoot the breeze. These spots tend to be along a major
village path and next to a communal threshing ground. They also tend to
be sunny spots, which are especially warm and nice during winter. When
a little crowd gathers at one of these spots it is said the spot has become
a "human market" (S. *rensher*). At these human markets villagers smoke,
knit, swap market information, tell stories, gossip, complain, and watch
their small children play. When older people gather, the more versatile
sometimes tell segments from the Romance of the Three Kingdoms (*sanguo*), Five Women Reviving the Tang Dynasty (*wunü xingtang zhuan*), or
other well-known stories. These informal storytelling sessions are called
"speaking about past dynasties" (*shuo guchao*). Nowadays fewer and
fewer people are capable of or are interested in speaking about past dynasties.

Most villages have a village temple, but because the village temple is
usually located on a hill at a distance from the center of village life, it is
generally deserted except during the temple festivals and when individual
villagers come to consult the temple oracle or to burn incense. The over-

whelming majority of village temples are what anthropologists would consider "popular religious temples," i.e., not strictly Buddhist or Daoist (more on this in later chapters).

Peasant Households and Peasant Homes

The most basic social unit in rural Shaanbei is the peasant family or household (*jiahu* or *zhuanghu*). The household not only is a political economic unit but also a sociocultural and ritual unit. Land is distributed according to the total number of family members in each household and agricultural tax is collected accordingly; rituals of importance such as funerals and weddings are staged by individual households; gifting commonly takes place between households, and each household keeps a ritual-gift account (*lizhang*) for important ritual occasions involving large amounts of gifts in cash and kind (see Yan 1996b); though much less elaborate than those found in Guangdong, Fujian, and Taiwan, there are also household-based ritual behaviors (e.g., the worship of the stove god, heaven and earth, and the earth deity) continually producing and reproducing the household as a symbolically integral unit (see Hsieh and Chuang 1985).

Peasant households have never been very large in Shaanbei; richer landlord families in the past had larger, multigenerational households, whereas poorer peasants tended to have nuclear families. In fact, many poor peasant men could not afford a wife and hence never formed their own households. After Liberation, the peasant nuclear family became the norm. In 1985 the average size of peasant households in Yulin Prefecture was 4.33 persons (4.8 in 1981) (YLDQZ: 129). Since the Land Reform, sons tend to set up their own households as soon as they get married (called "serial family division"; see Cohen 1992; Yan 2003), as opposed to the more traditional form of dividing the family at the retirement (i.e., loss of ability to farm) or death of the head of household (usually the father) (see Selden 1993: 148 for discussion of a similar trend in Wugong, Hebei Province; and Yan 1996b: 196–98, 248 for rural Heilongjiang[30]). It is interesting to note that in Shaanbei, weddings tend to take place in the winter agricultural slack season, and the family "splitting-off" (*fenjia*) by the newlywed couple usually takes place right before the spring planting season, i.e., one event almost immediately following the other.[31]

As mentioned earlier in the section on social stratification, most Shaanbei peasants do not harbor unrealistic dreams that their lives are going to improve drastically, or that their children can easily escape the life of a peasant. Unless they know of obvious channels of improving their life chances (e.g., having a relative who became a high official and who is willing to grant special favors to one's family), most would be content to be able to make ends meet and keep disasters at bay if possible.

Shaanbei peasant men's work is typically outside the home, in the field or going to the market. The cultural ideal for a man is to become a competent farmer, shrewd marketer, and congenial villager. Because he is the head of the household, the reputation of the household rests largely on his personal reputation. From a peasant woman's perspective, her responsibilities after marrying into her husband's family are to partner with her husband in making a living (i.e., in agricultural production and the occasional marketing of farm produce); support and treat her parents-in-law well; have children (especially sons, or one son under the current birth control policy); find a daughter-in-law for the son and marry the daughter off to a good family; cook meals for the whole family (and the pigs if there are any); keep the house clean; and maintain good relationships with neighbors, and upkeep her husband's "face" (i.e., reputation) and that of the household. Because the wife bears so much responsibility in running the household, I find that women are as sensitive to "face" issues as their husbands. In fact, it seems that women break into fights with female neighbors over perceived slights more often than men. One of the reasons is that as mothers they are in charge of the children and children, because of their inadequate knowledge of or unwillingness to follow social etiquette, frequently cause troubles (e.g., hitting other kids, saying mean things, etc.). Because women work more at home, their roles are often defined by the activities they do in the *yao* (home) or the courtyard. They are called "ones who mill around the stove counter" (S. *zhuanguo-taide*) or "ones who feed the pig(s) and beat (i.e., discipline) the dog" (S. *weizhu dagou*). When women do join the men in the fields, it is during agricultural busy season (e.g., spring planting and autumn harvesting).

Even though Shaanbei people are very individualistic in their family-centeredness (what some have called "household individualism," see Nee 1985), neighbors, agnates, and co-villagers often help out one another in agricultural work and social events. To help out is called "mutual(-aid) group" (S. *xianghuo*) and to exchange labor is called just that (S. *biangong*). A Shaanbei expression underscores the importance of mutual help: *lü ken bozi gong bian gong* (S. [just as two] donkeys gnaw each other's neck, [two men or households should engage in] work exchange for work). Good friends usually form lifelong and even trans-generational mutual-aid and labor-exchange arrangements. They work together during spring planting and autumn harvesting seasons, when building a house, as well as at each other's major social events such as funerals and weddings (more on mutual-aid principles in Chapter 7).[32] Because of the prevalence of single-clan villages, mutual-aid groups are often made up of brothers or close agnates such as cousins or uncles and nephews. Yet siblinghood and close agnatic relationship do not necessarily guarantee amicable and close friendship and mutual-aid arrangements. When Shaanbei people feel close to each other they say their "relationship is good" (*guanxi hao*). When they can get along they say their "relationship is just fine" (*guanxi keyi*). Bad relationships are just called bad relationships (*guanxi buhao*).

One of the most distinct features of the Shaanbei village landscape is the form of village homes. Traditionally Shaanbei peasants preferred to live on hill slopes because it was convenient and cheap to create their dwellings by digging large, arched caves (called *yaodong* or simply *yao*) into an artificially chipped vertical surface on the slopes. These cave-dwellings created out of the compact loess soil made excellent homes, cool in the summer but warm in the winter (see Knapp 1989 for architectural descriptions). Before Liberation only very rich landlords could afford to build their yaos using cut stones or bricks, whereas most peasants dreamed of but rarely succeeded in attaching a vertical layer of cut stones or bricks to the outside "face" of their yaos to make them look prettier and more respectable.[33] During the Maoist era many peasant families could "face-lift" their dirt yaos or even build stone/brick yaos, but it was only in the 1980s that a large number of better-off peasants began to construct stone/brick yaos. Traditionally Shaanbei homes, though scattered on different levels or locations of the slopes, tended to form little clusters of topography-conforming (thus "natural-looking"), irregular settlement formations. More recently (since the 1980s), however, some villages with flat land moved down the hills en masse and constructed straight, parallel rows of stone cave homes (*paiyao*). The orderliness and confined nature of these new constructions sometimes reminds one of military barracks or prison camps, and many inhabitants of such new homes would have preferred the more spacious traditional form of housing arrangement, even though they would not want to trade in the convenience of being located on flat land and closer to the main road.[34]

The typical Shaanbei peasant dwelling is the yao (yaodong) and its accompanying courtyard. The family yao is the center of domestic life. Typically a household would have at least three yao: one for the conjugal pair, one for receiving guests (like a living room), which doubles as a bedroom for other family members such as children and the elderly or for the occasional overnight guests, and one for storage.[35]

The hosts would extend their hospitality by inviting the guest to come inside the yao, saying "come sit inside the home" (*jiali zuo*). Once inside the yao, the guest would be invited to sit on the *kang* (*kangshang zuo*). The kang is the earthen raised platform inside the family yao. Shaanbei people sleep on the kang, eat and drink around a low, square table on the kang, and receive guests on the kang (especially because they are to serve the guests food and drink). It is usually covered with a layer of woolen rug.[36] Bedsheets and blankets are rolled out at night for sleep, and during the day they are rolled up and piled up along the edge of the kang against the wall at the far end of the yao. Right next to the kang is the family hearth, the stove counter (*zaotai* or *guotai*), where food is prepared. A flue system goes underneath the kang so the heat from cooking goes under the kang to heat it up before escaping out through the chimney. Cooking is done inside the yao in winter to supply heat to the kang. During the summer, however, Shaanbei people prefer cooking in a shed outside in the courtyard. Next to the stove counter are large water vats for storing water.

The courtyard serves as the outer layer of the physical household. Typically one finds in the courtyard the latrine, an underground cave for storing potatoes, a shed for storing farm equipment, a shed for goats, a pig-sty, chicken cages, a stone mill, a guard dog, a wheelbarrow or two, and perhaps a tractor. Nowadays Shaanbei people usually prefer having an enclosed courtyard for their homes so that they can have privacy. Separate courtyards minimize the possibility of conflict with neighbors over the use of space, because farm equipment and harvested farm produce are often spread out in the courtyard.

᠆᠆

Shaanbei society of the late 1990s had a generally upbeat feel about it. Even though the household registration system was still in effect, many peasants could live in towns and cities if they chose to, and many more were traveling up and down Shaanbei's motorways in buses, vans, and tractors, as there was no longer any need to apply to the authorities to even travel to the next town, as was the case during the commune era.

The mining of coal and drilling of natural gas and petroleum brought unprecedented prosperity to many parts of Shaanbei, and connections to the outside world were broadened. It is in the context of this larger social transformation that one should locate the story of folk cultural revivalism in general, and the revival of popular religion in particular.

CHAPTER THREE

Shaanbei Popular Religious Landscape

> Out of the 1.5 million people in the Shaan-Gan-Ning Border
> Region, there are still more than one million illiterates and two
> thousand spirit mediums; superstitious thinking is still affecting all
> of the masses.
>> —Mao Zedong, speech at a meeting with cultural
>> and educational workers (1944, Yan'an)

> People around here are still very superstitious; [it's all because] the
> quality of their minds is so low (*sixiang suzhi hencha*).
>> —A Professor of Political Education (*zhengjiao*)
>> at Yan'an University (1997, Yan'an)

Chinese popular religion has been much studied in the contexts of Taiwan, Hong Kong, and overseas Chinese communities; yet its contemporary expressions in the People's Republic of China are only beginning to
be covered in the Western scholarly literature in recent years. Difficulty
of field access is sometimes still a problem, the Chinese government
being unwilling to let foreign researchers study what it considers to be
"backward" and "superstitious" activities. On the other hand, research
on the history and the written traditions, i.e., the "Great Traditions," of
Buddhism, Daoism, and Confucianism is considered not only harmless
but also beneficial to the glorification of Chinese civilization. In contrast
to the great interest in popular religion among China scholars in the
West, PRC researchers have mostly found popular religion unworthy of
their attention[1], and it is only recently that local folklorists and scholars
have begun collecting and describing local religious activities such as temple festivals and ritual dramas, sometimes with foreign financial sponsorship and cooperation.[2]

The purpose of this chapter is not only to provide the background necessary for the story of the Dragon King Valley and the Black Dragon King
cult, but also to attempt an overview of the popular religious landscape
in Shaanbei so as to contribute to establishing a baseline knowledge for

any future research on popular religion in North and North-central China.[3] This chapter only serves as a general introduction to popular religion in Shaanbei. Many specific issues will be explored in later chapters in conjunction with the ethnography on the Dragon King Valley. I will first outline the history of the shifting fortunes of popular religion in 20th century Shaanbei. Next I will paint a broad-brush portrait of the popular religious landscape of Shaanbei with an emphasis on my area of field-work. This is then followed by a discussion on the building of temples and the organization of temple associations. Then I describe the central role two kinds of ritual specialists play in Shaanbei popular religion: spirit mediums and yinyang masters. In this chapter, I wish to address a broad range of important topics pertaining to Shaanbei popular religion, especially the extent to which it is *embedded* in Shaanbei society.

The Waning and Waxing of Popular Religion in Shaanbei in the 20th Century

Much like everywhere else in the PRC, popular religion in Shaanbei has experienced phases of decline and resurgence during the course of the 20th century. As the arch-signifier of antimodernity, popular religion has been labeled as feudal superstition (*fengjian mixin*) and has received bursts of attack nationwide ever since the fall of the Qing Dynasty in 1911 (see Duara 1991).[4] Advocating science and rationalism, new-style students, reformist intellectuals, enlightened magistrates, and elite Republicans of the May Fourth generation were the first to tear down temple statues, turn temples into schools, and condemn spirit mediums and "quack doctors."[5] In the 1920s and 30s the teachers and students of Shaanbei's first new-style secondary schools became the local anti-superstition vanguards. The militarization of parts of Shaanbei during the so-called Warlord Period (1910s to 1920s) also contributed to the demise of temples. During his tenure as commander-in-chief in Yulin City between 1922 and 1924, the Nationalist general Yang Hucheng ordered the destruction of many temples in the Yulin Region. And a number of temples and monasteries were turned into army barracks (Zhang J. 1993: 159). When another Nationalist general, Tang Enbo, was stationed in Suide in 1936, he registered the land and other properties of many temples and monasteries in Yulin and turned many of them (including the famous Yulin City Daixing Monastery) into schools and vocational schools (YLDQZ: 411). However, these efforts against popular religion were primarily confined to the small number of urban centers (i.e., county seats) in Shaanbei. Meanwhile, the unstable social milieu provided a hotbed for the growth of sectarian groups such as Yiguandao ("Unity Sect"), Hunyuanjiao ("Origin Sect"), Yaochidao ("Jasper Pool Sect"), and so forth.

In the 1930s and 40s, when Shaanbei was divided into the "red" and the "white" areas, the "red" areas were subjected to Communist anti-superstition drives whereas the "white" areas faced much milder anti-superstition efforts under the Nationalists. The Communists were particularly keen on eradicating the many spirit mediums in the Shaan-Gan-Ning Border Region, who were deemed parasites of society and upholders of feudal superstition.[6] However, some parts of Shaanbei that benefited from a bustling wartime economy witnessed unusually active popular religious activities. Gambling and opium dens became a prominent feature at temple festivals.[7] Many Shanxi opera troupes fled Shanxi, which was already under Japanese occupation, and crossed the Yellow River to Shaanbei to perform for temple festivals there. Guanzhong (i.e., area near Xi'an) opera tastes were brought to the Yulin area by Nationalist troops. When civil war broke out between the Communists and the Nationalists, armies and regimes crisscrossed the Shaanbei landscape, sending landlords fleeing to safer places and making travel (e.g., for pilgrims and opera troupes) generally hazardous. Many monasteries and temples were destroyed by the armies, which used the wooden structures as firewood and took out the bricks to build fortifications. Popular religion waned as a result.

Even though the chaos of Land Reform in the early years of the Liberation was not conducive to the recovery of temple activities, the ensuing peace and prosperity and the empowerment of ordinary peasants in the 1950s to a certain extent brought back popular religion to Shaanbei social and cultural life.[8] Rich landlords and merchants, traditionally sponsors of temple festivals, were eliminated, and temple properties were confiscated and redistributed; yet ordinary peasants were enriched and empowered to contribute to popular religious activities. One might say that there had been a democratization of popular religion, thanks to the Communist victory and the Land Reform.[9] Many temples that had been destroyed during the war or had fallen into disrepair were rebuilt or renovated. For example, the Daoist shrines on Yan'an City's Great Serenity Mountain (Taiheshan), which had been blasted out by Japanese bombing, went through two restoration efforts between 1956 and 1960 under the initiative of the Daoist priest Qiao Wenyi (Yan'an juan 1994: 534).

Even during a large part of the collectivization era temple activities carried on as usual. In Yulin Prefecture alone, close to twenty thousand temples existed in the early 1960s (Fan 1997: 100).[10] Only sectarian cults such as Yiguandao and Hunyuanjiao faced harsh treatment, as they were outlawed in 1957 and their leaders executed or imprisoned and their members disbanded (YLDQZ: 678–79). The Great Leap Forward years of the late 1950s and early 1960s must have negatively affected religious life, as people struggled to merely survive.[11]

In 1963, the state began to tighten control on popular religion. The impetus came from the Socialist Education campaign (also called the Four Cleanups). Temple festivals were banned and the manufacture of "superstitious merchandise" such as incense and paper money was prohibited. These were considered not only superstitious but also wastefully unproductive. Temple festivals were banned also because markets of all kinds were condemned as "taking the capitalist road." The "coup de grâce" for Shaanbei popular religion came in 1966, at the beginning of the Cultural Revolution, when temples all over Shaanbei were demolished or turned into granaries or storage. All Buddhist monks and nuns and Daoist priests were forcibly made to become commoners again (*huansu*). For more than ten years temple-based religious activities vanished without a trace. Only a few courageous spirit mediums and yinyang masters practiced their trade clandestinely while the majority of religious practitioners dared not risk becoming "counterrevolutionaries."[12]

Yet even in the middle of the antitraditionalist period, popular religious sentiments flared up occasionally. Consider the curious emergence of the spirit of the Canadian Communist doctor Norman Bethune at the height of the Cultural Revolution. Bethune became a volunteer doctor for the Communist army in the late 1930s and died of a blood infection on the battlefield in the northwest. Mao Zedong's essay praising his selflessness became one of the most widely read of Mao's works. My Shaanbei informants told me that in the early years of the Cultural Revolution the spirit/god of Bethune (*Baiqiuen shenshen*) was traveling around Shaanbei to cure people's illnesses. There was no temple dedicated to Bethune; people needed only to utter his name and light Yan'an brand cigarettes (supposedly Bethune's favorite cigarette or because he met Mao in Yan'an) to get his divine assistance.[13] In one village in Zizhou County, the mass of worshipers became so large that the local militia (*minbing*) had to throw a hand grenade next to the crowd to disperse it.

Religious activities in Shaanbei were only severely interrupted for a mere decade. The late 1970s marked the beginning of the shift in policy away from radical leftism and antitraditionalism. The actual brevity of this interruption of popular religious life is surprising, for it is often assumed that the interruption was much longer. As early as 1978, accompanying the return of markets, some temple festivals revived, often disguised as agricultural fairs and only with very timid religious overtones. Then, among other stimuli, the news of government-sponsored renovations of famous religious sites spread, and the impetus for reviving worship began. Throughout the 1980s and 1990s, Shaanbei people rebuilt and renovated their temples, and the scale and beauty of these temples often far exceeded that of the original ones. This large-scale religious revival in many ways resembled the post-World War II boom of the so-called "new religions" in Japan (McFarland 1967) and the religious boom in Taiwan in recent years (see Jordan 1994; Katz and Rubinstein 2003; Pas 1996). During the same two decades, many old spirit mediums and yinyang masters resumed their practice and many new ones appeared. It is interesting to note that, nowadays, when a Shaanbei peasant says that he or she believes in "superstition" (*jiang mixin*) there is often no sense of fear or embarrassment as there would have been during the Maoist era; the term "superstition" (*mixin*) has apparently been purged of its negative and derogatory connotations and become as normal as the word "customs" (*fengsu*).

Most of the well-educated elite and many of the Shaanbei urban dwellers, however, still frown on or make jokes of blatantly "superstitious" behavior (see the paternalistic remark made by a university professor quoted in the epigraph to this chapter). Popular religion is indeed a contested site through which different interpretations of reality compete for an audience, and the battle between modern atheist ideologies and traditional religiosity is an ongoing one. The difference between today and the Maoist era is that few people if any are willing to fight for the Marxist-atheist cause against the overwhelming masses of believers and the wide and fast circulation of miracle stories.

Popular Religious Landscape in Contemporary Shaanbei

Deities

Even though popular religion in Shaanbei is not confined to temple-based activities, temples built for different deities are the most visible testimonies to the level of intensity of popular religious life in contemporary Shaanbei. Temples and their accompanying opera stages (when they have any) are easily identifiable by their traditional architectural style of red wooden columns and plain gray or glazed golden-colored tiled roofs. When traveling in Shaanbei, no visitor will fail to notice the many temples that dot the landscape, on mountaintops, in the valleys, and alongside the roads. According to the estimate of a Yulin Prefecture government agency, by the middle of the 1990s there were well over ten thousand temples in the prefecture (Fan 1997: 98). Among these, three to five hundred had supra-local or supra-county influence, about one thousand were at township or rural district level, and the rest were village-level temples (ibid.).

Shaanbei people often identify famous temples not by temple name but by the name of the site, be it a mountain, a valley, or a stretch of desert. The most famous and the largest in scale of all temple sites in Shaanbei is the Daoist White Cloud Mountain (*Baiyunshan*), which, like many famous religious sites in China, is actually a cluster of temples.[14] The second most famous temple site is the Dragon King Valley (*Longwanggou*), which is the focus of this study. Other famous sites include the Great Harmony/Serenity Mountain (*Taiheshan*) in Yan'an City, the Dragon Bond Mountain (*Helongshan*) in Suide County, the Eastern Sand (*Dongsha*) in Yulin City, the Blue Cloud Mountain (*Qingyunshan*) in Yulin County, the Mountain Worship Top (*Jishanliang*) in Jingbian County, and the Ancient Spring (*Gushui*) in Hengshan County.[15] These famous sites typically have very impressive temple buildings and command a large temple ground. The overwhelming majority of temples in Shaanbei, however, are much smaller, one-hall, village temples.

Most of the deities worshiped in the past have been revived, even though some have declined in significance while some others have gained greatly in popularity. The most influential deity is still the Perfected Warrior Ancestral Master (*Zhenwu zushi*), who is the presiding deity of the White Cloud Mountain Daoist shrines and a score of other shrines all over Shaanbei. The other commonly worshiped deities include Guandi (*Guanlaoye* or *Laoye*), the Buddha (*Laofoye*), the Emperor of the Eastern Peak (*Dongyue dadi*), the Jade Emperor (*Yuhuang dadi*), the Three Pure Ones (*Sanqing*), the Three Divine Officials (*Sanguan*), Guanyin, the Monkey King (*Qitian dasheng* or *Dasheng*), the City God (*Chenghuang*), the Horse King (*Mawang*), the Three Heavenly Goddesses (*Sanxiao niangniang*), Sage Ancestor Lü (*Lüzu* or *Lü Dongbin*), various dragon kings (*longwang*), various fertility and child-related goddesses (*niang-niang*), the God of Medicine (*Yaowang*), the God of Wealth (*Caishen*), the God of Letters and Exams (*Wenchang*), the God of Insects (*Bazha*) (see Shu 1969), the Mountain God (*Shanshen*), fox spirits (*huxian*) (see Kang 2002), and various efficacious officials (*lingguan*) and immortals (*daxian*). The above-mentioned deities are all worshiped in temples, but there is a separate category of deities that are worshiped only inside the home or in the courtyard. They include the stove god, Heaven and Earth (*tiandi*, which is strictly speaking not a deity), and the earth god (*tu-shen*).[16]

There were very few ancestral halls in the past in Shaanbei and none have been revived in the reform era, even though there are isolated instances of the rewriting of lineage genealogies. Shaanbei people have never had domestic ancestral altars (except perhaps a few gentry families who might have brought this tradition from the South), even though in the past, as was common in North China, they kept collective ancestral tablets (*shenzhu*) or large cloth scrolls with drawings of ancestral tablets that they used during special occasions such as during the Lunar New Year's ancestral worship ceremony (Cohen 1990: 515–19). There are visits to the graves of the immediate ancestors a few times a year on pre-scribed occasions such as the Cold Food (*hanshi*) / Clear and Bright (*qingming*) (Third Month Ninth)[17] but Shaanbei people do not believe that their ancestors' souls are active forces capable of protecting, benefiting, or troubling the living. On those extremely rare occasions when the souls of "old relatives" (S. *laojiaqing*, meaning dead ancestors) do become active and seek to communicate with the living, it is a sign of trouble and certain divine intervention would be called upon. There are also cases of certain ancestors who have turned into gods and act as tutelary deities for spirit mediums who are usually their descendants (see below on mediumism).[18]

Similarly, few Shaanbei people believe in or care about ghosts. There are no rites, domestic or otherwise, to propitiate the so-called wandering ghosts. The Buddhist monasteries and Daoist temples which had staged exorcistic rituals for individuals or communities in the past have not, to my knowledge, revived these activities.[19] Shaanbei people in general do not perform any rites on Seventh Month Fifteenth (the *zhongyuan* festi-val in Daoist terminology), the supposed date to feed the hungry ghosts (see Teiser 1988). This said, however, I hasten to add that there are two kinds of ghost-like monsters that some Shaanbei people still say exist.

The first are the "paralysis monsters" (S. *tanjiezi*) who kidnap children's souls and cause them go into paralytic fits. The second are "hairy ghost gods" (S. *maoguishen*), mischievous monsters whose powers can sometimes approximate that of minor gods. They can employ different techniques to harm people and their property, making people fall ill or causing valuables to disappear. It is sometimes said that some spirit mediums secretly worship these *maoguishen* to harm people and to generate business. Nevertheless, the discourse on ghosts or monsters is not an elaborate one in Shaanbei.

One recent surprising development in Shaanbei popular religion is the erection in a few places of temple-like structures dedicated to the memory of the three most prominent deceased leaders of the PRC: Chairman Mao Zedong, Premier Zhou Enlai, and General Zhu De. These structures are built on temple grounds, adjacent to real temples, and they are built with temple funds. Supposedly these structures and the statues in them have been built to commemorate the great leaders but not for worship. The burning of incense and spirit money is explicitly prohibited inside these structures. Yet some visitors put lit cigarettes between the fingers of the statues; some explain that they do this because they think the Chairman, the Premier, and the General liked smoking cigarettes when they were alive (recall the cigarette offering in the Norman Bethune story recounted earlier). Even though it is not difficult to imagine some Shaanbei people asking the spirits of Mao, Zhou, and Zhu to bless and protect (*baoyou*) them—the prohibition against burning incense and spirit money hints at the existence of worship—I did not get the feeling that these were established and popular cults.[20] Even the Mao picture (sometimes with Zhou on the opposite side) traffic talisman fad that was all the rage in China in the mid–1990s died out in Shaanbei in the late 1990s. One function these commemorative temple-like structures do perform is to lend legitimacy to the popular religious temples on whose ground they stand.

Temples, Temple Associations, and Temple Festivals

Like Chinese people in other places, Shaanbei people build temples for their gods and goddesses both because they think the deities deserve a beautiful abode and out of communal pride. A beautiful and well-maintained temple and a "red and fiery" (*honghuo*) temple festival reflect well the strength and state of blessedness of the community.[21]

The variety of temples dedicated to different deities is quite astonishing, and an outsider observer would wonder why villagers in this village worship this set of deities whereas villagers in another village worship another set of entirely different deities. In a way the choice of deities of each village is largely a result of historical accident. Sometime in the past a deity might have appeared to a villager either in a dream or through a medium asking the villagers to build a temple for him (or her),[22] or a villager felt grateful for the help of a particular deity (e.g., the Perfected Warrior Ancestral Master) and decided to build the deity a temple in his own village, or a deity decided to make a villager his spirit medium by possessing the latter. Whether or not a temple would be built eventually depended on whether or not other villagers were convinced of the importance of the task and the availability of resources. The maintenance and expansion of the temple would then depend on how efficacious the deity had proved himself to be in responding to the villagers' requests. If the deity became less efficacious, his following and temple donations would dwindle, and eventually the temple would fall into disrepair and the cult would disappear. The same cult could revive, however, after years of disuse, if another villager made a convincing case for the deity. Thousands of temples were destroyed during the Maoist era in Shaanbei, but today a significant proportion of them have been rebuilt (though not necessarily in the same locations). More often than not, the initiation of the rebuilding of the temples depended on a miraculous reappearance of the deity to the villagers.

As tradition dictates, Shaanbei people stage temple festivals at least twice a year, one during the Lunar New Year and the other for the deity's birthday.[23] These temple festivals are organized by temple associations (*hui*), which comprise a small group of responsible and generally respectable adult men who are approved by the deity through divination. If the temple has a medium he will usually become a core member of the temple association. The members of the association are called "association heads" (*huizhang*), and the head of the association is called the "big association head" (*dahuizhang*).

Traditionally, every year in the first half of the first lunar month the temple association organizes a temple yangge troupe to "visit door to door" (*yanmenzi*) around the villages in the vicinity of the temple to greet the villagers and to collect donations for the temple.[24] On First Month Fifteenth the association oversees the communal festival at the temple. The temple festival on the deity's birthday is a much larger event, lasting typically for three days, and thus requires much more organizational effort. Depending on the level of prosperity of the temple community, different folk performing arts are staged for the deity as well as for the community. The goal of every temple festival, like that of other festive occasions such as weddings and funerals, is to produce "excitement and fun" (*honghuo*). If the temple commands a large sum of donations, the temple association will invite an opera troupe to perform folk opera, the culturally ideal choice for temple festivals in honor of deities' birthdays. But if the temple endowment is modest, the temple association will then only invite a folk music band or a storyteller to enliven the atmosphere. Lots of firecrackers are also a must.

Two genres of folk opera are popular in Shaanbei. In most parts of Shaanbei, Shanxi Opera (*Jinju*) enjoys the widest popularity because of the historical and cultural proximity of western Shanxi Province to Shaanbei. In fact, before Liberation there were not many native opera troupes in Shaanbei and numerous Shanxi opera troupes traversed the Shaanbei landscape to perform at temple festivals. In the southern part of Yan'an Prefecture and the western part of Shaanbei another folk opera genre, Qinqiang (literally "the tune or sound of Qin"), is more popular because of the cultural domination in these areas by the Guanzhong Plain to the south. Qinqiang is also quite popular in Yulin City, partly because it was enjoyed by soldiers from Guanzhong stationed in Yulin City during the first half of the 20th century. Unlike in some parts of Fujian, Guangdong, and coastal China (Dean 1994; Johnson 1989), ritual drama has never been an important part of Shanxi and Qinqiang opera repertoires. I also did not encounter any Mulian-themed opera performances. As in other parts of China, traditional dynastic and mythical stories are the most prevalent in Shanxi and Qinqiang operas. Traditional stories also provide the most common themes in Shaanbei storytelling at temple festivals. Folk music bands play a variety of festive music, overlapping with many tunes they play at weddings and funerals.

Many temple festivals in Shaanbei also serve as occasions for commerce. Zhao Shiyu (Zhao 1992, 1995) has argued that, because of the imperfect development of marketing networks in North China and the sparseness of permanent marketing towns, temple festivals in North China in late imperial China had substantial commercial significance. In many ways this is still true today, at least in Shaanbei, where itinerant traders bring their commodities to sell to temple festivalgoers.

All temple festivals entail some kind of pilgrimage, when people from outside of the regular temple community come to pay homage to the deity, meet old friends and relatives, and enjoy the excitement and fun. Daughters who have married out come back to their natal villages, and parents visit their daughters when their in-laws' villages are having temple festivals. When long-distance pilgrimage is involved and the number of outside visitors is high, the temple associations have to arrange accommodation for them. Large temples often have dormitories or build temporary structures for pilgrims. Sometimes when a large number of pilgrims come from one particular locale they will organize into groups to take care of themselves. A famous example of a locale-based pilgrimage organization is the "eight big congregations" (*badahui*) for going to Baiyunshan (the White Cloud Mountain) in Jia County.[25] Because the temple festival at Baiyunshan is so crowded, different congregations in different areas have to arrive on different days to be accommodated, fed, and received properly.

Ritual Specialists

Human intermediaries are often required in the interactions between Shaanbei people and their gods (spirit mediums) and when esoteric ritual knowledge and actions are needed, for example for funerals and burials (yinyang masters).

According to my informants, there are two broad categories of spirit mediums in Shaanbei. Both kinds are categorically called "horse lad" (*matong*, reminiscent of the *jitong* or *tang-ki* in Taiwan). When a deity possesses the medium it is said that the deity "descends from the horse" (*xiama*), and when the deity leaves he or she "mounts the horse" (*qima*). Temple murals often portray the deities as riding horses in the clouds. When possessed, the medium makes frequent horse snorting sounds.

One kind of medium is called *wushen*, whose tutelary deities are so-called "proper gods" (*zhengshishen*) such as the Monkey King. When this medium becomes possessed, the occasion is called "tripping (on?) the altar" (*dietan*). The wushen often uses a heavy, three-pronged wrought-iron sword (*sanshandao*) as ritual paraphernalia, which he shakes and waves. Some wushens, however, do not use the wrought-iron sword but merely fall into an altered state of consciousness when possessed. The other kind of medium is called *shenguan*, whose tutelary deities are ghosts-turned-gods, immortals (*daxian*). For ritual paraphernalia a shenguan usually beats a heavy drum made of wrought iron and goatskin (*yangpigu*) as he chants and dances. The dancing and performing is called "dancing the great god" (*tiao dashen*). In the past the shenguan used to have a fake queue on his head to dance with, hence the irreverent rhyme "Zhang shenguan, Li shenguan, their dicks waggle as they swing their queues" (*Zhang shenguan, Li shenguan, yangqi bianzi qiu dongtan*). My impression is that shenguans are usually found in northern Shaanbei and Inner Mongolia while wushens are usually found in areas further south. Systematic historical and field research needs to be done to ascertain the relationships and differences between the two kinds of mediums. My initial guess is that the shenguan mediums exhibit more influence from Mongolian shamanism, as suggested by the use of the goatskin drum, whereas the wushen practice is more indigenous to Han Chinese culture. During my fieldwork I heard a lot about different mediums but unfortunately witnessed only four in action, three of whom were drum-playing shenguans and one a wushen though without the sword.[26]

People go to see the mediums for all kinds of problems but mostly for treating illnesses. Regardless of the kinds of deities possessing them, all mediums seem to be able to cure illnesses. They are especially effective in treating illnesses that are considered "weird" and "wayward" (*xiebing*), not the kind that regular doctors can deal with. These illnesses include soul loss and disturbances by bad spirits such as the maoguishen ("hairy ghost gods") mentioned earlier, so exorcism is an important component of their repertoire.

The mediums are often the ones who initiate the building of temples for their tutelary deities. Many temples have "resident" mediums the clients can consult. The mediums usually do not live in the temple but at home, which is never far from the temple. The mediums can conduct séances either at home or at the temple, and they can always make house calls if the clients cannot come to visit them. When a deity uses a medium, the reputation of both the deity and the temple depends upon that of the medium. Popular mediums bring more donations to the temple, and the retirement or death of a medium always means a crisis for the cult unless a new medium is quickly chosen by the deity. When there is no medium, people would resort to conventional divination methods (described in Chapter 6). Some mediums can attain considerable fame as healers and diviners, thanks to the efficacious power of the deities that come down to them; and Shaanbei people love spreading and swapping tales of divine/medium efficacy, such as a miraculous healing, thus generating a whole regional lore about famous mediums and their tutelary deities. The fame of a medium may be measured by how crowded his or her "consultation sessions" are, from how far away people come to seek help (especially from outside of Shaanbei), and how many sedan cars (*xiaoche*, literally "small cars," signaling rich or high official patrons) often line up outside the medium's home.

Yinyang masters (or geomancers, called simply *yinyang* or *pingshi* in Shaanbei) form the other important category of ritual specialists, and are in fact much more important than mediums. Yinyang masters specialize in the determination of auspicious dates for weddings and funerals and auspicious sites for houses and graves. Many Shaanbei people might never in their lives consult a medium, but almost all, even most urbanites, will have to use the service of a yinyang because of the importance for Shaanbei people of death rituals. In rural Shaanbei, to build a house or to bury the dead without first consulting a yinyang is unthinkable. The ritual paraphernalia a yinyang uses are a compass (*luopan*) and a ritual almanac. The surface of the compass has many concentric rings of traditional directional signs for the purpose of, for example, making sure that a coffin is properly aligned in the grave or that the main gate of the house makes the right angle with the house. The almanac, not the regular kind available for purchase in bookstands, is for calculating dates according to the compatibility of personal and cosmic signs. During my fieldwork I did not have the opportunity to see how yinyang masters work on housing sites, but I witnessed many times their important ritual work relating to funerals and burials. They make the elaborate and colorful "soul-directing canopy" (*yinhunfan*) from paper, conduct the soul-calling ritual at the burial (so that the wandering soul of the deceased will come back into the body in the coffin), orchestrate the worship at the grave, pacify the earth god at both the burial site and the home of the deceased's family, purify the homes of the neighborhood after the funeral, and mete out other ritual prescriptions to ensure auspiciousness and ritual propriety.

Another important ritual both mediums and yinyang masters can perform on behalf of their clients concerns the protection of children. According to Shaanbei folk belief, small children before reaching twelve years old (traditionally a child is considered one year old at birth) are susceptible to all kinds of dangers, especially to those so-called "life-course obstacles" (*guan* or *guansha*, "obstacle/difficulty demons").[27] In the past, only those children who were very vulnerable to soul loss and other serious illnesses needed to go through the ritual called "passing the obstacle" (*guoguan*) or "exterminating the obstacle-demon" (*puo guansha*). But partly in response to the reduced number and increased value of children, today many parents feel the need to let their children go through the ritual, which is conducted at temple festivals annually for a small fee. At age twelve a child passes the last obstacle, at which point the parents present a white rooster to the deity as a token of gratitude for his or her protection. Both yinyang masters and mediums, and sometimes even laymen, can officiate at "pass the obstacle" rituals.

Unlike mediums, selected by deities as their "horse lad," yinyang masters have generally inherited their trade from their fathers. Usually one male child in each generation is picked to inherit the trade. Whereas there are many female mediums, there are only male yinyang masters. And while mediums practice their trade out of divine calling (ostensibly), yinyang masters are like Daoist priests or Buddhist monks who rely on esoteric knowledge. Apparently anybody can become a yinyang as long as he is able to get his hands on the right knowledge, hence the folk saying "it takes no effort for a learned man to become a yinyang" (*xiucai xue yinyang, yi bo jiu zhuan*). Shaanbei people often used this expression to compliment me on the apparent ease with which I understood what they happened to be teaching me.

Besides yinyang masters and mediums, there are a small number of Buddhist monks, nuns, and Daoist priests in Shaanbei who reside in officially registered monasteries and temples and are paid salaries by the local Buddhist or Daoist associations. Buddhism used to have a strong presence in Shaanbei before the 20th century, but today only a few monasteries in Shaanbei have permanent clergy. Their numbers are very small. Sometimes the monks are called to conduct a funeral service, but often lay villagers are hired to do similar Buddhist funeral ceremonies (the latter eat meat and drink alcohol at the funeral banquet just like the other guests).[28] There are even fewer Daoist priests, who are mostly concentrated in the White Cloud Mountain Daoist Shrines in Jia County. Despite the fact that both Buddhism and Daoism are "official religions" recognized by the state, their institutionalized expressions are extremely hampered by the latter. Ironically, it is the "feudal superstitious" elements of religion that enjoyed the most vigorous revival during the reform era. A yinyang once told me proudly that they [i.e., the yinyang masters] were the key actors in reviving folk religion and rituals in Shaanbei whereas the Buddhist monks and Daoist priests have not made a similar comeback.[29] Kenneth Dean (1993) has argued that in southern Fujian the Daoist liturgical framework helped spread and secure the influence of local popular religious cults. A similar symbiotic relationship between Daoist ritual specialists and popular religious cults is absent in Shaanbei. The reason might be that the Daoist priests in Shaanbei belong to the True Perfection tradition, which is more monastic and less well integrated into their surrounding communities as compared to the Zhengyi Daoist tradition in southeastern China.

CHAPTER FOUR

Beliefs and Practices

Shaanbei People's Religiosity and Religious Habitus

The Problem of Religious Belief

Looking at the rate at which temples and religious practices have been revived in Shaanbei, the impression one gets is that Shaanbei people are very religious. But what is the nature of Shaanbei people's religious beliefs? Perhaps we should question the very concept of "belief" in the Chinese popular religious context, as the concept carries with it enormous Judeo-Christian theological baggage.

It is always extremely difficult to determine people's beliefs. Inference from behavior ignores possible discrepancy between belief and practice. Direct interrogation may elicit falsehood. Concurring with R. F. Johnston's skepticism about Chinese religiosity, Arthur P. Wolf warned that it "should never be thought that people believe everything they tell the visiting anthropologist. Some do; others do not" (Wolf 1974c: vii). An additional vexing problem arises in the discrepancy between *actually experienced* beliefs and beliefs *constructed* by the anthropologist from *statements solicited from the informants about their beliefs*. Even more radically, Rodney Needham has famously asserted that unless a culture has a set of vocabulary to express and talk about religious belief we cannot assume that this culture has such thing as belief or the people actually "experience belief" (Needham 1972). To all of these I would add that even if the natives have a language for belief and really believe what they say they believe, we might still have the problem of explicating the nature of that belief.

It is not difficult to imagine that the tenor of belief in a monotheistic

God would be qualitatively different from a religiosity based on a variety of deities and spirits, as is the case in Chinese popular religion. But that is still assuming a phenomenological equivalence between *"believing in God"* and *"believing in* gods, goddesses, and spirits.*"* This is the kind of functionalist fallacy the early anthropologist Franz Boas fought against when he opposed the tendency in ethnological museums to display the "same category" of artifacts from different cultures side by side because of their functional equivalence and evolutionary progression (Boas 1974: 61–67).[1] For Boas, it would not do to put a New Guinea stick hoe next to a Chinese flat-blade hoe just because both are agricultural instruments. He argued that the significance and meaning of one category of artifacts cannot be understood without putting them within the total context of the culture from which they come, so he advocated displaying all of each particular culture's artifacts together organically and in relation to one another. Therefore in his view, Kwakiutl religious beliefs and practices could only be understood in the context of the whole repertoire of Kwakiutl culture and not when mechanically juxtaposed and compared with religious beliefs and practices of other cultures. While comparative studies have tremendous value when done properly, I think we should take Boas's advice seriously and not extract facile "categories" of seemingly similar phenomena out of context from very different cultural settings. In our case I suggest that we investigate the nature of belief in the context of Shaanbei society and culture. In an important sense this book is about how embedded religious ideas and practices are in their cultural and sociopolitical milieu.

But first let us look at the concept of belief in a classic Biblical passage: "Go out all over the world and preach the gospel to the whole creation. *He who believes* and is baptized will be saved; *he who refuses belief* will be condemned" (Mark 16:15-16; quoted in the *Catholic Encyclopaedic Dictionary* 1951: 187; emphasis added). As is evident in this key passage in the New Testament, one's belief in the gospel (there is God and Jesus Christ is the savior, etc.) is central to Christian religiosity and to one's ontological status, i.e., saved or condemned.

During the course of my fieldwork in Shaanbei, however, I seldom encountered any explicit talk of "belief in deities." Shaanbei people do have the word for the verb "believe" (*xiangxin*) as used in "I believe what you are saying," but they do not say "I believe in the Black Dragon King" or "I believe in gods and goddesses." Most important, they do not have the noun "belief" (as in "you have the right to hold your religious beliefs") or "faith" to refer to the totality of their "beliefs." In contemporary elite discourse in China there is the word "belief" or "conviction" (*xinyang*), but I have never heard Shaanbei people use it. So was Rodney Needham right, that because Shaanbei people do not have a language for religious belief they therefore do not think it is important and they do not experience belief as a psychological state? Needham might have given too much weight to linguistic representations as signs or proof of mental states, for there are many things in life that are too elusive to be captured by linguistic conventions (especially affective states). But we should heed his skepticism regarding an overly facile identification of a familiar psychological state (i.e., "belief") in otherwise unfamiliar places (a lesson similar to the one we draw from Boas). It goes without saying that when I use words in this book such as "believe," "believer," "worship," "worshiper," or "pray" the reader needs to be aware of the considerable linguistic compromise necessary in describing Chinese popular religious practices in the English language; these are merely linguistic shorthand.

Religiosity

Deities, temples, temple associations, and ritual specialists are all integral elements of the Shaanbei popular religious landscape, yet one cannot fully understand how these elements are mobilized without a careful understanding of Shaanbei people's religiosity and religious habitus.

By religiosity I mean the *manner and extent of religiousness* of the people under consideration. When we describe some people as being "very religious," we usually mean that these people's lives are infused with a heightened level of religiosity, and religious beliefs and practices suffuse their consciousness and daily activities. In the history of Christianity, a broad distinction has been made between two modalities of religiosity. The first modality, *ritualism*, is characterized by formalistic, behavioral displays of faith (e.g., elaborate church service with complicated manipulation of religious symbolism). The second modality, *piety*, emphasizes the internal state of devotional feelings but not conspicuous, ritualized expressions of such feelings (Quietism being one extreme form of such religiosity). The "piety believers," who chastise the "ritualism believers" for their "empty ritualism" seem to have gained the upper hand in the battle to define whose religiosity is a "higher," "better," and "truer" religiosity, and subsequently, who are better Christians (despite protests from the other camp).

One legacy of the victory of piety over ritualism in the Christian West is the modern craze for spirituality. "Being spiritual" transcends the rigidities of organized religion and even the required central tenet of belief in the one Christian God. Spiritualism thus helps establish a deep respect in the West for other religious traditions that are perceived to be spiritual (e.g., yoga in Hinduism, Japanese Zen Buddhism, Tibetan Buddhism). Spiritualism easily accommodates religious pluralism because it is believed that the different gods in different religious traditions are different manifestations of the same Higher Truth and that the paths might differ but they all lead to the same ultimate destination. For a contemporary, Western (Christian) spiritualist, the biggest threat to his or her sensibility therefore is not other religious traditions but atheism. This same sensibility thus to some extent explains the enthusiasm in the West that has greeted the religious revival in heretofore "Godless" Communist China.

But ritualism and piety are only two modalities of Christian religiosity. This admittedly oversimplified contrast serves to highlight the internal diversity of Christian religiosity. Other factors contribute as well to the often astonishing diversity found within Christian religiosity: national history, region and locale, historical period, political climate, socioeconomic condition, race, ethnicity, class, gender, and so forth. Just as it is difficult, if not impossible, to talk about an "average Christian," it is equally difficult to speak of an "average Shaanbei popular religious believer." I will discuss the problem of variation of the character and level of belief between individuals when I introduce the concept of religious habitus below, but first we need to explicate the nature of Shaanbei people's religiosity.

Shaanbei Peasant Religiosity and Religious Practices

Even though Shaanbei people do not speak of "belief" explicitly, they engage in activities that imply belief in the existence of supernatural forces and the magical power of the deities to bless them and to aid them when they are in distress. Their religiosity is largely based on a practical dependence on these deities. Unlike the average Christian who reads the Bible, goes to church, and prays to God regularly, the average Shaanbei popular religious "believer" does not own any religious text to read, does not form a congregation to meet at regular intervals, and does not pray to any particular deity with any frequency. His or her religiosity is normally diffused but is intensified by some personal or familial crisis.

Shaanbei people go to the deities or consult mediums when they encounter specific problems or crises. However, they employ a host of family ritual procedures to deal with a variety of simple problems. One may call these home magical remedies. One of the most common problems in Shaanbei peasant homes is soul loss of a child; the family ritual procedure involved is known as soul-calling (*jiaohun*). When a baby or young child cannot stop crying, especially at night, or acts listless, or refuses to eat, and the condition persists, some Shaanbei people would think that the soul of the child has gone astray. One family remedy is to draw on a sheet of paper an upside-down hanging donkey (*daodiaolü*) and write a rhyme next to the picture. This sheet is then pasted on a tree or lamppost on a main village road for passersby to read, so that the child's soul may be called back (this apparently being a very widespread practice; see Gates 1993: 251). The content of the rhyme is some variation on the following:

> The heaven is bright and the earth is bright;
> There is a child in my home that cries at night.
> If a passing gentleman reads this once;
> He [the child] will sleep all night till broad daylight.

Another simple remedy to call back the soul is employed if the first one does not work. This method works for both adult and child patients. The father and a sibling of the patient circle the village in the evening calling the soul. During their entire round the father cries out the name of the patient and the sibling replies in the voice of the patient: "I'm back." During my fieldwork I encountered unexpectedly this kind of soul-calling duo a number of times, each time being quite an eerie moment.

When simple family ritual procedures fail to effect recovery of the patient, most Shaanbei people go to a temple, consult a medium, bring the patient to see a doctor, or do a combination of all these, not unlike the Taiwanese in similar situations (see Gould-Martin 1975; Harrell 1974a). When visiting a deity or consulting a medium, Shaanbei people normally donate some incense money and make a vow to contribute more incense money, bring gifts, or sponsor opera performances if the deity or the deity possessing the medium helps the patient recover. Of course, illness is far from being the only problem Shaanbei people bring to the deities. Other problems include marriage prospects, changing jobs, promotion, travel or business plans, lawsuits, interpersonal problems, missing persons or goods, or any other troubles. Many Shaanbei people attend temple festivals specifically to honor their vows by bringing the promised amount of incense money donation. Occasionally personal troubles are diagnosed by mediums or deities to be caused by a former dishonored vow, sometimes even from past generations.

When Shaanbei people are not troubled by any specific problems, they go to the deities to give thanks and to pray for their continual blessing. The most commonly used phrases in the prayers are "[We or I] implore Your Venerability to bless/protect us so that we will have good fortune, every endeavor will go smoothly, and we will be free from trouble (*qiu ni laorenjia baoyou zanmen dajidali pingpinganan*). The "we" (*zanmen*) in this prayer generally refers to the immediate family of the person praying, and that is why the expression "our whole family" (*zanmen quanjia*) is often used instead. This "we" almost never refers to the larger descent group, the village, let alone even large collectivities such as province or nation. Even when the prayer (as in a rain prayer) refers specifically to "the myriad masses" (*wanmin*), the implied object of blessing is still the numerous families and their members.

Shaanbei people usually make the above-mentioned generalized requests on two different occasions: during the first lunar month and on a particular deity's birthday. The first thing many Shaanbei villagers do in the morning of the first lunar month is to pay respect to the local deity (usually at the village temple). On First Month Fifteenth yangge troupes of different villages and towns (and nowadays also schools) visit the temples and pray for blessing for the year, but this particular celebration is generally considered part of the New Year's festivities. And then there are the temple festivals celebrating the deities' birthdays. Shaanbei people say they go to a temple to "pay respect to the deity" (*jingshen*) instead of "worship" (*bai*).

Magical Efficacy and Religious Habitus

The single most important concept in understanding the Shaanbei deity-worshiper relationship is *ling* (magical efficacy). It refers to the ability of the deity to respond (*ying*) to the worshipers' problems, for example, curing an ill family member, pointing to the right direction for conducting business, enlightening one on a knotty personal dilemma, bringing down ample rain after a bad drought, and so forth.[2] Therefore, we can characterize Shaanbei popular religion as essentially *a religion of efficacious response* (*lingying*). Most thanksgiving plaques or banners at the Black Dragon King Temple, as in other popular religious temples in

Shaanbei, have the following stock expressions: *youqiu biying* (whatever you beg for, there will be a response), *shenling xianying* (the divine efficacy has been manifested), and *baoda shen'en* or *dabao shen'en* (in gratitude for divine benevolence).

If we reject the possibility of real divine power, we have to examine how *ling* is socioculturally constructed. Even though *ling* is constructed by people, people's experience of *ling* is real and is a social fact. A deity is *ling* because people experience his power and therefore say that he is *ling*. One deity is more popular and "powerful" than another because more people say the first one is more *ling*. A perceptive Taiwanese informant told the anthropologist Emily Ahern:

> When we say a god is *lieng* [*ling*] we mean the god really does help us. Word is then spread from person to person, each telling the other that the god helped. So it is really a matter of relations among men. . . . A change in the popularity of temples is not a result of change in gods' abilities. The abilities of gods don't change. People's attitudes toward them do, however. (Ahern 1981a, quoted in Sangren 1987: 202)

This understanding of deities' power would apply in Shaanbei as well. In other words, the more people experience a deity's *ling*, the more *ling* is attributed to the deity, which in turn contributes to the intensity of people's experience of the deity's *ling*, and so on. One deity's decline in popularity is usually caused by the rise in people's *ling* claims for another deity and the subsequent defection of incense money to the other deity.

On the one hand, *ling* is a deity's power in the abstract. On the other hand, *ling* inheres in concrete relationships, between the deity and an individual worshiper or between the deity and a community. It is meaningful to worshipers mostly in the second sense because *ling* in the abstract is only latent power, not manifest power, and the only meaningful way a deity manifests his or her power is through aiding a worshiper who is in trouble or who needs the blessing to weather life's many trials and tribulations. An allegedly powerful deity whom a person has nonetheless never consulted is without significance to this particular person. Like social relationships, the relationships people have with deities also need maintenance and frequent renewal, hence the visits to the temple in the first lunar month and on the deity's birthday.

Despite the great variety of deities worshiped in Shaanbei, there seem to be some very basic principles or postulates that inform Shaanbei people's religious beliefs and practices and form the core of their religiosity. These basic postulates are:

1. That there are gods (or that it does not hurt to assume that there are gods);

2. That people should respect the gods and do whatever pleases the gods (e.g., building them beautiful temples, celebrating their birthdays) and should not do anything that displeases the gods (e.g., blasphemy);

3. That the gods can bless people and help them solve their problems;

4. That people should show their gratitude for the gods' blessing and divine assistance by donating incense money, burning spirit paper, presenting laudatory thanksgiving plaques or flags, spreading the gods' names, and so forth;

5. That some gods possess more efficacy than others (or have specialized areas of efficacious expertise); and

6. That one is allowed or even encouraged to seek help from a number of different gods provided that one does not forget to give thanks to all of them once the problem is solved.

These six basic postulates underlie most of Shaanbei people's religious beliefs and practices, even though they are not systematically laid out as I have done here. For example, all temple festivals are expressly to celebrate the gods' birthdays, to show gratitude for a year's peace and prosperity or a good harvest, or simply to make the gods happy. Scholars of Chinese popular religion have attempted to categorize temples and their cults using criteria such as the deities' functional specialties (C. K. Yang 1961) or the temple-cult's membership spread, i.e., local or translocal (Baity 1975; Duara 1988a; Faure 1987; Sangren 1987). Yet despite these differences most Chinese people, or at least most Shaanbei people, seem to practice popular religion according to the above-mentioned postulates or principles.

Different people must have different degrees of faith in the power of different deities depending on their personalities and personal experience with these deities. In their comparative study of a Chinese person's and a Hindu Indian person's religiosity, Roberts, Chiao, and Pandey (1975) put forward the concepts of "personal pantheon" and "meaningful god set." According to them, a personal pantheon is "the aggregate of gods known to a single believer" (ibid.: 122), whereas this same person's meaningful god set refers to the most important subset and core of his personal pantheon, which comprises "gods who are particularly meaningful for the believer in the sense that they have personal significance and salience for him, but not necessarily in the sense that he loves or treasures them"

(123). The same approach was also applied to the determination of a personally meaningful set of sacred places (Roberts, Morita, and Brown 1986).

This person-centered approach is immensely useful to the proper understanding of Shaanbei people's religiosity. Even though the popular religious landscape in Shaanbei consists of a large number of deities, sacred sites, and religious specialists, each Shaanbei person's set of meaningful deities, sacred sites, and religious specialists is a limited one. The makeup of each person's "religious habitus" (concept inspired by Pierre Bourdieu's notion of "habitus"; see Bourdieu 1977)—that is, his attitudes toward, and behaviors concerning deities, sacred sites, religious specialists, religious rituals, and supernatural forces in general—is determined by whether or not, in what way, and to what degree the events in his personal life have brought him, in a meaningful way, to which of the deities, sacred sites, and religious specialists. It also goes without saying that each person's religious habitus changes over time. Because of their lack of life's many responsibilities and experience with deities' assistance, children and young people tend to treat deities with less respect, and they also know much less about different deities' legends and magical exploits.[3]

In his study of individual variations of religious belief and unbelief among Taiwanese villagers, Harrell also provided a useful, person-centered perspective on Chinese religiosity (1974a). Among the villagers he interviewed, Harrell found four basic types of believers (or what I would call believers with four basic kinds of religious habitus): intellectual believers, true believers, nonbelievers, and practical believers. Intellectual believers base their beliefs on intellectual coherence and systematic relatedness of religious ideas and practices and are extremely rare; true believers are characterized by their total credulity toward all religious ideas and are rare; nonbelievers are those who completely disregard or ignore the possible truth or usefulness of any religious tenets and are rare as well; and practical believers base their belief on the principle of practical utility and constitute the great majority of Harrell's interviewees. The religious attitude of the practical believers is one of "half trust and half doubt" (ibid.: 86, in Mandarin *banxin banyi*) or "better believe than not." Even though I did not conduct a similar, systematic study of individual variations of Shaanbei people's degree of belief and unbelief, my impression is that in Shaanbei too a great proportion of people are practical believers and many fewer are true believers or nonbelievers. Some Shaanbei urbanites I talked to also expressed the sentiment of practical and selective belief, as some of them told me that insofar as supernatural powers and stories of efficacious responses are concerned, "one should not not believe [what others say about the power of deities and other supernatural occurrences], nor should one believe everything [they say]" (*buke buxin, buke quanxin*). Another saying also testifies to the flexible attitude Shaanbei people hold toward deities and worship: "If you worship (literally 'honor' or 'respect') him, the deity will be there; if you don't worship him, he won't mind" (*jingshen shenzai, bujing buguai*).

Popular Religion and the Village Community

I have so far characterized Shaanbei people's religiosity as mostly based on private desires (individual or familial). Sometimes community concerns come to the fore and communal solidarity is the goal. At Chinese New Year, when a village *yangge* troupe visits the village deities and prays for their blessing, the villagers expressly petition on behalf of the entire village collectivity. At the annual temple festivals many villages also have a "sharing the sacrifice (sacrificed animal offering)" (*fensheng*) ceremony in recognition of each household's membership in the village community. In this ceremony or ritual, a pig is first brought to the village temple and ritually sacrificed to the deities (*lingsheng*), then brought back to the village, slaughtered, cut into small pieces, and divided into shares according to the number of households in the village. Representatives of each household pay for their share and bring the meat home. Most importantly, participation in sharing the sacrifice confirms all the households' membership in a moral community overseen by the patron deity.

Another occasion for the confirmation of community is the collective responsibility of staging and paying for the annual temple festivals honoring the deities' birthdays. In the nineteenth and early twentieth century, both Catholic and Protestant missionaries in many parts of rural China were engaged in aggressive proselytizing. Villagers who became converts invariably came into conflict with those who did not, especially over temple festival dues. The converts were instructed by the missionaries to perceive the village deities as pagan idols and to refuse to pay their share of the dues. The rest of the village argued that as long as these converts were still part of the village they were still responsible for their dues, especially because the entire community, including the Christian converts, benefited from, say, the rain brought by the village dragon god (Litzinger 1996). The same kind of conflicts also happened in Shaanbei.

However, it would be erroneous to conclude, based on the above-mentioned examples, that community solidarity is the primary concern of Shaanbei popular religion. The resurgence of popular religion in rural China, especially the reconstruction of village temples and the staging of temple festivals, persuades some China scholars that the rural communities are reasserting their autonomy vis-à-vis the state. In these accounts there is an emphasis on the collective, community-based, if not egalitarian, dimensions of popular religion (Anagnost 1994; Dean 1997, 1998a; Jing 1996; see also Judd 1994). Other scholars, however, have pointed out the selfish, familial-individualistic, and amoral dimensions of these resurgent popular religious activities (Bruun 1996; Chen 1995; Gates 1987; Siu 1989b; R. Watson 1988; Weller 1994a, 1994b). China scholars have recognized for some time now that Chinese people tend to evaluate and attend to human relationships according to degrees of social distance, with the family being the core of a person's concern and devotion (what the Chinese anthropologist Fei Xiaotong has famously called *chaxu geju*, i.e., patterns of differential relations). My Shaanbei data suggest that both personal-familial and communal dimensions are present, and it is important to distinguish between the two. Put simply, we can say that while collective popular religious activities (e.g., temple-building, temple festivals) are sporadic manifestations of assertions of community and the organizational capacity inherent in popular religion, *the familial-individualistic dimension is the perennial force motivating people to engage in popular religious activities*, be they collectivity-based or household/individual-based.

Popular Religion as an Idiom of Communal Hegemony

Insofar as the village temple belongs to the village community, the village as a whole worships the village deities as a community of believers. Membership in this community is assumed but also reaffirmed through personal worship, donation of incense money, participation in temple festivals, the sharing of the sacrifice, and other activities related to the deities. When it seems that everyone in the village is a member of the community of believers (disregarding the level of commitment and involvement), the worship of the village deities has achieved what can be called *communal hegemony*.[4]

A community of believers does not prohibit its members from seeking help from deities outside or participating in other such communities, but it would sanction against the absence of its members from its own communal worship. The above-mentioned conflicts among Christian converts and other villagers over temple festival fees are a good example of such sanctions. When there are explicit nonbelievers or blasphemers who challenge the power or even the existence of the deities and the validity of others' beliefs, the community of believers often employs coercive measures to attempt to bring these people back in line. They will recount stories of divine retribution and warn of bad death and suffering for the nonbelievers and their families. This kind of communal coercion is a very common practice among believers of Chinese popular religion and seems to be effective in at least subduing dissenting voices within the community if not actually stamping out unbelief.

As in many other Shaanbei temple revivals in the early 1980s, the initial period of the rebuilding and reviving of the Heilongdawang Temple also relied on the power of communal coercion. Here I give only one story relating to what had happened to a man who played an active role in destroying the Black Dragon King Temple during the Cultural Revolution.

Before Liberation, the Heilongdawang Temple was run by three neighboring villages. During collectivization these three villages became three brigades, and when the directive to "destroy the four olds" came from the commune in 1966, the brigades decided to take down the temple and use the much-needed building materials for civic purposes. They divided up the job; one brigade was to take down the main temple building, the other the entrance hallway, and the third the opera stage.

A young man from one of the brigades, a small-team leader, was in charge of the operation on the main building, where the Heilongdawang statue stood. In a flare of revolutionary zeal, he led the charge on Heilongdawang by hitting the large clay statue on the neck with his hoe, knocking off the statue's head. The operation on the whole was very smooth; there was no drama of Red Guards' storming the temple, clashing with protective peasants, as had happened in some parts of Shaanbei. No one sensed any ominous happenings looming ahead and indeed nothing bad happened after the temple was taken down, that is, not until quite a few years later.

Sometime in the mid-70s villagers were called to help build the runway of the nearby military airport. The same man, now in his late thirties and still a small-team leader, was in charge of leading a group of men to blast rocks on the riverbank. Three holes full of dynamite were ignited but only two went off. They waited for a long while for the third to explode but it didn't. The women came with lunch so the men stopped working. Lunch in hand, the team leader was finally overcome by curiosity and went over to the third hole to check what had gone wrong—only to have his head blasted off.

Some time after this tragedy, people began to comment on the causal link between this man's rash attack on Heilongdawang and his subsequent bloody and sudden death. The story of divine retribution quickly became a household tale in the area. Some even added the details: the head was blown from the neck at exactly the spot where he had struck Heilongdawang's neck with his hoe.[5] Today, the man's three sons and their families still live in the shadow of this incident and the village's communal discourse of divine retribution. The villagers all think that it was because of the father's bad deeds that the third son is a half-witted village idiot and the other two married sons have only daughters but no sons. The blasphemer's descendants have essentially become semi-outcasts in their own village.

Belief in deities is as much a personal psychological state as a public discourse. When the majority of a close-knit village community believe in the village deity, it is extremely difficult to publicly present dissenting views, much less knocking down the deity's statue. Members of the community who believe in the deity thus form a discourse community as well, enforcing a more or less uniform view on the efficacy of the deity, even if allowing different individual experience with the deity. If a person states that he doesn't believe in the deity and something terrible happens to him or his family, the believers will say that the person suffers because the deity is punishing him for his blasphemy and impropriety. Normally, very few people have the nerve or resolve to counter such a strong communal hegemonic force.

This communal coercion dimension of popular religion also partially explains the reluctance of local cadres to crack down on temples and temple activities. Theoretically, because all cadres are Communist Party members and presumably atheists, they should not be afraid of gods and divine retribution. In reality, however, as members of local communities and under the influence of the communal hegemony of believers (who are more often than not their close kin), local cadres are often believers themselves, which makes them unwilling to interfere with popular religious activities. In fact, many village temple bosses are current or ex–village Party secretaries, some devout servants of the village deities making up for having wronged the deities during the Maoist era.

It is widely known that the Communist government resorted to physical violence during campaigns against "feudal superstitions"; but too often scholars overlook the element of communal coercion inherent in the maintenance of popular religious communities. Community-based popular religious activities might have the potential to counter the state's penetration and serve as the locus of folk civil society, but we also need to recognize the implications of the communal hegemony dimension of Chinese popular religion.

The Bureaucratic Model and the Personal Model

Both natives and scholars alike have often characterized Chinese gods as the supernatural equivalents of official bureaucrats (Wolf 1974a). Historically, this symbolic bureaucratization of Chinese gods has been the result of the interaction of many forces. Religious Daoism found in the imperial bureaucracy a convenient model for organizing a hierarchical pantheon headed by the Jade Emperor. The imperial court realized that it could co-opt popular religious deities by bestowing on them imperial titles and bureaucratic ranks. And local cults welcomed these imperial favors and sometimes even invented them as markers of distinction and legitimacy. Feuchtwang (1993) has argued that the bureaucratic metaphor should best be seen in light of power pretensions predicated on the authority of history. The process of the bureaucratization of deities was so thorough that few deities in late imperial China were not touched by this bureaucratic metaphor. Even those deities known for their free-spirited personae (e.g., the Monkey King and the patricidal enfant terrible Nezha) are often depicted as engaging in battles with the divine bureaucracy and, in the case of the Monkey King, enthroning himself to be "the Great Emperor that Parallels Heaven."[6] And the Black Dragon King in our story evolved from a powerful local rain god to an imperially recognized, titled "King" (his title was actually Marquis of Efficacious Response).

Do Shaanbei peasants see their deities as supernatural equivalents of bureaucrats? Most Shaanbei deities are decorated with bureaucratic garb, especially City Gods and all the deities with bureaucratic or imperial titles (e.g., the Great Emperor of the Eastern Peak and the Marquis of Efficacious Response). But how do Shaanbei peasants perceive real bureaucrats? The relationship between local state agents and ordinary peasants in Shaanbei is strained, to put it mildly. Indeed, the image of the local bureaucrats in the minds of Shaanbei peasants is mostly negative: they take things away from you but rarely give anything back; the local officials are good-for-nothing and corrupt, spending all their time eating, drinking, singing karaoke songs, and dancing with prostitutes (see Gates 1991); the traffic police are too rapacious; the birth control work teams are so brutal with their fines and punishments that they are worse than the Nationalists before Liberation; doctors at the county hospital are asking for too much gift-money; and no one can hope to win a lawsuit unless he knows someone in the county or prefectural court (*youren*). In peasant eyes, the local bureaucrats are better at squeezing the people, not serving the people.

Because real bureaucrats in Shaanbei couldn't care less about serving the people, it is hard to imagine that worshipers perceive Heilongdawang or other deities as the celestial equivalent of bureaucrats, even though it is possible to speculate that they see in deities an image of *ideal* bureaucrats. But most important, the way Shaanbei people interact with the deities suggests that they operate on what Robert Hymes has called a "personal model" of divinity rather than the "bureaucratic model" (Hymes 2002). The bureaucratic model operates as pretensions of the Daoist priests who symbolically subjugate local cult deities and local communities by assuming a mediating role between the Daoist high gods and low-ranking local gods and humble earthlings. On the other hand, most popular religious worshipers establish dyadic personal relationships with deities and directly call on them for blessings and magical assistance. My Shaanbei findings support this "personal model" of divinity.

Modalities of "Doing Religion" in Chinese Culture

One of the best-known debates in the anthropological study of Chinese religion was on the question of whether there is one unified Chinese religion or many religions[7] (Freedman1974; Wolf 1974b; Sangren 1984b, 1987; Weller 1987a; Feuchtwang 1991). The debate originated in an exchange between Maurice Freedman and Arthur Wolf. Freedman suggested that because of China's long history of political and cultural unity, its religious life ought to have been unified into a system as well, and that the apparent gaps between elite and commoner ideas and practices are merely differences in expressions of the same underlying principles. He posited as a working hypothesis that "all religious argument and ritual differentiation [in premodern China] were conducted within a common language of basic conceptions, symbols, and ritual forms" (Freedman 1974: 40). So the task of the anthropologist of Chinese religion is to identify these ruling conceptions, symbols, and ritual forms.

Arthur Wolf countered by arguing first that because in China priests were not preachers, there cannot be such a thing as a Chinese religion (Wolf 1974b: 17). For Wolf, the esotericism of elite religious specialists and peasant practices cannot be reconciled into a unified system, implying that these two realms of ideas and practices are not merely "idiomatic translations of one another," as Freedman would have it (Freedman 1974: 21). The second reason Wolf objected was almost one of aesthetics: "Where belief systems are uniform, there is little to interest the anthropologist beyond the historical origin of the uniformity. Where belief systems vary, there is the endlessly fascinating question of why" (Wolf 1974b: 18).

Intuitively I am more sympathetic to Wolf's position, but on the other hand I also sympathize with the impulse behind Freedman's desire to find order in the confused mess of diverse Chinese religious ideas and practices. In a way my attempt to identify the nature of Shaanbei peasant religiosity and religious habitus can be seen as trying to determine elementary structures of popular religious practices, though not on a macro, systemic level. There are two ways to look at the "one or many Chinese religions" debate in a new light. First, instead of seeing premodern Chinese religious life as either unified or divided, it would be more useful to say that there were unifying and diversifying forces and tendencies at the same time (i.e., adopting a perspective that emphasizes process over structure) (see Sangren 1984b). So the task is not to find the common denominators or a generative core of Chinese religious ideas and practices (Freedman's proposition) or to identify differences in social structure and organization in explaining differences in religious beliefs (Wolf's proposition); rather, the task is to identify and analyze the forces that pull or push Chinese religious ideas and practices centripetally or centrifugally and see how these forces contest and negotiate with one another.

Another way to resolve the debate is to circumvent it. One important limitation of this "one or many" debate about the unity and diversity of Chinese religious life is its emphasis on religious conceptions rather than on practices. When religious practices are discussed, they are assumed to reflect similarities or differences in religious conceptions instead of themselves constituting the defining components of the debate (Weller 1994b; Shahar and Weller 1996). I suggest that we put aside religious conceptions for a moment and see how considering religious practices would help clarify the debate. I argue that in the long history of religious development in China, different ways of "doing religion" evolved and cohered into relatively easy-to-identify modalities. These are relatively well-defined forms that different people can adopt and combine to deal with different concerns in life; however, the contents within these forms can vary widely. These modalities of "doing religion" are:

1. Discursive/scriptural. People are attracted to this modality because of the allure of Confucian, Daoist, Buddhist Great Texts (classics, sutras, etc.). This modality obviously requires a high level of literacy and a penchant for philosophical and "theological" thinking.

2. Personal-cultivational. Practices such as meditation, qigong, alchemy, personal sutra chanting, and keeping a merit/demerit ledger belong to this modality. This modality presupposes a long-term interest in cultivating and transforming oneself (whether Buddhist, Daoist, or Confucian). Sometimes sectarian movements might precipitate out of these personal-cultivational pursuits (e.g. Falungong).

3. Liturgical/ritual. Practices such as exorcism, sutra chanting rites, *fengshui* maneuvers, and feeding the hungry ghosts belong to this modality. Practices in this modality aim at more immediate transformations of reality done in highly symbolic forms. This is the modality of the religious specialists (monks, Daoist priests, yinyang masters, Confucian ritual masters, spirit mediums, exorcist-dancers, etc.) and often involves esoteric knowledge and elaborate ritual procedures.

4. Immediate-practical. Practices in this modality also aim at immediate results but compared to those in the liturgical modality they are more direct and simple. There are minimal ritual elaborations. Examples include divination, getting divine medicine from a deity, charms, and consulting a spirit medium.

5. Relational. This modality emphasizes the relationship between humans and deities (or ancestors). Examples are building temples, making offerings, taking vows, spreading miracle stories, celebrating deities' birthdays at temple festivals, and pilgrimage.

These are frameworks for religious practice and action. At any one time in any corner of the vast late imperial Chinese empire, all of these modalities were available to be adopted by individuals or social groups, though factors such as class, gender, literacy level, accidents of birth and residence, position within different social networks, and temperament might channel some people toward certain modalities and not others. Most peasants in China, like those in Shaanbei, have traditionally adopted a combination of the relational and the immediate-practical modalities into their religiosity; sometimes they adopt the liturgical modality and hire religious specialists when the occasion requires (e.g., funeral, communal exorcism). Illiteracy and lack of leisure would largely preclude them from the discursive and personal-cultivational modalities. The traditional educated elite tended to adopt a combination of the discursive and the personal-cultivational modalities, but they too often needed the service of the liturgical specialists.

The most significant merit of this framework of modalities would be that it focuses on the ways in which people "do religion" rather than their religious conceptions, which can vary widely and in ways that defy any explanation; there are many flukes and accidents in the history of the evolution and interaction of religious ideas, and people's social experience and social structure do not always determine the contours of their religious imagination. Studying people's religious conceptions is important, but it will only yield a bewildering diversity; on the other hand, there are only a limited number of forms (modalities) that permeate the Chinese religious landscape. The varieties of Chinese religious life have resulted from the elaboration of differences within these forms as well as the different configurations of various forms; I suggest that the great variety in the symbolic contents of the Chinese religious world as well as the relatively small number of forms (modalities) and their lasting stability and versatility are both great achievements in the history of world religions. This framework of modalities of doing religion suggests a possible compromise between Freedman's position and that of Wolf: it can help explain the diversity as well as provide a unifying framework (admittedly not a system) for the understanding of Chinese religious life.

Legends and Histories

Heilongdawang and the Heilongdawang Temple

Sharp rocks, like ten thousand tablets, are pointing towards the sky;
Dark clouds black as ink are shrouding the body of the dragon.
Indistinctly, three pearl trees emerge at the beachhead;
Hidden behind the mouth of the lair are bushels of treasures.
As the dragon dips its head shimmering droplets hang from its jaw;
And when it summersaults in the deep pool the waves sparkle.
We prayed for rain at the Yulin Pass and the next day it rained all over;
It was only then that I believed there is god in the magical spring.
   —*The Black Dragon Lair* by Zhao Ke (Qing Dynasty) (YLFZ: 1650)

The Longwanggou Temple Festival of 1938 (a Historical Reconstruction)[1]

The year is 1938, or the 27th year of the Republic. The date is Sixth Month Thirteenth. The time is noon. Today is the big day for Longwanggou: the fourth and most festive day of the five-day temple festival, the official birthday of the Black Dragon King. From the mouth of the long, narrow valley up to the temple, throngs of worshipers, peddlers, and fun-seekers push their way forward and backward along the small dirt path. Unlike at temple festivals for other dragon kings, where women are strictly forbidden, at the Black Dragon King temple festival in recent years women have been allowed to come and watch the opera, though they are still excluded from the temple. A few years ago Longwanggou broke the no-female taboo by allowing women opera singers to perform onstage; it was a famous Shanxi troupe with women performers! To request the service of that opera troupe the temple association had to compromise its age-old gender principle. Through the temple oracle rod, the Black Dragon King agreed to let women come to the temple festival. So women, young and old, riding on donkeys or pushcarts, brighten the crowd with their colorful outfits.

But the overwhelming majority of the festivalgoers are male. Most are peasant men, with white towels around their clean-shaven heads to shield them from the sun and to soak up sweat. Many have come with fellow villagers and family members, including small children, who always enjoy the fanfare more than anyone else. Many men are also wearing military uniforms. They are Nationalist soldiers who are here looking for a good time. The soldiers are here also to maintain order during the temple festival and to keep an eye out for Communist agitators.

The fanfare of the temple festival barely covers Shaanbei's otherwise tense atmosphere. Three years earlier, after the Long March, the Communists arrived in Shaanbei, and last year they made Yan'an the headquarters of their Shaan-Gan-Ning Border Region. The Nationalists mounted sieges but failed to annihilate the Communists. Also last year, the Japanese began their offensive into the interior of China, taking most of Northern China, including large parts of Suiyuan and Shanxi. Chinese armies of all varieties retreated into Yulin Prefecture, whose military importance grew by the day. After the Xi'an Incident, the Communists and the Nationalists agreed to fight the Japanese instead of each other, and Shaanbei finally became a little more peaceful. Yet earlier this year, the Japanese army took western Shanxi and even attempted to cross the Yellow River into Shaanbei. It was beaten back by Nationalist and Communist forces.

Longwanggou lies midway between Mizhi Town to the south and Zhenchuan Town to the north, each a few li away. A little to the south of Longwanggou is a place called Wanfodong (Ten Thousand Buddha Cave), where a fortified military pass checks the traffic between the northern, Nationalist area, and the southern, Communist area. Village youth, organized into youth corps, help the Nationalist soldiers guard the pass.

The sun is fierce. It hasn't rained for more than two months. The peasants are especially anxious, fearing yet another drought and bad harvest. They have come to the temple from near and far not only to present offerings to the Black Dragon King on his birthday but also to pray for timely rain. They walk up the stone-paved stairway with incense and paper money and sometimes a string of firecrackers. They light the firecrackers next to the two stone lions guarding the temple, put the lit incense in the large stone incense pot, and burn the paper money while kneeling in front of the statue of the Black Dragon King. "Oh Dragon

King your Highness," they beseech the god, "We beg you to bless us. We beg you to grant us some rainwater, otherwise the crops are all going to dry up and die. We beg you." They then put some real money into the temple's collection box as a token of gratitude for the deity's blessing for the past year. Some of them have particular questions to pose to the dragon king, so they consult his divination set or the temple oracle roller.

In front of the temple stands an opera stage, with a famous Shanxi opera troupe performing historical and mythical dramas. At noon, they play the Black Dragon King's favorite opera: *Judge Bao Chopping Off Chen Shimei's Head*. Hundreds of people gather to watch.

Competing for attention with the opera are dozens upon dozens of gambling dens set up throughout the temple grounds, some operated by the Nationalist troops. For every dollar won at these gambling dens, ten cents go to the temple association for the opera performances. The rest of the festival expenses and the yearly operating fund come from a few local rich landlords, some Zhenchuan Town merchants, worshipers' incense money donations, rents from the temple's extensive landholdings, and the villagers of the three villages of Hongliutan, Chenjiapo, and Batawan, who have all paid a nominal per-household fee.

In opium-smoking sheds, customers can lie on wooden boards for a few puffs. Many prostitutes ply their trade among the largely male festivalgoers. Beggars and thieves, too, stream back and forth through the crowd. The whole atmosphere is one of abundance, joviality, and excess.

Power, Temporal and Magical

Shaanbei people resort to many deities when they have the need. Out of this long list, the dragon king is the agrarian deity par excellence, especially in drought-prone north China.[2] He is the provider of the most important agricultural resource, water (in the form of rainfall). Heilongdawang has been a local rain god administering the Zhenchuan general vicinity. Compared to the throng of village dragon kings, Heilongdawang was considered a much more powerful rain-granting god because he has an imperially decreed official title (more on this below). In the past, peasants in nearby areas who had failed to obtain rain from the lesser dragon kings came to Heilongdawang for help.[3]

The wish for a good harvest is only naturally paralleled with the wish for peace, because the threats of drought, war, and civil disturbance are

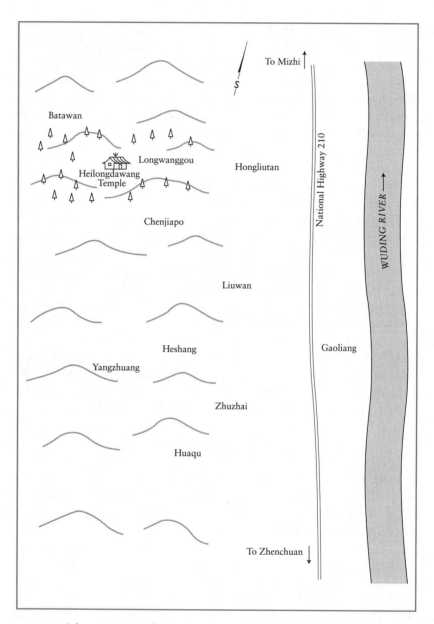

MAP 2. Schematic Map of Longwanggou and Surrounding Areas

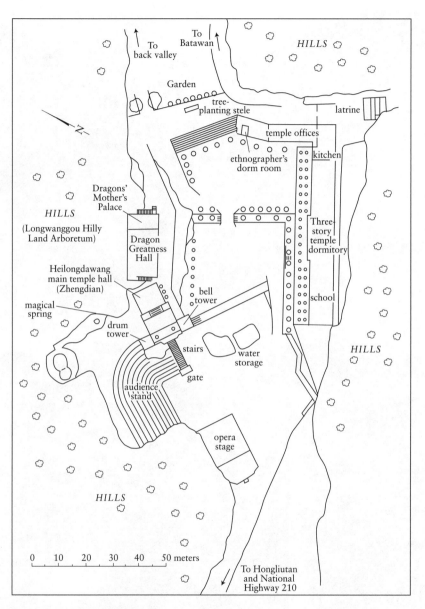

MAP 3. Bird's-Eye View of Longwanggou Temple Ground. Based on a drawing by Kurihara Shinji (National Museum of Ethnology, Osaka, Japan), printed in Luo Hongguang, *Kokuryuutan: chyuugoku hokubu nooson ni okeru zai wo meguru gireiteki katei no kenkyuu*.

Above: A quiet winter day at the Black Dragon King Temple. *Below:* Plaques donated by worshipers thanking the Black Dragon King and praising his magical efficacy.

Statues of the Black Dragon King and his attendants in the new subsidiary hall dedicated to the five dragon king brothers and their mother.

often immediate and real. The couplet on the two frontal columns of the Heilongdawang Temple reads: "Out he comes from his dragon palace, the winds are gentle and the rains timely; Back he goes hiding in the sea, the country is peaceful and the people without troubles" (*chu longgong fengtiao yushun; ruhai cang guotai minan*). In fact, in the past as well as today, believers come to Heilongdawang to pray for divine assistance for all kinds of problems. In the past decade or so, however, more and more people ask Heilongdawang to help them with their businesses, to bless them so they will get rich.

Razed completely during the Cultural Revolution and rebuilt from scratch in 1982, the temple has been expanding in grandeur ever since. Its fame really took off in the mid- and late-1980s, when stories of Heilongdawang's efficacy spread widely in Shaanbei, and when the Heilongdawang Temple began to host during the annual temple festival by far the longest, the most diverse, the best, and the most expensive opera performances in Shaanbei history. The temple coffers swelled as Heilongdawang's fame grew phenomenally. It is now the richest non-government-managed temple in Shaanbei, receiving more than a million yuan in donations from worshipers each year.[4]

In temple boss Lao Wang's office, two rooms down from my dormitory room, a framed glass plaque (*bian*) hung on the wall. Over a picture of a garden were written, in red paint, four large characters: *shenling renjie*, meaning "[here at Longwanggou] the god is powerful/efficacious and the people are brilliant/outstanding."[5] The plaque was a gift for Lao Wang and the temple from the Yulin Prefecture Forestry Bureau a number of years ago. The praise on the plaque nicely evoked the two sources of Longwanggou's power: the magical efficacy of the god (Heilongdawang) and the extraordinary ability of the temple leadership (especially Lao Wang).

The power of Longwanggou can indeed be viewed as having two broad sources, one temporal and the other magical. The temporal or secular source of the power lay in the temple's organization, particularly its leadership. The magical or divine source of the power lay in the magical efficacy of Heilongdawang, *believed in* and *activated* by worshipers. Spatially, the temporal power resided in and emanated from the offices of the temple association, which were in the dormitory building on the south side of the valley. The magical power, on the other hand, resided in and emanated from the temple buildings, the magical spring next to the temple, and the overall geomantic configurations of the temple surroundings.

In this chapter, I first situate the Heilongdawang Temple in its local context. Then I recount the legends surrounding Heilongdawang's origin and his magical accomplishments, evoking the history of the temple through selected historical scenarios (historical "snapshots," the first one being the historical reconstruction of the 1938 temple festival at the beginning of the chapter). The Black Dragon King exists in material form as a statue in the Black Dragon King Temple, but he also exists in legends and local histories, and in the recounting of these legends and histories of his origin and his efficacy. In other words, Heilongdawang is constructed from both clay and discourse. I will introduce the concept of text act as a way to account for the prominence of textual representations at the Heilongdawang Temple.

The Heilongdawang Temple in Its Local Context

Though the Heilongdawang Temple is hidden in a long, narrow valley, its recently constructed carved-stone main entrance gate (*pailou*) stands majestically right on the east-side curb of Shaanbei's only north-south thoroughfare. The route connects the ancient Silk Road cities of Baotou in Inner Mongolia and Xi'an, a metropolis since the Han Dynasty, and now the provincial capital of Shaanxi. The thoroughfare is now called National Highway 210 (*eryaoling guodao*), recently aggressively upgraded to a second-grade highway (*erji gonglu*). The Wuding River (literally "river with no fixed course"), one of the major rivers in Shaanbei, flows south along the west side of Highway 210. Some 120 kilometers later it joins the south-flowing section of the Yellow River, the natural boundary between Shaanxi Province and Shanxi Province.

At the mouth of the Dragon King Valley is the village of Hongliutan (i.e., Red Willow Beach, population around 450), and next to it the village of Chenjiapo (i.e., Chen Family Slope, population around 600). Over one of the ridges of the Dragon King Valley is the village of Batawan (i.e., Eight Towered "Bay," population around 300). Batawan, an offshoot of Hongliutan since the mid–19th century, is the smallest. Chenjiapo is the largest, occupying a long strip along the Wuding River and the mouth of a valley much deeper and wider than the Dragon King Valley. These three villages cooperated in running the temple before it was taken down in 1966. Chenjiapo led them because before Liberation a couple of its landlords actively sponsored the temple festivals and perhaps also because the village was the largest of the three. Chenjiapo thus was the "First Association" (*yihui*) and Hongliutan and Batawan together formed the "Second Association" (*erhui*) and the two associations alternated yearly responsibilities for the temple and its festivals.

Since the revival of the temple during the early 1980s, six more villages have been added to the temple association. Liuwan (Willow Bay), Gaoliang (High Ridge), Zhuzhai (Zhu Family Fort), Heshang (On the Creek), Yangzhuang (Yang Family Village), and Huaqu (Flower Canal) lie to the north, all on the same, eastern side of the Wuding River.[6] Adding the other six villages was a strategic move on the part of the then temple association leaders in a time of dire need for labor and monetary resources for rebuilding and of great vulnerability in the face of uncertain official attitudes.[7] However, representatives from the original three villages still form the core of the temple association, and now only one association runs the temple.

According to the villagers, the Heilongdawang Temple was initially located somewhere else up north, closer to Zhenchuan, and the present site of the temple is the Dragon King's third and, it is hoped, permanent

home. Nobody knows for how long the Dragon King had been worshiped in the first site, but one day long ago the worshipers discovered
that the Dragon King's title plaque (*shenweipai*) was missing. They
looked for it everywhere and finally found it in a spot in Chenjiapo. Although they returned it to the temple, the next morning it vanished again,
reappearing in Chenjiapo. This to-ing and fro-ing continued until the
worshipers decided that the Dragon King liked the new place better. A
second temple was built in the new place.[8]

Nobody knows how long Heilongdawang was worshiped at the second site. Eventually it moved to a third site, where it stands today. To the
worshipers, the reason why Heilongdawang preferred the third site seems
easy to explain: the pools of spring water at the current temple site. The
original temple was very small. Lao Wang, who engineered the rebuilding
and expansion of the temple in the early 1980s, described the remains of
two previous foundations, one smaller than the other with different quality of stones. The smaller rectangle was presumably the older one because
of the foundation stones' irregular shapes and rougher craftsmanship,
and because one assumes that the temple had expanded rather than
shrunk over the years.[9] Including the present edifice, the temple has gone
through at least three incarnations on the same spot, each bigger than the
last.

The "natural" advantage of being right on a major highway has certainly helped the Black Dragon King Temple attract visitors. But the temple does not just stand on a highway (so do many other temples); it is
near a major nodal point of transport and commerce. Zhenchuan is a
town of major commercial significance in Yulin Prefecture, second only
to Suide, 50 kilometers to the south. From the mid-Qing onwards and
especially during the Republican period, it was already famed for its role
as an entrepôt between the pastoral and semipastoral hinterland to the
north and west of Shaanbei (the so-called *xilubianwai*, i.e., the west
beyond the walls, YLSZ, p. 358) and major cities in the north China
plain, especially the coastal city of Tianjin (for export). Pelts, wool, car-
pets, processed intestines (for making sausage casings), Chinese herbal
medicine ingredients, salt, and so forth were stored in Zhenchuan before
going east and south, while tea bricks, grain, textiles, alcohol, and other
consumer goods went north and west. The traffic in opium (*dayantu*) in
the 1920s and 30s only followed well-practiced trade networks and made
an already bustling town teem further with the excitement of quick

wealth. Now, after the Maoist hiatus, Zhenchuan has regained its status as wholesale entrepôt and is actually nicknamed the "little Hong Kong of Shaanbei" (*Shaanbei xiaoxianggang*). Zhenchuan is about three li to the north of the Black Dragon King Temple, and the three villages that have traditionally run the temple belong to the Zhenchuan township.

The fate of the Black Dragon King Temple has been intricately tied to that of Zhenchuan. During the Republican period, the temple began to gain wider fame by hosting the best and the most expensive opera performances in the area during temple festivals. A large part of the expenses was met by a couple of Zhenchuan merchant sponsors from Chenjiapo, one of the temple's three villages. Today, many of the petty capitalist entrepreneurs who donate large sums of money have extensive business dealings in Zhenchuan. Lao Wang, the current head of the temple association, has a "small hundred things" wholesale business (*xiaobaihuo menshi*) in Zhenchuan, and he says that the money he earns there keeps him from worrying about a livelihood so he can concentrate on temple affairs.

Legends of Heilongdawang

The Legend of Heilongdawang's Origin: An Earthy Folktale

Even though the Shaanbei landscape is full of dragon kings distinguished only by the five colors, yellow, azure, white, red, and black, each dragon king usually has his own origin story. Unless he is explicitly recognized as a replica of another Black Dragon King, each Black Dragon King is unique. The origin story of the Heilongdawang of Longwanggou goes like this:

Once upon a time, in a village called Gejiagelao (i.e., Ge family hole), ten or so li upstream from the Dragon King Valley along the Wuding River and not far from Zhenchuan, lived a landlord's beautiful teenage daughter. One day she went with her older sister-in-law to the little creek next to the village to wash clothes. Suddenly a big, red, fragrant peach bobbed down the creek from upstream. The girl grabbed the peach and hurriedly took a bite. Just as she wanted to hand the peach to her sister-in-law for a bite, the peach slipped into her mouth. For this sign of greediness she was more than embarrassed. Soon she discovered that she was pregnant and she became very scared. Though she tried to hide it, her belly did not escape her mother's notice. So the girl confessed to her mother about the swallowed peach. The mother was kind and forgave her daughter, but the girl's belly got bigger and bigger and her father also found out He thought his daughter had done something immoral and unmentionable and that the scandal would ruin the family's name. He became so angry he beat the girl up very badly. The girl finally said to her father: "Please bind me up with a rope and take me to the hills. You can drop me where the rope breaks." Too ashamed to let anyone know about it, the father tied up the girl with a rope that evening after dark and piggybacked her up to the hills behind the village. He walked and walked and suddenly the rope broke, and he left the girl there and came home. The whole night the mother cried and blamed the husband for being so cruel. Early the next morning both mother and father went to look for the girl. When they found her she was already dead, and out of her mouth, nostrils, and ears climbed five snakes, red, white, yellow, azure, and black. The father and mother were very frightened and ran away. The five snakes were actually five dragons and they flew in five different directions and settled in different places in the vicinity of Zhenchuan.

Like other folktales, this story has many variants. In another version, for example, the girl ran away from home by herself instead of being tied up and piggybacked to the hill by her father (Huo 1996: 5–6). I recorded the above-mentioned version of the legend from temple boss Lao Wang when he recounted the story to members of an environmentalist group from Beijing who came to Longwanggou to plant trees (more on this tree-planting event in Chapter 11). The temple guardians and longtime worshipers never tire of telling new visitors the legend.

The story is as much about the birth of Heilongdawang as the apotheosis of the girl, who became the mother of the five dragon kings and was subsequently worshiped as a fertility goddess, Dragons' Mother (*Longmu Niangniang*), in her natal village Gejiagelao to the north of Longwanggou. Like Heilongdawang, the other four dragons also became rain gods and dragon kings, and were worshiped in different locales around Zhenchuan. The Azure Dragon King (Qinglongdawang), worshiped in Yingou (the shaded valley), has traditionally had a closer relationship with Heilongdawang. The two dragon kings would invite each other to their temple festivals.[10] Among the five dragon "brothers," the Azure Dragon is the eldest; the Black Dragon is the youngest but the most powerful and popular. So far as I know, the other three brothers are not too close to Heilongdawang so their temples do not have relationships.

The "No Flies" Legend

During my fieldwork in Shaanbei, I heard the Longwanggou "no flies" legend countless times, on buses, at temple festivals, and in restaurants. Reputedly, not a single fly would appear in Longwanggou during the hot summer days of the temple festival, despite its many food stalls, watermelon stands, and garbage mounds. It is like this every year, for Heilongdawang is "extremely efficacious" (*keling la*). Just this "miracle" alone would often draw the curious to Longwanggou. Some people from Longwanggou's rival temples told me that this "no flies" legend was Longwanggou's most powerful propaganda.

The Legend of Heilongdawang's Patriotism and Divine Power

The back wall of the Heilongdawang Temple's main hall is decorated with colorful flying dragons in relief, while the walls on the left and the right depict Heilongdawang's divine accomplishments, similar to the so-called "Pictures of Divine Traces" (*shengjitu*) in temples dedicated to famous divine figures such as Confucius, the Emperor of the Eastern Peak (*Dongyue dadi*), the Perfected Warrior Ancestral Master (*Zhenwu zushi*), Guandi, or the Daoist deity Lü Dongbin (see Katz 1999; Murray 2002). All of the temple decorations and statues were commissioned by the temple association and done by the best craftsmen in Shaanbei.

The story of Heilongdawang is shown in frames of individual scenes (left to right and top to bottom), with painted background, some scenery in high relief, and freestanding figurines. Under each frame is a small wooden plate with a one-line written annotation. The vividness of composition and the attention to detail make these murals first-class among similar murals in Shaanbei.[11] The story is essentially the same as the legend told in the temple stele inscription (see below), describing the background of Heilongdawang's "promotion" into imperial officialdom (or enfeoffment) by the Guangxu Emperor of the Qing Dynasty. The scenes are summarized as follows:

(1) Japanese pirates attack Taiwan; Government defenders are defeated repeatedly;

(2) General Zhang Yao anxiously strategizes into the night; Heilongdawang appears in his dream and advises him;

(3) As the General follows Heilongdawang's strategies, the god commands thunder and lightning to help the Chinese troops; the Chinese troops win and repel the invaders;

(4) The General returns to the capital and reports Heilongdawang's great patriotic deed to the emperor;

(5) The emperor grants Heilongdawang the title (or enfeoffs him as) "Marquis of Efficacious Response" (*Lingyinghou*), personally writing a plaque in praise of the Dragon King;

(6) The plaque and half a set of imperial processional insignia (*luanjia*) and other imperial gifts are sent to the temple; local people welcome the procession with firecrackers;

(7) [Years later] an official coming to Yulin City to assume the post of Yulin City magistrate is welcomed by Heilongdawang in the shape of a beautiful black cloud;

(8) The new magistrate and his aides kneel and worship Heilongdawang.

The double theme of, first, Heilongdawang's patriotism and his role as local protector and second, official recognition of his power and virtue, is common in the hagiography of local cult deities in traditional China. The invocation of an official title granted during a "feudal"—and over-thrown—dynasty does not seem to present any problem for anyone to-day: Heilongdawang's patriotism transcends dynastic changes. More importantly, the temple leaders emphasize the *official* title, which reminds worshipers that Heilongdawang is superior to the throngs of ordinary dragon kings and other minor deities that populate the vast Shaanbei, and for that matter, Chinese, rural landscape. Two stone gate columns at the foot of the flight of steps leading up to the main temple hall carry an inscribed couplet, dating to the Republican era, lauding the Dragon King Marquis:

> [He/You] were once granted a high title by the Qing emperor;
> No wonder that the masses spread [his/your] mighty name.
> (*yeceng qingdi feng gaojue; wuguai limin shuo weiming*)[12]

The grandness of Heilongdawang's patriotic act and the subsequent imperial reward contrast sharply and curiously with his humble origin, as recounted in the virgin-girl-and-peach story earlier. One is presented as history (with historical details such as emperor's and general's names to back up the story), while the other is a mere folktale (with the "once-upon-a-time" opening). What makes the factuality of the "history" suspect is the existence of a few other versions of the same story with Heilongdawang helping to fight different foreign invaders and being rewarded by different emperors. For example, in one version collected in a local folklore volume (Wang and Ma 1990: 41–42), the foreign invaders are Westerners and the emperor is not Guangxu but Kangxi; the general's name is still Zhang Yao, though he is fighting the invaders in the heart- land of China (*zhongyuan*), not Taiwan. The Western invaders in this ver- sion put live human hearts into full goatskins and make them into invin- cible goat-skinned robots (*yangpiren*) who kill and kill without stopping until General Zhang enlists Heilongdawang's divine assistance. In an- other version the enemies are Chinese Muslims (*laohuihui*).[13]

The imperial state had a long history of granting official titles to local, "worthy" deities, sometimes elevating these local deities to regional or even national fame (Watson 1985). This practice was particularly preva- lent during the Qing Dynasty. As titles and honors were bestowed on them, local deities transcended their humble local origins and became prominent in the state-endorsed system of cults, though often still mostly powerful at the local or regional level (Duara 1988a: 34).

When I first encountered the honored-by-the-emperor story, I was skeptical. I assumed it was a legend locally fabricated to boost Heilong- dawang's standing among the Shaanbei pantheon. The City God of Yuhe Town up north from Zhenchuan also boasts an imperial title of Marquis of Efficacious Response. At both places all the original evidence of impe- rial favor, i.e., the plaque with the emperor's calligraphy and the half set of processional insignia, was conveniently destroyed during the Cultural Revolution. I also thought the fact that Heilongdawang flew to Taiwan to help fight Japanese pirate invaders was very odd and even overly imag- inative. Could it be that the temple leaders during the late Qing or the Republican era invented this legend or changed the identity of the in- vaders to Japanese as a patriotic response to Japan's assault on China? One is reminded of the first Sino-Japanese War in 1894–95 when Japan destroyed the entire Chinese navy and took Taiwan (through the infa- mous Shimonoseki Treaty of 1895) and strategic parts of Manchuria.

Though many times tempted to check the Qing Dynasty imperial archive to see if Heilongdawang was indeed granted an imperial title, I did not pursue the matter. True history or fabricated legend, it does not matter. What is important is how the locals promote and advertise Hei- longdawang's power to the outside world. In the juxtaposition of "low" and "high" legends, the Heilongdawang case also exemplifies what Duara calls the "superscription of symbols" and what Katz calls the "cogeneration and reverberation" of interpretations (Katz 1995, 1999), i.e., when different social groups ascribe different attributes to the same deity thus contributing to the deity's versatility and appeal to different audiences (Duara 1988a: 146; 1988b). Ultimately, the average worshiper cares only about Heilongdawang's efficacious responses to his or her own personal problems and situations.

The Temple Reconstruction Commemorative Stele

To the right of the main temple hall's door one finds a stone stele installed on the wall. It is an essay, written in classical Chinese, commemorating the rebuilding of the Heilongdawang Temple. I present the complete text here because this commemorative essay eloquently conveys the temple's official version of "the story" of Heilongdawang, Longwanggou, the temple, the temple's destruction, and its eventual revival. It integrates both the "high" and "low" legends of Heilongdawang, and delves into an elaborate exaltation of Longwanggou's geomantic properties. Its mix of legend and history and the use of classical Chinese and flowery, sometimes stilted language are typical of such records. The text is as follows:

> In Commemoration of the Reconstruction
> of the Black Dragon Temple

> Tracing back in time, ever since the times of Pangu, who stabilized Heaven and Earth, the Three Divine Rulers who set the world in order, and the Five Sage Kings who governed the nation, this sacred land of Huaxia China has seen many upheavals; generations upon generations of descendants of the Yan and the Yellow Emperors have come and gone for thousands of years. When one looks at the growing prosperity as well as the declining fortune of the times, the happy reunions as well as the sad farewells of the common folks, one feels that these are like the waning and waxing of the moon and the relays of the cold and warm seasons; all these are determined by Heaven on high and cannot be comprehended by ordinary people. Yet there are gods who are so mighty and so full of virtue that people pray to them sincerely and erect stelae in commemoration of the gods' great deeds; this they do of their own accord and are forced by no one. The gods are best at punishing evil and vice and commending loyalty and goodness. Therefore if we praise and worship the gods it not only goes well with heavenly reason and human sensibility but also befits the current flows of civilization; on the higher level [worshiping gods] can guard the nation against dangers while on the lower level it can protect the people so that they are healthy and happy and without worries. Since [worshiping gods] has so many benefits, ridding us of bad things and promoting good things, shouldn't we be happy to do it?

Thus the Preface.

The ancients said: it doesn't matter how tall the mountain is, as long as there is an immortal it will be famous; it doesn't matter how deep the water is, as long as there is a dragon, it will be efficacious. That is why the Dragon King Valley has been called the best of all magical domains in Yulin. The dragon god who dwells here has done so many mighty deeds that no other god can ever match him. His greatness is as bright as the sun and the moon and as everlasting as Mount Tai. It has been said that in the beginning, the dragon's mother swallowed the magical peach and gave birth to five dragons. The Black Dragon roamed into the hills to the north and often demonstrated his power on Tower Temple Ridge in Chenjiapo. In awe of his magical efficacy, the villagers built him a small shrine and worshiped him. It was like that for a few hundred years. Later on, the dragon god chose for himself as dwelling place a secluded valley with nine dragon pools to the east of Hongliutan. This valley has the shape of a golden bowl. On four sides the hills point upwards and circle around; purple vapors float atop them and colorful lights shine and shimmer. The valley presents nine pools and the springs flow and jump. Orchid-green, the water is so clear that one can see the bottom of the pools; there are tiny ripples running across the surface and a chill rises from the depth. At the bottom of the valley there is a peculiar rock called "Water Beauty" (shuixiu), a precious treasure. North-east of the valley there is a protruding cliff, on the left side of which there is a natural egg-shaped spring mouth called "The Sea's Eye" (haiyan). It is six cun [Chinese inches] or so wide and of unfathomable depth. A clear thread of springwater drips down from it all year round and it is never exhausted. It looks like a dragon spitting out a string of pearls and it just flows and flows. This is called "Dragon Hole Hiding Treasures" (longxue cangzhen) and is a great sight at Longwanggou.

The Heilongdawang Temple was first built during the reign of the Zhengde Emperor of the Ming Dynasty. Rebuilt and expanded a few times during the Guangxu reign of the Qing Dynasty and during the Republican era, it was made more perfect and magnificent. Rising above the pools were built the main temple hall, the entrance hallway, the bell tower, the drum tower, the stone lions, the flagpoles, the stone arch, the opera stage, and so forth. The layout was orderly and precise; the architectural and building techniques were refined and the results impressive; the structures were elegant and evocative of ancient simplicity, showing the special talents of the artisans. It was truly a fine work of tradition. The main hall of the dragon god reclined on the north hills, and it climbed up the dragon pools as if it were washing its feet in them; it appeared as if the dragon were playing with the water in the pools, jumping out and diving in. In the main temple hall the Dragon King's gilt statue wore an embroidered silk robe and an official cotton gauze hat. He stared out with the eyes of a tiger, making people look at him in awe and solemn respect. Over time, the efficacious god increasingly showed his power and he became famous near and far. When rain was requested, rain there would be; when illnesses were consulted, health would be restored. The country people who came to burn incense and pray were so numerous that they formed endless streams. Inside the temple flags and procession umbrellas were like forests and everyone fought to hang their plaques of praise. It was an incredible sight. There were a hundred or so mural paintings inside the temple, one of which recorded the historical event of the Dragon King going to Taiwan to help General Zhang Yao beat the invading Japanese pirates and accomplishing a patriotic deed for the nation. The Guangxu Emperor of the Great Qing Dynasty looked up to the divine power and granted the Dragon King the official title of "the Marquis of Efficacious Response" (*lingyinghou*); the emperor also gave a gift of a golden plaque, with his personally written exaltation: "Mighty Savior of the People, Your Loyal Contributions Have Been Put Down in Records" (*gongbu weilin*); also conferred was half a set of imperial processional insignia to honor the Dragon King's meritorious deeds. Years later, because he had successfully prayed for rain, the magistrate-examiner of the Yulin Prefecture honored the Dragon King with a gift of a colorful plaque with sculpted human figurines.

In 1966, Longwanggou experienced a violent calamity in which the cultural relics and ancient remains were almost completely destroyed. During that period of time the god left and the water dried up; everywhere there were merely crumbling walls. It looked so sad that words could hardly describe the scene. The Heavenly net casts widely but surely: evil people were punished for their crimes and foolish people were brought back to their senses before it was too late. A decade or so later, the dragon god's magical power reappeared, and people from all around crowded back here to worship and pray. The temple leaders of the nine surrounding villages decided to rebuild the temple. When people knew about the plan, countless numbers of them helped out with money and labor. On an auspicious day in the autumn of 1981 the foundation was laid, and in early Sixth Month the next year the preliminary construction was completed. The main hall for the Marquis of Efficacious Response and the entrance hallway were rebuilt; two mountain-guarding stone lions and one three-tier stone incense tower were carved; and the statue of the Marquis of Efficacious Response was also resculpted. On Sixth Month First that year the "Opening the Light" (*kaiguang*) ceremony welcomed the god. The Dragon King's sedan chair finally came back to the palace, and the god's power and virtue were both bolstered. People thank the god for his divine power; the god blesses people's livelihood; the god and people complement each other and live side by side. Such is the auspicious sign of an era of peace and prosperity for the nation and the people and of a great reign of all under Heaven.

To record so as to last forever

> The Longwanggou Temple Association;
> dedicated in the Sixth Month of 1982

The stele text was written by Mr. Ren, who serves as the official literatus consultant for the temple. Mr. Ren is a well-educated man about the same age as temple boss Lao Wang (mid-fifties in 1997), and he and Lao Wang were primary school classmates. He works for the Zhenchuan

Town Cultural Station, collecting folklore and writing articles and plays. In the early 1990s, he organized an opera troupe that folded after two years. Mr. Ren is thus an official local cultural worker. Because of their old school ties, Mr. Ren agreed to help Lao Wang with temple affairs whenever his literary and performing arts talents were needed. The temple reconstruction commemorative stele text is Mr. Ren's major contribution to the temple, a splendid example of a government cultural worker and official socialist propagandist defecting to folk cultural production.

To understand rural cultural struggle in China, one needs to examine the role of the grassroots cultural brokers like Mr. Ren—village school teachers, ritual specialists, community cult leaders, village headmen, local officials in charge of "culture work," local representatives of the Women's Federation, members of itinerant opera troupes, peasant intellectuals—who were organic members of village communities (cf. Feierman 1990; Mallon 1995; Pickowicz 1994). The government first subjected these grassroots cultural elites to socialist cultural propaganda while mobilizing them to transform peasant traditions. Surprisingly, however, many of them were also the first to revive local traditions as soon as their role as symbolic-ideological missionaries was temporarily forsaken. A full account of the role of these local cultural elites in the socialist cultural project and peasant cultural revivalism is beyond the scope of this book. I only wish to suggest that perhaps their simultaneous embodiment of both socialist culture and peasant culture allowed them to "disarticulate" the two cultures and preserve the integrity of the latter. This situation contrasts sharply with that in traditional China, when cultural brokers, e.g., gentry elites, used to serve as integrative agents of elite culture and peasant culture.

Text Acts

Stelae like the one at the Heilongdawang Temple are very important, standard features of Chinese temples (see Katz 1999; Vermeer 1991). They legitimize the temples by putting them in the larger contexts of the reign and even cosmic forces and by linking them to the Literati Tradition elements of solemn texts and fine calligraphy. However, very few people who come to the temple to worship pay much attention to the stele I just described. The people who do try to read it are educated visitors who can understand the often obscure, classical prose. For the majority of temple-goers, who are mostly illiterate or semiliterate peasants, the stele is one more awe-inspiring part of the temple structure. One can argue that the *physical presence* of the stele and its text is more important than the actual contents of the text.

In fact, the temple has many kinds of texts inscribed in many different places in the temple ground. I have already mentioned the plaques, couplets, and the commemorative stele that are found in the main temple hall. Toward the back of the temple building, between the temple and the dormitory building, a large section of the rock slope was shaved to make vertical sheets of flat surfaces on which many sayings and poems have been inscribed. These are traditionally called "cliff inscriptions" (*moya shike*), and are very widespread in China at famous temple sites and on sacred mountains. The most prominent and eye-catching inscription is about 15 feet wide and 7 feet tall, with eight giant characters written in forceful and beautiful calligraphy, the strokes chiseled deep into the rock surface: *gongguo shifei, ziyou pingshu* (Merit or demerit, right or wrong, it is to be decided and commented on [in the future]). It is a thinly veiled reference to the building of temples and whether this kind of "superstitious activity" should be judged right or wrong. Other inscriptions are much smaller. There is the famous poem on the Heilongdawang written by a Qing Dynasty local official, cited as the epigraph for this chapter. Most of the other inscriptions are laudatory remarks made by "important" visitors (officials, foreigners) to Longwanggou over the years commenting on the temple, the locale, the reforestation project, and the local people's hospitality.[14]

Seen as a whole, these different genres and mediums of texts (including the orally transmitted folklore and legends) present a cacophony of voices. It is difficult to determine which are dominant voices and which are subordinate ones. It is as if all these messages were coexisting in one social space, not so much competing with one another as presenting different facets of Longwanggou as a "macrotext" (Katz 1999). Katz (1999) presents a detailed and insightful study of the different kinds of "texts" (including temple inscriptions and murals) at the Palace of Eternal Joy in Shanxi dedicated to the Daoist immortal Lü Dongbin. He concludes that different texts were produced in specific social contexts with different intended audiences in mind and eliciting both intended and unintended readings (and sometimes, may I add, non-readings). Texts created by cultural elites such as Confucian literati and Daoist priests and hagiographers can never fully supersede and dominate those earthier, sometimes "dirty," and more efficacy-oriented "texts" created by illiterate and semi-literate worshipers. Similarly, in the Longwanggou case, no "interpretive community" has emerged out of the cacophonous and "saturated" jumble of texts to present clearly "precipitated" meanings and ideological or theological statements (Weller 1994b).

The cultural and political significance of texts and writing in China has long been recognized. Traditionally, scholars in the fields of history, literature, religious studies, and philosophy study the *contents* of texts, while art historians study the artistic *forms* of writing (e.g., calligraphy).[15] What has not received adequate attention is how certain texts exert their power in the social world not necessarily or simply through their rhetorical/discursive power or artistic beauty but more importantly through their sheer presence (e.g., seals, inscriptions on stone or cliff surfaces, tattooed characters, talismans, slogan banners, Maoist big character posters). The presence of these texts assumes a fetishistic power. They act upon their audience and produce effects (awe, submission, recognition, etc.). More than (and sometimes rather than) reading these texts, the audience *feels* the force of their presence. I suggest that we call these acts of writing and inscribing *text acts*.[16]

Traditionally anthropology tends to emphasize the oral, and treat texts mostly as dormant documents.[17] However, in China, because of its long history of writing, text acts have become a pervasive aspect of most social domains. Text acts are especially abundant and power-laden in religious and political domains, for in both power is at issue; writing has been endowed with so much power in China not least because traditionally most subjects of the empire were illiterate or marginally literate. In the case of Longwanggou, it is quite clear that most of the text acts are for the purpose of visualizing and displaying legitimacy, both in the political sense (blessed by representatives of the state and by powerful people) and in the cultural sense (blessed by [feigned] literati high culture) (see Bourdieu 1991). The proliferation of text acts has helped set Longwanggou apart from the average village temple, even though it will be a long time before Longwanggou can match the number and quality of text acts that major monasteries and temples in China typically exhibit.

As a text act, the commemorative stele also aims at government officials who happen to read it: "[O]n the higher level [worshiping gods] can guard the nation against dangers while on the lower level it can protect the people so that they are healthy and happy and without worries. Since [worshiping gods] has so many benefits, ridding us of bad things and promoting good things, shouldn't we be happy to do it? ... People thank the god for his divine power; the god blesses people's livelihood; the god and people complement each other and live side by side. Such is the auspicious sign of an era of peace and prosperity for the nation and the people and of a great reign of all under Heaven." If deity-worship has so many benefits and is a sign of good times, why would any government want to oppose it?

CHAPTER SIX

Provisioning Magical Efficacy and Divine Benevolence

In this chapter I examine the organizational structure and operations of Longwanggou as an example of a folk cultural institution. First, I describe the most important "religious" aspects of the temple complex, e.g., the main temple hall, divination methods, and the magical spring.[1] Which of the spots in the temple ground is the most powerful? How do people communicate with Heilongdawang and receive divine assistance? What are the daily routines of efficacy provision at Longwanggou? Then I look at the ways in which incense money is handled at the temple. I attempt an interpretation of Longwanggou as an example of a service provider of magical efficacy (*ling* or *lingying* or *lingyan*).

The Main Temple Hall and the Zone of Ritual Interaction

If there were one place at Longwanggou that had the most magical power, it would be the main temple hall, or the *zhengdian*. Here one finds the imposing statue of Heilongdawang, the sculpted dragon-motif decorations and stories of Heilongdawang's divine accomplishments and hagiography on the walls, the altar always with offerings laid on top, the incense money donation cabinet, the paper money burner, the incense burner carved from stone, the prayer mat, the divination sticks, and the oracle roller tray. Here worshipers are brought face-to-face with the Dragon King; here incense sticks are lit and paper money burned; real money donated; wishes wished and problems consulted; magical power evoked and sought; praises sung and pleas aired; thanks given and pigs and goats sacrificed. For a brief moment, as people kneel down in front of Heilongdawang's statue, they become worshipers; the magical realm and the human realm interact.

Nine feet tall, the seated figure of Heilongdawang is made taller and even more imposing because it rests on a four-foot-tall platform at the center back. Like many deities in the Chinese popular religious pantheon, Heilongdawang appears in official dynastic garb, and is additionally clad in layers of colorful embroidered robes. His face is gilded; he wears a beard and has thick black eyebrows. His eyes are huge and bulging, and they stare out in a solemn way. At the front of his hat over his forehead a small round mirror reflects light. The face and the whole statue emit an air of dignity and awesomeness. On either side of Heilongdawang stands a statue of a child-servant, one holding Heilongdawang's official seal and the other a record scroll. The statues of Heilongdawang and the child-servants are protected by a large glass case.

In front of the glass case and flanking the altar on each side are statues of two official attendants, both six feet tall. The military attendant holds weapons and looks fierce while the civil attendant holds a book and a brush and looks stern. Looking up, one sees a black dragon curled around the top of the glass case, holding a human head in its claws. Bloody and disheveled, the sculpted human head seems so real that it never fails to scare unguarded visitors, especially women and children. It is a graphic reminder that, according to temple lore, Heilongdawang is a fierce god (*xiongshen*) who punishes evildoers.[2]

In front of Heilongdawang's statue sits a four-foot-tall altar table with offerings such as cookies, fruits, and candies, a copper incense burner, a bowl-shaped copper bell, a porcelain bowl containing small yellow packets of Heilongdawang's magical medicine, a little pile of Heilongdawang's yellow paper amulets, red threads for tying the amulets, incense, paper money, and various other small items. Flanking the altar are two red electric lamps, kept lit all the time. The altar's wrought-iron base serves as the incense money cabinet. It has three narrow horizontal slits in the front for donations. In front of the altar is another incense burner, carved out of stone and much bigger than the copper one on the altar. Used more often, it is filled with a thick layer of incense ashes. To the right (from the perspective of the worshiper) of the stone incense burner an oil lamp offers a flame for lighting paper money, and next to it an iron bowl receives the burning paper money. In front of the stone incense burner are two divination devices and two kneeling mats. To interact with Heilongdawang, worshipers always kneel on these mats, especially when they consult the divination devices. I call this the *zone of ritual interaction*, a universal feature in all Chinese temples. In my estimation nine out of ten worshipers consult either or both divination devices when they visit Longwanggou.

The first device is a set of divination sticks, a common feature in Chinese temples. Each of one hundred individually numbered bamboo sticks in a wooden container corresponds to a different divine message that is printed on a small slip of paper. Both the set and the individual bamboo sticks are called *qian*, and the container *qiantong*.[3] To address a particular problem the consultee shakes the container until one bamboo stick drops or shoots out of the container. This action is called "drawing the divination sticks" (*chouqian*). The consultee notes the number on that stick and gets the divination poem slip (*qianzhi*) from a back room.

A variety of stick divination sets are found in Shaanbei, some very local but some with considerable regional spread. Each major deity has his or her own stick divination set, for example the True Marshal Ancestral Master Magical Divination Set (*Zhenwu zushi lingqian*), the Lord Guan Divination Set (*Guan laoye qian*), the Black Dragon King Miraculous Divination Set (*Heilongdawang shenqian*), and the many different fertility goddess divination sets (*niangniang qian*) and those of different city gods. When a deity is of only local relevance and significance, his divination set is parochial indeed, often being one of a kind. But when a deity is influential on a regional scale, his divination set can be duplicated in many places. The Heilongdawang stick divination set presents an anomaly: the deity is influential on a regional scale yet the divination set is found only here at the Heilongdawang Temple. In fact, the temple tries to prevent any person or other temples from duplicating the set. I was told that even if some people successfully duplicated the set and used it somewhere else it would lose its power and no longer be efficacious; "It's because Heilongdawang only lives *here*." Significantly, the locals are not going to allow duplicate Heilongdawangs to diffuse their temple influence and income.

Worshipers consult the divination sticks for many reasons, the most common of which I list in descending frequency (according to my observation):

1. Business fortunes (*shengyi*), which might include specific business decisions such as going on a long-distance trading trip, buying a truck, or setting up a business partnership;

2. Financial fortunes (*caiyun*), which may be business-related or not;

3. Current general fortunes (*shiyun*);

4. This year's fortunes (*liunian yunqi*), or fortunes of the first half year (*shangbannian*) or the second half year (*xiabannian*);

5. Marriage (*hunyin*), or more specifically, time to get married or not (*hundongle me*);

6. Marital discord or divorce, often euphemized as "domestic affairs" (*jiawushi*);

7. Young people looking for or waiting for (desirable) jobs (*gongzuo*);

8. Examination and enrollment fortunes (*kaoxue*);

9. Lawsuits (*guansi*), or the prospect of someone's being released from jail;

10. Interpersonal relationships (S. *churen*);

11. Illness (*jibing*);

12. Fortunes in officialdom (*guanyun*);

13. Birth/children fortunes (*qiu ernü*)[4];

14. Missing persons or things (*xunren, xunwu*);

15. Chance of switching jobs (*diao gongzuo*), and others.

The other divination device at the zhengdian is an oracle roller called the *gua* (with obvious reference to the Daoist octagram *bagua*). The gua is a short, fat wooden roller with eight segments along its sides (so the two ends are octagon-shaped). It is about 10 inches long, and the middle is a little thicker than the ends. Each segment has a different four-character message inscribed in the wood. The consultee with a particular problem holds this roller in both palms and rolls it horizontally in a wooden tray about 12 inches wide and 22 inches long. This action is called *tang-gua* (S. literally rolling the gua). When the roller stops, the characters on the top segment are the message Heilongdawang wants to communicate to the consultee.[5] The eight four-character messages are:

—Extremely auspicious (*shangshang daji*);
—Not so good (*xiaxia zhongping*);
—Not clear how you would thank me for the help (*kouyuan buming*);
—Go home soon if traveling (*xingren zaohui*);
—Not in accordance with god's ways (*buhe shendao*);
—Pray with a sincere heart (*qianxin qidao*);
—Bring the medicine with magical water (*quyao daishui*);
—Will get well after taking the medicine (*fuyao nenghao*)

The simplest application of this oracle is to ask a yes or no question. For example: "My brother and I are planning to take a trip to Wushen

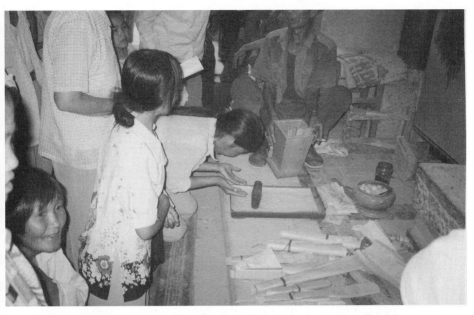

A worshiper consulting the Black Dragon King using the oracle roller. The wooden box next to the roller tray contains the 100 divination sticks.

Banner [of Inner Mongolia] to sell some clothes. Your Highness the Dragon King, do you think we will make some good money? If yes, give us "extremely auspicious"; if no, give us "not so good." Then the consultee rolls the roller. If Heilongdawang's answer is "not sure how you would thank me for the help," the consultee either puts more money in the donation box or makes a vow, promising that he will bring a certain amount of incense money if he makes money on the trip with Heilongdawang's blessing. Sometimes the consultee promises ten percent of his profit or even higher. It is like entering a partnership with Heilongdawang. If the answer is "not in accordance with god's ways," the consultee needs to reflect on whether his business plan is going to break the law or offend the god. Other yes or no questions can be: "Has my marriage luck come?"; "Will grandma get better or not?"; "Will I get assigned a good job?"; and so forth.

The reference to medicine and magical water on the oracle roller indicates that this gua is the medicine gua (*yaogua*), most often used when consultees want to request Heilongdawang's divine intervention in treating their own or their family members' illnesses. Heilongdawang has another gua that is only used when, on increasingly rare occasions, there are requests for rain. It is called the rain gua (*yugua*). On it the two medicine-related messages on the medicine gua are replaced by two rain-related messages: "will rain today" (*jiri youyu*) and "will rain within three days" (*sanri youyu*). To my knowledge all dragon kings in Shaanbei have a similar rain gua.[6]

The Zhengdian Caretaker and Heilongdawang's Magical Medicine and Magical Water

To the left of the incense burner and the divination devices is an old sofa. Congminr, a thin humpbacked old man from Chenjiapo and caretaker of the main temple hall, sits every day in his comfortable sofa and assists the worshipers. He is, so to speak, Heilongdawang's receptionist. Though not a ritual specialist by any means, he oversees all the ritual interactions between the worshipers and Heilongdawang and often mediates in these interactions, especially during divination sessions. As a worshiper approaches the zone of ritual interaction in front of the altar to consult the divination set, Congminr tells him to kneel and report to Heilongdawang his name, age (preferably with moment of birth in traditional reckoning), and home (e.g., which village or town) before raising his problem. Congminr usually shakes the divination container for the consultee unless the latter chooses to do it himself. When the divination stick "answer" jumps out, Congminr writes down the number of the stick on a small piece of paper and hands it to the consultee, who gets the divination slip. He also makes sure that the anxious consultee does not rush away with the divination stick; all one hundred sticks must be in the container for the divination to work properly.

Consulting the medicine gua involves even more assistance from the caretaker. Heilongdawang agrees to help cure the illness by showing the consultee either one of the two medicine messages on the gua: "bring the medicine with magical water" (*quyao daishui*) or "will get well after taking the medicine" (*fuyao nenghao*). Either message indicates Heilongdawang's consent to grant his magical medicine and the magical water. The magical medicine is in tiny yellow packets folded from incense paper. Each packet holds three smaller packets. Nothing is wrapped inside these packets: they themselves are the medicine, to be burnt and the resulting ashes mixed with water. The medicine can be taken orally or it can be used to rub on parts of the body for an external ailment. Like a pharmacist who dispenses medicine according to a doctor's prescription, Congminr gives out the medicine packets and instructs the consultee on how to take the medicine. If the consultee has not brought a bottle to bring home the magical water, Congminr hands him a cleaned beverage bottle for a 0.5 yuan fee.

The magical water refers to the trickle of springwater dripping from a small hole on the side of a 15-foot-high overhanging cliff next to the *zhengdian*. The hole, about 6 inches wide and 2 inches high, is called the "ocean's eye" (*haiyan*). It is said to connect to the rivers and the ocean. Inside the hole lives the Black Dragon King. The constant small trickle of water drips into a carved-stone container in the shape of a trough. A couple of big bowls lie on the wooden plank on the container for water-drinkers, and a plastic funnel facilitates bottling of the water. This miraculous divine water (*shenshui*) is arguably the strongest selling point of the temple. It is said that the electromagnetic field is so strong around the "ocean's eye" that a number of *qigong* masters who came to Longwanggou claimed that they could not deliver *qi* (*fagong*) there.

The Divination Slips Room and the Divination Poems

The divination slips room was once a simple *yao* dug into the side of the hill, along with a few other yao that served as temple dormitory and storage rooms. When the large, new, two-story structure was built in the location of the old dirt yao, the divination slips room was upgraded to a spacious, bright room behind the zhengdian. Though it is no longer a yao, the room is still called the divination slips yao, *qianzeryao*, both because the internal structure of the room resembles that of a yao and by inertia of usage.

When a worshiper walks into the qianzeryao, she sees a large *kang* at the end of the room. A large wooden rack leans against the wall facing her, with the one hundred divination poems in small packs hanging from the rack in sequence. Near the window are two desks and two chairs. Since this room is the most *honghuo* (frequented by people, exciting) spot on the temple ground, a few people are usually hanging out here. The divination message decipherer, Lao Chen, greets the worshiper, who hands him the number of her message. Lao Chen tears one copy of the corresponding poem off the rack and asks for the small 0.5 yuan fee. If the worshiper is literate, she reads and interprets the divine message on her own. If she is illiterate or not literate enough to read the semiclassical style of the message, Lao Chen will interpret the message for her. Most people prefer to have Lao Chen interpret.

All of the Black Dragon King's 100 messages follow a set structure of six components: (1) the number of the message (from 1 to 100); (2) the level of auspiciousness of the message (from great great down through medium medium to bad bad—nine levels); (3) the title of the message in the form of a condensed, four-character, *chengyu*-like idiom with historical or legendary references; (4) a poem explicating the often obscure title idiom (the poems are always in the form of four seven-character lines); (5) another poem further explicating the meaning of the message (these are always in the form of four five-character lines); and (6) a succinct summary interpretation of the message and a suggestion for action for the consultee. To illustrate the divine message I provide a full translation of a few of the slips:

EXAMPLE ONE:

Slip number 9. Bad bad (*xiaxia*). The New *Mang* Usurping the Liu.

> It is widely known that your sin is as serious as covering the entire sky,
> Yet you still congratulate yourself by claiming that you are following the examples of sage kings and the virtuous.
> If you return the country to its former rightful owner,
> You may be able to save your life and home.

Also said (*you yue*):
> When you do things to the extreme,
> Seeing that disaster is upon you,
> If you don't have any thought of regrets,
> Your two lines of tears would be shed in vain.

Interpreted as saying (*jie yue*):
> You who have drawn this divination slip have accumulated a lot of evil deeds and a great disaster is upon you. If you could repent and start doing good deeds as soon as possible, you would be able to turn back Heaven's rage.

EXAMPLE TWO:

Slip number 19. Great Great (*shangshang*). The two Song brothers succeeding in the civil exam in the same year.

> Your ancestors have left a long-lasting merit,
> And now it is shining brighter than ever.
> Two trees of laurel blossoming at the same time;
> Every leaf and every flower spreading fragrance far and wide.

Also said:
> Flying side by side out of the nest,
> You are writing essays of equal brilliance.
> Like the locust blossom in the spring and the laurel flower in the autumn,
> The two brothers are enjoying great fortune.

Interpreted as saying:
> You who got this slip: If you are brothers, partners, or friends and can work together with one heart you will be successful and prosper together. If you are inquiring about exams it is especially auspicious.

EXAMPLE THREE:

Slip number 24. Medium to bad (*zhongxia*). Mingfei (Bright Lady) went beyond the Frontier.

> In order to stop the fighting you have decided on the peace-making marriage strategy;
> How can you endure the pain, now that the beauty is leaving the Han palace.
> She can never come back again once she journeys beyond the Goose Pass;
> Only in a painting will you be able to see her.

Also said:
> Whatever you do you can never hold your stance;
> Shamefully and in vain you adopt crisis-solving measures.
> Yet the more you try the more there are crises;
> In the end all you can do is swallow your sobs.

Interpreted as saying:
> If you got this slip: You can't stand straight even under ordinary circumstances. When there is a crisis you sacrifice yourself to please others and act stupidly without calculating the cost. You will have the grave misfortune of losing your wife or servant.

If the consultees bring a wide variety of particular problems to consult the Black Dragon King divination set and the divination poem is alluding to a particular historical event, how then do the consultees make the connection between their particular problems and the particular historical event in the message? The secret is in the moral lesson derived from the particular historical event, which can be generalized across time and space and be connected to another completely different situation of the here and now. The consultee, with the help of the divine message decipherer if needed, tries to get whatever she can out of the message relating to her problem (see Luo 1998).[7] Following Zeitlin (2001), I see this kind of "text-based" divine message interpretation as a "dialogic" process during which the message decipherer takes the role of indigenous critic and helps the consultees clarify their problems and weigh the pros and cons of different paths of action.

Building on the bureaucratic model of Chinese deities mentioned in Chapter 4, Emily Ahern (1981a) has proposed that Chinese divination rituals are learning games through which the peasant learns how to deal with the bureaucracy, given that the structure of communication between worshiper and deity is analogous to that between subject and magistrate. However, one is hard put to explain why most commoners are always frustrated with the state when they are brought to interact with it despite the fact, if Ahern is correct, that they have practiced and rehearsed so much with the deities. I think one can propose the very reverse of Ahern's position: that people's relationship with the deities is what their relationship with the state is not, and that they feel drawn to consulting deities about all kinds of personal problems while being extremely reluctant to deal with any parts of the bureaucracy (see also Dean 1993: 183). Perhaps Chinese divination is not so much learning to deal with the officials as learning to respect the written word and the authority behind it. In other words, divination poems are also examples of text acts that, in an agrarian environment where most peasants are illiterate or barely literate, inspire awe and submission to the cultural mystique of literati culture and the magical efficacy of the deities.

The Organizational Structure of Longwanggou

In terms of everyday forms of organization and division of labor, Longwanggou is comprised of five parts: general management or temple association proper, the temple, the Longwanggou Hilly Land Arboretum, the kitchen, and the Longwanggou Primary School. Theoretically, the overall temple association (*dahui*) is comprised of the core managing committee members (introduced below) and three representatives (usually the village Party secretary, village head, and accountant) from each of the nine participating villages. All members of this larger association meet only a few times a year for elections and other extremely important matters. Otherwise, the core members of the managing committee take care of all temple operations.

Members of the core managing committee include Lao Wang and six other temple officers. Lao Wang from Hongliutan is the temple boss (*dahuizhang*), directing and overseeing all the operations. All temple officers, including Lao Wang, are in their forties or fifties. Zhu Xurang from Zhuzhai is the accountant (*kuaiji*) who keeps track of temple income and expenditures. He is known as a meticulous accountant and has been the village accountant of Zhuzhai for 25 years. Zhang Yuhou from Hongliutan is the treasurer (*chuna*) who oversees all the financial transactions at Longwanggou. He is also Hongliutan's village medic, running a home pharmacy—with the help of his wife—and attending to minor illnesses or emergencies in the village. Liu Jinhou from Hongliutan is the electrician (*diangong*). Electricity was extended to Longwanggou during the rebuilding of the temple and an electrician is essential to the proper operation of the temple, especially during the temple festival. Chen Baolin, also from Hongliutan, is the custodian (*baoguan*). Baolin keeps all the keys to all the rooms in Longwanggou and is in charge of keeping an eye on temple properties.[8] Because of the nature of his job he is often sought after by people who want to get this or that from the rooms when they don't have the keys. "Baolin! Baolin!" One often hears people shouting and looking for him around the temple buildings. Yang Zhibiao from Yangzhuang, or Yangnao by nickname ("goat head," playing on his family name "Yang," a homophone of "*yang*," or goat), is the purchasing agent (*caigou*). He is responsible for purchasing most of the supplies Longwanggou needs for its operations, especially food, including live pigs and goats for occasions such as sacrifice to Heilongdawang. Zhang Zengyou from Batawan, nicknamed Mandur ("full grain hamper"), is the driver (*siji*). The temple has two trucks, one new and the other recently "retired," and Mandur is the only person allowed to drive them. Because he drives and is often present at temple external affairs (e.g., submitting to the prefectural government the application to become an official Daoist shrine or picking up important guests), Mandur is also nicknamed the temple diplomat (*waijiaoguan*). These seven men are the brains of Longwanggou and they are always together, engaged in serious discussions of temple matters or just idle bantering.

As described earlier in this chapter, Congminr of Chenjiapo is the zhengdian caretaker, and Lao Chen, also of Chenjiapo, is the divine message interpreter, in charge of the divination slips room. Lao Zhu of Zhuzhai is the caretaker of the new temple halls in the back of zhengdian, the Dragon Greatness Hall (*Longshengdian*) for the five dragon brothers and the Dragons' Mother Palace (*Longmugong*) for their mother the fertility goddess. Liu Zhihou from Liuwan is the forestry technician who manages the Longwanggou Hilly Land Arboretum. Lao Cai watches the arboretum against thieves (there are many fruit trees in the arboretum) and chases away the occasional hunters of small game. Weiping waters the trees and is the temple's general laborer for all kinds of chores. Lao Gao takes care of the temple garden with its many species of flowers and plants. Chen Shengxiao of Hongliutan is the chief cook of the temple canteen, assisted by Batawan's Si Laohan the second cook.[9] The Longwanggou Primary School employs ten teachers. Only two teachers are on government payroll (*gongpai*), whereas the rest are all on Longwanggou payroll, as the so-called "people-run school teachers" (*minban jiaoshi*). On top of this long list of people who are regular, paid employees—Lao Wang is the only person in Longwanggou who does not receive any salary, which is his choice—some other people help out at the temple whenever the need arises: Yaling the computer operator, Ai Shi the bulldozer operator, Lao Ren the artistic director and "court literatus," Wang Baowen the auditor, Lao Yao the opera contractor, not to mention a small army of day laborers and volunteers when there are large temple building projects. The largest mobilization of people is during the six-day temple festival of Sixth Month Thirteenth (usually in July) (see Chapters 7, 8, and 11 for details on temple festivals).

Managing the Incense Money (I): Handling Money

Money can be a very sensitive issue in Chinese society. Because I knew of the large amount of money that ran through the temple, I had prepared to be very cautious in approaching my informants at Longwanggou on matters relating to temple finance. I did not want to be perceived as having an inordinate interest in things monetary, even though I *was* extremely interested to know how it all worked. Therefore I did not try to pry into that mysterious realm and instead just let the knowledge "happen" to me. My dormitory room at the temple was only a few rooms away from some of the temple offices (see the map of the temple layout), and when the temple officers gathered there I "naturally" joined in the group, listened, and observed, as would any good anthropologist. It did not take long for me to find out which room was the accountant's office and treasury with the big green safe.

One afternoon during the first month of my residence at Longwanggou I went up to the divination slips room (S. *qianzeryao*) intending to chat with Lao Chen the divination message interpreter, and as I went in the room, lo and behold, I chanced upon a few of the temple officers sitting on the *kang* around a big pile of money! My heart was filled with a sudden burst of excitement. Here it is, I thought to myself, the *money*! There were six temple officers, two of whom I had not chatted with yet. They all gave me a brief look when I came in and resumed counting the money without the slightest fuss. Then I noticed that not only Lao Chen was there but also a few old men who were *qianzeryao* regulars, as well as a couple of worshipers who were getting their slips. There was not the slightest unease in the air, except perhaps my own momentary surprise and excitement. Apparently that was the way they had always counted the donation money: in full view of anyone who happened to be in or near the *qianzeryao*. I was surprised at this transparency, but quickly understood that such a conspicuous transparency was probably a necessary gesture for the public, just as the total figure of donations during the temple festival was always public knowledge.

I half-sat at the edge of the kang and just looked at them count the money. It was a huge pile of *renminbi* bills large and small. Most of them were wrinkled and many were soiled. Some small bills (*maomaoqian*, literally fractions of a yuan) were so worn that the patterns were hardly recognizable, and a few even broke into pieces when picked up. The officers were Yuhou the treasurer, Xurang the accountant, Baolin the custodian, Jinhou the electrician, and another two I only later knew as Pingr from Heshang and Lougangr from Huaqu. They divided up the task and each would pick out and count only one or two kinds of bill: the hundreds and the fifties, the tens, the fives, the twos, the ones, and the *maomaoqian*, which was the most numerous (fifty cents, twenty cents, ten cents, and even coins of smaller value). "A fake fifty yuan!" Jinhou exclaimed. "Let me see," said the others, who all wanted to examine the bill. "Definitely fake!" Jinhou held the bill at one end and gave it a hard and sudden wag in the air before passing it on to the others. It seemed that the bill was a little too crisp. They each looked for the watermark and the in-seam thread and massaged the bill with their hands. I had a look at it too. The verdict was that it was definitely fake. They told me that they would always find a couple of fake bills in the pile, and they did not think the worshipers who donated the money knew that they were donating fake bills. "No one would dare to cheat the venerable dragon king (*Longwangye ta laorenjia*), you know." I wondered whether the temple would try to spend the fake bills or just destroy them.[10] After all the different kinds of bills were counted and tied into bundles with elastic bands, they added up the total: 17, 368 yuan and 72 cents. Then Yuhou left the 72 cents in the *qianzeryao* drawer for Lao Chen (because he would need it to give people change when they bought the divination slips) and wrapped the bundles in the red cloth that had been spread underneath the pile of money. They all went to the treasury (i.e., the office of the accountant and the treasurer), put the money in the big green safe, and, after much casual chatting and bantering, went upstairs to the kitchen for dinner. I for obvious reasons never asked during the course of my field-work how much money there was in the big green safe, and whenever I was in that room I consciously avoided sitting too close to it or looking at it when it was open. I only knew that the temple kept most of the money in a bank in Mizhi Town and the safe probably never had too much money in it.

In the course of the year I was at the temple I witnessed similar money-counting sessions many times. The session took place once every ten days (sometimes every five days when the donation was estimated to be large) and was always on the ninths of the lunar month, i.e., ninth, nineteenth, and twenty-ninth, which were all Zhenchuan Town market days.[11] The session was called *diangui* (counting of the cabinet), and was divided into three segments: opening the incense money cabinet (*kaigui*), counting the money, and entering the amount into the book and the safe. As mentioned earlier, the incense money cabinet (*gui*) was the big, reddish-brown, wrought-iron cabinet in the main temple hall that sat right in front of Heilongdawang's statue. It had a wooden top and doubled as the altar and offering table. There were three narrow, small, horizontal slits in the front of the cabinet for worshipers to tuck in their donations. The door that opened at the front had three installed locks and three different keys were required to open the cabinet. Three officers held these three keys, and all three of them had to be present to open the cabinet. The three officers were Yuhou the treasurer, Xurang the accountant, and Lougangr from Huaqu. Obviously there were precautions against possible mishandling of the money by individuals. Usually the three officers were joined by two or three others to count the money. They did this so often that it had become a routine for them (about thirty-six times a year for many years). First they would go to the main temple hall, spread the red cloth in front of the cabinet, open the cabinet with the three keys, and dig out all the money in the cabinet. Then they would carry the red bundle of bills to the *qianzeryao*, open the bundle on the kang, and start counting. Sometimes, when they felt like it, they would even do the counting outside the *qianzeryao*, under the overhanging balcony of the

Longwanggou temple officers count the donation money.

Dragon Greatness Hall (*Longsheng dian*). And finally they would bring the money to the treasury, chat and banter, and go upstairs when dinner was ready. Lao Wang was usually at the temple on a cabinet-counting day not only because he needed to know how well the temple had been doing but also because on these days most temple officers were around so they could discuss temple business together.

Also on these cabinet-counting days, receipts were checked and expenses approved by temple boss Lao Wang. Lao Wang was the only person at Longwanggou who could approve expenses. He oversaw all the temple finances large and small, and he was rightfully called the "man who is in charge of the cabinet" (*zhangguide*).[12] Let us look at a couple of examples to see how temple finances worked at Longwanggou. A few days before the annual temple festival the temple would buy wholesale a couple of thousand *jin* of watermelons for treating guests, the opera performers, employees, and volunteers. The lucky watermelon seller would truck the watermelons to the temple. Baolin the custodian and a few helpers would weigh the melons and store them in the storage rooms. The total cost would be noted and written on an IOU, with the temple and the seller each keeping a copy. The temple copy of the IOU would then be brought to Lao Wang for approval. Lao Wang of course had approved this transaction beforehand so he would just check the amount and legitimate the transaction by signing his name on the IOU. The IOU was idiomatically called *tiaozi* (i.e., the slip), and Lao Wang's action of approving was called *pi tiaozi*. The signed IOU would then be brought to Yuhou the treasurer if the money needed to be paid right away. Whether paid right away or at a later time the signed IOU would have to go to Xurang the accountant to be recorded in the account book under the paid or yet-to-be-paid column. If the watermelon seller was to be paid at the end of the year, he could come back to the temple at that time, present his copy of the IOU, and get paid the amount the temple owed him. His copy of the IOU would get a temple chop "PAID" in blue: end of transaction. Temple income moved in a less complicated manner. After each cabinet-counting session the amount would be entered into both the treasurer's and the accountant's books, the former because he had taken in the actual money and the latter because he had to record all incomes under the income column. It was the treasurer's job to keep track of how much money was in the safe and how much money was in the bank. He was also responsible for having the money ready for timely payment of salaries and repayment of debts. I did not try to find out how banking worked at Longwanggou. I imagine there had to be cautionary measures against individual mishandling of funds. The temple also had its own auditor, who checked the accounts once every season. The books had to be well tended because the Bureau of Investigations (*jiancha yuan*) of the Yulin City government had the right to check them on a regular basis, even though I did not investigate how often they had indeed checked.

Managing the Incense Money (II): Temple Income and Expenses

The temple donation coffer is at the heart of all of Longwanggou's activities: No money, no activity. Yet it is also true that if there were no temple activities, especially the annual temple festival, not much money would come in either. The reputation of the temple hinges on both the amount of donations and the level of activities sponsored by the temple (including temple expansion projects). Many worshipers are interested in the income figures as well as the expense figures. People are often awed by the unbelievably high amounts; they publicize them, and make the

Heilongdawang Temple even more famous. The logic is simple: so many worshipers donate so much money to the temple, therefore Heilongdawang must be efficacious.

Because of the constant relay between spending money on temple activities and receiving money from worshipers, these monetary cycles seem to have become the raison d'être of the temple: spending, receiving, spending more, receiving more, spending yet more, receiving yet more . . . As these relays of money spiral upwards, the amounts can reach a formidably high level. In the early 1980s during the first years of the temple's revival, the annual temple donation income was a few tens of thousand yuan. In 1998 the amount was estimated at around 1.4 million yuan, more than 50 times larger than that of fifteen years ago. It is worth noting that the average annual gross income per capita in the rural areas of the Zhenchuan Town vicinity at this time was barely one thousand yuan. How was this large sum of money managed?

Let us first look at all the categories of income and expenses at Longwanggou. The income was composed almost entirely of incense money donations (*bushi*). A little income was generated by occasional interest from loans from the temple to individuals or businesses, though this was never substantial because loaning out money was neither a regular nor a significant temple activity. There was also the income from renting out space to vendors during the temple festival, though this again was not much. Incense money can be viewed as being divided into two kinds: that which trickles in on a daily basis and that which pours in on special occasions such as the New Year's days, the First Month Fifteenth *yangge* fest (*zhengyue shiwu nao yangge*), the Dragons' Mother's birthday (Fifth Month Fifteenth), and the annual temple festival (Sixth Month Thirteenth). The five-day-long temple festival in 1998 alone drew more than six hundred thousand yuan, almost half of that year's annual donation income total. How well the temple festival does in a particular year in terms of donation income always sets the mood for the entire year, and so far the Longwanggou Temple Festival has never failed. On a "slow day" in between these special occasions, however, the donations can be as low as a couple of hundred yuan.

The temple expenses fall into the following broad categories:

ROUTINE TEMPLE OPERATIONS
— Salaries of temple employees, including the schoolteachers;
— Food (for the daily operation of the temple canteen);

— Supplies (including gas for the temple trucks and bulldozer);
— Electricity (including that which was used for pumping water for watering the trees);
— Maintaining the Arboretum (renting land from villagers, buying seedlings, hiring laborers);
— Business travels of temple officers (e.g., trips to contract opera troupes);
— Receiving guests (liquor, cigarettes, and gifts), etc.

SPECIAL TEMPLE OPERATIONS
— Hiring opera troupes for the annual temple festival;
— Hiring folk music bands (*chuishou*) on the Dragons' Mother's birthday, during the temple festival and on other special occasions;
— Compensation for yangge troupes that performed during the First Month Fifteenth yangge fest;
— Food for serving large groups during the temple festival and other special temple events;
— Compensation for service rendered by local police force during temple events;
— Temple expansion and repair projects;

LOCAL CAUSES
— Donation to local schools, public works projects, and other worthwhile causes (e.g., publication of local history).

Hiring the opera troupes for the temple festival constitutes the largest expense on the temple annual budget. In 1998 the four opera troupes (two famous provincial level troupes and two local, regional troupes) cost more than three hundred thousand yuan (including transportation costs), which was around half of the donation income during the temple festival. But some temple expansion projects can cost more, though they are usually multiyear projects. For example, the side temple building completed in 1998 cost nearly six hundred thousand yuan, and the second and larger stone gate (*shi pailou*), half-finished in 1998, would eventually cost close to 3 million yuan. Food costs quite a few tens of thousand yuan annually, and so do the salaries for temple employees. The rest, when added up, also consumes a sizable portion of the budget. As the temple accountant said to me: "Ten or twenty thousand here and three or five thousand there, and the money is all spent!" It is clear that the donation money is always "reinvested" in temple operations and there is a tendency toward avoiding a sizable surplus, not least to avoid additional squeeze from the local state. In fact, the two large projects mentioned above plunged the temple into debt beginning in 1996. The temple would still be repaying the debts related to these two projects in 1999, and possibly in 2000. Yet these are seen as investments that would soon pay off by attracting more worshipers and hence more donation money.

The fiscal year at Longwanggou, like in rural Shaanbei at large, begins with the first month of the lunar calendar and ends with the last month. The end of the twelfth month (*layue*) is the second busiest time at Longwanggou in terms of monetary transactions—*the* busiest time is during the temple festival (see below)—because this is when all outstanding salaries are paid and, theoretically and ideally, all debts are collected or repaid. Following traditional practice, the salaries of temple employees and the schoolteachers are paid on an annual basis, even though they can always "borrow" an advance payment when they have urgent need for cash, and they usually do in the course of a year. For example, the annual salary for Chen Shengxiao the chief cook in 1997 was set at six thousand yuan (five hundred monthly) but he only received two thousand or so at the end of the year because he had already "borrowed" a large portion of his salary for, among other things, treating his wife's chronic mental illness. The cumulated daily wages of non-regular temple employees such as the hired laborers are also paid at the end of the year even though, again, many of them would have already taken out some advance payments.

At the end of 1997 Longwanggou does not have any debt to collect; on the contrary, it has many debts to repay. Among Longwanggou's creditors are the gas station the temple trucks frequent, the shops and stores in Zhenchuan Town from which the temple usually gets its food and supplies, the artisans and contractors who work on temple projects, the local opera troupes which performed at the 1997 temple festival, and some other miscellaneous ones. Earlier I mentioned that debts are "theoretically and ideally" repaid at the end of the year because often they are not, especially in the case of Longwanggou. Because of its high local status as a corporate body, Longwanggou can afford to delay its debt payments, and it often does, until the middle of the first month of the next year when the temple would have another large wave of donation income. Few creditors are in a position to complain and they graciously tolerate this minor inconvenience to ensure continued patronage by the temple. Sometimes even the salaries, and bonuses if there are any, of the schoolteachers are paid after First Month Fifteenth.

Sometimes portions of large debts are repaid as late as during the temple festival because that is when the temple has the most money to go around. During the few days of the temple festival the donation money is collected and counted a few times each day and some of it immediately goes to repaying these outstanding debts (the creditors always come to the temple festival). The opera troupes the temple hires from outside the local area (e.g., those from Xi'an and Zhouzhi of Shaanxi, Taiyuan of Shanxi, Kaifeng and Zhengzhou of Henan) are always paid immediately after the temple festival. And, perhaps according to tradition, all the folk music bands are also paid immediately after their service during special temple events.

Longwanggou as Corporation

Scholars of Chinese society and culture have long noted the adeptness of the Chinese in organizing strong and enduring civil collectivities beyond the household/family (see Sangren 1984a). These collectivities can take the forms of lineages, shops and companies, sworn brotherhoods and sisterhoods, secret societies, guilds, native-place associations, monasteries, nunneries, and shrines, temple associations of village and regional cults, literati poetry clubs, alumni associations, rotating credit clubs, etc. Some of these civil collectivities are more enduring than others, and many hold properties that help ensure their financial strength. Hill Gates (1996) theorizes on the long history and the contemporary relevance of the capacity of some of these civil collectivities to form corporate structures and operate on petty capitalist principles to eke out a living and a social space under the shadows of the tributary state.[13] The township- and village-owned enterprises (the so-called TVE), territorially based and often kinship-based in their organizations and operations, are merely contemporary elaborations of a very ancient practice.

The organizational and operational practices of the Heilongdawang Temple and the Longwanggou Complex also bear the marks of this long tradition of civil corporate organizations. The Heilongdawang Temple had its own extensive trust land before the Land Reform broke it all up to give away to poor peasants. The trust land generated rent in the form of food and money for sponsoring temple activities, most important of which was the annual temple festival. Back then the incense money donation was minimal compared to the rent income. The leaders of the temple association took care of the finances and other temple operations. It was a classic case of a popular religious corporate body.

After the temple was deprived of its trust land, it relied more on donations generated from yangge troupe trips during the first month of the lunar year and even on spreading (*tan*) the cost among the production teams and brigades. Incense money donation from visiting worshipers during this period (i.e., 1950s to early 1960s) was minimal. The leadership of the temple association was taken over by leaders of the teams and brigades. The corporate status of the temple was greatly compromised, mostly because it hardly had an autonomous existence. Since its revival in the early 1980s, however, the temple has not only resumed a corporate existence but also greatly expanded the scope of its operations. Still, the temple does not have any land of its own, because all land in rural China is owned by the villages, and ultimately by the state. But this matters little now because of the huge income from incense money donations.

Longwanggou is a corporate body in three senses. First, it is an organization engaged in institutional behaviors and it has clearly understood, if not clearly articulated, missions: self-perpetuation and continual expansion. Second, and as a component of the first sense, it has an institutional budget of income and expenses; the more autonomous the budgeting, the more independent and corporate-like is the organization. Third, and as a component of the second sense, even though it is theoretically a nonprofit organization, Longwanggou "makes" money, or desires as much money as possible. It is also in these three senses that Longwanggou resembles a business corporation, even though few Shaanbei people would view it this way. Because of the high financial stakes at Longwanggou, conflicts naturally arise regarding the disposition of the funds or the temple leadership (treated in later chapters).

Longwanggou as Religious Service Provider

Recall the divine retribution stories I related in Chapter 4. Vivid as they are, the apparently very entertaining as well as horrific divine retribution stories are a small part of the collective "divine lore" among the growing number of worshipers of Heilongdawang. Since many worshipers have only recently joined the fold of the cult and may have come from faraway places (sometimes hundreds of miles away), they are more primed into the lore of Heilongdawang's benevolence and wisdom rather than his fits of anger against violators. Indeed, worshipers and pilgrims never tire of telling one another their own experience of having been well served by Heilongdawang. One can see temples as places where people interact with deities and receive divine assistance; one can also see temples as providers of divine assistance or magical efficacy (ling). Different temples quite consciously compete with one another in promoting their own deity's magical power, and in the process different ways of provisioning ling are invented, modified, or expanded. The case of Longwang-gou presents several examples of these kinds of conscious manipulation of what is called "business models" in the world of business (i.e., ways of generating revenue). Of course, any innovation should still be framed in culturally acceptable idioms or one risks provoking cynicism and losing support of worshipers.

In the past, people consulted the divination sticks only when there were very grave problems because it was a lot of trouble to find an interpreter for the divine message, given the low literacy rate. The divination roller was used more often instead. But ever since the temple's revival in the early 80s, a permanent interpreter in residence became available to help consultees understand what lies behind the often obscure historical references and semi-literary flair in the divine messages. What's more, instead of merely reading from a big, heavy, hand-copied divine message book bound in red cloth, the kind many small temples in Shaanbei still feature today, the consultee can now take home the message slip printed on paper for a small fee of half a yuan. Thus *convenience* is a key issue in efficacy service. For many years now the few old folks taking care of the temple have been cleaning used beer and soft drink bottles and storing them in the temple so that they can give them to people who want to take the divine water home, for only, again, half a yuan. And the medicine packets are now premade and prepackaged, unlike in the past when each individual medicine-seeker had to spread joss paper underneath the burning incense and wait for a long time for the divine medicine to come down. I had spent many hours packing these medicine packets with the old men at the temple under the warm Shaanbei sun.

In an effort to further expand the temple's service repertoire, temple boss Lao Wang decided a few years ago to build an elegant, new temple hall for Heilongdawang's mother, Longmu niangniang, so that people with problems and anxieties relating to reproduction and child rearing who would normally go to goddess temples could come to the Heilongdawang Temple for help. Images of one-stop shopping easily come to mind. Lao Wang's strategic move is even more significant when seen in the context of the birth-control policy being really tightened up in Shaanbei in the past few years and the anxiety level of son-favoring peasant men and women mounting to an all-time high.[14]

I have shown how people brought a wide array of problems to consult Heilongdawang. But what about Heilongdawang as the rain-granting god? Aren't dragon kings supposed to grant timely rainfall, regulate the wind, and stop hailstones? Heilongdawang is still *the* deity in the area to ensure good harvest with adequate and nicely timed rainfall, but this function has receded into the background for two reasons. First, since his rain-granting function is his prima facie function and is understood as such, people are only reminded of it when there is a really bad drought. Second, rainfall and good harvests are communal and generalized wishes compared to individualized problems such as an illness, a bad husband, or bad luck with money. As worship at temples in Shaanbei becomes more and more individualized and devoid of community concerns, the dragon kings' rain-granting function will undoubtedly be less stressed.

Hill Gates (1996) argues that folk cultural expressions are not timeless givens. Instead, they gain and retain a tenacity only in particular political and economic milieus. She argues that a lot of what we know as Chinese folk culture are largely products of Chinese petty capitalism, which is a mode of production in constant interaction with another, more dominant tributary mode of production throughout the history of late imperial China until today. An extremely vibrant and competitive petty capitalist economy and its concomitant desires and anxieties are the basis of folk cultural expressions such as complementary beliefs in fate and hard work, bribing the gods, competitive display of wealth and status, and valuation and manipulation of kinship ties (see also Bruun 1996, 2003; Chan, Madsen, and Unger 1992; Gates and Weller 1987; Harrell 1987; Weller 1994a; Yang 2000). Gates sees the revival of folk cultural traditions in the PRC as a reflection of the revival of petty capitalism during the reform era.

Attention to how larger political economic processes affect peasant sociocultural lives steers us clear of the pitfall of imputing a primordial status to folk cultural traditions such as popular religion. Activities surrounding temples support many related petty capitalist businesses: ritual paraphernalia shops; makers of incense, spirit money, firecrackers, commemorative plaques, and flags; printers of divination slips; folk music bands and private opera troupes; restaurants and guest houses along pilgrimage routes, etc. More specifically, Gates contends that popular religions often are sometimes very much themselves petty capitalist enterprises, embedded as they are in intricate petty capitalist socioeconomic networks. Fund-raising activities of temples in Taiwan in particular exemplify petty capitalist ingenuity (Gates 1996; 231–42). Similarly, we can view Longwanggou as a petty capitalist enterprise based on the provisioning of Heilongdawang's efficacious responses, and increasingly in a manner resembling convenience stores and one-stop shopping malls.

Longwanggou's move toward multiplication of functions in one temple is not new; traditionally larger temples and monasteries have always expanded their repertoire of services by erecting more statues and incorporating functionally differentiated deities. Longwanggou was merely following the model of a long venerated tradition. In fact, Lao Wang had planned to build a separate temple hall for the God of Wealth, apparently aiming at attracting more businesspeople and wealth-seeking worshipers to Longwanggou, but was persuaded by his associates not to because, they argued, Heilongdawang had already become a God of Wealth over the years.

Alan Cole (1998) has argued that medieval Chinese Buddhists revolutionized Chinese family values by elevating the mother-son tie over the conventional Confucian father-son tie, and promulgated what Cole calls a "Buddhist biology" in which motherhood (i.e., giving birth) was polluting and damning for the mother and in need of the son's ritual expiation. And conveniently, the Buddhist monasteries provided ritual services that would expiate the very sins that were the constructs of Buddhist propaganda. Studying the rise of Daoists as professional ritual specialists providing service to individuals and communities, Robert Hymes (2002) proposes to view the Daoists and other religious professionals as competing in a religious market, and the rituals they provide as religious commodities to be selected and bought. In their struggle for market share and attempts at monopoly, different religious specialists and institutions (Daoists, Buddhists, geomancers, even Confucians) enter into sometimes fierce competitions or relations of domination and subjugation, negotiation and accommodation, absorption and syncretization. Perhaps the best ethnographic example of religious consumerism and the provisioning of religious services is Marc Moskowitz's study of the myriad ways to deal with haunting fetus ghosts in contemporary Taiwan (2001). In this newfound religious niche market, Daoist exorcists compete with Buddhist monasteries, and a street-side noodle-vendor-turned-seer works side by side with sorcerers who manipulate desperate uncared-for fetus ghosts. Recall my suggestion in Chapter 4 to examine Chinese religious life from the angle of "doing religion" rather than merely through making sense of religious conceptions; much of the "doing" involves the provision of various religious services, by ritual specialists or temples.

My purpose in this chapter has been to highlight the service-provision aspect of popular religion in Shaanbei. Heilongdawang *is* perhaps like a bureaucrat because he has been granted an imperial title and wears bureaucratic garb (see Wolf 1974a; also Shahar and Weller 1996). Yet I have tried to show that he is *more* like a versatile service provider, a doctor, a pharmacist, a psychiatrist, a counselor, a caretaker, and many other things all rolled into one (though he only speaks vicariously through the divination set, the oracle roller, or the divine message interpreter). With the Heilongdawang example I have hoped to illustrate the sociocultural construction of divine efficacy, of particular kinds of service, and of patterns of religious consumerism. Like a famous doctor, Heilongdawang is a deity of choice for many Shaanbei people, just as brand names and quality service are for consumers of secular goods. But I want to emphasize that presenting popular religious temples as religious service providers should in no way be seen as denigrating their role in the sociocultural lives of peasants; rather, it is a way to see beyond, and beneath, the apparently "religious" activities in popular religion.

CHAPTER SEVEN

Modes of Social Organization and Folk Event Productions

Social Organization of Folk Cultural Traditions

An important contribution the anthropologist Robert Redfield made to anthropology is the concept of "the social organization of tradition" (Redfield 1956). According to Redfield, any tradition is actualized through the "social organization" of *institutions* (e.g., schools, temples, temple associations, pilgrimages), *specialists* (e.g., priests, spirit mediums, epic reciters, storytellers, musicians, opera singers), and *cultural products* (e.g., religious epics, sutras, symbols, ideas). In the words of Redfield's colleague Milton Singer, who exemplifies Redfield's approach with his study on Hinduism in Madras, "[a] cultural tradition needs to be conceived both culturally as a cultural structure and societally *as a social organization*" (Singer 1972: 192).

A folk tradition such as Shaanbei popular religion does not simply exist; it needs to be produced and reproduced. Drawing on Redfield's insight, we can view popular religion as involving the social organization of folk social institutions (e.g., temples, temple associations, opera troupes, folk music bands, pilgrimage networks), diverse social actors (e.g., ritual specialists, opera performers, spirit mediums, storytellers, worshipers, festivalgoers, sponsors), and a wide range of folk cultural products and event productions (e.g., opera performances, temple oracles, temple festivals, deity legends, efficacy stories, charms). The key is to look at the *mechanisms of social organization that actualize popular religion.*

In Chapter 4, I tried to show that the relationship Shaanbei people have with the deities can be understood in terms of social relationship, only in a different register (the relational modality of "doing religion").

In dealing with deities, as in dealing with people, one relies on and follows important social values such as trust, respect, and reciprocity. I then examined the organizational structure of the Longwanggou temple complex in Chapter 6. I argued that popular religious institutions can be understood as efficacy service providers, and there is nothing particularly religious about the ways in which they are organized. Religious organizations are ultimately social organizations, and this is especially true in the case of popular religion. In this chapter I focus on the principles and mechanisms of staging important popular religious events (e.g., funerals and temple festivals): volunteerism based on principles of reciprocal labor assistance, division of tasks among helpers and specialists, and the symbolic weight put on the importance of being a good host. These principles and mechanisms complement those that are embodied in more formal folk social institutions such as temple associations. In particular, I introduce two key concepts, "event production" and "hosting," to highlight the social aspects of popular religious activities that have not received adequate scholarly attention. The overall argument is to show how much of popular religion is thoroughly social: not only socially embedded, but also *socially produced*. After introducing some theoretical frameworks informing this discussion, I will compare and contrast a funeral and a temple festival observed in my field site in Shaanbei. The temple festival was the annual birthday celebration for Heilongdawang at Longwanggou. The funeral took place in Batawan, one of the three villages around Longwanggou.

Hosting and Event Productions

First, I propose the expression "event production" as a broader term to refer to all kinds of cultural productions that are set apart from the everyday life. Event production as a category of social life includes all rituals, but not all event productions are rituals. For example, the Olympic Games are a gigantic modern event production that is not quite a ritual (even though one can certainly analyze it as a meta-ritual). A temple festival is a peasant event production that includes many ritual components (e.g., the presentation of offerings, exorcism), but cannot itself be reduced to a ritual. Event production can better characterize some of the social phenomena that hitherto have been glossed as ritual (or ceremony).[1] *Second*, I suggest that any event production (e.g., a funeral) typically consists of two parallel aspects: the *ritual-procedural or liturgical aspect* and the *hosting or guest-catering aspect*. I argue that the concept of *hosting* is useful in highlighting some of the hitherto neglected elements of event productions due to the overemphasis on the ritual-procedural aspect.

A focus on the hosting aspect of event productions affords us the opportunity to discover that the principles and mechanisms of producing large-scale "religious" events (e.g., a temple festival) are the same as those used in producing small-scale "religious" events and secular events. The most basic element of the social organization of popular religious events in Shaanbei is *volunteerism based on understandings of reciprocity and the division of labor among the helpers and specialists*, which is found in the social organization of all important social events in rural life such as funerals, weddings, or house construction. Only the degree of complexity and the specific kinds of specialists used vary. In Chapter 2, I discussed the prevalence of mutual help between different peasant households based on the idioms of "labor exchange" (*biangong*) and "helping out" (*xianghuo*). These same idioms are used in staging event productions. For example, to help out at a funeral or wedding is called "helping at the event" (*xiangshi*). Temple officers of one temple might help out at the temple festival of another temple and vice versa when the two temples have good relations. Worshipers volunteer at temple festivals and say they are "helping out" the deity (i.e., the supposed real host) in staging the festival. Redirecting our analytical gaze away from ritual procedure to hosting has important theoretical implications: it complements the traditional anthropological search for meanings behind symbols and symbolic actions with a search for *the cultural basis (cultural logic) of social intercourse and cultural performance*. I will use ethnographic examples from Shaanbei to illustrate and support my propositions.

Hosting is arguably the most important social activity for Shaanbei people.[2] There are two broad kinds of hosting activities. The first kind is the more mundane, small-scale hosting of a few friends, neighbors, or relatives visiting the house. These minor hosting occasions are numerous and recurrent, and they are crucial to maintaining social relations (*guanxi*) and long-term sentimental attachments (*ganqing*) (Kipnis 1997). I also include under this category hosting occasions such as the first-month celebration of a child, feasting the helpers and laborers after finishing constructing a house.

The second kind of hosting occurs on the few occasions of highly significant household events (in descending order of significance): funerals for parents (*mai laoren*, literally "burying old people"), weddings for sons (*yin xifu*, literally "bringing in the daughter-in-law"), and weddings for daughters (*jia nüzi*, literally "marrying off the daughter").[3] These occasions are far more important because they are traditionally assigned ritual significance. Both funerals and weddings have procedures and valences theorized by Confucian literati thinkers in the past, and following the right procedures has been an important marker of a Han Chinese identity (Watson 1988b). Watson has called this "doing it right" cultural imperative "orthopraxy," in contradistinction to the relative unimportance of knowing and believing the actual references of particular ritual symbols and procedures (i.e., orthodoxy). I would like to argue that hosting these major household events (or event productions) successfully most importantly constitutes the personhood and identity of the head of household and by extension establishes and confirms the standing of the household in the community. Building upon Watson's insight, I suggest that there are actually two aspects of the funeral that the host household has to "do right": the ritual-procedural (Watson's emphasis) and the hosting (my focus in this chapter).

Hosting important household events such as weddings and funerals is scripted into every peasant's life. But how is a Shaanbei peasant's life scripted? In other words, what is the culturally ideal path for a peasant to pass from birth, childhood, through adulthood, and to death, and what are life's obligations?[4] The answer is obviously different for men and women because of the persistent patrilineal ideologies and patrilocal marriage practices. Simply put, ideally, a peasant man should get married, have sons (at least one son, and maybe some daughters too), bury his parents properly, get wives for his sons, and marry off his daughters to good families. A woman, on the other hand, should be a good daughter before marriage, and be a good and helpful wife after marriage and assist her husband in fulfilling the above-mentioned life obligations. She is equally implicated in the successes and failures of these household events as the wife of the head of household. A man's (and his wife's) status within the community gradually increases as he fulfills these obligations one by one, and his sense of his identity also consolidates over time. A man and his wife will not feel fulfilled and accomplished until they have buried both of the man's parents,[5] gotten wives for all their sons, and married off all their daughters.[6]

Each of these moments entails hosting an event production: a funeral or a wedding. In Shaanbei to stage a wedding or a funeral is called "doing an event" (*banshir*). The household that is hosting the event is called "the host household" (*zhujia*). In "doing an event" the host household is fulfilling a *ritual* obligation as well as a *social* obligation. As mentioned earlier, the traditional ritual procedures for a funeral or a wedding have to be followed.[7] Yet equally important, these are also occasions where the host household has to engage in largely prescribed social interactions with many guests who come to the events to pay respect to the dead or to congratulate the newly married couple. The zhujia has to host and feast the guests well.

On these hosting occasions the "sovereignty" of the zhujia is the most manifest and celebrated. Just as imperial Grand Sacrifice and imperial guest rituals fashioned the imperium and the emperor as supreme host and lord of the realm (Zito 1997: 26–30; Hevia 1995: 212), peasant household event productions (which are guest rituals in crucial aspects) fashion the zhujia as a sovereign (and solvent) social unit and the head of the household as the lord or master (*zhu*) of this unit. Even though the guests have to be well treated and respected, it is the zhujia that accrues social prestige, "face," and symbolic capital by being the host.[8]

But assertions of household sovereignty have costs. Hosting these major household events can be extremely expensive. In the Longwanggou area where I conducted most of my fieldwork, an average funeral cost over 5,000 yuan, and an average wedding over 3,000 yuan (not counting brideprice), each amounting to many years of careful economizing and saving.[9] If a couple has many sons, their financial situation can be particularly precarious because getting wives for their sons also means building and furnishing houses (*yao*) for all of the sons. Traditionally, a man in his thirties would face the greatest challenges of his life because that is when both of his parents might die and all of his sons would reach marriageable age. So a man has to start saving money literally as soon as he is married and becomes the head of his own household in anxious anticipation of all these large ritual expenses. Shaanbei parents see these required occasions of hosting as both onerous burdens and proud moments. Many adult peasant men have grumbled to me about the burden of financing these events. However, even if these men have to go into debt (and many do), they cannot afford not to put up a good show on these crucial occasions. The host and "sovereign" is obliged to be generous and magnanimous.[10] Fortunately, the zhujia can always count on the help of many people when they host a household life-course event (most crucially in labor, and also in cash).

Below I will describe and analyze a typical Shaanbei funeral, and then compare and contrast it with the hosting of a temple festival. Funerals are of course very different events compared to temple festivals, but comparing the two can help illuminate two related issues: first, their common modes of organization; and second, their common cultural logic (the idiom of hosting, the desire to stage a honghuo event). In addition, traditional forms of staging a funeral revived at around the same time as temples did in the early 1980s, and, as I will show below, funerals manifest equally strong popular religious ethos.[11]

Funerals as Event Productions

Shaanbei people treat funerals very seriously. Funerals are called "white events" (*baishi*), white connoting mourning, whereas weddings are called "red events" (*hongshi*), red connoting happiness and celebration.[12] A red event is relatively easy to organize because it is usually considered a success as long as the guests are properly banqueted with a lot of good food, cigarettes, and liquor (despite the fact that there are also a wide range of symbolically significant ritual procedures). It is the organizers' duty to create a joyous and festive mood through their hospitality. By the time of the wedding ceremony itself most of the troublesome matters of negotiating marital exchanges have already been settled.[13]

White events are different. Unlike a wedding, a funeral entails more intricate ritual procedures, which necessitate the hiring of a ritual specialist, the yinyang. Also unlike in a wedding, members of the household staging the funeral cannot be involved in the actual process of the funeral as organizers because they are supposed to concentrate on mourning the dead and because they have specific roles to play in the rituals, not as organizers but as key ritual participants (e.g., kowtowing to the guests who pay respect to the deceased). Therefore the household has to find a chief organizer and a whole team of assistants to help them stage the funeral. Typically, when a household has a very old and ill member, it begins planning for the funeral as early as possible because many things need to be considered. The funeral clothes and coffin for the dead need to be made. The burial site needs to be prepared. The entire funeral needs to be carefully budgeted. A funeral is likely to be the biggest cash outlay in the life of a household, so the household needs to save up for funerals for many years. Everywhere in rural China, funerals are social events in which social debts are incurred and repaid, gestures of sentiments are expressed and reciprocated, social ties are reaffirmed and reproduced, and most importantly, *the social and moral worth of the household in question eval-*

uated and judged. To mismanage a major social event such as a funeral is to lose face in a major way for the household. One cannot afford to fail (S. *langan*, literally "rotten stalk").

So many things could go wrong at a funeral. The food might not be plentiful enough or might be badly cooked; the affinal guests might complain about ritual impropriety; some guests might get too drunk and cause trouble; the band might be too lazy to play properly (if they are not treated with respect and care); the yinyang master might be incompetent and negligent; and so forth. Therefore the chief organizer and assistants need to be carefully chosen so that everything will run smoothly.

The head of the zhujia chooses the chief organizer first and discusses with him whom to invite as assistants. The chief organizer, called the "chief director" (*zongling*), is in charge of the entire event. He is usually an experienced, well-respected male co-villager (never a female because of male dominance in village public life) with strong leadership abilities. The chief director helps select the right individuals for each assigned role in the production of the funeral. These assigned roles are as follows (based on an actual funeral I attended in Batawan in the summer of 1997 with around one hundred and fifty guests):

— chief director of the event (*zongling*): one person
— guest inviter (*qingke*): one person
— caretaker of the spirit shed (*lingpeng* or *lingqian*): one person
— attendant to the yinyang master (*kanyinyang* or *daipingshi*): one person
— attendant to the musicians (*kanchuishou*): one person
— recorders of gifts (*shuli*): two persons
— cooks in charge of meat dishes ("meat wok," *hunguo*) including one head of meat wok (*hunguotou*): six persons
— cooks in charge of vegetarian dishes ("vegetarian wok," *suguo*) including one head of vegetarian wok (*suguotou*): nine persons
— water boiler (*shaoshui*): one person
— distributor of cigarettes and liquor (*yanjiu*): one person
— waiters to serve the guests (*kanke*): eight persons
— plate carriers (*chipan*): five persons
— table cleaners (*jingzhuo*): two persons
— dish washers (*xiwan*): two persons (with one person doubling as table-cleaner)
— grave diggers and coffin carriers (*tugong*): eight persons

Sometimes a list of the assigned roles with names of all the responsible individuals is written down on a large sheet of red paper and posted on the wall for all to see, partly to hold these individuals accountable and partly to publicize the fact of social reciprocity performed or repaid.

A standard funeral in today's Shaanbei lasts for a day and a half (abbreviated from the pre-Liberation three-day standard).[14] On the first day, from morning to dusk, guests come to pay respect to the dead by burning incense and spirit money in front of the dead person's spirit tablet and kowtowing to his or her portrait. The family members of the dead person kowtow back in gratitude. The host provides three meals that day.[15] After dusk the mourners, led by the folk musicians, carry the spirit tablet outside the village, ritually feed the spirit of the dead, and provide for its transit through the netherworld. In the morning of the second day, after a final round of respect paying, the coffin is brought out of the spirit shed and carried to the burial site. It is buried with the yinyang's direction and accompanied by many graveside rituals. Then the host provides another meal that ends the funeral proper. The chief director and all the assistants are feasted lavishly at the end of the whole event and are given gifts of liquor and cigarettes as tokens of gratitude for their help. The host family members have other ritual observances to perform in the days and months that follow according to the advice of the yinyang.

The chief director orchestrates the whole event, but is especially in charge of proper timing of the major ritual procedures. The guest inviter makes sure all relevant guests are informed of the death and invited to the funeral. He also receives the guests outside the household gate. The spirit shed caretaker sits next to the spirit tablet of the dead person in the spirit shed, making sure that the incense sticks are lit, the offerings are properly laid out, and the bowl for burning spirit money is emptied out regularly. He also plays the standard PRC funeral music on cassette tape when the band is resting. The attendant to the yinyang takes care of the yinyang's needs, fetching the necessary ritual paraphernalia to be used in the many rituals during the funeral. The attendant to the musicians serves members of the band tea and cigarettes and invites them to eat and drink after the other guests have dined (according to tradition band players eat last). The band members' job is the most tiring, so they are to be treated nicely. The recorders of gifts need to be literate because they need to write down on the gift account (*lizhang*) the names of the gift-givers and the kind of gift or the amount of cash gift. Every guest brings a gift or cash gift according to a locally set formula of reciprocity.

Burning paper offerings at the new grave site.

The meat dish cooks prepare and cook all the dishes with meat (chicken, pork, lamb, and sometimes even beef). The vegetarian dish cooks make steamed buns (S. *mo*), pressed noodles (S. *helao*), sweet cakes (S. *gao*, consumed the morning after the burial, the sound punning on the word for "high," which denotes advancement), and other nonmeat dishes. The water boiler attends to the big stove for water and tea. The cigarette and liquor distributor oversees the proper apportioning of packets and cartons of cigarettes and bottles of hard liquor (and sometimes beer) among the tables of banqueters and between the yinyang, musicians, and other special guests. The plate carriers bring the dishes from the kitchen to the tables. The waiters make sure plates and bowls of food are properly served and the wine cups of the guests are always filled. The table cleaners and dishwashers quickly make the tableware clean and available for the next round of guests, as the number of tables is limited and the guests have to take turns to eat. Eight strong men are invited by the host household to dig the grave and to carry the coffin from the family courtyard to the burial site. These are usually ordinary co-villagers and not funerary specialists, there being no strict taboo against death pollution as among the Cantonese (Watson 1988a). Many of the banquet assistants, especially the young men, double as funerary procession assistants to carry balls of fire lamps (bunches of corn cob soaked in tar) to brighten the way (for the procession as well as for the soul of the dead) and to throw firecrackers along the way to ward off evil spirits.

On top of this large ensemble of director and assistants are the yinyang and the folk band of five to seven members. The yinyang makes the "soul-calling canopy" (*yinhunfan*), determines the dates of funeral, burial and post-burial offerings, sites the grave and aligns the coffin according to fengshui principles, performs graveside rituals, propitiates the disturbed earth god, and exorcises harmful influences from the host's and neighbors' homes after the funeral. The band plays music during the entire funeral, selecting different tunes for its different segments. It also accompanies the coffin to the grave.

Not counting the yinyang and the musicians, forty-eight people are involved in producing the particular, standard-sized funeral I witnessed in Batawan. Clearly the production of a funeral entails the organization of labor around a set of well-defined tasks. I will attempt an analysis of the different elements below.

Ritual-Procedural Aspects Versus Hosting Aspects of a Funeral

Funerals in Shaanbei typically involve the following standard procedures[16]:

Upon the death of the family member:
— Public notification of the death of a family member, planning the funeral (hiring the yinyang master to determine auspicious dates to conduct the funeral and for other services during the entire funeral; hiring the musicians; asking friends and neighbors for help with the funeral; preparing the burial site; assembling all the ritual paraphernalia needed for the funeral and the burial such as spirit money and firecrackers);
— Donning of mourning attire by mourners;
— Ritualized cleaning of the corpse, clothing the corpse in "longevity" clothes, and putting the corpse in the coffin;
— Preparation and installation of a soul tablet for the dead; setting up a temporary altar in front of the coffin in a temporary shed called a "spirit shed" (*lingpeng*);

The first day of the funeral:
— Mourners and guests paying respect to the deceased;
— Procession of spirit tablet to the edge of the village in the evening (feeding the hungry ghosts) (*sa ludeng*, literally "spreading road lamps")

The second day of the funeral:
— Departure of the coffin for burial in the morning; dismantling of the spirit shed;
— Burial of coffin; offering at the grave;[17]
— The ritual cleansing of the zhujia household and the neighbors' household by the yinyang master

This list of activities shows the standard sequence of ritual actions that relate directly to the deceased. However, what this list of "death ritual" procedures does not show is how much activity is going on to feast and host everyone at the funeral on both days. I would like to argue that activities at a funeral that are not explicitly ritualistic or do not relate directly to the dead are not peripheral to the focus of the funeral; rather, these activities (banqueting, socializing) are central to the funeral. I suggest that we look at a Shaanbei funeral as comprising two parallel, simultaneously occurring threads of activities: ritual-procedural (or liturgical) and hosting (or guest-catering).

Anthropologists studying Chinese funerals have tended to focus on the ritual-procedural aspects and relegate the hosting aspects to the sidelines (Watson and Rawski 1988). At most these anthropologists noted the role of commensality in promoting kinship and communal solidarity and left it at that. The ritual-procedural aspects, with the accompanying "forest of symbols," attracted our analytical gaze and subsequently became equated with the funeral as a whole. I would like to argue, however, that the hosting aspect, though much more prosaic, also deserve our attention. Staging a funeral (including both the ritual-procedural and hosting aspects) as a material, social, and symbolic activity has an overall aggregate meaning (for the zhujia as well as the guests and others): that the head of the household and by extension all members of the household are moral persons not only in relation to the deceased as a filial son but also in relation to his kin and community as a generous host.

A funeral has five mutually related yet distinct concerns: What to do with the body of the deceased? What to do with the soul of the deceased? What to do with the inauspicious impact of the death (death pollution)?

How to enact proper relations between the different categories of people (descendants, agnatic and affinal kin, friends, neighbors) who have converged to the time-space of the funeral within this particular ritual context? How to treat the guests well?[18]

First, what to do with the body of the deceased? This question can be called the "geo-corporeal concern," for it deals with transferring the body of the deceased, in a coffin, out of the village to the grave site and burying the body in the ground. The zhujia hires the yinyang master to take care of these procedures. As I mentioned in Chapter 3, the yinyang master is entrusted with the task of "siting" the best location and orientation for the house of the living (yangzhai) as well as the dwelling of the dead (yinzhai). He (always a male) is also responsible for aligning the coffin properly (with his geomantic compass), arranging in-grave utensils, and appeasing the earth god for having disturbed him with the digging of the grave.

Second, what to do with the soul of the deceased? This question can be called the "salvation concern," for it deals with the passage of the soul through hell and its prospect of reincarnation or going on to the Western Paradise (*shang xitian*).[19] Traditionally in Shaanbei, Buddhist monks would have been hired to take care of these aspects. The rite they conducted was called "doing the merits" (*zuo gongde*), referring to chanting scriptures to accrue more merits for the deceased so that he or she would receive less severe punishments in the courts of hell and be reincarnated into better stations.[20] But because of the lack of sufficient Buddhist clergy in Shaanbei today, the yinyang master or the master of ceremony would conduct the minimally required procedures (e.g., feeding the hungry ghosts the night before the burial).[21]

Third, what to do with the inauspicious impact of the death (death pollution)? This can be called the "pollution concern." Traditionally Daoist priests specialized in exorcising evil influences and restoring communal or household peacefulness. Again, because of the lack of sufficient Daoist clergy in Shaanbei today, the yinyang master takes care of the exorcistic rituals at the end of the funeral (after burial). He goes from door to door in the immediate neighborhood of the zhujia with three ad hoc assistants (chosen from the many adult helpers at the funeral).[22]

Fourth, how to enact proper relations between the people who have converged to the time-space of the funeral (descendants, agnatic and affinal kin, friends, neighbors) within this particular ritual context (i.e., funeral)? This can be called the "ritual-social propriety concern," for it deals with the ritually proper enactment of social relationships between the mourners and the deceased, between the zhujia and the other mourners, and between the zhujia and the guests (including the hired professionals).[23] The chief director (master of ceremony) is in charge of ensuring ritual propriety among all present: the stylized wailing, the graded mourning clothes,[24] funeral music, the prostrations and kowtows, the proper sequencing of ritual phases, and so forth. Traditionally a local literatus would be hired to sing some stylized elegies but this practice has not been revived, at least not in the Longwanggou area. These concerns about propriety are largely of Confucian derivation, and their near standardization in late imperial China was due both to a long history of literati promotion and the commercial diffusion of ritual handbooks (Naquin 1988; Rawski 1988; Watson 1988b).

Fifth and last, how to cater to the guests' needs and treat them well? This "guest-catering concern" has received the least attention from scholars because there seems not much to be said about feeding and entertaining people beyond the most obvious: that commensality promotes social solidarity, and the feasting rejuvenates the household, the clan, and the community after the loss of a senior member. I would like to argue, however, that in the mind of Shaanbei peasants, this guest-catering concern is the most serious concern, and that when the zhujia plays the host, they are primarily talking about hosting in the sense of guest catering. I am not suggesting that the other four concerns are not serious, but the zhujia entrusts the responsibilities to the specialists and so they don't need to worry about those concerns (though they are full participants). The success of the funeral rests on addressing satisfactorily all five concerns, but it is the guest-catering aspect that the zhujia worries about the most. The zhujia's worries are justified because the guests will evaluate the event primarily based on their perceptions of how well the host has treated them (e.g., by gestures of respect; quality and quantity of food, drinks, and cigarettes), all the while also not paying too much attention to the intricacies of symbolic actions conducted or orchestrated by the ritual specialists relating to the other four concerns.[25]

A look at the distribution of categories of funeral expenses reveals how important the hosting aspect is in the whole enterprise. The yinyang master's service typically cost around 200 yuan, the folk music troupe between 200 and 300 yuan. The coffin can cost anywhere between 300 yuan and over a thousand depending on the quality of wood, amount of decoration, and quality of craftsmanship. Other funeral materials such as paper offerings, firecrackers, incense, and so on cost about 200 yuan. A full-grown pig costs between 1,000 and 1,200 yuan. Three or four goats cost about 800 yuan in total. Other food items such as chickens, vegetables, flour, and spices cost about 300 yuan. Cigarettes and liquor cost between 600 yuan and 1,500 yuan (depending more on variation in quality and brands than variation in quantity). So it is clear that a lot more money is spent on food, liquor, and cigarettes for the guests than on "ritual" items. Using Georges Bataille's notion of "ritual expenditure," Mayfair Yang (2000) analyzed the seemingly excessive ritual consumption among rural people in coastal Wenzhou (Zhejiang Province) in the reform era; it appears that much of the ritual extravaganza involves spending an enormous amount of money on hosting.

The importance of hosting guests is also revealed in the large number of helpers involved in preparing food, cooking, cleaning, and waiting on the guests (see the earlier list of personnel at the funeral). Anthropologists have paid attention to weddings and funerals as important occasions for presenting gifts in relationships of reciprocity and mutual good feelings (Yan 1996b). I argue that the contribution of labor to the zhujia is as important as gifts from guests in understanding peasant conceptions of social relations and reciprocity. In addition, an overly transactional perspective on such mutual help and gifting scenarios might obscure the fact that these event productions are also occasions for the *production* of relations (not just exchanges). Unlike gifts, which are recorded in gift registries and should be reciprocated on equal terms, labor cannot be quantified as easily. So the zhujia owes the helpers not so much an equal amount of labor hours in the future as a morally salient gratitude repayable only in kind: helping out at the helpers' household events. Now I turn to a description and analysis of the social production of a temple festival to illustrate how temple festivals and funerals are based upon similar social-organizational principles.

Producing the Longwanggou Temple Festival

The hosting idiom is also used in staging temple festivals.[26] Theoretically the host would be the deity himself or herself because he or she resides in the temple and is therefore the zhujia. But the situation is a little complicated. First of all, even though the temple is supposed to be the deity's domicile on earth, the deity might be roaming somewhere in the celestial realm, or, in the case of dragon kings, in rivers, oceans, springs, or on clouds. So in a sense on the occasion of the temple festival, the deity becomes an honored guest, invited to come down and enjoy the opera performances and offerings and listen to prayers and praises.[27] Also, because the deities cannot really act to organize the temple festival, the temple associations host the event production on their behalf. For example, at Longwanggou the temple officers and other volunteers would say that they are "helping out the venerable Dragon King to produce the event" (*gei Longwangye ta laorenjia banshi/xianghuo*). As a result, how well the festival is organized reflects the ability of the temple association and the sponsoring villages; and more importantly, it ultimately reflects on the capability and magical efficacy of the deity. The motivation and enthusiasm of the worshipers to organize an exciting (honghuo) festival is supposed to be directly proportional to how well they feel they have been blessed by the deity. A Shaanbei folk expression goes: "people depend on gods and gods depend on people" (*ren ping shen, shen ping ren*); on no occasion is this principle of mutual reliance between god and people more highlighted than in the organization of the temple festival.

A standard Shaanbei funeral is a folk event production for a couple of hundred people who are related by agnatic, affinal, and friendship ties. A temple festival, on the other hand, is a folk event production for thousands of unrelated people. In the case of Longwanggou, it is for hundreds of thousands of people, lasting not for a day and a half like a funeral, but for six days,[28] and the spatial range is not within a courtyard but over a couple of square kilometers from the temple ground to the mouth of the Dragon King Valley. Now I turn to a description of the Longwanggou temple festival of 1998 to show how the work was divided up and how this grand festive occasion was realized by the aggregation of relatively simple tasks.

Preparations for the annual temple festival usually begin immediately after the First Month Fifteenth festivities (*zhengyue shiwu*, usually in February). Two or three persons are sent out to book opera troupes (called "writing the opera," *xiexi*). The experienced Lao Yao of Gaoliang is usually the leader of this trip. They follow the suggestions made at the large temple association meeting, seek out the right opera troupes, check their dates of engagement and their repertoires, and reserve them for the Longwanggou temple festival. They make a sizable down payment and make preliminary requests for particular opera pieces. They also agree on the details of picking up (*jiexiang*; picking up the trunks) and seeing off (*songxiang*; sending back the trunks) the opera troupes and their equipment. Because Longwanggou invites famous, provincial-level troupes, Lao Yao and his assistants often travel to Xi'an, Taiyuan, Shijiazhuang, Kaifeng, Zhengzhou, and other major cities in north and north-central China. Longwanggou also invites a local opera troupe each year in addition to the outside ones as a gesture of goodwill. Usually it is the Yulin Prefectural Opera Troupe or the Yulin City Opera Troupe. Writing the opera is arguably the most important part of the preparation because of opera's crucial role in all temple festivals.

After the opera-writing team comes back with good news, the temple officers can relax for a few months. About a month or two before the temple festival, they book the fireworks (to be shown on the night of Sixth Month Thirteenth, always a highlight for the festivalgoers). They make appropriate gifts to the local electricity personnel to ensure that there will be no power outage during the festival. The festival would be irrevocably spoiled in case of a power outage because the opera performances, the lighting, and the hundreds of stalls all rely on electrical power. They also negotiate with the local Public Security Bureau and the Traffic Police Brigade (*jiaojing dadui*) to arrange for the police officers to come and help maintain peace and order. If the police are not happy one is sure that they will cause enough trouble to wreck the festival, for example, by blocking the traffic, by simply not granting permission for a large gathering, or even by cracking down on "superstitious activities."

In the two weeks before the festival, villagers from the nine villages begin to pester the temple officers for the best spots in the temple ground to set up their temporary stalls to sell noodles, candies, icicles, watermelons, and the like during the festival. Villagers from Hongliutan, Batawan, and Chenjiapo naturally have an advantage over villagers from the other six villages. A week before the festival, the temple officers draw up stall plots on the ground with numbers and assign them to the different bidders. Rooms in the temple dormitory are cleaned up, bedding dusted and sunned, and rooms are designated for the four different opera troupes, the police force, special invited guests (local officials, the occasional foreigners, journalists, top officers from brother-temples), and the temple officers. Because the primary school is in summer recess, all the classrooms become dormitory rooms, with chairs and desks turning into makeshift beds. Webs of electrical cords are connected and tested. Loudspeakers are set up on each side of the opera stage.

The entire temple ground is swept clean. New auspicious couplets on red paper are pasted on columns. The two large public latrines are cleaned out. Posters of black ink on red paper announcing the temple festival are posted in Zhenchuan Town, Mizhi Town, Yulin City, Suide Town, and other nearby towns. These posters list the names of the opera troupes and preliminary programs of their performances. Residents of these towns begin talking about the scale of this year's festival, judging from the statuses of the opera troupes. Sometimes another notice is pasted next to the poster, alerting people to the existence of scoundrels collecting money in Heilongdawang's name. A large quantity of food is bought. Meat is put in the freezers and vegetables pile up and line the outside walls of the canteen. A large quantity of ritual items (charms, red threads, divine medicine packets, water bottles) are prepared and brought to the zhengdian. New copies of the divination slips are made, and additional divination sets and oracle rollers are brought out. All along the valley, itinerant performing troupes (song and dance, freak show, circus, etc.) set up their tents. All kinds of other vendors and game-show conmen pour in and compete for prime spots. The temple registers all vendors and charges them lot fees (*changdifei*) according to the size and location of their spots.

A couple of days before the beginning of the festival, helpers from a brother temple in Ansai County of Yan'an Prefecture come to Longwanggou. They refer to themselves as "people who came up from Yan'an" (*Yan'an shanglai de*). They are officers of the Ansai Zhenwu Zushi Temple with their entourage of about forty pilgrims, and they have been helping out at the Longwanggou temple festival for more than ten years.[29] Each year they have the honor of heading the offering-presenting procession that begins in Zhenchuan Town. Lao Wang, the other temple officers, and the Yan'an people have a meeting and discuss the details of the three-hundred member procession, such as the route and the order of different participants (including offering-bearing pilgrims, folk music bands, drum troupes, yangge troupes, and firecracker squads).

On Sixth Month Ninth, the opera performance opens (*qixi*) and the temple festival officially begins. For the next six days, worshipers come in buses, minivans, trucks, tractors, motorcycles, and bicycles and pour into the valley, which is filled with hundreds of stalls and peddlers. Noodle and snack stands and games circles sit side by side with religious trinket hawkers, fortune-tellers, and tooth-pullers. Many mini gambling mats materialize in the corners here and there. Song and dance troupes and freak show doormen attract festivalgoers with the blare of their loudspeakers. Quite a few beggars and prostitutes also mingle in the crowd. Especially numerous are the incense hawkers with their baskets full of incense, spirit money, and firecrackers. All worshipers buy incense and spirit money as offerings to Heilongdawang. They first pay their homage at the zhengdian before wandering off to watch the opera or tour the temple ground. The four opera troupes take turns staging uninterrupted performances from early morning to midnight. Uniformed agents of the local Taxation Bureau (*shuiwuju*) and Industry and Commerce Bureau (*gongshangju*) descend upon the valley to exact taxes and fees from all the vendors.

At this point, the regular temple employees are joined by close to a hundred volunteers, some from the nine sponsoring villages but many from outside as well, who are fulfilling their vows. The majority of these volunteers are men. The zhengdian and the two other temple halls are manned by a dozen or so people who assist worshipers with divination and hand out charms and medicine packets. Lao Chen, who is in the divination slips room, is joined by nine or ten volunteer divine message interpreters, some of whom are experienced and some who are just trying their skills. Five or six people take care of the magical spring and the dispensing of magical water. Five or six more conduct passing-obstacle rituals (*guoguan*) for children. Two dozen people fill the kitchen, all helping Chen Shengxiao and Si Laohan make noodles, soup, and other dishes. All eight large fire stoves are operating at full power. Another dozen people help clean the tables and dishes. Worshipers or families who make sizable donations (e.g., over a hundred yuan) at the zhengdian are given meal tickets so they can eat a free, simple meal at the temple canteen. The temple thus feeds thousands of people each day. Nine people handle the three huge boilers on the temple ground, providing free boiling water for worshipers to make tea. A dozen or so people help regulate the flow of the crowd and act as security guards. Another dozen help the police manage traffic on Highway 210 and direct cars to parking spaces, all on empty fields next to the stone gateway at the mouth of the valley. They charge parking fees as well. Five or six people take care of the needs of the opera troupes and the police (e.g., bringing them hot tea, cigarettes, and liquor). Two or three men on motorcycles bring new posters announcing opera programs to the nearby towns every day. A few local cultural workers help write the opera program posters and other materials. Meanwhile the temple officers busy themselves with entertaining important guests and responding to crisis situations.

At night the temple provides basic accommodation for festivalgoers who stay overnight. When the weather is good and warm many people without dorm room accommodation sleep outside. When it is cold or raining people crowd into the large meeting room under the Dragon Greatness Hall or whatever sheltered spots they can find. Many pilgrims come from far away, e.g., Inner Mongolia, Shanxi, Yan'an Prefecture, and stay overnight for many nights. Therefore even at night the temple ground is full of people.

Two-dozen middle-aged and elderly women begin preparing the offerings (decorated food items, flowers, flags, plaques, liquor, tall incense, etc.) in Zhenchuan a couple of days before Sixth Month Thirteenth, the main day (*zhengrizi*) of the temple festival. In the early morning of Sixth Month Thirteenth, the offering procession leaves the sports ground of the Zhenchuan Middle School and advances slowly along the main street of Zhenchuan, Highway 210, and finally into the Dragon King Valley. Once in the valley, the procession moves even more slowly, as the yangge and drum troupes show off their repertoires of dance formations to the festival-going crowd, which now numbers tens of thousands. The procession finally reaches the zhengdian and worshipers present their offerings on behalf of individuals as well as entire communities. Each of the seven yangge and drum troupes performs an offering-presentation number, with the leader singing a short praise of Heilongdawang. They then proceed to the Dragon Greatness Hall and the Dragons' Mother's Palace to present offerings to all the brothers of Heilongdawang and their mother. At night, the temple stages an exuberant, half-hour-long fireworks show, which is the climax of the festival.

The next day (Sixth Month Fourteenth), the festival winds down and the last opera pieces are performed to a much dwindled audience. The pilgrims leave; the opera troupes are thanked, paid, and seen off; and the police are sent away with their compensation and more gifts. Temple association officers and all other important organizers get together at the canteen to enjoy a celebratory feast (*qinggongyan*) with much high-spirited drinking, playing of fist-swinging drinking games, and honghuo-making. Then there are days of cleaning up of the numerous small mountains of festival waste. After that the temple returns to its normal, less glamorous everyday routines.

Common Modes of Organization and Common Cultural Logic

When an outsider observes the Longwanggou temple festival, he sees mostly a chaotic festival-going crowd and random social interactions (I discuss the atmosphere of the temple festival in more detail in Chapter 8). But the whole event is actually very carefully orchestrated, though based on simple principles of division of labor. The temple association is at the center of action, assigning tasks to temple employees and volunteer workers. However, very few formal directions are given because much implicit knowledge is assumed. Most people know what their tasks are as soon as they arrive because they are veteran volunteers of many years, not only at Longwanggou but also at other temple festivals. From the above description of the organization of the Sixth Month Thirteenth temple festival, we see that it extends and elaborates on the *same principles and mechanisms of organization* as a funeral or wedding. I argue that this organizational simplicity is one of the most crucial factors underlying the survival and revival of popular religion. The table overleaf compares and contrasts the salient features of funerals and temple festivals in chart form.

C. K. Yang (1961) famously proposed that in China elements of popular religion are diffused into core secular social institutions such as the family, socioeconomic groups such as trade guilds, communities such as villages and native-place associations, and the state. He argued that the diffused religious ideas and practices provided an air of sanctity to, and thus helped uphold, these core institutions. I suggest that the symbiosis between secular institutions and religious life is even more intimate, that the same principles and mechanisms for organizing ordinary social life are used in organizing popular religious life. The building of temples, the staffing and management of temple personnel, and the staging of temple festivals rely on volunteerism (based on an understanding of mutual aid and reciprocity), division of labor, a combination of paternalism and folk democracy, and a system of informal networking and contracting (e.g., the hiring of specialists). These are the same mechanisms, social skills, and cultural know-how used in building a family house, managing the household, staging life-course events such as weddings and funerals, finding a spouse for one's child, and rural marketing. Similarly, the same cultural values or desires that are realized in folk social life are replicated and enacted in popular religion (e.g., the significance of hosting and the

Aspects of a Funeral and a Temple Festival Compared and Contrasted

	Funeral	Temple Festival
Cultural logic for event production	hosting the funeral so as to fulfill ritual obligation to the deceased and social obligation to the community and kin	hosting the temple festival so as to give thanks to, and please, the deity
Host	zhujia (host household)	temple association and sponsoring villages
Guests	agnatic and affinal kin, neighbors, co-villagers, friends of deceased	deity, villagers of the sponsoring villages and all other worshipers
Venue	the home of the zhujia (mainly courtyard)	temple ground
Time/Occasion	death of a family member	"birthday" of the deity or *Yuanxiao* (the first Month Fifteenth)
Modes of organization	—ad hoc funeral organizing committee —volunteer helpers drawn from agnatic kin and co-villagers	—temple association —volunteer helpers from sponsoring villages and from outside
Cultural logic behind volunteering (helping out)	—maintaining good relationship (guanxi) and emotional ties (ganqing) with zhujia —as part of ongoing cycles of mutual help	—maintaining good relationship (guanxi) and emotional ties (ganqing) with the deity —as part of ongoing cycles of blessing and magical assistance from the deity and respect and help from the worshiper
Major ritual-procedural aspects	—the "geo-corporeal concern" —the "salvation concern" —the "pollution concern" —the "ritual-social propriety concern"	—sacrifice to the deity (pigs and goats) —procession of offerings —paying respect to the deity (burning incense and spirit money, setting off firecrackers) —consulting the deity's divination set and oracle roller
Ritual professionals involved	—yinyang master —chief director —(Buddhist monks or Daoist priests)	—(spirit medium if the deity has one) —(Buddhist monks or Daoist priests if the temple has professional clergy)
Major guest-catering aspects (guests include hired professionals)	—banqueting the guests —entertaining the guests (music band) —giving gifts to helpers —complex meals for many people	—banqueting the guests —entertaining the guests (opera performance) —giving gifts to chief invited guests (e.g., police) —simple meals for a huge number of people
Modes of producing excitement (honghuo)	—convergence of people —folk music band —firecrackers —feasting (including drinking and playing drinking games)	—convergence of a lot of people —opera performance —firecrackers —eating, drinking, playing, gambling, etc.

pursuit of red-hot sociality). Sangren (1984a) has argued that the Chinese virtuosity in forming cooperative associations lies in the fact that Chinese social organizations such as the lineage, the trade guild, the deity association, the ritual association, the native-place association, and the alumni association employ similar organizational techniques and operational norms (such as the rotation of leadership positions, decision by consensus, hierarchy of committees). I have built upon Sangren's insight in highlighting the transferability of organizational principles and idioms across different domains of Chinese social life (in this case from secular domain to popular religious domain).

Even though the social-organizational forms of popular religion might be simple, it is an undeniable fact that some of the contents in popular religion might be quite elaborate, sophisticated, or even esoteric (e.g., as expressed in divination poems, opera performances, specific ritual procedures, etc.). However, the ways in which popular religious activities are socially organized make it seem that it doesn't matter how elaborate and sophisticated the contents are. Shaanbei peasants, as do most Chinese peasants, I would argue, readily concede to the professionals for their specialized services (e.g. yinyang masters for identifying optimal locations for houses and graves, Daoist priests or spirit mediums for manipulating cosmic forces and expelling evil influences, Buddhist monks for buying off hungry ghosts and accumulating merits for the dead, musicians and opera singers for entertaining the gods, etc.). The way a peasant household hires and uses a ritual specialist is no different from the way it hires and uses a professional carpenter: the extent of esoteric carpentry knowledge has no direct bearing on the ways in which the carpenter and his specialist knowledge are mobilized for the purpose of building a new house. Specialists and their specialist skills are respected and used whenever needed; the key is knowing when and how as well as having the resources to mobilize them (see Hayes 1985).

The mechanisms that go into the *social organization* of popular religious activities are as important as the specific contents of the religious traditions. I would like to suggest that the ease of transferring of organizational mechanisms, social skills, and cultural know-how from the realm of ordinary social life to the realm of religion is one of the main explanations for the apparent ease of popular religious revival, not just in the reform era but in other periods of Chinese history as well. In other words, the resilience of popular religion in the face of persecution (by orthodox Confucianism, elitist Daoism or Buddhism, or by the Communist government) lies in its intrinsic socially embedded nature and organizational simplicity—or perhaps ingeniousness. Therefore I have called Chinese popular religion a minimalist religion (see Chapter 4). As I discussed in Chapter 3, organized religion such as monastic Buddhism and Daoism has not been revived as much as popular religion has in Shaanbei, as probably is the case in other parts of China (but see Dean 1993, 1998b), most likely because of the difficulty of recruiting and training qualified religious specialists, the state's continued suppression of organized religion (despite the rhetoric of legality), and, as compared to popular religion, an over-elaboration of form and content. So in the context of contemporary China, organized religions such as Buddhism and Daoism are victims of their own historical success achieved during dynastic times.

CHAPTER EIGHT

Red-Hot Sociality

Popular religion is not simply or even primarily about relationships between people and deities; it is also about relationships between people and about forms of sociality. This is brought out most poignantly by the exuberance of temple festivals. Describing the high-spirited, chaotic scenes typically found at local temples in Taiwan and invoking the southern Hokkien term *lauziat* ("heat and noise," i.e., renao, honghuo), Robert Weller aptly calls Chinese popular religion "hot and noisy religion" (1994b: 113–28). Similarly, Shaanbei people are drawn to temple festivals because the latter provide an occasion when they can produce and experience what in their culture is the most desirable mode of sociality: red-hot sociality (heightened excitement).

Before I proceed, a working definition of sociality is in order. Anthropologists usually define sociality as the capacity for social life (among humans or other animals). I define sociality more specifically as *the condition of social co-presence*, i.e., the gathering of a group of people in one social space. Sociality may encompass but is distinct from both social interaction and social relationship. Social relationships can exist without the parties' being brought together. For example, kin are still kin because of blood relatedness even if they are dispersed. Social interactions, so eloquently studied by symbolic interactionists (e.g., Ervin Goffman), are usually premised on dyadic interactional pairs or small group dynamics, to the exclusion of large groups. In other words, sociality can happen even without the people present having any preexisting social relationships or interacting with one another in any substantial or meaningful way. And even when the people are related to one another and do interact, their relatedness and interactions do not necessarily constitute the character or make up the entirety of that particular occasion of sociality. An exemplary mode of sociality in modern life is the cinema: the cinema-goers are all in one social space and even though they might not be related or interact, they feel one another's social presence and often derive pleasure from such a co-presence. Substituting the movie screen with the deities' statues, we will find that while the worshipers all have personal relationships with the deities, they at the same time produce and share social co-presence with all the other temple festivalgoers. I shall argue that this intense co-presence, which might be called social heat, endows popular religious sites and the deities with heightened aura and appeal.

Different societies in different historical periods have different configurations of sociality. In contemporary American society, typical modes of sociality include going to the movies, going to the mall or department store, going to church, watching baseball or basketball with friends (at home or at the stadium), going to the gym, partying, clubbing, entertaining guests at home, socializing in cafes or bars, and so forth.[1] Urban Chinese today share many of the same modes of sociality. But what about Chinese peasants? How do they socialize within as well as beyond the confines of the family and the village? How do they conceive of group social life? How and when do they have fun?

Studies of peasant sociality have traditionally been focused on *guanxi* maintenance and *ganqing* exchanges (Kipnis 1997; Yan 1996a, 1996b). I suggest that we need to shift our attention from a heretofore (over)emphasis on interpersonal or inter-household transactions (what can be called a transactional model of peasant sociality) to *productions of affect and subjectivity in group life* (an affective model of peasant sociality). Peasant worldview is not only made of rational calculations of profits and losses and models of reciprocity (material or emotional). In this chapter I present one oft-ignored aspect of Chinese peasant worldview and related practices: peasant sociality, particularly the production of excitement on important social occasions.

Honghuo (Red and Fiery)

The word honghuo is the most important native concept for understanding Shaanbei peasant sociality. Honghuo literally means "red and fiery," and it can be variably translated as red-hot, fun, lively, crowded, hectic, chaotic, confused, messy, exciting, enthusing, hustle and bustle, festive, carnivalesque, intense, frenzied, sensational, social heat, red-hot sociality, or even "collective effervescence" (Durkheim 1965). Honghuo is a state of being that is most desired in Shaanbei social events such as funeral and wedding banquets or temple festivals. The concept embodies a native conception of social life that values the convergence and intermingling of a lot of people and the collective production and consumption of loud noises, vibrant colors, fragrant smells, savory tastes, radiant heat, and heightened excitement.

The word honghuo is composed of two characters: *hong*, meaning red, and *huo*, meaning fire. Different colors are endowed with different meanings in different cultures. Red is the most highly valued color in Chinese culture. It is the color of happiness, success, and good fortune. Red is thus the dominant color at weddings and the Lunar New Year. On these occasions people wear red clothes, give out red packets with gift money inside, hang couplets written on red paper, release red-coated firecrackers, and generally indulge in red-themed merrymaking. The everyday colors of peasant life in China have traditionally been gray (e.g., earth in winter), brown (e.g., earth, dwelling), blue (e.g., clothes), green (e.g., crops), and yellow (e.g., earth, crops near harvesting time), which further accentuate the vibrancy of red in happy events.[2] The opposite of red is white: the color of death and lifelessness (not purity as in Western cultures). White is the dominant color at funerals; mourners wear white clothes and headdresses, and no bright and vibrant colors (such as red) are allowed. Fire (huo) symbolizes the stove, hearth, warmth, heat, and excitement. In northern dialects and in Mandarin, people use the word huo to describe some phenomenon that is becoming really popular (e.g., an actress, a restaurant, a product): "*Huo zhe ne! Te huo!*" (So hot! So popular!).[3]

Honghuo is the Shaanbei colloquial equivalent of the Mandarin word *renao* and the Minnan (southern Hokkien) word *lauziat* (which is the inverse of the same two characters in the Mandarin word). Since the ideas embodied in the word renao are the same as those embodied in the word honghuo, it might be instructive to explain the semantic field of renao as well.

The word renao is composed of the two characters *re* and *nao*. Re means hot, heat, heady, emotional, passionate, fervent, or feverish. In Maoist China, re was usually coupled with *lie* to form the word *relie* (to do something enthusiastically), e.g., enthusiastically welcoming (*relie huanying*) dignitaries from Communist brother countries; enthusiastically celebrating (*relie qingzhu*) the October First National Day, and so forth. But being feverish is not always good. One is prone to act irrationally when one's head becomes suddenly hot (*naodai yire*). In reform-era China re is most often used to describe different kinds of "fever" or "craze" when people rush to do the same thing because this thing suddenly becomes really popular, whether it is investing in the stock market (*gupiaore*), going to the disco (*disikere*), learning English (*xueyingyure*), going abroad (*chuguore*), consuming and discoursing "high culture" (*wenhuare*), or doing rustic yangge dance in urban China (*yanggere*).[4]

Nao means to stir up and connotes a wide range of excitement: rambunctious, agitated, hustle bustle, playful, busy, noisy, conflicted, exuberant, colorful, to express dissatisfaction, to vent, to plague, to turn upside down, to be naughty, to make a scene. For example, traditionally at weddings friends and relatives are supposed to "stir up (rouse? inflame?) the nuptial room" (*naofang* or *naodongfang*); a busy market is called *naoshi*; to make trouble or cause a disturbance is called *naoshi* (different *shi* than the one in the previous expression); *naohong* (red troubles) referred to early Communist "disturbances" in Republican China; *naogeming* is to do revolution in a noisy and exuberant manner; *naochang* (stir up the field) or *naotai* (stir up the opera stage) refers to dance or music numbers that serve to attract the audience. Shaanbei people also use the word nao in similar ways.

In Shaanbei, as is most likely the case in other Chinese cultural settings, honghuo (or renao) describes a condition of social life that is exciting and highly desirable. This condition is the desired goal and outcome of staging and producing events such as New Year's celebrations, temple festivals, banquets, drinking parties, business opening ceremonies, and even political campaigns and public executions.[5] If these events are not honghuo they are not considered successful or satisfactory. An event that is not honghuo is a failure and will bring shame and disgrace to its host. An event that is honghuo will not only bring satisfaction to all the participants but also prestige and status to the host.

It does not take a Lévi-Straussian structuralist to notice the obvious binary oppositions set up by the expressions honghuo and renao. In typical Chinese correlative fashion of conceiving the world, redness (hong) is set against colorless plainness; fire (huo) is set against dark, damp, coldness; hot (re) is set against cold; and noisy (nao) is set against quietness and loneliness. The first terms of these pairs are desirable and the second terms not.

Some non-Chinese societies have concepts similar to honghuo or re-nao. Ortner describes the Sherpas' fondness for parties because good parties are *hlermu* (fun, pleasurable, exciting) (Ortner 1978: 81). Speaking of the Balinese value of *ramé*, Geertz writes: "Ramé means crowded, noisy, and active, and is a highly sought-after social state: crowded markets, mass festivals, busy streets are all ramé, as, of course, is, in the extreme, a cockfight. Ramé is what happens in the 'full' times (its opposite, *sepi*, 'quiet,' is what happens in the 'empty' ones" (Geertz 1973: 446). Just like ramé, the Indonesian/Malay word *ramai* and the Torajan word *marua'* express similar conditions of the crowded, noisy, hot, excited, tense sociality desired in ritual events and social gatherings. Among the Toraja people of Sulawesi Volkman studied, the worst thing that could happen at a ritual event was that very few people showed up and it consequently was quiet and lonely (*makarorrong*) (Volkman 1985: 69). Shaanbei people would be able to recognize such an event as a failure because it is not honghuo. On the other hand, the kind of crowd-inciting royal pageantry in pre-modern Bali (Geertz 1980: 98–102) would have appealed to Shaanbei people immensely.[6]

Drinking and Finger-Guessing Drinking Games

In Shaanbei, drinking is always a social activity, and many social events incorporate drinking and drinking games to heighten the honghuo level. Liquor is used to treat visitors and guests.[7] Drinking can take place anywhere, at home, in a restaurant, and at banquets and temple festivals. There are no social institutions specifically dedicated to drinking such as a bar or tavern, so common in many agrarian societies (e.g., in the Mediterranean and Latin America). There is no drinking age in China, so teenage boys learn how to drink as they begin to participate more actively in social life. Women usually do not drink. A few women might indulge in a cup or two on festive occasions but it would be considered improper if they drink more.[8] The most common alcoholic drink is clear, distilled liquor (from grains such as sorghum, millet, wheat) that is called "spicy liquor" or "burning liquor" (*lajiu* or *shaojiu*). Shaanbei has its own distilleries, but the most commonly consumed shaojiu is from the neighboring province Shanxi. In recent years beer has made its way into the social drinking scene, but shaojiu is still far more preferred on festive occasions.[9]

Liquor is a crucial ingredient in honghuo-making not only because it causes a burning sensation in the throat and warms up the body. It is also the most important medium of intensified social interaction between men.[10] Liquor is usually served with small, white porcelain shot cups put in front of each person around the table. The cups are always filled as soon as they are emptied. No one is supposed to drink from his cup by himself unannounced. A call to empty the cups together has to be made, or someone invites a particular person with a toast to drink up with him in a pair (called *jingjiu*, i.e., to pay respect to you via the invitation to drink up). In other words, the very act of raising one's cup is always social and relational. Drinking together reaffirms and deepens existing relationships (*guanxi*) and builds new ones.[11]

Drinking is also an art form in Shaanbei. Instead of using words, Shaanbei men often sing a short song to invite their drinking partners to empty their cups. The lyrics of these songs (called *jingjiuge*, drink invitation songs, or *jiuqur*, liquor tunes) are often composed on the spot to existing folk tunes, and others usually have to sing back a song in a return invitation to drink up. The singing immediately raises the honghuo level of the occasion. Sometimes at restaurants a professional hostess is hired to sing liquor tunes and help persuade the guests to drink.[12]

But it is the finger-guessing drinking games that really raise the noise level and honghuo level of the occasion. These games are played almost exclusively by men. In fact, older men typically tend to be savvier at these games, a result of decades of practice. Men play these games whenever they drink alcohol. There are a few different kinds of drinking games but the most common is called "*huaquan*" (literally, swinging the fists).[13] The game is played by men in pairs. Both simultaneously swing out their right hands with varying numbers of fingers and shout out a number which each thinks would be the sum total of all the fingers in both men's hands.[14] The one who has guessed it correctly wins and the loser has to drink up a cup of shaojiu or a glass of beer. These drinking sessions most commonly take place at engagement, wedding, or funeral banquets but also transpire in restaurants, homes, or at temple festivals. Playing drinking games is probably the most important social skill for Shaanbei men. Being good at swinging the fist is a sign of cultural competence and mastery of good human relationships (it has to be played with appropriate courtesy and good humor). It is also one of the most important means of fostering brotherhood and friendship among male peers (usually one only drinks and plays the drinking game with partners of similar age and of the same generational cohort). The clamorous noise the men make together and the red-hot sociality they create and share infuse them with a sense of camaraderie and vitality.[15]

Honghuo as Social Heat

The key component of honghuo is people; the more people the more honghuo. Embedded in this belief is a premium put on the warmth or heat generated from human sociality and a fear of, or distaste for, social isolation, which is associated with loneliness and coldness.

Shaanbei people often asked me if I was married or had any children. I told them I was married but I didn't want to have any children. A few urban persons understood that it was my choice not to have any children and that in the West and urban China it is quite common for couples to choose not to have children. But every peasant I mentioned this to felt indignant and admonished me. They said that just as trees set down their roots, it is important for people to beget children. Here they were obviously reiterating the patrilineal imperative to have descendants. They then said that having no children is not honghuo (*bu honghuo*), making a household cold and desolate and its occupants feeling lonely and sad; a lot of children add honghuo to the household. They were genuinely puzzled when I told them that I didn't plan to have children because I considered children too noisy. They must be thinking: Noisy? Children crying and running around screaming? But that's precisely what makes the household honghuo! For the same reason, Shaanbei people resent the family planning policy because one child is not honghuo.[16] The ultimate happiness and good fortune in traditional Chinese culture is expressed by the phrase "the hall (house) filled with sons and grandchildren" (*ersun mantang*). It is not good enough if one has many sons and grandchildren if they are dispersed; the cultural ideal or ideal imagery is to have them all (crowded) under one roof.

The opposite of a full, crowded, and joyous house is living by oneself: the worst fate imaginable. When a man's parents have passed away, his sisters have been married out, his brothers have established their own households, and he himself has not been married, he is most likely to live by himself.[17] Sometimes an old person lives by himself or herself because the children have moved away and only visit on important dates such as Lunar New Year. During my fieldwork in rural Shaanbei I encountered a number of people who lived by themselves. Other villagers often told me how they sympathized with these lone persons because their homes were not honghuo. These people's homes tended to be cold, damp, dark, messy, filthy, and lifeless.

The stereotypical figure of the sad, lonely, poor, and miserable person in Shaanbei is the unmarried adult shepherd (S. *lanyanghan*, literally the man who blocks the sheep/goats; shepherds in Shaanbei are always male). The life of a shepherd is that of loneliness. In the early morning he rounds up different villagers' flocks of sheep or goats into a big flock and takes it to the hills and comes back to the village only at dusk. All day he has only the animals to talk to. I got to know a few shepherds during my fieldwork but unfortunately did not get to know them well. Their situation seemed to confirm the stereotype. They were all unmarried and poor. One that I encountered during a temple festival in Shenmu County doubled as a village clown. The villagers asked him to do an imitation spirit medium session for the benefit of the visiting anthropologist, and he complied, to the delight of the huge crowd of fifty or so adults and children. I later learned that he did the clown version of the well-respected village medium whenever people requested it on festive occasions to add to the honghuo atmosphere. Later that day I saw him again, this time being invited to drink together with some of the temple association officers and a few guests from outside of the village, including myself and a gregarious policeman from the nearby town. The shepherd was assigned the responsibility of helping to entertain everyone by playing finger-guessing drinking games with everyone in turn and singing drinking songs. The situation reminded me of a scene from the film *The Yellow Earth* (*Huangtudi*), which is about Shaanbei in the 1930s, in which a poor shepherd is asked to sing some songs to further brighten up the honghuo atmosphere of a wedding banquet.[18]

A household that has too few people is considered "*bu honghuo*" (cold and desolate), as is a household that is far away from its neighbors. Yulin Prefecture has twelve counties. The six southern counties (Mizhi, Suide, Hengshan, Wupu, Zizhou, and Qingjian) have been settled by Han people for much longer and the landscape is comprised of the typical hills and valleys of the loess plateau. Villages in these counties are usually older, with *yaodong* or houses clustered together. Large parts of the six northern counties (Jingbian, Dingbian, Shenmu, Fugu, Yulin, and Jiaxian), on the other hand, are characterized by a flat and sandy landscape similar to the Inner Mongolian steppes (the territory north of the Great

Wall was traditionally Mongol land). As I noted in Chapter 2, the Han settlement in these areas is much more recent. Because of the much larger farming plots, households in the rural areas of these northern counties tend to be spread out. Sometimes one's nearest neighbor is a good 10 or 15 minutes' walk away. Many Shaanbei people in the southern counties told me how they could not imagine living in the northern counties because the way the settlements are spread out is not honghuo.

A desire for honghuo within the home and in settlement patterns is the more prosaic modality of honghuo desire. The more dramatic modality of honghuo desire lies in the contrast Shaanbei people make between the dull and bland drudgery of everyday life and the lively and exciting social events such as funeral and wedding banquets or temple festivals. These social events are honghuo because there are always large gatherings of people, people doing any number of things: milling around, talking and shouting, eating and drinking, smoking, playing, singing, dancing, drumming, setting off firecrackers and fire-works, burning incense, gambling, or simply watching and being part of the scene.

Crowdedness is the necessary condition for honghuo-making. It is as if the simple convergence of many people will generate honghuo, which is why I choose to translate honghuo not simply as "exciting," but also as "social heat" or "red-hot sociality."[19] The convergence of people generates honghuo, and honghuo generates a greater convergence of people because people are disposed to be attracted to the noise and colors of honghuo. A small crowd is sure to generate a bigger crowd. Shaanbei people say that they are "in a hurry to get to or rush to a honghuo event" (S. *ganhonghuo*) the same way they say they are "in a hurry to get to or rush to the market" (*ganji*). They hurry to the market because the most honghuo time of a market day is in the early morning; by noon most people have dispersed. They hurry as well to a honghuo event such as a temple festival because they fear that they might miss the action, miss the honghuo. If they are not the protagonists in a honghuo event (e.g., a brawl or a funeral procession in the street), they rush to the scene so that they can "watch the honghuo" (S. *kanhonghuo*; Mandarin: *kanrenao*). But by rushing to the scene they become part of the honghuo and partake in producing a bigger honghuo. So the expression "to watch the honghuo" somehow makes people misconstrue themselves as mere spectators whereas they have actually become full participants. Often, it is not the incident or scene itself that is honghuo but rather the crowd that surrounds it.

The generation of social heat bears a striking resemblance to the generation of physical heat. According to thermodynamic laws, when molecules are compressed mechanically they generate more heat due to increased collisions between molecules. So when people converge they generate more social heat (i.e., honghuo). One may call this native conception of sociality a *sociothermic theory of sociality*. Presumably one may even "measure" the honghuo level of a social event on a sociothermic scale (how many people are present? how noisy and excited are they? how much social heat are they generating?). At least Shaanbei people have an intuitive sense according to which they judge the honghuo level of different social events they participate in or "watch." The temple festivals at Longwanggou have certainly ranked at the top of the honghuo scale.

Honghuo and the "Convergence Model of Event Production"

A household filled with many family members is a honghuo household, yet daughters get married out and leave, some members get sick, age, and die, other members have to go to distant lands to work, and all households eventually have to be divided among the married sons. A household grows in size as the couple has more children, but over time it dwindles in size as new households are split off from it.[20] A pleasurable banquet has to end and people must part company. Anthropologist Charles Stafford calls the inevitability of separating from one's loved ones or treasured companions the "separation constraint" (Stafford 2000). Springing from this separation constraint is a highly elaborated sentimental desire for the reunion of people long separated, even if the reunion is temporary (the fact is that most reunions are temporary). This reunion can take the form of a Lunar New Year family reunion, a daughter's visit to her natal family (*huiniangjia*), or events such as weddings, funerals, or temple festivals where friends and relatives see one another again after having been separated for a long time. Those who have been separated must be brought back together. This sentiment or cultural value might be called the "reunion imperative."

Building on Stafford's insights and rephrasing his terminologies, I would argue that just like separation, *dispersal* is a human universal, which might be called the "dispersal constraint," which in turn spurs a "convergence imperative," which includes, but is not limited to, reunions. From this convergence and dispersal model of social life I have derived a "convergence model of event production," which allows us to see ritual and event productions in a new light.

Ever since the publication of van Gennep's *The Rites of Passage* (van Gennep 1960), anthropologists have used the "rite of passage" model to study all kinds of rituals. Victor Turner (1967, 1969) and others have enriched this model with elaborations on the rich symbolisms that infuse these rituals. According to this model, any ritual is composed of three distinct stages: separation, transition, and reincorporation. The initiates (or participants) are first separated from the normal contexts of society, enter a sacred space and time of transition and transformation (the ritual proper, usually involving the shedding of the initiates' old identities and the infusion of new identities), and finally the initiates reenter society with a new identity. Victor Turner was particularly influential in applying this model of analyzing rituals, especially with his insights on the transition phase of rites of passage (he introduced concepts such as liminoids, communitas, anti-structure, etc.). The rite of passage model has enabled better understanding of the "ritual process" across cultures (Turner 1969), but does it obscure aspects of rituals that other analytical models might illuminate? And, is it equally useful in elucidating large-scale events such as temple festivals, where there are diverse happenings beyond ritual actions (see Fernandez 1986; Grimes 1976)?

I suggest that a "convergence model of event production" will help elucidate dimensions of rituals that have been sidestepped by the rite of passage model. In Chapter 7 I introduced the concept of event production to better characterize some organized social happenings that have usually been glossed as ritual. Here I argue that what all event productions share in common is the convergence of people (hence the convergence model of event production). This convergence of people manifests different kinds of sociality (social co-presence), depending on the nature of the event production. And, most important, even if the core of an event production is a ritual (e.g., an initiation ritual for a group of boys), the sociality that is produced and shared by the participants is not necessarily an intended or articulated part of that ritual. I therefore suggest that *we look at the modes of sociality that are generated by the convergence of people at event productions* in addition to examining their symbolisms and procedures, the latter having been anthropologists' main concerns in studying ritual life. Think of how differently event productions such as weddings, funerals, parades, or political conventions will appear if we compare and contrast the modes of sociality their participants generate. We have been seduced by the elegance of the rite of passage model (and that of the rites themselves) as well as the exuberance of native symbols while neglecting what is felt but often not remarked upon, experienced but poorly articulated: sociality.

There are many different modes of sociality and not all are "hot" (e.g., think of Buddhist group meditation sessions). For our purpose I will focus on red-hot sociality, i.e., the heightened excitement at many event productions, such as temple festivals. It was Durkheim who first expounded on the role convergence plays in generating intense sociality (Durkheim 1965: 245–52). The Australian aboriginals are dispersed most of the year as separate family units in search of food, but at regular intervals they gather into a larger group (the totemic clan) and celebrate. The dispersed state is characterized by "very mediocre intensity"; it is "uniform, languishing and dull." On the other hand, when the group comes together, "everything changes."

> The very fact of the concentration acts as an exceptionally powerful stimulant. When they are once come together, a sort of electricity is formed by their collecting which quickly transports them to an extraordinary degree of exaltation. . . . [W]hen arrived at this state of exaltation, a man does not recognize himself any longer. . . . [E]verything is just as though he really were transported into a special world, entirely different from the one where he ordinarily lives, and into an environment filled with exceptionally intense forces that take hold of him and metamorphose him. (Durkheim 1965: 246–47; 249–50)

This intense sociality has been known as "collective effervescence." Durkheim was speculating on the origin of religious beliefs, arguing that early humans, just like the Australian aboriginals, were enthralled by the very convergence of members of the clan, and religious ideas were born as people began worshipping this effervescent collectivity, i.e. society itself (ibid.: 250). Even though we might never know how religious ideas began and Durkheim's speculations remain speculations, he certainly highlighted the power ("exceptionally intense forces") that inheres in the convergence of people and heightened sociality that this convergence generates.

The convergence model of event production (or the "rite of convergence" model) spurs us to ask questions that are usually relegated to the background of ritual studies: Why do people converge on a particular occasion (i.e., What are the idioms of convergence?)? How often do people converge? How many people converge on different occasions? From how far away do people come? What kinds of people are allowed to converge and what kinds of people are excluded? What do people do when they come together? What are the mechanisms of convergence and dispersal? Who is in charge? What modes of sociality are encouraged or suppressed during the convergence? What effects does the convergence have on the participants? What kinds of subjectivities are presupposed, produced, and reproduced through the convergence? How does the event production encompass different rituals? What symbols and actions are used to convey what messages? The convergence model can complement the rite of passage model and is particularly useful for examining event productions that do not have an explicit ritual structure or when rituals are embedded in a larger "event structure": dance parties, festivals, parades, political campaigns, imperial or royal pageantries, World Fairs, the Olympics, and so forth. I will explore in the last section of this chapter the political implications of temple festivals' having become one of the most important "rites of convergence" in today's rural China.

Temple Festivals, Sensations, and Sociothermic Affect

Temple festivals, being rites of convergence par excellence, epitomize what Weller calls an "aesthetics of 'heat and noise'" (Weller 1994b: 118). The purpose of a temple festival is to hail all worshipers of the deity to come and celebrate the deity's "birthday." Temple festivals are "hot" events.[21] When worshipers converge at a particular temple festival, they experience red-hot sociality.[22] They will find themselves bombarded by an overwhelming amount and variety of sensory stimulation. Below I will try to evoke the sensory ambience of the temple festival at Longwanggou. Admittedly the Longwanggou temple festival is a lot more grand in scale and richer in sensory stimulation than most other Shaanbei temple festivals, but the difference is only in degree, not in kind. All temple festivals are honghuo events replete with noises, sights, smells, tastes, and ambient sensations (see Dean 1998b, chapter one).

Noises. Tractors, motorcycles, minivans, and buses are constantly bringing people into and out of the festival site; on the roads leading to Longwanggou the bus operators are shouting: "Longwanggou! Longwanggou!"; at the mouth of the valley the bus operators heading out shout out the destinations or directions: "Mizhi! Mizhi!" "Yulin! Yulin!" "Zhenchuan! Zhenchuan!"; the diesel motors are relentless with their staccato "tok tok tok tok tok tok tok," rhyming with the different pitches of honking; loudspeakers tout people into freak show or song-and-dance tents; people are shouting, laughing, chatting, playing games, gambling; firecrackers explode; drums, gongs, trumpets of the yangge troupes are playing; the sacrificial pigs and goats squeal; the sounds of opera singing and music pierce the air. . . .

Sights. People are everywhere, people in festive, colorful clothes; an ocean of people, some one knows but most one doesn't; game stands, trinket sellers, incense and firecracker sellers, watermelon stands, noodle tents, freak show tent, song-and-dance tent, fortune-tellers, folk music bands; men, women, children, old people; people climbing up the steps to the main temple hall; people kneeling down in front of the deity, burning incense and spirit money, praying and offering thanks, and putting money into the donation box or bowl; the pile of bright yellow spirit money burning like a bonfire; the brightly lighted opera stage and the opera singers in colorful costumes; the yangge performances; the fireworks at night; the dazzling chaos. . . .

Smells and tastes. The smells and tastes of all kinds of food: noodles made of wheat and potato flour, griddle cakes, goat intestine soup, stir-fried dishes, garlic and scallion, vinegar and red pepper, watermelons, small yellow melons, ices, soft drinks, burning liquor, beer; the pungency of diesel exhaust, firecrackers, freshly slaughtered pigs and goats, and their warm raw blood; the mixed fragrance and pungency of incense and burning spirit money; the faint smell of sweat from so many people squeezing through the main temple hall. . . .

Ambient sensations (heat, proprioception, kinesthetics, etc.). The worshiper gets off the bus or tractor-truck, whichever is his means of transportation to get to the temple festival, follows the swarms of other worshipers up and along the valley, passing through noodle stands, watermelon stands, gambling circles, song-and-dance tents, buys a few bundles of incense and spirit money from the incense hawkers, climbs up the steps to the main temple hall, throws the spirit money into the bonfire, lights a string of firecrackers, kneels and prays, burns incense, puts some money in the donation bowl, shakes the divination cylinder and gets his divination slip number, gets immediately pushed aside by worshipers coming up from behind, goes to the divination slips room and has the divination poem interpreted, then squeezes his way through the crowd to catch a glimpse of the opera performance, and wanders through different parts of the festival ground, snacks or eats a bowl of noodles, chats with acquaintances and co-villagers or complete strangers, plays a few rounds of

Above: Festivalgoers enjoying an opera performance at the Longwanggou Temple Festival. The opera stage is directly across from the Black Dragon King Temple. *Below*: Worshipers climbing a flight of steep stone steps to the temple to burn incense and pay respect to the Black Dragon King; people in the background are watching the opera.

Worshipers bringing offerings (elaborately constructed and decorated food towers) to the Black Dragon King.

games, watches the fireworks at night, and always finds himself in the company of tens of thousands of other worshipers. . . .

The English language has words for someone who receives sensory stimulation with eyes or ears (spectator, listener, audience) but does not have a word to describe someone who is experiencing intensely his surroundings through all his senses. I suggest that we call this person a "sensoric." We are all sensorics at all times because we always experience the world with all of our senses, even though in most of our life situations our surroundings are not characterized by heightened stimulation. But at temple festivals, all kinds of sensory stimulation literally assault and saturate the senses of the worshiper. The temple ground is a huge sensorium. The worshiper is a moving sensoric, feeling and experiencing with all his senses, and taking in the whole honghuo event at all of its points of excitation (in the main temple hall, in front of the opera stage, amidst the crowd, burning incense and setting off firecrackers, eating and drinking, etc.).

Even though the festivalgoers are super-loaded by sensory stimulation,

I must say that most of them do not become frenzied. Even though they might experience a mild form of what Durkheim called "collective effervescence," it would be going too far to suggest that they, like the Australian aboriginals described by Durkheim, are metamorphosed and can no longer recognize themselves. The festivalgoers do not appear ecstatic, as many people around the world might during intense ritualistic situations (e.g., going into trance, being possessed by spirits, dancing and singing, convulsing, foaming at the mouth, eyes rolling, etc.). Many festivalgoers look excited, happy, and engaged, while some others are quite calm; some look awed, even disoriented and confused; many seem not to know where they are or where to go, and are simply being pushed by the momentum of the crowd to wherever there is action; and some look tired or simply exhausted. It is difficult to assess or characterize precisely the kinds of affective state the festivalgoers are experiencing, but one may speculate that they are suffused with some kind of *sociothermic affect* (more diffused than "feelings" and more complex than simple excitement) that resonates with the kind of sociothermic affect they experience at wedding and funeral banquets, crowded markets, and other temple festivals.[23] The source of this affect is not only all the sensory stimulation at these honghuo events, but more important, the very convergence of a lot of people.

My emphasis on affect rather than symbols and meanings is in response partly to the actual ethnographic situation of temple festivals and partly to what might be called the communicative or semiotic approach to analyzing rituals and event productions. The main analytical strategy in ritual studies has been heavily influenced by Victor Turner's symbolic approach and Clifford Geertz's cultural interpretivism. Both approaches interpret the ritual process and symbols as if they were texts; the analyst performs cultural hermeneutics and tries to uncover what rituals and their component symbols "mean." While attempting to uncover these often hidden meanings, an anthropologist sometimes runs the risk of overinterpreting and finding many more meanings than are really meaningful to the natives. These hermeneutic approaches also often sidestep experience, bodily sensations, and affect due to their semiotic and cognitive emphases. What are meaningful to the natives at ritual events are often not necessarily "meanings" lying behind "symbols" but rather aggregated sensations and affects psychosomatically experienced. By highlighting the social construction of sociothermic affect, I have hoped to heighten our appreciation for the natives' sensorial world, in this case Shaanbei people's desire for, and experience of, collectively generated "red and fiery" sociality.[24]

Honghuo and Magical Efficacy

How does Shaanbei people's desire for and construction of honghuo at temple festivals relate to their religiosity and their conceptions of magical efficacy (ling)?

The fact that a temple festival is an elaborate event production rather than a ritual should be quite clear. At a temple festival there might be a pre-arranged program for the opera performance or a set sequence for some organized groups to pay homage to the deity, but there is no strict plan for individual worshipers to experience certain things in a certain manner, as is the case for most ritual participants. There are no prescribed "ritual actions" other than the minimal sequence of paying respect to the deity, which is a small part of the entire temple festival experience for any worshiper. It is utterly impossible to control or predict the many different encounters, experiences, sensations, pleasures, or frustrations of different worshipers. This absence of structure (as opposed to Victor Turner's famed "anti-structure") allows one person's trajectory through the time-space of the temple festival to be quite different from that of another; as a result no one's experience at the temple festival is ever the same as that of another.[25] (I will explore the political implications of this absence of structure below.) Also unlike a ritual, an event such as a temple festival does not have a clear beginning or a clear ending: the momentum builds up to a crescendo, and then it tapers off and dies out completely. People come and leave as they wish. Each person can have his or her idiosyncratic moments and loci of excitement. But just like rituals, events are also judged as successful or unsuccessful, though not in terms of effectiveness in delivering the desired result as in rituals (e.g., healing, adulthood, exorcised state) but in terms of *felt satisfaction*: a sense of having been part of intense red-hot sociality.

Most worshipers spend the better part of a day at a temple festival, coming in the morning (most likely after breakfast) and leaving in the evening.[26] Out of the entire day of activities at the festival, the act of paying respect to the deity and consulting the oracle usually takes only three to ten minutes. One can argue that the explicitly "ritual aspects" (paying respect to the deity, the offering-presenting procession) are not even the most central aspects of the festival, though they might appeal to anthropologists as the most central aspects because of their symbolic weight (I discussed this in the last chapter when I attempted to deconstruct the ritual centrality of the funeral ritual sequence). Therefore it is important to recognize that activities that are not directly related to "worship" are not peripheral to the focus of the temple festival; as a matter of fact, the whole festival is an *assemblage* of rituals and happenings that is experienced as a whole by worshipers.

Many Shaanbei peasants related to me the most honghuo funerals, weddings, or temple festivals they had been to, their eyes glowing in excitement as if they were reliving the honghuo atmosphere in their minds. It was not uncommon for some members of the audience to recount *their* experience of honghuo events as if in competition to see who had the good fortune of having seen or participated in the most honghuo events. On one such occasion of casual bantering and storytelling at Longwanggou, an old man who described the funeral for the mother of a very rich man in Zhenchuan during the Republican era beat everyone else in the group. Clearly honghuo events become memorable events to be savored long afterwards, and it is almost as if participants or witnesses become imbued with honghuo as an intangible quality the way a person is endowed with *mana* (life force, vitality, spiritual power) in Melanesian societies (see Firth 1967).

Taiwanese pilgrims who go on long and often arduous pilgrimages to centers of divine power to attend temple festivals (e.g., the Mazu temple at Beigang) experience similar feelings of the endowment of renewed energy and personal vitality. They even liken the experience to dead batteries' getting recharged (Huang 1994). Even though they believe the power comes from Mazu, it is equally plausible that they derive renewed vitality from the extreme social heat (i.e., honghuo, or the Minnan expression *lau-jiat*) generated at the crowded and exciting temple festival scene. Sangren (2000) has convincingly argued that the masses of worshipers at Mazu festivals constitute a kind of collective testimonialism that confirms and authenticates an individual worshiper's faith in the magical efficacy of the deity. The same can be said about Shaanbei deities, temple festivals, worshipers, and magical efficacy. Temple festivals are not simply expressions of people's relationships with the deities; they at the same time construct and affirm such relationships.

Honghuo-Making and the Agrarian Public Sphere

Even though banquets and temple festivals are both honghuo-making events, there are important differences between the two. The number and kind of people at a funeral or a wedding are limited and restricted; one cannot just show up at anybody's wedding or funeral without an invitation. On the other hand, temple festivals are what can be called "open events"; anyone can come to any temple festival. Even though there is an underlying assumption that people who come to the temple festival are those who have benefited from the deity or might want to establish a relationship with the deity, no one will question anyone about his or her identity or experience with the deity. Because of the sheer scale of a temple festival (from a few thousand to a few hundred thousand people), the occasion provides both a place and a time for the gathering of a large crowd of people who often do not know one another. For the duration of the temple festival they form an ephemeral co-presence (red-hot sociality), but they eventually disperse, and segments of the crowd may reconstitute with segments of other crowds at yet another temple festival in the region. Yet year after year most members of the same crowd reconstitute at the same time and at the same place for the next birthday celebration of the same deity, without necessarily getting to know one another better despite possible chance interactions. Therefore worshipers at temple festivals do not form a community in the sense of an organized and self-conscious collectivity. Nor do they constitute an "imagined community" (Anderson 1991) of worshipers because no attempt is made to construct such an imagination (unlike nationalism, ethnicity, or sectarian cults, for example). However, the strongly felt co-presence might help construct an unarticulated, vague sense of shared well-being that might be consciously or subconsciously attributed to the divine power of the deities. As such it is a powerful affirmation of the conception of a world in which one can freely worship deities without fearing government suppression, a world in which one thanks the deities but not the Party or the state for one's blessedness and good fortune. And this conception of the world can be read as either an implicit critique of the failure of the socialist state to care for the people or a happy approval of the current policies of economic reforms and much softened ideological work. Or both?

The largely unstructured form of the temple festival contrasts sharply with the highly structured forms of Maoist-era political rituals and event productions. The most common Maoist political rituals were humiliation and struggle meetings, political study and self-criticism sessions, public executions, and ritualized collective endeavors such as production campaigns. These were also rites of convergence, where one of the most important tasks was to assemble (*jihe*) the masses for purposes of production, education, devotion, or even consumption (e.g., the collective canteens). Unlike the temple festival, these rituals were much more structured with predetermined procedures and predetermined (desirable) outcomes. They were political dramas, and words and communication were paramount.[27] The preferred mode of political indoctrination and ideological control was the small group (*xiaozu*), where a group of ten to fifteen people gathered to study Mao's or other party-state writings and engage in intense discussions and self-criticisms (Whyte 1974). But there were also frequent larger assemblies (*dahui*) to both educate the masses and to use the power of the people to intimidate class enemies or other targets of political struggle. And of course there were parades and other forms of ceremonial rites to demonstrate the beauty and accomplishments of socialism.[28]

The Communist leaders were obviously aware of the political potential of honghuo-making; the red-hot pageantry of the Tiananmen Square parades and large-scale struggle meetings attested to their conscious manipulation of sociothermic affect. However, sometimes the masses' enthusiasm for honghuo overflowed and carried many political campaigns beyond their original stated goals. The overzealous participation in the Great Leap Forward and the Cultural Revolution might be partially interpreted as the masses' hijacking the political campaigns for their own honghuo-making purposes. I suspect that peasants preferred the big rallies to small group political rituals because they could hide in the crowd and "watch" the honghuo. Many Shaanbei peasants told me that they tried their best to avoid speaking up at political meetings, and when they had to speak they spoke as little as possible. Liu (1998) recounted similar situations in another rural locale in north-central China. He found that the traditional arrangement of space in rural areas prevented the effective transformation of peasants' consciousness during Maoist political campaigns. In other words, the persistence in form became an impediment to changes in content.

Honghuo-making event productions such as temple festivals and wedding and funeral banquets certainly constitute an important component of what I have called the agrarian public sphere. But are the temple festival or the honghuo-seeking crowd as traditional forms conducive to the development of political communities that can negotiate with the state?[29] In later chapters of the book (chapters 9, 10, and 11), I will show that the rise of the temple association and temple bosses as local elites has significant political ramifications as they interact with the local state and even forces beyond the immediate locales. However, at this stage it is difficult to say that religion-based sociality will bring about major changes in political culture and shifts in state-society power relations.

CHAPTER NINE

Temple Boss and Local Elite

The Story of Lao Wang

The flying dragon mounts the clouds and the *t'eng* snake wanders in the mists. But when the clouds dissipate and the mists clear, the dragon and the snake become the same as the earthworm and the large-winged black ant because they have lost that on which they ride.

—Ancient Philosopher Shen Tzu,
quoted by Han Fei Tzu (Ames 1994: 74)

Am I not a mere peasant after all?

—Temple Boss Lao Wang

"People Depend on Gods and Gods Depend on People"

One day in early spring of 1998 I stayed over at the divine message interpreter Lao Chen's home in Chenjiapo. The next morning I had a hearty breakfast of millet and green bean porridge (*xiaomi lüdouzhou*), pickles and *ganlur*[1] with Lao Chen and his wife. Erhu (Second Tiger), the big boy from next door, came to fetch me as he had promised the night before, and off we went to climb the little hill overlooking the village. Erhu wanted to show me the construction of the temple association cave dwellings (*huiyao*) at the site of the two Chenjiapo temples up on top of the hill.[2] When we reached the top of the little yet steep hill, I was already sweating profusely and out of breath. But the panoramic view of the village and the surrounding areas was worth the effort. There was quite a bustle up there. Six men were busy digging the ditches for the "legs" (*yaotui*, i.e., foundation) of the planned cut-stone caves. Another man was transporting stones up the hill with his bull-cart and unloading them next to the temples. There was already a large pile of neatly heaped stones; there must have been thousands of them. Three other men were cutting and chipping the stones into shape for the construction. And Erhu's uncle, one of the heads of the Chenjiapo temple association, was supervising the work. They were all Chenjiapo villagers except one of the stonemasons.

I looked on, listened to their bantering, and asked questions about the temples, the construction, and the much-anticipated Third Month Third temple festival. Then it was rest time and we all squatted or sat down together and chatted over cigarettes and pipes. They told me they would try to ask Longwanggou to help out with the expenses of the construction of both the caves and the new, widened road for the Chenjiapo temples. In the late eighties, Longwanggou had helped out financially with the reconstruction of the two Chenjiapo temples. The men had heard that Longwanggou was in the red because of its own ongoing construction and wondered if this time Lao Wang would agree to subsidize theirs at all. Then the discussion turned to an evaluation of Lao Wang and his extraordinary abilities in reviving the Heilongdawang Temple. One older man who had just finished telling us about his participation in the early years of Longwanggou's revival suddenly sighed, drew a long puff from his pipe, and said:

"People depend on gods and gods depend on people (*ren ping shen, shen ping ren*). Hongliutan is sure lucky to have a capable man like Wang Kehua."

I sensed the more than slight envy in this old Chenjiapo villager's tone. It reminded me of the fact that historically it had been Chenjiapo that controlled the affairs of the Heilongdawang Temple, but ever since the temple revival in the 80s the people of Hongliutan have gained de facto control, thanks to Lao Wang's leadership and the fact that the temple stands on Hongliutan land.[3] This old man and some other Chenjiapo villagers must have felt humiliated to be "begging" Lao Wang for money to subsidize the work on their village temples.[4]

However, I was more drawn to the old man's idiomatic expression "People depend on gods and gods depend on people." This was not the first time I heard this wonderfully lucid idiomatic expression concerning the mutually dependent relationship between human and god. I had heard it a few times before in other parts of Shaanbei and continued to hear it uttered in similar discussions about gods, temples, temple association leaders, and worshipers. What this expression meant was that even though humans are dependent on the efficacy of the gods to protect them from misfortunes and bring them good harvests, health, and prosperity, the gods themselves have to rely on people to worship them (of which donation of incense money was an indispensable part) and to spread their names. The gods were dependent especially on dedicated and capable temple association leaders to build, run, and continue to expand the temples, thus "making manifest" (*xian*) the power of the gods. Without the clouds and mists to ride on, the flying dragon and the *t'eng* [i.e., leaping] snake would be the same as "the earthworm and the large-winged black ant." A proper understanding of the revival of Longwanggou is therefore not possible without an understanding of temple boss Lao Wang because of his instrumental role in the life of the temple complex since its revival.

This chapter tells the story of Lao Wang. It treats the following questions: Who is Lao Wang? What kind of man is Lao Wang? How did Lao Wang become the temple boss? What is the relationship between Lao Wang's identity and his involvement in the temple? What is his leadership style? How do his associates/colleagues view him and his leadership style? Why did he want to be the temple boss? What are his political ambitions? More than just a portrait of a village-level local elite, this chapter tries to relate Lao Wang's story to larger patterns of the emergence of a new kind of rural local elite as well as those of local power configurations in contemporary China. This chapter also serves as a background for the ethnography in the next two chapters (chapters 10 and 11), which look at the connection between village politics and temple politics at Longwanggou and Lao Wang's strategies of legitimation for both himself as the temple boss and for his power base, the Black Dragon King Temple.

Who Is Lao Wang?

Lao Wang is fifty-seven years old in 1998, though he looks much younger than his age.[5] He is taller than the average Shaanbei man and is of medium build. His face is tanned, like all Shaanbei peasants, though less so than those who toil daily in the fields. His features are quite refined, and he is always clean-shaven. His lips are thin and his voice high-pitched and very distinctive. His eyes are very bright and attentive, and they smile and look mischievous when he is about to crack a joke or tease someone. He can appear as a different person depending on situations: quiet, pensive, and serious when with strangers and social superiors, while jovial and talkative when with friends or colleagues. He does not smoke, which is rare for a man in Shaanbei. He usually does not drink either, even though he is famed for being able to down one *jin* (equivalent

Temple Boss Lao Wang speaking to a group of temple association members and volunteer yangge dancers who are preparing for the First Month Fifteenth celebration.

of half a kilogram in weight) *lajiu* (high-degree liquor) in one sitting. He likes to wear a dark blue Zhongshan suit (also know as a Mao suit), a relic from the Maoist era, even though the Zhongshan suit has long become unfashionable even in Shaanbei, having been replaced by casual jackets and Western-style slacks. In winter he always wears a big, heavy sheepskin coat.

Lao Wang is very fond of his motorcycle, an old, small, military-green, Japanese-made Suzuki, and he rides it mainly between Zhenchuan Town, his native village Hongliutan, and the temple. He never rides the motorcycle on long-distance trips, though, preferring to ride on the temple pickup truck or to take the bus. He sometimes walks the one *li* unpaved road between his home in Hongliutan and the temple. He usually walks with a slow, casual pace, looking down as if in deep thought, and he sometimes massages his lower back with a hammering motion with his fists as he walks. Though he gives an overall impression of middle-aged "steadiness and assuredness" (*wenzhong*, as the Chinese have it), Lao Wang is in fact known as having an unpredictable temper. People say, and he admits himself, that because of his quick temper and sharp tongue he has lost quite a few good friends and helpful colleagues as well as alienated many potential allies. During the course of my fieldwork I witnessed many episodes of Lao Wang's flare of temper and each time I could not help but marvel at his command of mean expressions. Once I saw him shower one of his younger brothers with such vicious sarcasm that his brother almost cried in public. But most of the time he has good reasons to be upset, and he certainly is an expert at scolding people (S. *jueren*).

Though not the richest person in Hongliutan, in 1998 Lao Wang is undoubtedly one of the most well-to-do people in his village. Like most well-to-do people in the Zhenchuan area, he runs a wholesale business in Zhenchuan Town, and as he has set up another home in Zhenchuan Town he is clearly spending more and more time in the town rather than in the village. But because of the need to attend regularly to the affairs of the temple and also to see his aging and ill mother, who chooses not to live in the town, Lao Wang still often stays at his Hongliutan home. Lao Wang has three sons and no daughters. None of his three sons are living with him. The eldest son married a Guanzhong woman and lives and works in Xi'an. The second son married a Yulin City woman and lives and works in Yulin City. The youngest of the three sons is attending a police academy in Nanjing in the South. Though his father, now deceased, was a Communist Party member, Lao Wang never joined the Party.[6] In 1998 he is serving his third year as the village head of Hongliutan.

Lao Wang's Early Years

The Wangs are "old households" (*laohu*) of Hongliutan, probably having lived there for a few hundred years.[7] They had a lineage genealogy in the past but it was destroyed during the Cultural Revolution. Like most lineages in Shaanbei, the Wangs never had an ancestral hall. The lineage did, however, own a few *mu* of collective land whose income was used to sponsor the annual "grave gathering" (*fenhui*) during the "Eat Cold" (*hanshi*) and "Clear and Bright" (*qingming*) Festival, which was their only collective activity relating to ancestors. The activity was called "eating at the grave gathering" (*chifenhui*). Lao Wang once mentioned casually that one of his ancestors had earned a local level degree under the Qing, except that he did not know what exactly the degree was. It was probably a county level *shengyuan*. During the Class Struggle years of the Maoist era Lao Wang's family was classified as a lower-middle peasant household (*xiazhongnong*).[8] There were no landlords in Hongliutan and only a few rich peasants.

Lao Wang's father once served in the People's Liberation Army – he might have been a lower-ranking officer—and after he was demobilized he came back to Hongliutan and, thanks to his status as an ex-"revolutionary soldier" (*geming junren*), became a village-level cadre. Presumably he joined the Communist Party when he was in the army. He served as the Party secretary of the brigade for many years during the collectivization era and was of reasonably good reputation. During the Four Cleanups and the Cultural Revolution he was criticized and became a member of the so-called "Loyalists" (*baohuangpai*) vis-à-vis the "Rebels" (*zaofanpai*). He had four brothers (he was the third), one of whom had been a yinyang master (*yinyang*) before "superstitious activities" were completely banned during the sixties.

Lao Wang himself was born in Hongliutan in 1942, the first of an eight-member, all-male sibling set.[9] It was three years before the Japanese surrendered and four years prior to the liberation of Zhenchuan by the People's Liberation Army. Lao Wang remembered how, when he was a small child, he and his family went hiding in the "hide-from-the-rebels caves" (*cangfan yaoyao*)[10] in the hills as the Communist and the Nationalist armies passed back and forth along the Wuding River on the edge of the village. He also remembered vividly witnessing some of the struggle sessions during the land reforms of 1947 in nearby villages, in which some landlords were hung up on tree branches and beaten.

Without doubt, Lao Wang was very intelligent from a young age. He studied in the Chenjiapo Primary School,[11] and because his grades were so good he was one of the very few pupils who could go to the secondary school in Zhenchuan Town (the commune seat). After having graduated from junior high school with distinction in 1957, Lao Wang decided to become a teacher and went on to study in the Suide County Teachers' School (one of the two teachers' schools in Yulin Prefecture). In 1960, he graduated and started teaching at the neighboring Zhuzhai Primary School. He taught for about two years and had once won a county-level model teacher certificate. Those were very difficult times in rural China with widespread famine caused by natural disasters and "human errors." Lao Wang, however, because of the monthly 32 yuan he earned from his steady, state job, did not suffer much. In 1962 a state policy to reduce state-sector personnel sent him back to his native village.

At first he farmed with his fellow villagers in the collective fields and, for a year, tended the brigade's livestock. In 1965 he left with a band of Hongliutan villagers to contract out their labor (*langong*) as stonemasons (*shijiang*). Initially he was a mere "small laborer" (*xiaogong*), earning a very low wage. Learning fast, he soon became a skilled laborer (*jianggong*).[12] He and his fellow laborers cut and carved stones, did woodwork, mixed mud and cement, painted, and built houses, bridges, roads, canals, embankments, and dams. He learned and worked for four years (1965–1969), contributing to his brigade two thousand and four hundred yuan, while keeping the remaining earnings to himself.[13] Because of his wide experience and connections gained through these years, he later became a brigade labor contractor himself and traveled and worked in ever more distant areas in Shaanbei, Guanzhong, Inner Mongolia, and Ningxia Hui Autonomous Region. Between 1970 and 1972, while still a labor contractor, he made and sold clothes for the brigade. During the tumultuous years of the Cultural Revolution from the late sixties to the early seventies he traveled widely and, like so many people during that time, gambled along the way. He said once he brought back home a "large hemp bag full of small notes" (*yi mabao maomaoqian*). In the mid-seventies he landed a large contract: building the aircraft hangars for the military airport which was being built to the north of Zhenchuan Town.[14] This project and many others before it must have helped Lao Wang accumulate the capital he needed for his investments in later years. Lao Wang was an adolescent and then a young adult during his father's tenure as Party secretary (the fifties until the early seventies). It is reasonable to assume that Lao Wang had benefited from his father's intra-village as well as extra-village influence and connections. For example, it must have been easier for Lao Wang, son of the brigade Party secretary, to obtain permission to go out and earn cash instead of staying behind to earn work-points.

Then it was the reform era. Markets gradually began to be opened after 1979, and full-scale de-collectivization began in early 1982. Lao Wang, then forty years old, energetic, experienced, and full of hope, was one of the first people to open a shop in Zhenchuan Town. Together with his wife, he made and sold clothes he designed himself. Later they switched the business into a "small hundred items" (*xiaobaihuo*) wholesale store. But what really changed Lao Wang's life was his involvement with the revival of the Heilongdawang Temple from the beginning of 1981.

Lao Wang Became the Temple Boss

In the beginning it was only a handful of elderly villagers who took up the task of reviving the temple. It was a very risky business, and they were once dispersed and investigated by the local government officials. One was jailed for a few months; another fled and did not dare to come home for a few months. Then slowly the government seemed to acquiesce to the obvious mass enthusiasm for reviving temples. The organization of the Heilongdawang Temple Association quickly took shape and Lao Wang, because of his organizational and technical expertise in design and construction work, was elected the leader of the reconstruction operations. He then put all his experience as an artisan to good use, revamping the whole topography around the temple, designing the new temple buildings and organizing and contracting out different phases of the work. During the reconstruction he had put in 100, 000 yuan of his personal funds, in the form of loans to the temple to finance the operations (including buying a bulldozer).[15] In 1984 the new Heilongdawang Temple proper was completed. Meanwhile, electricity was finally brought up from down the valley in Hongliutan to the temple ground. At a meeting with all the representatives of the nine participating villages, Lao Wang was elected the chair (*dahuizhang*) of the temple association. The vice-chair, the treasurer, the temple property custodian, the supplies procurer, and other core members of the temple association managing committee were also elected on that occasion. At that time Lao Wang was forty-two years old, and most of the committee members were of the same generational cohort.[16]

The work of building and expanding Longwanggou consumed much of Lao Wang's time and energy. Yet he tried to find time to tend to his business. From 1988 until 1990 he, like so many merchants in Zhenchuan, rode the waves of the prosperous wool trade between Inner Mongolia and Shijiazhuang.[17] He also invested some money in a taxi service company in Xi'an, though he quickly lost all of it; he was cheated, or "devoured," by his savvier city partners (*gei renjia chi le*). In 1988, at the suggestion and with the help of Zhu Xubi, a native of Zhuzhai and a forestry specialist working at the Yulin Prefecture Forestry Bureau, Lao

Wang began the reforestation project in Longwanggou. It became so successful that it would become Lao Wang's most recognized achievement for years to come (Chau n.d.).

Just as things were going very well for him, Lao Wang encountered a major personal setback. Lao Wang was charged with embezzling public funds and was put in jail for four months in 1990 (more details on this in Chapter 10). Though he was subsequently acquitted and released from jail in March of 1991, Lao Wang was much embittered by the experience. It took him some time to recover from the shock and humiliation. But he resumed the leadership of Longwanggou as soon as he came back, putting an end to the chaotic strife that had resulted from his absence. Maybe because of the insecurity he felt, he also launched a few purges to rid the association of the people with whom he had problems. Meanwhile the businesses in Zhenchuan continued to thrive. Lao Wang and one of his brothers decided to enter into partnership to open a wholesale shop in Zhenchuan's newly constructed market compound. However, because Lao Wang was often busy with work in Longwanggou, the running of the business depended on his wife, his brother, and his brother's wife.

As the reforestation project (the Longwanggou Hilly Land Arboretum) slowly took shape, it attracted positive attention from different quarters. This was at a time when environmentalism became all the rage in public discourse on a national level. Lao Wang began to realize the value of the reforestation project and took the initiative to promote the success of the arboretum. In the summer of 1990, Longwanggou received the first foreign visitors to have heard about the temple and the arboretum. A few Japanese were the first to come, and they were followed by a steady trickle of foreigners of different nationalities. Not many foreigners had visited Shaanbei because much of it was still officially closed to foreigners. Therefore their visit to Longwanggou conferred importance and recognition on Lao Wang and his colleagues' enterprise. Quite a few of these foreigners were journalists or academics and they wrote about Longwanggou after they went back to their own countries. Because of the friendship Lao Wang struck up with a key foreign contact, he was invited to become a Chinese member of Inter-Asia, a Japanese-funded, pan-Asian, non-governmental organization that organizes regular transnational activities to promote friendship among the common people of Asian countries. As the leader of Longwanggou, he participated in national and even international conferences on forestry, environmentalism, and sustainable development. In 1996, as part of an aggressive expansion program for Longwanggou, Lao Wang founded the Longwanggou Primary School. In the same year, he was invited to go to Japan to take part in a conference as well as a short study tour, both organized by Inter-Asia, thus making him one of a handful people in Yulin Prefecture who had ever gone abroad. He liked telling the story of how he was questioned at the Chinese immigration booths before boarding the plane: "You? A peasant? What are you going to Japan for?"

Despite the fact that such expansive developments had hardly been anticipated in the beginning, Lao Wang welcomed these opportunities with great enthusiasm. Just as he had done when he was a young man learning different trades, he now eagerly absorbed new knowledge and made new friends and allies. It was at this expansive moment of both Longwanggou and his personal life that Lao Wang welcomed me, a doctoral student of anthropology from the United States, to do research on the temple and to use Longwanggou as a base camp for my research in Shaanbei. He wanted Heilongdawang (and presumably himself also) to be known in the United States too. However, the spread of Heilongdawang and Lao Wang's names abroad had not been matched by similar enthusiasm from the local government. Lao Wang once grumbled that he and his efforts were more acknowledged abroad than at home. Although he was elected a member of the Yulin County branch of the People's Political Consultative Conference (popularly known as *Zhengxie*) in 1993, he felt that the Yulin county and prefecture governments had not been paying enough attention to his great accomplishments.[18]

Lao Wang as Master Artisan

Once I asked Lao Wang what he would do if, hypothetically, the government decided to close the temple in another anti-superstition campaign. He laughed, and said, "What would I do? I'd pick up my hoe and farm (*shouku*) again. Am I not a mere peasant after all?" He then went on to tell me why he thought my imagined hypothetical situation would never happen.

I knew Lao Wang was most likely joking when he said he was, after all, a peasant. He was undoubtedly a peasant by origin and upbringing, and by status on his residence booklet (*hukou ben*), identity card (*shenfen zheng*), and passport.[19] However, he was so much more than just a peasant that he was already not a real peasant. Even though he still had his share of land in his village, he hadn't farmed it for more than ten years, after having asked one of his brothers to take care of it. The occasional work in his small courtyard garden hardly counted as farming. But if Lao Wang was no longer a peasant, what was he? Could he be called a merchant because he had a wholesale store in Zhenchuan Town? He was rarely at his store to take care of its day-to-day chores. Could he be called a religious functionary because he was the temple boss? Unlike a Buddhist abbot, a Daoist priest or a spirit medium, there was nothing strictly speaking religious about what he did at the temple. Lao Wang never received any training in religious doctrines or rituals nor did he need any training to be the temple boss; theoretically anyone from the village could be the temple boss. As I have suggested in earlier chapters, temple-based popular religion is a "minimalist religion," and the organization of Longwanggou is very much a secular one, resembling that of an ordinary *danwei*, or work unit, in Chinese society. Therefore the position of the temple boss is like that of the *danwei* boss, be it Party secretary, manager, chairman, or director. Still, although Lao Wang enjoyed being the temple boss and treasured the status and perhaps the privileges attached to the position as well as all the titles he had accumulated related to Longwanggou, it seemed that "temple boss" was hardly the core of his identity.

I only slowly realized that Lao Wang most probably saw himself as an all-around master artisan or folk engineer. Lao Wang was a skilled builder, stonemason, carpenter, painter, decorator, tailor, and he was the engineer in chief of the entire *new* Longwanggou since the beginning of the revival of the temple. Not only did he design the new temple buildings (which included the main temple, the entrance hall, the new wing to the temple, the bell and drum towers, the opera stage, and the dormitory building) but most important of all he put forth and carried out the ambitious and visionary plan of filling in a stretch of the valley to make room for the building projects of the temple as well as for its many expected visitors. His engineering feat was the most difficult, and its results the most spectacular, of any contemporary temple building in Shaanbei. Among his contributions in Longwanggou, Lao Wang was most proud of the huge, four-column stone entrance gate (*pailou*) on the edge of the highway and at the mouth of the road leading up the valley, which attracted every traveler passing by along the highway. In 1996 Lao Wang began building another stone gate, this time with six columns and on a scale much grander than the first one, halfway between the first gate and the temple. He said that he wanted this gate to be the largest stone gate in the whole country.[20]

Building or decorating projects were always going on in Longwang-gou, and Lao Wang was always involved in the planning as well as the minutiae of the execution of these projects. Recent undertakings included the second temple building made up of the Dragon Greatness Hall and the Dragon Mother Palace, both with elaborate interior decorations, the aforementioned stone gate, the partial paving with asphalt of the road leading up to the temple from the highway, and the new carvings and in-scriptions on the cliff. When Lao Wang was not overseeing some bigger projects, he was often busy designing smaller objects for the temple or looking for craftsmen who could execute his designs. His recent small projects included large silver talismanic seals (*fuyin*) for both the Longmu niangniang and Heilongdawang, a copper ritual bowl-bell for the altar to Heilongdawang in the main temple hall, small copper bells for the eaves of the temple buildings, a large copper bell for the bell tower, a huge cop-per bell to replace the large copper bell, and six different stone stelae. It seemed that Lao Wang was very happy to be able to apply his artisan's skills to different domains, as well as to learn new skills along the way. Most of the books at his Hongliutan home were art, calligraphy, and ar-chitecture books he collected for reference. Not unlike the Renaissance master artisans, Lao Wang developed and used his "extended compe-tence" in diverse artistic domains that the revival of Longwanggou had afforded (see Chastel 1991: 186).[21] The number of projects, large and small, seemed only to be limited by the availability of funds. As a matter of fact, in the past couple of years Longwanggou had been in the red be-cause of the large expenses the numerous projects incurred.

To give the reader a sense of how much Lao Wang enjoyed solving the practical problems of artisanal projects, I will present one brief example. It concerns the problem of estimating the weight of a giant copper bell. One morning in early March 1998 an old man, probably in his sixties, appeared in the temple canteen. As we lined up with other people in the kitchen to get our noodles for brunch, I made his acquaintance. I found out that he was a master coppersmith from a town near Xi'an and it was he who, half a year ago, had made all the small copper bells for the eaves of the temple buildings and the copper bell for the bell tower. This time he was summoned to come up to Longwanggou to talk about a new as-signment with Lao Wang. I learned that the copper bell then hanging in the bell tower, though working very well, was to be replaced by a much larger one. As I and a couple of the temple officers chatted with him, Lao Wang came, got his bowl of noodles, and squatted down right next to Fu *shifu*, the master coppersmith. After a little casual chat Lao Wang took out a piece of paper and spread it out on the kitchen floor in front of Fu shifu. It was a carefully hand-drawn picture of a traditional and complicated-looking bell including all the dimensions. The two of them then began a lively discussion of the techniques of alloying, melting, and molding, which I found very technical and difficult to follow. This occasion deepened my realization that nothing at the temple was as simple and easy as it might have seemed. Then the problem of cost came up. Fu shifu had to know how much the bell would weigh in order to calculate how much copper he had to use, which in turn would determine the cost of material for the project. Lao Wang took out a pen from his jacket pocket and was about to start calculating the weight of the bell when he looked up and around, and saw me and a few of the Longwanggou Primary School teachers. He jokingly asked the teachers and me if we were interested in having a contest to see who could get the correct answer in the least amount of time. The teachers were not interested, perhaps seeing no point in losing precious leisure time over what was, to them at least, a meaningless problem. I, on the other hand, was thoroughly intrigued by the problem and took up the challenge.

It turned out to be a very complicated problem of geometric mathematics and I, with the additional handicap of not having a calculator at hand, was soon lost in a morass of multiplications and divisions. Before I could figure out where my own calculation was going, Lao Wang had already come up with the answer: around 900 *jin* (i.e., 450 kilograms). I did not believe he could do it so quickly and asked him to explain to me and to Fu shifu how he had done it. He proceeded to explain to me his simplified way of calculation and it sounded brilliantly simple and elegant. "Ha, you useless university student!" Lao Wang teased me.[22] Determined to calculate the answer the hard way, I went back to my room and spent more than an hour on the problem, and my answer came out so close to Lao Wang's that I had to admire his quick mind and his artisan's practical "instinct," accumulated over many years of solving similar problems.

Lao Wang as Peasant Intellectual

In his attempts to theorize the social formation of intellectuals [in Europe, that is], Gramsci claimed that "the peasantry does not elaborate its own 'organic' intellectuals" (Gramsci 1971: 6). Is this claim applicable to

China? The case of Lao Wang seems to present us an example of a peasant intellectual who has grown out of the agrarian context "organically" (see Feierman 1990). If we follow Gramsci's definition of intellectuals as people in any significant social group who perform "directive, organizational, and educative" functions (ibid.), Lao Wang and other temple bosses like him are certainly intellectuals. Because he was born and raised as a peasant, had lived in a peasant community almost all his life, identified with his own community and ways of life, had been a leader of a quintessential peasant institution (i.e., the Black Dragon King Temple), Lao Wang was a peasant intellectual par excellence.

Significantly, Lao Wang was to have become an educator, had he not been laid off from the school he was teaching at due to state personnel-reduction policies in 1962. Had he continued his vocation as a teacher, he might have become an accomplished teacher in one of the village primary schools in Zhenchuan Township or even in Zhenchuan Town itself. He could have studied for a higher degree (say, a high school teacher's diploma) and become a junior high or high school teacher. A career in teaching would have taken Lao Wang away from his native village, his peasant background and surroundings, and made him into an intellectual but not a *peasant* intellectual. So it was thanks to Maoist state policies (including the household registration policy) that he returned to his native village and became a peasant again.

Lao Wang's pursuit of an artisan's training and skills was based on both economic and intellectual considerations. As a member of the brigade labor gang and later as a labor contractor he continually learned new things, especially because of his extensive travels and the wide variety of people he met. He respected people who knew things that he did not know, and he relished the opportunities of being told and taught new things. That surely was one of the reasons he welcomed visitors like me who could bring new knowledge to him.

Lao Wang readily embraced high technology as he had embraced practical know-how. As the temple boss, he had to decide how to keep the technology in Longwanggou up-to-date to meet the many demands of temple activities. Professional audio and loudspeaker systems were among the first high-tech equipment the temple purchased so as to better coordinate large-scale activities such as temple festivals. A video cassette player and recorder followed. The temple did not need to buy a video camera because the Zhenchuan Cultural Station chief Lao Ren was a good friend of Lao Wang's and took care of videotaping when needed.

Then, in 1997, one of the early visitors to Longwanggou and by now a good friend of Lao Wang's from Beijing donated his computer to the temple, complete with printer and Chinese-language software. Lao Wang was thrilled by the promise of the computer, and immediately hired a computer-savvy vocational high school graduate to try to make the computer useful for the temple and the primary school. Lao Wang also wanted to learn how to use the computer and asked me to give him lessons. We tried a few times but since he had never learned to use the alphabetical letters—he went to school before the popularization of the pinyin system—we got stuck at the almost insurmountable difficulty presented by the keyboard, Microsoft Windows (Chinese version) notwithstanding. But I managed to demonstrate to him the basic features and uses of the computer.

Even though he did not continue to be a teacher, Lao Wang was extremely interested in education. According to him, he founded the Longwanggou Primary School so that the village children would get a good education and thereby have a better chance to "get out of here" (S. *chuke*, i.e. *chuqu*). "There won't be enough land to go around. The more kids can get jobs outside, the better." When Lao Wang said "jobs outside," he meant nonagricultural jobs in towns and cities. Because there were very few village enterprises in Shaanbei and they could rarely provide employment to more than a handful of villagers, Lao Wang's educational strategy was certainly farsighted. Ever since the founding of the school in 1996, it had consistently been the best primary school in Zhenchuan Township. When I was leaving Longwanggou in the summer of 1998, Lao Wang was already actively planning to open a junior high school in Longwanggou.

Because of his role as the leader of Longwanggou, especially that of the Hilly Land Arboretum, Lao Wang had been invited to attend a number of conferences in major Chinese cities and even abroad to share Longwanggou's experience of reforestation and nongovernmental social activism. These experiences further widened his intellectual outlook and knowledge base, and whenever he came back from these trips he would share informally his experiences with his colleagues and friends. In 1997, Lao Wang went to Japan to participate in a pan-Asia conference on "green development" as well as a short study tour organized by Inter-Asia. During my fieldwork I heard him talk about his experiences and encounters in Japan with his colleagues in Longwanggou on many occasions. Lao Wang was quick in learning about new trends in the larger

world, both inside China and beyond, and he was always ready to capi-
talize on his new understanding and to try new things, which made Longwanggou such a dynamic and exciting place.

Seeking Fame and Influence

When I asked Lao Wang why he spent so much energy on the temple,
he told me in a straightforward way: "Because I want to leave a name.
You see, one comes to live in this world only once, so one has to leave a
name. It doesn't matter whether it's a good name or bad name; one has
to leave a name." I was sure he himself wanted to leave a good name. In
fact, I discovered that the desire to leave a good name for posterity was a
very strong motivating force for most Shaanbei people. Older people
often talk about how they have tried all their lives to make sure that their
children are properly married and how they have performed impeccably
other social obligations so that they would die "without leaving a name
to be reproached" (*mei liuxia maming*). For Lao Wang, it is obviously not
enough just to leave a name beyond reproach; he wants to be remembered as *the* architect (in both its narrow and broad senses) of the
revival of the Black Dragon King Temple. This desire for posterity underlies his attempt to have his name inscribed on various surfaces of the
Longwanggou Complex: the temple stelae (as temple boss, chief architect, and initiator of the arboretum project), the bronze bells (as de-
signer), and the inscription cliff wall (as temple boss). His name is not
only inscribed into these hard, almost permanent surfaces (i.e., metals
and stone); it is also recorded in the temple documents and newspaper articles.

However, leaving a good name for posterity is only part of the ratio-
nale behind Lao Wang's will to fame. More important is his desire to be
famous *here* and *now* and to reap the benefits of fame *here* and *now*.
This desire, however, is less readily articulated. Or perhaps it is a matter
of course? Why not seek fame, power, and influence, as one would
money and a comfortable life? These goals seem to be part of the natural
order of things in Shaanbei, and probably no one ever doubts that a well-
endowed man like Lao Wang would pursue them.

The trajectory of Lao Wang's pursuit of fame and influence is best illustrated by the gradual accumulation of his official titles—"official"
here includes all formal titles, not just those granted and recognized by
the local state. In Shaanbei, as elsewhere in China, official titles are often

indicators of one's social prominence. The titles, which often appear in the concrete form of lines on name cards, communicate the symbolic capital of the owner of the titles. Theoretically, titles imply positions, which in turn imply power.[23] By 1998, Lao Wang had accumulated quite a few official titles, all of which were related to his leadership role in Longwanggou. In 1984, soon after the new Heilongdawang Temple had been formally dedicated, he was elected the chair (*dahuizhang*) of the temple association. In the same year, the Cultural Bureau (*wenhuaju*) of Yulin City appointed Lao Wang to be the chief (*suozhang*) of the Longwanggou Cultural Treasure Management Office (*Longwanggou wenwu guanli suo*). In 1988, when Longwanggou began the reforestation project, Lao Wang was appointed the chief (*yuanzhang*) of the Longwanggou Hilly Land Arboretum by the Yulin city government. In 1995, he was selected as one of the few members of the Chinese chapter of the Japanese-funded NGO Inter-Asia. In 1996, he was elected a member of the Yulin County branch of the People's Political Consultative Conference. In the same year, he was elected the village head (*cunzhang*) of his village, Hongliutan. Also in 1996, he founded the Longwanggou Primary School and became its honorary principal. In August 1998, as the Religious Affairs Bureau of the Yulin prefecture government granted Longwanggou the official status of the "Longwanggou Daoist Shrine Management Committee" (*Longwanggou daoguan guanli weiyuanhui*), Lao Wang became the committee's chair (*huizhang*).

That is eight official titles at the same time! However, the concentration of so many official titles on one person should not surprise anyone familiar with contemporary Chinese society and political culture. As mentioned above, titles convey a person's sociopolitical worth, and therefore there is a tendency for a power-seeker to concentrate official positions on himself and thereby accumulate as many official titles as possible. I occasionally received name cards with more than a dozen titles, printed on both the front and the back of the cards. Lao Wang, however, does not make any name cards. Given his rustic-and-proud attitude, he probably considers exchanging name cards a silly urbanite practice. But he might have to play this ritual game as his social contacts include more and more people carrying name cards in their wallets.

Both Chinese people and Western political scientists have observed the sociopolitical significance of official positions (*guanzhi*) in contemporary Chinese society. Cadres occupying a strategic official position are capable of exercising considerable personal power and reaping considerable personal gain because they have the power to allocate scarce resources and key benefits (e.g., an official approval to start an enterprise). The power that they derive from their office is called "position-power" (*zhiquan*), which they often abuse (*lanyong zhiquan*).[24] Corruption is ubiquitous and is simply part and parcel of the repertoire of a large number of Chinese officials' life-advancement strategies. The desire for the occupation of many strategic positions explains the tendency for power-seekers to scramble for more positions and thus more titles. Even when the positions are not strategic and power-conferring ones, the titles still "sound nice to the ear" (*haoting*) and reaffirm that one is somebody.

Lao Wang's numerous positions are of course outside of the local government bureaucracy. Even though they are different titles, they in fact all say the same thing: that Lao Wang is the boss in Longwanggou. Indeed, all eight positions hinge on the fact that he has been elected the temple boss. In Longwanggou as well as in Longwanggou's interactions with the outside, people pay little attention if any to Lao Wang's various titles; all they know or need to know is that Lao Wang is the boss and therefore only his say and his decisions matter.

Lao Wang's position as the temple boss not only gives him real power in Longwanggou but also lends him social "face" (*mianzi*) (see Jacobs 1980; Wilson 1994). It is as temple boss that he receives visitors in Longwanggou, and it is as temple boss that he makes political connections and alliances with people beyond Longwanggou. Especially after his bitter prison experience, Lao Wang makes sure that he has powerful figures in the political hierarchy to protect him from further harm from his enemies. Among his useful political allies are Lawyer Liu from Yulin City and Investigator Zhao of the Zhenchuan Township government. As we shall see in Chapter 11, Lao Wang is extremely concerned with legitimating and buttressing his power as temple boss.

"Local Emperor" or Feudal Patriarch? Or, Lao Wang's Leadership Style

Social critics of different eras had referred to local strongmen in agrarian Chinese society as "local emperors" (*tuhuangdi*), pointing to the formidable power they were able to yield within the confines of their turfs (see Madsen 1984). Because of his physical proximity, a local emperor was more feared by the people than the emperor himself, who was "as far away as the mountain was high" (*shan gao huangdi yuan*). A term of abuse and derision, "local emperors" stood for bad local powerful figures, who could be a landlord, a lineage patriarch, a guild boss, a commune Party secretary, a village headman, or a bandit. Was temple boss and village headman Lao Wang a local emperor?

Lao Wang could be perceived as a local emperor, especially in the eyes of his enemies. Once, a teacher at the Longwanggou Primary School complained to me about Lao Wang's authoritarian leadership style and characterized Lao Wang as a local emperor. But what I found most interesting in Longwanggou was the fact that Lao Wang was sometimes referred to not as a local emperor but as *the* emperor (*zhuwang*)! This usage came out of folk operas, which had a large repertoire of "historical" stories about emperors and ministers (the so-called "emperor-minister stories," *junchen gushi*). People around Longwanggou were very familiar with the opera stories because of extended exposure to folk opera performances at temple festivals. Typically, it was the temple officers and employees who used this kind of opera metaphor to comment on their relationship with Lao Wang (behind his back, of course). Just as in most emperor-minister stories, there were the emperor, good ministers (*zhongchen*) and bad ministers (*jianchen*) in Longwanggou. The good and bad ministers played out their conflicts, each vying for favor and support from the emperor. For example, Lao Chen, the divine message interpreter, had a long-standing problem with Congmir, the main temple hall guardian. According to Lao Chen, Congmir was very quick-witted but mean-spirited, and often complained to Lao Wang about this or that employee. If the emperor really listened to the bad minister, Lao Chen surmised, there would be a lot of trouble for everyone. Plus, the emperor lately had been pretty misty-headed (*hun*). "Is it not true," Lao Chen asked me rhetorically, "that ever since the ancient times good ministers have always been wronged?"

Lao Wang's leadership style can be characterized as charismatic, authoritarian, and paternalistic. As mentioned earlier, though taciturn and reserved with strangers and social superiors, Lao Wang was usually very talkative and lively when with temple officers, fellow villagers, or friends. Because of his wide worldly experience and practical wisdom, he was generally well respected by his peers and fellow villagers (except his enemies, of course). When he talked, other people listened. It also seemed that, compared to other Shaanbei people I knew, Lao Wang had command of a wider and more lively vocabulary of the Shaanbei colloquial. Perhaps it was because he scolded people more than others and thus had more opportunities to use curse words and other mean idiomatic expressions. It was always a pleasure for me to listen to, and watch, Lao Wang talk (not just when he was scolding someone). Most of the time when Lao Wang scolded people, whether to their face or behind their back, he had a legitimate reason to do so. For example, he always lost his temper whenever he learned that the temple chefs wasted food, or a temple officer did not carry out assigned duties according to his wishes. On these occasions he would go on and on and literally gave the person a lecture using quite mean and sometimes unforgiving words. At other times he would scold people because he was in a foul mood, or, I suspect, simply because he enjoyed it. I was told that because of his bad temper and mean mouth, Lao Wang had lost quite a number of old friends and allies. I once asked Lao Wang about his temper and he sighed, turned to me, and said: "They need the scolding occasionally. Otherwise they'll do what they like. You can't please (*taohao*) everyone. Things here [i.e., in Longwanggou] are so much trouble (*mafan si le*)!"

Some of the teachers at the Longwanggou Primary School were the severest critics of Lao Wang's leadership style. Most of the teachers, who were in their twenties, were recent graduates of regular high school, teachers' high school, or teachers' college (two year). Because of the age and power difference between them and Lao Wang, Lao Wang sometimes treated them like children and talked down to them. Even though Lao Wang was only the honorary principal of the school, he was the de facto decision maker, often rendering the actual principal a figurehead at best. After all, most of the teachers, including the principal, were employees of the temple and Lao Wang was the temple boss. "He runs the school and the whole place [i.e., Longwanggou] like a feudal patriarch (*fengjian jiazhang*); well, he's really like a local emperor (*tuhuangdi*)," one teacher complained to me. As members of the educated class, the teachers probably felt more acutely the humiliation of disrespect.

But my account would not do justice to Lao Wang if it showed only the authoritarian side of his leadership style. Despite his often-severe demeanor in front of his colleagues and employees, Lao Wang was also capable of relaxed and sometimes even jovial interactions with them. Even though he forbade drinking and gambling on temple grounds, occasionally he kept one eye closed and let his colleagues enjoy themselves, especially after major temple events such as the temple festival. He too joined in on these occasions and drank and played drinking games with others. As the temple boss and superior, Lao Wang also showed ample paternalistic care for his subordinates. For example, when temple employees got sick or when someone died in their families Lao Wang always showed concern. He was also very generous with monetary assistance, from his own pocket, to help employees with financial problems (e.g., funding a funeral). It seemed that many of the temple officers and employees got to know Lao Wang so well that they genuinely liked to work for him and thus tolerated with good humor his sporadic bursts of temper.

Genealogy of Power?

Scholars have generally agreed that elite status, once achieved, is usually maintained through many generations (e.g., Esherick and Rankin 1990). Does Lao Wang's case fit the pattern? Did he in any way "inherit" his elite status from his forebears? And how had he tried to pass his elite status down to his own children? Though Lao Wang once mentioned an ancestor who had won a local degree, the title could not have been a very high one because otherwise Lao Wang would have provided at least a few sketchy details about this ancestor's achievements. Lao Wang's grandfather could have been a yinyang master because one of Lao Wang's uncles was a yinyang master and the profession typically runs in families. In any case, the grandfather could not have been well off because Lao Wang's father's class background was that of a lower-middle peasant. Local elite status for the Wang family began with Lao Wang's father, who was a brigade-level cadre during the Maoist era. His was a typical army-man-turned-local-cadre case in the early years of PRC history, when the new regime desperately needed strong, competent, and most important of all, reliable and politically loyal local managers of society and implementers of new policies.[25]

Even though Lao Wang must have derived certain benefits from his father's local elite status during the early and crucial stages of his life, his subsequent upward mobility and the development of his own local elite status largely depended on his own personal efforts as well as on the changing times. It can be argued that had the Maoist pattern of local elite succession continued, and assuming that Lao Wang's father did not make grave political mistakes and retired honorably and that Lao Wang was reasonably competent, it would not be unthinkable that Lao Wang could "inherit" his father's sub-commune leadership position.[26] However, Lao Wang made a name for himself thanks to the combined effects of his talents and shrewdness, and, as the Chinese would say, "Heavenly timing, advantageous earthly forces, and people's enthusiastic support" (*tianshi, tili, renhe*).

Lao Wang's attempts to get closer to mainstream political mobility pathways indicate a desire to obtain the conventional advantages of becoming an elite in the Chinese tributary system: status (i.e., *zungui*-ness; see Wen 1991), political alliances, and protection, among other things (see Gates 1996). However, an aversion to being controlled and disciplined and perhaps a general dislike of the Communist Party had prevented him from seeking Party membership, and as a result his ability to move upward in the mainstream political hierarchy was highly circumscribed.[27] The story of Lao Wang is, however, an ongoing one. It remains to be seen how in the future he manages to maintain and augment his status and influence in Longwanggou and beyond. One thing is certain, though, that Lao Wang will continue to use Longwanggou as his power base, and his fortune, especially political fortune, will be to a considerable extent tied to the fate of the temple.

Considering how important Longwanggou was to Lao Wang's personal fortune, it is interesting to note that he did not prepare any of his three sons to help him manage temple affairs. Instead, he was satisfied to have sent them away from the countryside to the city and found them, or prepared them for, state jobs. This in itself was a great accomplishment on the part of Lao Wang. The eldest son used to work in the provincial forestry bureau in Xi'an but now works for the regional branch of the China Travel Agency (*zhonglüshe*), also in Xi'an. The second son was a secondary school teacher in Yulin City for a few years but later, through Lao Wang's connections (*huodong*),[28] he began working in the Yulin Prefectural Personnel Bureau (*diqu renshiju*). The third son first studied forestry in Xi'an but is now studying at a police academy in Nanjing, the switch having been motivated by considerations of future job security and, perhaps, by Lao Wang's hope to have at least one son in the crucial police-prosecutor-court sector (*gongjianfa*) to ensure he has adequate official protection against his enemies.[29] The third son would most likely be assigned a position in the police force in Yulin City—this again needing some pulling of strings—after graduation from the police academy.[30] Given what I know about the abilities of Lao Wang's three sons, I suspect that none of them would ever be able to supersede Lao Wang in their personal achievements.

Studies of the Local Elite and Lao Wang
as a Local Elite Type

So what kind of local elite is Lao Wang? How does my study of Lao Wang relate to local elite studies in anthropology and China studies? What does the story of Lao Wang tell us about the structure of local elite dominance and the process of local elite formation in post-Mao China? Is there a return to more traditional forms of the accumulation and expression of local authority and power?

To the extent that Lao Wang is a local elite, my study of him constitutes an elite study (as well as a study on social mobility). Yet he is not the kind of elite usually studied by scholars of China: literati-officials, Confucian scholars, the gentry, the religious elite (famous priests or monks), party-state leaders, and intellectuals (including writers and artists). These elite individuals typically wrote and/or were written about, thus leaving substantial amounts of documented evidence for historical reconstruction and interpretation.[31] In contrast, local elites like Lao Wang, not unlike the ordinary masses, easily disappear into the shadows of Chinese history, only occasionally cropping up as mere names on a broken temple stele or the tattered pages of a surviving guild ledger. But just like the ordinary masses, local elites like Lao Wang make history, though on spatial and temporal scales smaller than those of the "supralocal/translocal" elite.[32] Yet because of their sheer numerical weight, their role in determining the character of Chinese society—which comprises countless local societies—is extremely important.

Robert Hymes defines local elite as those "whose access to wealth, power, or prestige was, *in the local scheme of things*, especially privileged: whose control of material resources, hold over men's actions and decisions, or special place in the regard of their contemporaries, set them apart from . . . society as a whole and made them people to be reckoned with" (italics mine, Hymes 1986: 7). But how local is "local"? Most China scholars seem to agree, though rarely explicitly, that the "local" in "local elite" refers to elite of the prefectural level (sub-provincial) or below. In other words they are the elite of *zhou* (prefectures, or *diqu* in contemporary China), *xian* (counties), *zhen* or *xiang* (townships), and *cun* (villages). In addition, to qualify as the local elite they usually have to be *rooted* in a substantial way in the locale in which they exert influence. For example, a prefectural chief who is from another place and is only stationed in a certain prefecture would not qualify as a "local" elite, even though he might have considerable influence in local affairs as the official administrative chief and act as a patron of the local elite. On the other hand, the same prefectural chief is often considered a member of the local elite of his own native place, especially when he actively involves himself in various affairs happening back home or when he returns to his native locale after retirement.

Because of the importance of the local gentry in Chinese history, historians of China have tried to capture the lives of local elite in their works. Robert Hymes studied the elite of Fu Zhou of Jiangxi of the Song Dynasty (Hymes 1986). Timothy Brook looked at the relationship between the patronage of Buddhism and the formation of county-level gentry society in the late Ming period (Brook 1993). Esherick and Rankin's edited volume on the local elite (Esherick and Rankin 1990) not only included numerous case studies of the local elite of different historical periods but also attempted to delineate common patterns of dominance and elite formation across time and space. Evident in these works are the complementarity and the tension between lineage/group-centered and individual-centered case studies.

Studying the local elite of the past, historians have the advantage of access to documents of completed life histories and events and are thus able to trace continuity and change through long time spans, sometimes across hundreds of years (e.g., Meskill 1979). Anthropologists, on the other hand, have the advantage of actually knowing the local elite individuals they study and of having observed the latter in action, though often just over a year's duration (unless there are additional longitudinal studies). Anthropologists have had an interest in the study of the local elite because as they conduct their fieldwork in a local community (which is still the predominant form of fieldwork despite recent shifts toward studies on transnationalism and larger social processes), the local elite are the most visible and powerful figures in the local sociopolitical landscape (see Friedrick 1986). There are many diverse portraits of local elite individuals (e.g., spirit mediums, chiefs, village headmen, patriarchs) in the anthropological literature.[33] In China anthropology, my study of Lao Wang the temple boss has been preceded by other biographical accounts of popular religious leaders, such as Stephan Feuchtwang and Wang Mingming's detailed case studies of four temple leaders in Fujian and Taiwan (Feuchtwang and Wang 2001), Gary Seaman's study of a rural Taiwanese temple boss (Seaman 1978), Hill Gates's study of an urban

Taiwanese temple master and spirit medium (Gates 1987, 2000), among others (e.g., Jochim 1990; Jordan and Overmyer 1986). Studies on the local elite during the Maoist period were few and far between because relevant information was hard to come by; at that time, almost all Western social science research on China was conducted "off-shore," based on press materials and later émigré interviews. One prominent example of such studies was Richard Madsen's examination of issues of morality and power among the elite of a Guangdong farming village (Madsen 1984). Following the opening up of the People's Republic of China to Western social scientists, there have been a number of important portraits of the local elite in agrarian China. Among these portraits are found a Party secretary in a Fujian village near Xiamen (Huang 1998), another Party secretary in a Henan village (Seybolt 1996), yet another Party secretary in a Hebei village (Pickowicz 1994), a group of temple managers in a Gansu village (Jing 1996), the managers of a heavily corporatized Sichuan village (Ruf 1998), and so forth. My study of Lao Wang is situated in the above-mentioned literature on the local elite in anthropology and China studies. It is clear that local activists like Lao Wang would snatch any opportunity and resource to realize their personal goals. Had the avenue to becoming a temple boss not been open to him, Lao Wang would have probably succeeded in doing something else. But it seems that he has found his niche and calling.

We still need many more similar studies on the local elite before we can arrive at a general picture of the processes of reform-era local elite formation. It is hoped that Lao Wang's story has helped point to pertinent areas of inquiry concerning the local elite. One such area is the role of "tradition" in the emergence of the reform-era local elite, a topic that is integral to the present study. Prasenjit Duara has argued that, since the beginning of the 20th century, as the state penetrated deeper into local Chinese society, the traditional "cultural nexus of power" came to be replaced by mercenary, naked power devoid of culturally sanctioned legitimacy (Duara 1988a). Duara and other scholars also argue that, with the further penetration into agrarian local society by the Communist party-state, traditional modes of elite leadership were replaced by the socialist mode of poor-peasant class domination and revolutionary Party "commandeerism" (see Chan, Madsen, and Unger 1992; Friedman, Pickowicz, and Selden 1991; Madsen 1984; Siu 1989a). Has the reform period brought back the traditional cultural nexus of power? A number of schol-

ars have argued that the retreat of the socialist state from radical anti-traditionalism has created room for the return of more "traditional" forms
of authority and power (Anagnost 1994; Feuchtwang 1993; Feuchtwang
and Wang 2001; Jing 1996, 2002; Luo 1997; Wang 1996). The story of
Lao Wang to a considerable extent supports this line of argument.[34] But
the agrarian political landscapes of the 1980s and 1990s are a far cry
from those of the Republican and late imperial periods. Can Lao Wang
really resemble a temple boss from two hundred years ago? Or, can Lao
Wang be *that* different from a temple boss from two hundred years ago?
The challenge for the social scientist is of course to see the underlying
continuity below the surface changes, and to spot real transformations
below the surface constancy.

  Another pertinent area of inquiry opened up by Lao Wang's story is
the importance of "the locale" as the power base of the local elite. Because of the fame and influence Lao Wang had garnered over the years as
the temple boss, he became a prominent figure, a "somebody" in the local society of Zhenchuan Township. However, he did not play an active
role in the politics of "downtown" Zhenchuan (referred to locally as
gaili, i.e., "in the street"), perhaps because of his status as a recent resident of the town. Though a member of the association for Zhenchuan
wholesale merchants, he was not an officer and kept himself away from
the affairs of the association. In fact, even though he was widely known
among people in Zhenchuan and even Shaanbei people outside of
Zhenchuan, his real sphere of influence was more or less confined to
Longwanggou and his native village Hongliutan. His political ambitions
might take him beyond Longwanggou, but because of his reliance on
Longwanggou as his power base, Lao Wang would remain a village- or
township-level local elite. Other studies have also shown that the local
elite must rely on local resources (e.g., village enterprises, community
temples, local supporters) as their basis of power. Only very few village-
level elite can ever rise to become members of the trans-local national
elite. Even as some local elite do achieve national fame and prominent
positions in "the Center" (e.g., Daqiuzhuang Yu Zuomin's rise to "the
Center" as a representative to the *national* People's Consultative Conference; see Gilley 2001 and Lin and Chen 1999), they have done so because
of their achievements in their particular locales.

  To conclude, I want to draw the reader's attention to the double allu-
sion of the epigraph (i.e., the Shen Tzu quote) that opened this chapter.
Just as the Black Dragon King depends on human worshipers to "make

manifest his efficacy," Lao Wang too depends on his colleagues, supporters, and "face-givers" to continue to be the temple boss. Without the clouds and mists to ride on, the flying dragon and the *t'eng* [i.e., leaping] snake would be the same as "the earthworm and the large-winged black ant." Without his support base in Longwanggou, Lao Wang perhaps would indeed have been a "mere peasant."

CHAPTER TEN

Longwanggou and Agrarian
Political Culture

The revival of popular religion in Shaanbei is not merely a matter of "the religious," whatever that may mean. Because of the socially embedded nature of popular religion, its rise in visibility is a sign of radical changes in the larger sociopolitical environment. And on the other hand, popular religious activities themselves are also factors in bringing about these changes. For example, the channeling of large sums of money into a "ritual economy" (Yang 2000) makes temples sites of contestations of local political factions. The inherently legally ambiguous status of popular religious activities also lends itself to opportunistic charges that the activities constitute revivals of "feudal superstition." The rise of temple-connected local elites might also be perceived as posing a threat to grassroots-level political control by the party-state. And the kind of red-hot sociality realized by popular religious activities such as temple festivals might harbor political potential antithetical to the state's wishes. This chapter and the next deal with the power dynamics aspects of the revival of popular religion in Shaanbei. In this chapter I analyze the nature of politics in Longwanggou and how it articulates with its local milieu. My purpose is to show how temple politics reflects and in turn impacts the larger sociopolitical domain.

The Articulation of Temple Politics and Village Politics

Because most popular religious temples are village collective properties and are run by ordinary villagers, the politics within the temple is normally also part of the politics within the village.[1] However, some temples

become more autonomous over time and become increasingly disarticu-
lated from the villages to which they originally belonged. Longwanggou
is such an example. Because it is a temple corporation run by representatives from nine villages, the politics within the temple straddles a social
space wider than a single village. Even though Longwanggou is physically
part of Hongliutan Village, temple affairs were at least theoretically separate from Hongliutan village affairs because of the temple's supposed
autonomy. In an important sense, Longwanggou's autonomy was even
confirmed legally by the establishment of the Longwanggou Daoist
Shrine Management Committee in 1998 (more on this in Chapter 11).
Yet a complete disarticulation of temple and village affairs has never been
achieved, and probably never will be achieved. Hongliutan villagers will
always view the temple as their own resource and resist any attempt on
the part of the temple to secede from the village. A complete secession is
not beyond one's imagination. For example, the Yulin City government
could decide one day that Longwanggou ought to be run by professional
Daoist priests together with the county tourist bureau, and that the entire
Longwanggou property would have to be handed over to the government
with some minimal compensation. Even though the scenario sounds
highly improbable, it is still within the realm of the possible; it would
only take another political campaign or simply some local state administrative fiat.

When I described the above scenario to temple boss Lao Wang, he
flatly rejected the possibility and said: "They [i.e., the officials] don't have
the guts to do that [i.e., to take over the temple from the village]. They
are too afraid of Heilongdawang to meddle with (*peng*, literally 'to
touch') the temple. You see, they are precious people (*guiren*), and their
lives are more valuable than those of ordinary people. They are more
afraid of Heilongdawang than anyone. Even though the high officials
don't come to the temple to worship because they are afraid that people
would know, they secretly send their subordinates or relatives to bring
money to Heilongdawang. Otherwise, where do you think some of the
big-sum donations come from? Besides, now we [i.e., the temple] have
the Hilly Land Arboretum, and the land belongs to the [village] collective. It's not that simple [for the government to take over the temple]."
Perhaps Lao Wang's evaluation of the situation was well-founded, but it
should at least be assumed that Hongliutan villagers and their leaders will
not let go of the temple to outsiders without a fight.

Neither completely embedded in village politics nor completely dissociated from it, temple affairs at Longwanggou articulate with Hongliutan village affairs (and those of the other eight participating villages) through what might be called the *temple/village political nexus*. Because the temple boss and most of the temple officers come from Hongliutan, it has the strongest engagement with the temple. Lao Wang occupied the most crucial nodal point in the nexus because he was at once the temple boss and the village head. Another clear sign of how closely Hongliutan intertwined with the temple was the fact that the Hongliutan village office was actually situated in the so-called conference room (*huiyishi*) in the temple building compound (right above my dormitory room).[2]

For many years there had been two factions that divided Hongliutan, as I have alluded to in earlier chapters. These factions coalesced along lines of personal grudges, multigenerational conflicts between households, and perceived political and economic stakes in the power field. Gradually village factionalism in Hongliutan solidified and turned into a protracted fight between two main blocs: one under Lao Wang and the other under a certain Zhang Xuezhi. These factions did not have definite political platforms. The main goal of the fight was to prevent the other faction from achieving their goals. Lawsuits became more frequent, and tension continued to mount as more and more villagers became involved in the fight. Secret meetings were held now and then, and intrigues were in the air all the time.

To a considerable degree the temple precipitated more factional conflicts because of the fight over the control of the temple and its considerable income, and the temple provided an additional site in which the two sides fought each other out. Anthropologists usually take delight in natives' conflicts because from observing conflicts and their resolution (or non-resolution for that matter) we can peep into not only the natives' political world and legal system but also their "moral ontology," that is, how they distinguish right from wrong and how they understand the nature of their world, especially relating to causation and liability (Just 2001).[3] Below are some scenes of conflicts I observed while living in Longwanggou. Besides giving us a flavor of village politics, these stories of conflict also reveal the penetration of law (such as lawsuits and imprisonments) and formal financial institutions (such as state-owned banks) into the lives of Shaanbei peasants.

Village Factionalism and Lawsuits

It was not too long after I had entered the world of Longwanggou that I realized the existence of temple boss Lao Wang's enemies. The new school building lay half-finished on the edge of Hongliutan Village. When I asked the village storekeeper when the Longwanggou Primary School could move down from the temple dormitory building to its new building he told me that he did not know. As the Longwanggou Primary School is their village school I was surprised that he did not know about something so important. Sensing my surprise, he immediately explained, "Some people in the village have disagreements with Wang Kehua and they are not allowing him to finish the building." He used the expression "having disagreements" (*naoyijian*), which I knew was a standard euphemism for some serious problems. My initial hunch was correct. The people who had "disagreements" with Lao Wang were actually suing him for, possibly among other things, illegal appropriation of village arable land for building the school. Last time, back in 1990, they had actually managed to put Lao Wang in jail for mishandling government funding for the village water-supply works, as I mentioned in the last chapter. Lao Wang was in jail for four months before the court was convinced by Lao Wang's lawyer to reverse the verdict and release him.[4]

The story I heard from various sources went like this: In 1990 Hongliutan was granted a provincial governmental subsidy to build a water-supply network for both people and domestic animals. When the government funds came, however, it was right during village election time, and there were no suitable financial personnel to keep the money. It could not be put in the Heilongdawang Temple account because of possible confusion. After consulting with the branch director of the Zhenchuan Town Credit Union (*xinyongshe*), Lao Wang decided to open a bank account as the chair of the temple association and save the money under his name. This was somehow made known to Lao Wang's enemies. Arguing that according to the law public subsidy funds must not be in private accounts for more than a week, they sued Lao Wang for embezzlement of public funds. Lao Wang was convicted and put in jail in Yulin City in November of 1990. Had it not been for the efforts of a very capable lawyer and the petitions of his colleagues and co-villagers he would have stayed in jail for many years.[5] Ever since this incident Lao Wang had become more mistrustful and was always on the alert so as to detect possible trouble.

One day in the spring of 1998, Lao Wang came to have brunch at the temple. The school teachers and a few temple officers were present. Lao Wang started berating the "bad people" (*erren*), i.e., his enemies, again, and asked all of a sudden if it was true that Mandur, the temple driver, was involved with a group of villagers filing a new lawsuit against him and the temple for taking up farmland to build the new school. He said he had heard it from someone. I was shocked at his paranoia and lack of trust in one of his most loyal and able subordinates. Other people all said it must have been a vicious rumor.

That night I visited Mandur's home in Batawan. While having dinner, Mandur, his wife, his father, and I talked about this rumor. Mandur, always a taciturn person, looked grave and contemplative and just chain-smoked. Mandur's father, a former village Party secretary and a well-respected old man, sighed at Lao Wang's lack of sagacity. Mandur's wife broke out into a torrent of comments: "That boss of yours is no boss at all! You work so hard for him and are so loyal to him but now he thinks you are backstabbing him. What kind of joke is that? If he got rid of you it would be like he was chopping off his own right arm." Now talking to me, she said, "We Batawan people are the most loyal supporters of Wang Kehua. You can't find people in our village who want to screw Wang Kehua over. Least of all Mandur! You know Mandur, (he is) so guileless and reliable. Wang Kehua is being such a bully (*qifu ren*)!"

Batawan people were all grateful to Lao Wang because, among other things, Lao Wang agreed to let Batawan children go to the temple primary school, thus raising the standard of Batawan children's education tremendously. Batawan people regularly volunteered to help out at the temple whenever the need arose. Besides Mandur, another villager from Batawan was also an important temple employee: Fourth Uncle (one of Mandur's uncles) who was one of the two cooks for the temple canteen. The rumor about Mandur's involvement in the lawsuit against Lao Wang was quickly dispelled, but the vicious village factionalism continued.

Conflicts over Housing Plots

One afternoon in late summer of 1997, I was awakened from my afternoon nap by the noise of a big commotion outside. I got up, went outside, and saw a small group of about a dozen or so people outside the temple offices (right next to my dorm room) having a heated argument. Among them were a few temple officers including Lao Wang, Hongliutan villagers, and three well-dressed city folk. At that time I already knew many of the villagers and all of the temple officers, so I just squatted down in the raised corridor next to the crowd and listened in. From people's arguments and from occasional probing, I pieced together a picture of the problem at issue.

As Hongliutan's population increased, many more people needed to build new houses. However, there was a limited amount of land for housing. The entire village had moved from the foothills down to the flatland about fifteen years before, so building more houses meant taking more flatland, i.e., good agricultural land. To make things more difficult, a new national Land Law (*tudifa*) had just been promulgated that year to strictly limit the turning of agricultural land into nonagricultural land (e.g., for building houses). Along major roads all over Shaanbei, one could see half-built houses left unfinished because the builders feared that their new houses, built on flat, good farmland would be proclaimed illegal and demolished.

Earlier that year, before the new Land Law was proclaimed, twenty-one Hongliutan families—almost a quarter of all the families—petitioned to the village council to build more houses, but many other villagers were against the plan, arguing that Hongliutan was already suffering from a scarcity of farmland. Conveniently, a large piece of flatland had become available the year before. There was a village orchard of apple trees, occupying a former graveyard. The orchard had been contracted to a small group of villagers. Though the orchard business was turning a profit, fights broke out between the partners over alleged private profiteering and uneven distribution of revenue. Lawsuits followed and locked some people into an ongoing bitter exchange of accusations and counteraccusations.

Then all of a sudden the apple trees began to die. No one knew why, but rumors had it that somebody had poisoned the trees. Since the orchard was no longer profitable the village hired someone to bulldoze all the apple trees. The twenty-one families wanted the now-empty plot to build their new houses on, while some other villagers wanted the plot to be divided equally among all the households for farming. In either case, however, there was the problem of clearing out some old graves underneath. What twisted the story more was the fact that the graves did not belong to any of the Hongliutan families; they belonged to some Chenjiapo families. It turned out that during the commune era Hongliutan had taken this piece of land from Chenjiapo. Because the graves belonged to former landlord families no one cared to relocate the graves, not even the families concerned, for fear of official reproach.

Representatives of the twenty-one families gathered that day at the temple office to discuss strategies to thwart any attempts by their opponents to claim the plot. They were going to help the Chenjiapo families open the graves and dig up the bones to be relocated somewhere in the hills. There is a strong cultural taboo against touching other people's ancestors' bones, which is considered very polluting, so why would they want to do it? This turned out to be part of a clever plan because then they could say to their opponents: Look, we went down there and dug up other people's ancestors' bones, so the plot is ours; You want part of the plot? Okay! How much are you going to pay me for having cleared the plot up? For having touched other people's ancestors' bones?

Another strategy they used was to put down deposits at the local bank for building the houses. That is why there were a few well-dressed urban folk at the meeting. They were clerks from the bank in the nearby town of Mizhi, who had come to collect these deposits. Each of the twenty-one families had to put down six thousand yuan as a deposit, partly to demonstrate their resolve to build the houses and partly to cement an alliance among the house-builders: no one was to take their deposit back until all twenty-one families got to build their houses. The bank had no role in financing their housing project; its clerks were there only to collect and safeguard the deposits.

A couple of weeks after the debate in front of the temple office, I went down to the old orchard site. Now all the apple trees were long gone, and a bulldozer was plowing up and down at one corner of the site. A village group meeting had just been held next to the site, where villagers of one of the four groups of Hongliutan Village were distributing the rent they received from the temple for the land they gave up for the reforestation project. Many of the villagers stayed behind and gathered around the bulldozing site and started debating about the plot. Many of Lao Wang's enemy faction villagers were in this group, and some of them were saying that they would just go ahead and claim their fair share of the plot. One middle-aged man challenged the house-builders: "I am going to plant some sorghum seeds next week on MY piece of land right here; I'll see who would dare to plow them up!"

Meanwhile, the house-building villagers were helping the Chenjiapo families to dig up their ancestors' bones from the opened-up graves. According to Shaanbei burial custom, dead people are buried at least nine feet below the surface of the earth. Since the aboveground markers of the graves had all been removed a long time ago, the villagers had to rely on the bulldozer to scrape off layers of dirt before they could find out where the graves were. Altogether seven graves were found. Most of them were paired burials, with couples buried together in one grave. One grave had only one coffin, which indicated that the dead person's family was probably too poor to provide a wife for him, or even a spirit spouse (i.e., a woman's body to bury with his). Some of the unearthed coffin pieces were quite elaborate and ornate, and two graves were lined with cutstones, i.e. a mini cut-stone burial yao.

From the unearthed burial tiles and bricks the villagers could tell when the dead people had been buried. When they could be certain of the identity of the dead, the related Chenjiapo family members crawled into the graves and picked up the bones from the crumbling wooden pieces of the coffins. When no Chenjiapo villager came to claim them, the Hongliutan house-builders helped gather the bones. These bones were dusted off and arranged in wooden burial boxes much smaller than the standard coffin, and then they would be reburied according to the dictates of the yinyang master on auspicious dates at auspicious sites. The struggle over the old orchard plot dragged on for a long time. It was still not resolved by the time I left Longwanggou at the end of the summer in 1998.

Did Lao Wang Commit Sorcery?

What makes a legitimate leader? How much dissent among the constituency makes a leader illegitimate? Did the existence of rivals in his village and in Longwanggou make Lao Wang an illegitimate temple boss? How did Lao Wang's enemies challenge him? What kinds of counter-legitimation maneuvers did they engage in to discredit and shame him? We have already seen how Lao Wang's enemies launched one legal attack after another in their attempt to dislodge him from power. But they were attacking through proper, official institutional channels (i.e., the court). Here I will present an example of counter-legitimation assault that was done through a highly unusual, informal idiom: written public denunciation. Specifically, it is a vengeful diatribe against Lao Wang and a public exposé of his alleged sorcerous ritual against his enemies, penned by Xu Wensheng, one of Lao Wang's former colleagues in the temple association.

Xu Wensheng, or Wer, as people called him, was about 60 years old. I first met Wer in the divination slips room during the first months of my fieldwork. Maybe because he looked sullen or maybe because I was busy asking other people questions, we did not talk. Later, I saw him on a couple of occasions, when he hobbled around in front of the zhengdian (main temple hall) with his long walking staff, angrily shouting strings of unintelligible words. I had seen a few crazy people come to Longwanggou, especially during the temple festivals, so I did not pay him too much attention. Later I pieced together the story about Wer from different sources.

Wer was not a Hongliutan villager. He was from Heshang ("on the river") Village, one of the nine villages that contributed to the rebuilding and the running of Longwanggou. He was one of many villagers who helped Lao Wang. A few years earlier Wer had had a stroke and became half-paralyzed. Apparently he had soon realized that it might have been caused by the fact that he had helped Lao Wang produce a petition (what he called "a curse," more properly called a ritual "indictment"; see Katz 2004) to Heilongdawang in 1989. He subsequently asked Lao Wang for compensation but only received a small amount of "charity money." Feeling that he had been wronged and betrayed by Lao Wang, he came to Longwanggou as often as he could to shout out his grievances in front of the temple. But because of his partial paralysis, he had a serious speech impediment and could not make himself understood. The shouting to no avail, he launched an even more public campaign against Lao Wang by posting many copies of his denunciation on the streets of nearby towns. The text was written by Wer himself in black ink on large sheets of white paper, reminiscent of the big character posters of the Maoist era. Below I present the text in whole:

> A "Death Notice" (*fugao*) for the Masses:
>
> The ex-convict Wang Kehua sits in the Dragon Valley. He is famous in the region and has his gang in the county. Everyone knows about his fame, and he himself knows that. He uses the arboretum to protect the god, the god to protect himself, and the money to protect his power. He has been in control of the temple for eighteen years. To enrich himself he has done so many things. He has a corrupt morality. He has done rotten and criminal deeds to oppress the masses and to spoil the Party and the government. He had wanted to kill some people to silence them at the Palace of the Dragon King. I am now posting this death notice to tell everybody about it.
>
> You have always done bad things. In 1958, who was it that smashed one of Black Dragon's big bells to sell at the Zhenchuan Provisions Co-operative for living expenses? Who was it that drove a car on the highway like a bully and said, "I can run you over and thirty or forty thousand yuan would be enough to compensate"? All right, do you make sense just because you are a descendant of a military officer? You talk bullshit! You do things that violate the country's laws. Incense temple and arboretum? What will humans depend on for food? Land cannot be used whichever way one likes. What is a proper matter? What is other people's business? At the National People's Congress in 1997, the spirit of President Jiang's talk repeatedly emphasized family planning, the control of the growth of the population, and other big matters such as wrongful use of land because people depend on it for livelihood. And

you! You use money to buy fame! That arboretum of yours? There are too many people and too little land in Hongliutan. How much flat land and hilly land per head? Turning huge pieces of good farmland into forestry land for the god? You think about it yourself!

You treat the Marquis of Efficacious Response like a small kid and a rubber ball, kicking it out and then kicking it back. You have enriched yourself in the process. You asked through divination to buy back a piece of temple property at two hundred and one thousand yuan [sic]. Then you sold it? You yourself bought it at the original price. In the process the temple didn't even get back the original cost. And the temple paid for the mortgage loan. How did all these money transactions happen? Who could know? We invite Mr. Wang to return the property to the temple's care as soon as possible, unconditionally and without cost. This way it will meet the masses' approval. Please do not commit crime upon crimes!

You are in a godly mountain and blessed land. You have your back on the gold mountain of the Marquis of Efficacious Response and you have grabbed a million yuan and more. You are a fierce wolf in the hills and woods, opening your bloody mouth wide whenever you see money! The in-coming and outgoing accounts were not balanced. The masses were angry and it had caused turmoil in the temple. But you used oppressive measures to protect yourself and to keep on enriching yourself. To people outside you used renminbi to buy their hearts and souls; to the people inside you burned pieces of curse at the dragon palace. In the 21 pieces of curses you had included 12 village Party members, cadres, and ordinary villagers. They were Chen Shengguang, Zhang Xuezhi, Zhang Guohua, Zhang Guojun, Li Shiyun, Chen Shengfa, Chen Guodong, Shen Shiying, Zhang Taichuan, Zhang Baozhou, Gao Zhonggang, Ren Fuguang. These comrades had supported and contributed a great deal of effort to the rebuilding of the temple but they were all cursed by Wang Kehua's poisonous hands through the 21 pieces of curses burnt at the dragon palace.[6] To enrich himself, he not only did not repay the debt of gratitude to these people but instead treated them like enemies. Such is the criminal evidence of a heartless person and poisonous hand, Wang Kehua.

The person who wrote the curses for him was Mr. Zhao Suoliang of the Third Secondary School of Mizhi. He was rewarded with 500 yuan. It was me who brought back the payment receipt to Wang Kehua. He was also the principal schemer behind writing the material to sue the village cadres in Hongliutan Village. He is an expert in things literary, and he writes very well. He is now 74 years old and has already retired. He used to live in the Mizhi Secondary School.

The water is clear and one can see the fish play; better to use long fishing thread to catch the big fish. It was all because of that piece of paper you gave me back then that destroyed me. Now all I can do is to let you know: you blast the bridge after having crossed the river! Heartless man. Your home is full of riches and your power is great; You are one rung higher than everybody else; You have a lot of money and a lot of power; Your legs are long and your roads are wide; For you heaven is high and the earth thick; There is no one in your eyes: "I am number one under heaven!" You oppress and bully the masses; You walk around everywhere like a hooligan; You murdered people to silence them at the dragon palace all for your own reign!

Wang Kehua, it was because of you asking me to burn the 21 pieces of curses at the dragon palace that destroyed me. Now I am just a breath more than a dead person; I can't take care of myself; I have a mouth but have no meal; I have things to say but nowhere to say them; there are roads but I have no legs to walk them; there are not even pennies in my hands; my household is poor and I am powerless; I am not able to finish preparing for my own af-ter-death matters; I thus caused harm to both my ancestors and my descen-dants and this makes me very anxious. My heart has been swamped by blood and tears. I came to ask you for a little bit of money to live on but you called me a half-dead handicap and told me to go die. You not only gave me no money but you told the police and the court to suppress me and to protect you. In 1997 I made a case at the court to sue you but nothing came of it even in 1998. Was it even filed? Because you have a lot of money the court was biased toward you. They even said to me: "What? You want to wrestle with Wang Kehua?" Yes! Of course I will wrestle with him until the end, even risk-ing my life! Mr. Wang Kehua is not afraid of me? I am not afraid of anything either, after having been made into a half-dead, dragging-along useless man. Now I am going to list the reasons behind asking you for money:

1. To live in society one has to have human reason and sense and worldly ways. Each family has its rules and each country its laws. The police and the court are not supposed to be superstitious, but they should at least have con-science. They should examine the nature of burning curses at the dragon palace! They should examine its consequences! You must talk about your rul-ing over the temple for 18 years. Otherwise who would talk about it?

2. When you asked me to burn the curses at the dragon palace, you told me: "As long as I am at the temple you will be fine. Your son is already getting big but you have no housing for him to get married? When the time comes it will only take me, Wang Kehua, one word to lift you up." Now the time has come. Pay me the salary you had promised me!

3. How much money did you, Wang Kehua, give Ren Fuguang during his illness? And how much did you give after he died? What are the differences be-tween me and Ren Fuguang? It's just that he was an official of the People's Government and I am a peasant. Based on what rationales had you given Ren Fuguang so much money? Please answer!

4. Mr. Wang Kehua, you had said that you would not use a person for free, that you would pay him money. How would you pay for this one? Let's pay me according to your high-standard, specialty-technical-work salary to balance this account.

Postscript: Mr. Wang Kehua, this is too harsh on you? Don't say that I am nasty! The rock overhang is three feet high and you are a five-foot tall man; I'd like to see how you, Mr. Wang, can pass without bending your back? Ever since the beginning of the world and the founding of the country, among the famous people in ancient and modern times, which "heartless man" has ever lived on? I am not being unreasonable. I talk according to human reason and worldly ways. I use reason to convince people and to risk my life to settle accounts with you! I know that you are tough [S. *pi'ning*, literally meaning "skin is hard"], with helpers and protection from outside and the formidable money of the Marquis of Efficacious Response. But I am not scared of you. I have already predicted that you are just like early morning dews.

If there were incorrect things in what I have said I'd let my head be chopped off for everyone to see!

Xu Wensheng
20th April, 1998
Written by self, with heart swamped with blood and tears.

Wer's poster was a strongly worded, heartrending plea for compensation and justice. The imagery of the half-paralyzed and penniless Wer against the powerful Lao Wang must have provoked sympathy from the readers of the poster. He accused Lao Wang of being a hypocrite (selling temple property in 1958 and later becoming the temple boss) and bully, of subjecting him to a dangerous ritual action (i.e., the "curse"), betraying him after having used him, using the temple to enrich himself, taking valuable agricultural land for temple construction and reforestation, bribing officials, and most damning of all, ritually "cursing" twelve co-villagers at the temple, which could be interpreted as committing sorcery.

Apparently written under oath ("… my head be chopped off for everyone to see!"), the accusations were meant to be true, despite the emotionally charged rhetorical excesses in the text. I did not probe into the details of all the accusations. However, a Batawan villager did explain to me the real estate purchase intrigue in Wer's text. A piece of land in Zhenchuan Town used to be temple property before it was expropriated during the Land Reform. In the early years of the temple's revival, the temple association bought back this piece of land at a cheap price. Much later, Lao Wang decided that the temple should sell this land. With the temple association's consent, he bought the land himself at the original price, which was much lower than its market value. The Batawan villager felt even though Lao Wang's action in this matter was highly irregular and disputable, he nevertheless deserved to derive some benefit from running the temple. "After all, Lao Wang invested a lot of his own money in the temple in the beginning." Recall also that in the eighteen years of being the temple boss Lao Wang had not received any salary, unlike the other temple officers. Here we are in the gray area of an informal economy where the degree of appropriateness and legitimacy of financial transactions is judged by folk understandings of the personal character of the individuals involved and the nature and circumstance of their actions. Even though Wer himself participated in producing the "curse" (he brought back the written "curses" from Mr. Zhao to Lao Wang and assisted Lao Wang to burn them), he alerted the authorities, i.e., the court and the police, to Lao Wang's alleged sorcery and hoped that they would arrest him and punish him for engaging in dark, superstitious activities. However, the local state agents did not take any action against Lao Wang, which further depressed Wer. The point of including this text here is to highlight the counter-legitimation challenges Lao Wang constantly had to face, and the diverse modes of political and moral contestation that are available in agrarian political culture. In Chapter 11, I will look at examples of Lao Wang's legitimation strategies in response to the pressures from his rivals and detractors.

〜

No longer a mere village temple, the Black Dragon King Temple had entered a much larger social and political field following its revival and growth into the Longwanggou Complex. The articulation of temple politics and village politics has also drawn in forces from beyond the temple and the village, for example, agencies of the local state (the Public Security Bureau, the local court, the bank, the Religious Affairs Bureau, the Land Bureau, the Education Office, etc.). I will explore the politics of legitimation involving the temple and the temple boss in the next chapter.

Appendix to Chapter 10

Lao Wang's Petition to Heilongdawang

Below is the full text of the petition Lao Wang allegedly burned in 1989 to implore Heilongdawang to help him stop his enemies from obstructing temple activities. The format of the petition is similar to Daoist petitions or memorials (*biao* or *shu*) (see Lagerwey 1987; Schipper 1974) or even an exorcist mantra. The text was reproduced by Wer as proof that Lao Wang had cursed his co-villagers.

> Heilongdawang:
> I am here burning this piece of respectful petition.
> Your excellency the Marquis of Efficacious Response Black Dragon of Longwanggou: Throughout the dynasties and over the generations people have been passing down this saying about you: As you come out of the dragon

palace the wind blows gently and the rain comes at the right time; As you go back hiding in the ocean the country and the people enjoy peace and prosperity. You have received the worship and incense of the masses and your formidable name has been spread everywhere under heaven.

During the Qing Dynasty, the Manchu government was corrupt and impotent. Then the foreigners invaded the central heartland. The people suffered in all kinds of ways. They had nothing to put on their bodies and nothing to put in their mouths. There was no way that they could survive. But while bones of people frozen to death lay about on the streets, the Manchu Qing government officials had heaps of meat and wine rotting in front of their doors. At this moment of extreme difficulty for the people, the Black Dragon stepped on the cloud and flew into the sky. He gathered a black cloud and made a shower of cold rain, which beat the foreigners dead in the cow puddles. Aiya! The efficacious god in heaven and under the earth, you showed your power and our country's army won the battle. They gathered up and went back to the capital, and the general reported to the emperor so as to pay back the divine favor. At night the Black Dragon appeared in the general's dream to tell him that it was the Black Dragon of Longwanggou of Zhenchuan Fort that had offered divine assistance. The general hurriedly reported the dream to the emperor. Emperor Kangxi then ordered that the Black Dragon be sent a dragon gown with a golden border to be worn in the dragon palace, as well as half a set of processional insignias to attend him on the left and the right. The Black Dragon of Longwanggou was granted the official title of the Marquis of Efficacious Response Who Protects the Western Mountain. Subsequently your formidable name has been spread wide and far.

But later on, due to the way things were going, the temple of the Marquis of Efficacious Response was completely destroyed. Nothing remained except a decrepit valley and heaps of disorderly rocks. No one came to burn incense anymore, and no one came to worship you anymore. Then there was a village youth from Hongliutan called Wang Kehua who was courageous, loyal, and honest. He assumed the leadership to revive the temple. He rose up early and slept late; he was not afraid of the sun or the rain. He weathered through those bitter and hard days and finally he succeeded in rebuilding the temple for you, even more splendid than before.

But there was a band of people who came to the temple to stir up trouble, causing the construction to stop and preventing the organization of the temple festival. They were: Chen Shengguang, Zhang Xuezhi, Zhang Guohua, Zhang Guojun, Li Shiyun, Chen Shengfa, Chen Guodong, Shen Shiying, Zhang Taichuan, Zhang Baozhou, Gao Zhonggang, Ren Fuguang.

The Marquis of Efficacious Response, unless you show your divine power, your temple festival cannot be organized and the construction will stay interrupted. I, your disciple, come here to burn this respectful petition. Show your divine power! Show your divine power! Show often your divine power! Your disciple Wang Kehua, I worship your excellency. Please let the temple festival be carried out as usual and the construction of your temple be resumed so that we can successfully finish rebuilding your beautiful domicile.

I wish that the Marquis of Efficacious Response your excellency's temple festival will be full of luck and blessings. Let all the masses come burn incense and worship you.

Your disciple Wang Kehua wrote the above respectfully. I kowtow to you respectfully.

CHAPTER ELEVEN

The Local State and
the Politics of Legitimation

The reform-era socialist state is willing to open up to popular religion a space that had been closed off in the past. This space seems to be one of the current regime's "zone(s) of indifference" (Tang Tsou's phrase, quoted in Shue 1995: 93), as the state is embroiled in other difficulties, such as the problems of money-losing state enterprises, massive de-employment of their employees (*xiagang*), birth control, the "Taiwan Question," and the like. However, the state still *can* and sometimes does, if it so chooses, exert brute force over popular religion, if only to periodically "make its power visible" (Anagnost 1994: 244). Anagnost calls these sporadic bursts of crackdowns on popular religion (or other "vices" such as prostitution, corruption, smuggling, piracy, crimes) "fetishized demonstrations of political efficacy" (ibid.). The recent crackdown on Falungong (Dharma Wheel Practice), Zhonggong (abbreviation of Chinese Divine Practice), and other qigong sects shows clearly how relentless the party-state can be if it chooses to parade its power.

Despite its immense popularity, popular religion carries with it an aura of illegality and illegitimacy, in Shaanbei as in other parts of China. Not properly Daoist or Buddhist, which are among the officially recognized religions (the other three are Protestantism, Catholicism, and Islam), popular religion consists of theoretically illegal, superstitious activities. All the village compacts (*cunmin gongyue*) I had seen in Shaanbei stated explicitly that villagers should not engage in such superstitious activities as deity worship, consulting spirit mediums or fortune tellers, and so on. Public Security Bureau (i.e., police) officers told me that they are supposed to crack down on superstitious activities just as they would on gambling, prostitution, drug trafficking, and crime. In reality, however, the police almost never crack down on popular religion; in fact, ironically, they are often invited by the temple association to attend the temple festivals and help maintain order and direct traffic. Besides the local police, many other agencies and members of the local state insinuate themselves into the burgeoning agrarian public sphere for control and spoils. The Religious Affairs Bureau is the most prominent local state actor in registering and regulating temples and religious activities.

How have Shaanbei people managed to maintain such high visibility for their illegal, popular religious activities without incurring the wrath of the party-state, which is no less atheistic today than during the high socialist era? How do temple bosses convince the authorities that they are legitimate leaders of the village communities and pose no threat to the regime or the officially sanctioned village leadership structure (i.e., the village committee as well as the Communist Party committee)? This chapter attempts to address these questions of legality and legitimacy through analysis of the case of Longwanggou and temple boss Lao Wang. I argue that the revival of popular religion in China should not be seen simply as the retreat of the state or the resistance of local communities against the state. Rather, both "state" and "local community" as categories need to be unpacked. In Chapter 9, I attempted to address the rise of local elites related to popular religion, using the portrait of Lao Wang as a case study. In this chapter I concentrate on looking at the actions of the local state and the frequent mutual accommodation, negotiation, and collusion of interests between the local state and popular religion. In particular, I analyze the ways in which Longwanggou and Lao Wang captured local state agencies' support and legitimation and harnessed translocal forces, the "powerful outside," to consolidate power and efficacy. To do so I present two examples of "legitimation rituals" at Longwanggou.

The first example of Lao Wang's legitimation maneuvers is the production of a stele inscription commemorating the tree-planting events co-organized by Longwanggou and Friends of Nature, a cosmopolitan nongovernmental environmentalist group from Beijing. I, the visiting anthropologist, was mobilized to help write the text of the inscription. The second example involves the ritual conferring and hanging of an organizational plaque and a speech Lao Wang made on that occasion: the plaque-hanging ceremony marking the founding of the Longwanggou Daoist Shrine Management Committee during the annual temple festival in August 1998.[1] Featured prominently in the two examples are what I have introduced in Chapter 5 as text acts: one a stele inscription, another a plaque with an inscription of the newly conferred organizational title. These examples show that text acts are always produced with specific political and social purposes for specific occasions.

The Role of the Local State in the Revival of Popular Religion

The Chinese socialist state has two guises: the policy-making central party-state and the *local state* that implements and often bends the policies. Relevant to this case study on Longwanggou, the local state takes the forms of township-, county-, and prefectural-level government bureaus and bureaucrats (what I call local state agents). Due to administrative and fiscal decentralization in the reform era, the local state has increased its power and autonomy considerably vis-à-vis the central state.[2] Because of its nested interest and embeddedness in the locale, the local state necessarily behaves differently from the central state. Local state agents have a large space in which to negotiate, bend, modify, or simply ignore central government policies.

So what characterizes the relationship between the local state and popular religion in Shaanbei? Freedom of religious worship is protected by the PRC constitution, but superstition is not. Much of Shaanbei popular religion hovers in the huge gray area between legitimate religion and illegitimate, thus illegal, superstition. Who makes the decision to categorize one activity as proper religion (*zhengdang zongjiao huodong*) and another as feudal superstition (*fengjian mixin*)? After Liberation, religious affairs in Shaanbei used to be part of the job of the Yulin and Yan'an Prefectural Civil Affairs Bureaus (*minzhengju*), which have branches in the county governments. Recently, a Religious Affairs Bureau (*zongjiaoju*) has been separated from the Civil Affairs Bureau in reaction to the growing prominence of religion in Shaanbei society.[3] Theoretically, it is the officials of the local Religious Affairs Bureau who make the distinctions, following directives and religious policies set by their superior offices (i.e., the Religious Affairs Bureaus at the provincial and central levels) and the central government. Once the distinctions are made, the same bureau is responsible for supporting proper religion by registering and supervising religious institutions and personnel while leaving the local police to crack down on superstition. However, on the concrete, local level,

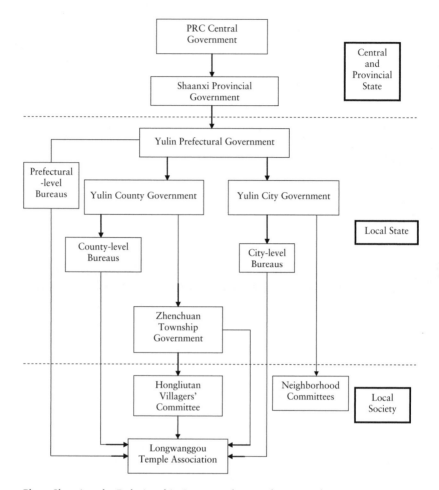

Chart Showing the Relationship Between the Local State and Longwanggou

explicit decisions to separate proper religion from superstition are not easily made, and the enforcement of this distinction is not easily carried out. To my knowledge, there has been no crackdown on superstitious activities in Shaanbei since the 1980s, which partly accounts for the vibrant popular religious life there. Yet so much of Shaanbei popular religious life (e.g., divination, spirit mediumism, rain prayers, symbolism of hell and divine retribution, etc.) would qualify as superstition according to criteria of the Maoist era.

The criteria that distinguish "real religion" from "superstition" are

The headquarters of the Mizhi County Branch of the Communist Party and other county-level bureaus.

still the same. But the behavior of the local state has changed. Nowadays the agents of the local state (e.g., officials of the Religious Affairs Bureaus and the Public Security Bureaus) are not interested in cracking down on superstition because they do not derive any benefit from doing so. Unlike during the Maoist era, being fervent (*jiji*) in stamping out superstition is no longer a sign of political rectitude and good political performance (*zhengzhi biaoxian*). In fact, a fervent anti-superstition attitude is so connected in people's minds with the ultra-leftism of the Cultural Revolution era (which has been officially declared as aberrant and wrong) that it has earned a bad political reputation. And it is quite plain to everyone in the local state that cracking down on popular religion, no matter how superstitious it looks, will meet with popular disapproval and even resistance; it "will not win people's hearts" (*bude renxin*).[4]

The shift away from radical anti-traditionalism to regulatory paternalism is best demonstrated by the act of registering temples by the prefectural Religious Affairs Bureau.[5] Theoretically, only temples that are legitimately Daoist or Buddhist can be approved to become institutional members of the official national Daoist Association or Buddhist Association. However, it is extremely difficult to ascertain Daoist or Buddhist qualities of different temples on the ground. The overwhelming majority of Shaanbei temples do not have a clergy or a set of doctrines for easy identification. And the range of religious activities at any one temple can be quite wide and confusing for anyone who is looking for some pure Daoist or Buddhist characteristics. Even historically Daoist or Buddhist temples have accommodated elements that are "impure." In a word, most Shaanbei temples are what scholars of Chinese religions have called folk or popular religious temples that exhibit a hodgepodge of different practices that have their origins in different traditions. Adding to the problem of apparently indiscriminate Daoist and Buddhist syncretism is the presence of clearly "superstitious" activities at many temples such as spirit mediumism, which is condemned by not only the Religious Affairs Bureau but also by the official Daoist and Buddhist associations. Despite these apparent difficulties, the process of temple registration was in full swing in the 1990s, probably to catch up with more than a decade of mushrooming of temples. In 1999, an official of the Yulin Prefecture Religious Affairs Bureau was named a provincial-level model worker for his outstanding work registering temples, a far cry from the high-socialist era when a cadre would have been praised for having smashed a lot of temples, not registering them. In a sense the Religious Affairs Bureau cadres have to work with the categories that are available. They can assign only one of the two labels (Daoist or Buddhist) to a popular religious temple, even if they are aware that the nature of these temples defies such easy categorization.[6] In fact, it seemed that these bureaucrats had no deep appreciation or cared to have such an appreciation for the complexity of the religious landscape that they had to work with.

Talking to temple officers of different temples that were in the process of applying to be registered, I found that this process always took considerable time and a lot of effort. Typically, a temple association had to treat the official representatives of the local state – from the Religious Affairs Bureau and other related bureaus and offices—as guests of honor at temple festivals, at banquets, and on other occasions. The relationship between the local state and the temples is thus one between patron and clients: its officials support temples that pay them respect and tribute. Besides these informal ways to benefit from temples, local state agents also benefit financially from collecting fees and taxes from merchants and peddlers who come to do business during the temple festivals. Members of the local police station, who *must* be invited to festivals to maintain peace and order, are paid for their service with money, free lodging, good food, cigarettes, and liquor. Small wonder that the police do not crack down on temple activities. Jean Oi (1999), studying the political economy of reform-era rural China, has highlighted the active role of the local state in enabling local economic growth. She calls this phenomenon local state corporatism. I suggest that the behavior of the Shaanbei local state toward the temples can be interpreted in a similar light: Temples are like enterprises that generate prosperity for the local economy (especially if they are regional pilgrimage centers) and income for the local state. It is thus in the interest of the local state to protect local temples the way they would local enterprises. The local state's new, regulatory relationship with local society is characterized by practical mutual dependence. Registering temples and making "superstitious" local cult centers into respectable, official Buddhist or Daoist "places for religious activities" (*zongjiao huodong changsuo*) is an act of indulgence, granting these local temples protection against any possible future anti-superstition campaign coming from the central government. It is instructive to note here that while the imperial government attempted religious control by frequent granting of majestic-sounding titles to individual deities (e.g., Mazu, Guandi; see Watson 1985), the same strategy is not available to the secular state today. But the state needs to register the temples in order to regulate them if necessary, which is a strategy that it has inherited from the late imperial state.[7]

Another way to protect illegal superstitious activities is to render them into quaint and harmless "folk customs" (*fengsu xiguan*) or "traditional culture" (*chuantong wenhua*) that are not worth any government's trouble to crack down upon. These customs, though "primitive" and "laughable," can serve as colorful regional cultural attractions for tourists. With the burgeoning domestic tourist industry, Shaanbei has in recent years jumped on the tourism bandwagon to promote and sell Shaanbei's charming peasant culture and scenic beauty. Images of Shaanbei's rusticity have appeared on TV, in newspapers, in novels, and in movies. Local folklorists have begun to sing Shaanbei's praises (e.g., He 1998; Zhang 1993). And scholars arrive from afar to do research on Shaanbei folk culture.[8] The temples, however, have to be vigilant and guard against any excessive appropriation and encroachments from the emerging tourism bureaus, a new feature in some local states.

One possible misconception about the local state is that somehow all

the different agents in different local state bureaus act in concert to indulge the revival of popular religious temples. Different local state bureaus and agents have different kinds and varying degrees of involvement
with the temples, though they might share a common predatory interest.[9]
For example, the township and county Industry and Commerce bureaus
(*gongshangju*) and Taxation bureaus (*shuiwuju*) are primarily interested
in collecting fees and taxes from the merchants who conduct business at
the temple festivals; the police (*gong'an*) and traffic police (*jiaojing*) are
primarily interested in maintaining order and collecting what might be
called protection fees from the temple associations; the Religious Affairs
Bureau has a duty to implement the government's religious policies
(*guanche zongjiao zhengce*) by registering temples (all the while squeezing as many gifts and other benefits from the temples as possible); the
Electricity Bureau (*dianliju*) officials also expect gifts before the temple
festival or else the electrical supply to the temple might just "by accident"
get cut off, disabling the opera performance and basically the entire festival. Most other local state bureaus actually have nothing to do with temples or temple festivals, though they probably wish that they too could
share a piece of the bounty.

It is useful here to contrast the local state's behavior concerning popular religion and birth control. Local state agents also know that the birth
control policy is extremely unpopular among the masses, yet they have to
enforce it. Serious consequences for their career ensue if they do not. For
example, during the period of my fieldwork many counties in Shaanbei
received serious warnings from the provincial government about their
poor birth control work (*jihua shengyu gongzuo*): the township or even
county top administrators could lose their jobs on the spot (*jiudi chuzhi*)
if, upon inspection, they were again found ineffective. Subsequently a
wave of drastic, sometimes draconian, measures were adopted by officials in the Shaanbei countryside to curb illegal pregnancies and births
(e.g., raiding or tearing down offenders' homes when they failed to pay
fines). By contrast, the higher-ups did not reprimand local officials for
laxity toward superstition. As a result the local state was extremely relaxed about popular religion. One county official told me that as far as
he could remember the issue of religion or superstition had not been mentioned even once in county government meetings since the beginning of
the reform era.

Another factor behind the permissiveness the local state shows towards popular religion is the local cadres' possible fear of the conse-

quences of offending the deities. Birth control resisters are merely people; some actors in popular religion are gods. Theoretically, because all cadres are Communist Party members and presumably atheists, they should not be afraid of gods and divine retribution. In reality, however, as members of local communities and under the influence of the communal hegemony of believers (who are more often than not their close kin), local cadres are often believers themselves, which makes them unwilling to interfere with popular religious activities. The temple caretaker at Longwanggou told me that many officials came to the temple to donate incense money in fulfillment of their vows, but they often came under cover of darkness for fear of being seen by others. And as I mentioned in Chapter 10, Lao Wang also told me how some cadres would have their subordinates or family members bring donations to the temple. Apparently some of the really large donations were from these officials. Many village temple bosses are current or ex-village Party secretaries, some devout servants of the village deities making up for the sins of having wronged the deities during the Maoist era.[10]

Longwanggou and the Politics of Legitimation

Two major interrelated issues always confronted temple boss Lao Wang: *first*, the legality and legitimacy of the Heilongdawang Temple (and the Longwanggou Complex) and *second*, the legitimacy of his own status as temple boss. Lao Wang was aware of the forceful tearing-down or closing of some temples in Sichuan, Henan, and some other places as news of these events were sporadically broadcast on the radio or TV. He also knew that sometimes the government could simply decide to appropriate a temple when it deemed it lucrative to do so. For example, in the 1980s the Jiaxian (a neighboring county) county government took over the control of the White Cloud Mountain Daoist Shrine, which is the most famous religious site in Shaanbei. Without the Heilongdawang Temple, Lao Wang would lose the basis of much of his power, so the most important task for him was to protect the temple against local state encroachments and against the possible charge that the temple was a venue for "feudal superstitious" activities, which might lead to unwanted official intervention.

On the other hand, it would be an even worse scenario for Lao Wang if somehow the temple thrived but he was no longer the temple boss, and the control of the temple fell into the hands of his rivals in the village.

Since the revival of the temple, all Hongliutan villagers had benefited from the temple's money in the forms of a first-rate primary school, improved irrigation system and roads, increased income (e.g., being employed by the temple, selling things during the temple festival, and renting farmland to the temple for the Hilly Land Arboretum), and generally a good village reputation. Some villagers, however, benefited in more ways than others and had become Lao Wang's clients and staunch political supporters. Those who felt left out or slighted by Lao Wang became embittered. It also became clear to all village power contenders that whoever controlled the temple resources could also exert tremendous influence in village politics. Subsequently a loosely cohesive oppositional clique against Lao Wang had formed in recent years, as I delineated in Chapter 10. They had launched frequent attacks on Lao Wang's reputation and would be only too happy to see him go down. As a result of this constant threat, Lao Wang was extremely concerned with legitimating and buttressing his power as temple boss. He had to make sure that he was adequately protected from attacks by his enemies and was equipped to launch any counteroffensive if needed. It was clear that Lao Wang's desire to protect the temple was predicated on the maintenance of his leadership position. In other words, protecting himself was the most important political task. The questions to ask are: What strategies had he been employing to legitimize his power? What material and symbolic resources had he been mobilizing to maintain his temple boss position? What were the relationships between his strategies to protect the temple and his strategies to protect himself? How successful had these strategies been? What can these strategies tell us about the larger structure of authority and power in Shaanbei local society today?

As can be seen from the above description, Lao Wang's leadership legitimacy and the temple's legitimacy were intimately intertwined; therefore the legitimation strategies he had engaged in often had an impact on both. Legitimation (in the form of validation, recognition, endorsement, and support) for the temple and for Lao Wang came from two broad sources: local people (villagers in his own village and those in the other eight villages) and people and institutions from beyond the immediate surroundings of Longwanggou.

Hongliutan villagers' support for the temple was strong and broadly based because of all the benefits the village was getting due to the temple's success. Even though the temple had achieved regional fame and wide appeal, Hongliutan villagers still considered it their village temple, similar to a village-run economic enterprise (see Ruf 1998), and therefore their support for it is not surprising. Support from the other eight villages was strong as well, because these villages had also benefited from the temple's success (e.g., in the form of financial subsidies for irrigation projects and schools).[11] Because Lao Wang played the most crucial role in making the temple successful and he had the ultimate power to decide on how to allocate temple resources, most locals pledged their support for Lao Wang partly out of genuine respect for his contributions to local welfare and partly as a conscious effort to trade support for potential benefits. In other words, Lao Wang had entered into patron-client relationships with many local individuals and communities. In addition, Lao Wang had been elected by the representatives from the nine villages and his position had been ritually confirmed by divination, which meant that Heilongdawang endorsed the decision. So not supporting Lao Wang was tantamount to challenging the divine endorsement. The most poignant expression of local villagers' support for both the temple and Lao Wang was the large number of people who volunteered to help out each year at the temple festival. Even though Lao Wang had enemies in Hongliutan, he was elected Village Chief (*cunzhang*) in 1996, which attested both to the level of his popularity and to his desire to consolidate his power with an official public office.

People beyond the immediate surroundings of Longwanggou showed their support for the temple by frequent visits to it, enthusiastic participation in the annual temple festival, and donations to the temple in gratitude of the Heilongdawang's blessings and divine assistance. Stories of Heilongdawang's magical efficacy had been spread far and wide by believers, and his power was amply attested by the number of people who worshipped him and the incredible amount of incense money they donated to the temple each year (over a million yuan annually since the mid–1990s, a staggering sum by Shaanbei standards).

Even though popular enthusiasm was an important source of legitimacy for the temple, it was not enough to ensure that the temple could survive another anti-superstition campaign like those during the Maoist era. Official endorsement from the government was a must for such an assurance. So Lao Wang and his associates had endeavored to secure official institutional status for the temple from the very beginning of the temple's revival to legitimize the whole enterprise. These endeavors required temple officers to go beyond their home turf and to interact with local state agents at the county and prefectural levels and with other social actors even farther afield.

In 1982, the recently rebuilt temple was blessed by the Yulin County Cultural Bureau (*wenhuaju*), which designated it a county-level cultural treasure (*xianji wenwu*). The Longwanggou Cultural Treasure Management Office (*Longwanggou wenwu guanlisuo*) was established as a result. The temple could garner this "cultural treasure" (*wenwu*) status not because of the newly constructed temple site, despite its magnificence, but because of the beautiful Republican-era stone temple gate that was spared destruction during the Cultural Revolution. Even though strictly speaking the temple's protected status rested only on the value of the stone gate as a cultural-historical artifact, at least the temple now had an officially sanctioned status.

In 1988, soon after Longwanggou initiated the reforestation project, the Yulin Prefecture Forestry Bureau (*linyeju*) granted the project an official name: the Longwanggou Hilly Land Arboretum. The significance of this project has to be seen in the larger context of rising national environmental concerns in the reform era and in Shaanbei's harsh environmental setting. Yulin County and many of Shaanbei's northern counties face constant threats of desertification and dust storms (part of the Maowusu Desert of Inner Mongolia extends southward into Shaanbei), and because of the long history of human settlement and dry climate Shaanbei has a severe tree shortage. As a result reforestation has always been a high-profile issue in Shaanbei. The Longwanggou reforestation project capitalized on the moral virtue of environmentalism and quickly gained regional, national, and even international attention as the first civic (nongovernmental) hilly land arboretum in China. Newspapers reported on the arboretum; officials and foreign dignitaries visited it; botanists, forestry specialists, and other scientists came to bestow their approval and marvel at this folk initiative; environmentalist groups from Beijing and NGO groups from Japan came to plant trees. One cannot overestimate the aesthetic and emotional appeal of the green hills around the temple set against the frequently parched landscape of Shaanbei's loess plateau. Because the reforestation project would not be possible without the money from donations to the temple, the establishment of the arboretum justified the superstitious activities of the Heilongdawang Temple. The success of the arboretum was a huge boost to the official status and image of the temple, and the temple had been riding on this success ever since. In the 1990s a few other Shaanbei temples had followed suit, using temple funds to initiate reforestation projects.

In 1996, Lao Wang founded the Longwanggou Primary School to replace the original Hongliutan village school. The neighboring Batawan village was only too happy to close down their small, dilapidated village school and send all their children to the new Longwanggou school. The classrooms and teachers' offices of the new school were housed on the third floor of the new and spacious three-story temple dormitory building, and the children used the large temple courtyard as a playground. The temple is situated midway between the two villages so the children had to walk a little more than they had to before, but that was a small price to pay for a much better school. Founding the school involved getting approval from the Yulin County Education Bureau (*jiaoyuju*). All school expenses were covered by temple funds. With the exception of two teachers who were on the government payroll, all the rest of the dozen teachers were on the temple payroll. The parents of the schoolchildren needed to pay only a minimal fee for tuition and books. Because of the better and well-funded conditions at the Longwanggou Primary School compared to other local schools, it quickly became the best primary school in the entire township of Zhenchuan in academic achievements, even outdoing the long-established and well-equipped government schools in Zhenchuan Town. The Longwanggou Primary School is a non-government-operated (*minban*) school. As China's reform-era educational policies allowed increasingly more "societal forces" (*shehui liliang*) to support education, the founding of the school was also capitalizing on a national trend. The school's accomplishments, just like those of the arboretum, would not have been possible without temple funds. As a result the school also provided ample justification for the temple activities, despite the apparent incongruity between secular education and folk religious tradition.

Though important in the legitimation of the Heilongdawang Temple, the above-mentioned official endorsements of the temple had been indirect. None was really granted to the temple per se. However, in 1998, a long-awaited blessing finally came: The Yulin Prefectural Religious Affairs Bureau granted Longwanggou the official status of the "Longwanggou Daoist Shrine Management Committee" (*Longwanggou daoguan guanli weiyuanhui*). In other words, the Heilongdawang Temple was now officially a Daoist temple, and Heilongdawang a Daoist deity. From then on, the temple itself was finally legitimate and enjoyed the legal protection of the PRC constitution (more on this in the next section). As popular religious deities, dragon kings have traditionally hovered at the edge of official Daoism, not quite members of the Daoist pantheon. But these were just minor details that both the temple association and the Religious Affairs Bureau officials were willing to ignore. The "Daoification" of the Heilongdawang Temple and other similar popular religious temples in a way made these temples "legible" to the state (Scott 1998) even if it involved a willful misreading.

Instrumental in obtaining the above-mentioned official statuses and endorsements were the temple association's cunning dissimulation strategies to protect the temple by highlighting its cultural-artifactual, environmentalist, educational, and official-religious aspects. In other words, these officially sanctioned statuses were clever covers for temple activities that would otherwise have been condemned as superstitious activities (e.g., provisioning divine springwater and divination, two of the temple's key appeals).[12] Anthropologists studying popular religion in Taiwan had noticed Taiwanese people's ingenuity in cleverly disguising their rituals to make them more palatable to the authorities that intended to repress or reform the rituals (Ahern 1981b; Weller 1987b). Similar techniques have also been at work in China, where some compromise was struck between complete submission to party-state ideological control (presumably atheism) and total assertion of popular religious autonomy. The temple officers willingly subjected the temple to state regulation only so as to be able to do what they liked. The local state agents, on the other hand, permitted what was permissible and turned a blind eye to those practices that were not. Both parties came out of the negotiation happy.

Being the temple boss and central figure who initiated most of these legitimation maneuvers, Lao Wang became the primary beneficiary of these local state endorsements. Because he was the paramount leader of the temple association, he naturally assumed the leading position of all of Longwanggou's official institutional designations. As I have already mentioned in Chapter 9, subsequently he became the director of the Longwanggou Cultural Treasure Management Office, the director of the Longwanggou Hilly Land Arboretum, the honorary principal of the Longwanggou Primary School, and the chairman of the Longwanggou Daoist Shrine Management Committee. In addition, Lao Wang acquired a few other positions, which were all related to his temple work. In 1995, thanks to the international connections he had cultivated, he was selected as one of the few members of the Chinese chapter of Inter-Asia, a Japa-

nese-funded NGO that organizes regular transnational activities to promote friendship among the common people of Asian countries. In 1996,
he was elected as a member to the Yulin County branch of the People's
Political Consultative Conference. Also in 1996 he was elected the village
chief. Lao Wang's numerous positions are of course outside of the local
government bureaucracy, yet his leadership has been repeatedly bolstered
and legitimated by official titles conferred by the local state. All these titles legitimized Lao Wang's further interactions with forces in the sociopolitical worlds beyond Longwanggou. They also increased the stake
of the power contestation between Lao Wang and his rivals: Lao Wang
would risk losing all of his titles if he failed to assert paramount control
of the temple.

Connecting with the "Powerful Outside": Erecting a Commemorative Stele

Over the course of my fieldwork in Longwanggou I slowly came to
know a few of Lao Wang's enemies, but upon the advice of Driver Zhang
and some other people at the temple I decided it was in my best interest
not to get too close to them. The result was that I was never entirely cog-
nizant of their side of the story. All I knew was that it was because of Lao
Wang's generosity and goodwill that I was able to use the Heilongdawang Temple as a base for my dissertation fieldwork and as far as I
had observed and heard Lao Wang was an upright person. I deliberately
decided not to probe into the history of the conflicts. But I still heard a lot
about them just by being in Longwanggou and around talkative informants. As an anthropologist, I was acutely aware of professional ethical
codes against taking sides in local political conflicts in one's field site. But
the time came when I had to demonstrate my allegiance to Lao Wang and
his projects.

The leaders of Friends of Nature (*Ziranzhiyou*), an internationally famous nongovernmental environmentalist organization based in Beijing,
had heard about the achievements of the Longwanggou reforestation
project and decided to bring some of their members as well as some Beijing secondary school students to Longwanggou to plant trees. They discussed the matter with Lao Wang on the phone in early 1998, and
decided to come in spring, during the May Day vacation (*wuyi lao-
dongjie*).[13] The director of the organization was Dr. Liang Congjie, a university professor and a well-known member of the National Political

Consultative Conference (*Zhengxie*). As Lao Wang was a member of the Yulin County Political Consultative Conference, Dr. Liang and he were also linking up as members of the same nationwide organizational system (*xitong*), though at two very different levels. Lao Wang seemed very excited about their imminent visit. He told Dr. Liang that he wanted to erect a stone stele to commemorate this important event. He also cordially asked Dr. Liang to tell him what message Friends of Nature would like to inscribe on the stele. Meanwhile he ordered some people to look for a good piece of stone for the stele. Not satisfied with what they found in the local area, Lao Wang finally decided to buy a piece of very nicely polished black granite from Shandong Province. It measured about five feet in width, three feet in height, and eight inches in thickness. It cost the temple more than 1, 000 yuan. Lao Wang also commissioned Zhengr, the young master craftsman, to prepare the base for the stele with local stone. Apparently Lao Wang was very serious about the stele.

In late April two members of Friends of Nature, Miss Zhao the program officer and Mr. Sun the school trip organizer were to come to Longwanggou to finalize the schedule of the event. As a gesture of courtesy and goodwill, Lao Wang sent Mandur (Driver Zhang, nicknamed "Longwanggou's diplomatic officer") and me to welcome the two Friends of Nature representatives. Mandur and I got up at 3 a.m., took the temple truck, and drove for 9 hours to meet up with Miss Zhao and Mr. Sun at the train station in Taiyuan, Shanxi Province, and spent another 9 hours driving back to Longwanggou.

Miss Zhao and Mr. Sun brought the message Dr. Liang had written for the stele: *Chinese Civic Environmentalist Organization Friends of Nature Planted Trees Here First of May 1998*. I was there, together with some of the temple officers, when the two Friends of Nature representatives gave Lao Wang the paper slip with Dr. Liang's message. Lao Wang's face registered a combination of shock, amusement, and dismay. After Mr. Zhao and Mr. Sun left the room for lunch at the temple canteen, Lao Wang, the temple officers, and I broke out into a heated commentary on the message.

Murmuring under my breath, "Friends of Nature planted trees here," I could not contain myself either. "What do they mean 'here'? Where? *Here* is not just *anywhere*." We quickly reached a conclusion: Dr. Liang's message was too simple, and it had ignored to mention Longwanggou. We needed something more to go with it, even on the back of the stele if necessary (the back side of a stele being inferior to the front side), to describe the event in a more detailed fashion and to highlight Long-wanggou's role in hosting this event. They all suddenly looked at me, and Lao Wang asked, half-smiling, "Why don't you help us write something?" I knew I could not refuse, despite my wariness of being implicated in not just local political conflicts but also local cultural productions. Yet I owed Lao Wang and the temple that much, and I knew I could demonstrate my gratitude by writing the text they, or rather Lao Wang, wanted.

I went to my room, sat down, and drafted the stele text (*beiwen*) in one stroke. I was elated to be mobilized as a resource, to be useful to Lao Wang and the temple in such an intellectually stimulating way. I knew my task was not just to describe the event, but to make the "description" serve a political purpose: to further legitimize the existence of Long-wanggou and Lao Wang's temple boss status. The stele text, in addition to the event itself, was to signal to Lao Wang's actual and potential enemies that Longwanggou had powerful connections with the outside world, and not just any outside world but Beijing, the national political center. I also knew this message had to be conveyed tactfully so it would not seem too blatant. I had to mention both Lao Wang's and Dr. Liang's names in the text, Lao Wang's because I knew he wanted to leave as many traces of his name as possible for posterity, and Dr. Liang's because he probably would like to have his name mentioned but was too polite to suggest it himself. And it seemed necessary to discursively pair Dr. Liang with Lao Wang to make Dr. Liang, a national-level politician, "lend" Lao Wang some symbolic power.[14] On the other hand, I tried to make Long-wanggou appear just a little bit more important than Friends of Nature. After all, there was nothing new about cosmopolitan-based environmentalism, whereas Longwanggou was truly one of a kind. In short, I went through quite some rhetorical labor while writing the stele text.[15]

I showed Lao Wang the draft. He seemed very pleased with it and did not suggest even a single alteration. Miss Zhao and Mr. Sun recommended a few minor changes in vocabulary and sentence structure. After that, the complete text was inscribed on the black granite by Hao Shifu (Master Hao), one of the best stone carvers and inscribers in Yulin Prefecture. Despite the tight timing, Hao Shifu managed to finish inscribing the more than five hundred characters in a week. The stele was erected on time and ready for the "revealing the stele" ceremony (*jiebei yishi*) on the last day of the Beijingers' visit. On the front of the stele is carved Dr. Liang's (or Friends of Nature's) brief message in very large characters:

Chinese Civic Environmentalist Organization
Friends of Nature
Planted Trees Here
First of May 1998

On the reverse side of the stele is carved the text written by the resident anthropologist and guest cultural worker:

For thousands of years, to eke out a living, the Chinese common folks have been using their diligent hands to open up farmlands one piece after another; to pass on their seed and continue their lines, they have given birth to generations upon generations of hope. But accompanying the birth of yet another baby and the felling of yet another tree is the destruction of nature. The ecosystem has thus lost balance, causing the environment of our ancestral country to moan and pant under the heavy population pressure. The ecosystem of Shaanbei's yellow loess plateau is very delicate. Because of severe erosion, everywhere one sees deep gullies, broken slopes, and marks of the struggles between human and nature. In 1988, in order to return greenness to the yellow earth, Wang Kehua of Hongliutan on the Wuding River bank and colleagues led enthusiastic peasant masses and established in Longwanggou China's only mass organized hilly land arboretum. They utilized the traditional folk belief in Heilongdawang to gather funding for the arboretum, and within the short span of ten years they have already made more than two thousand mu of the yellow earth green and full of life. This achievement has created strong reactions both within China and internationally, and it has become a model for those people with a vision who wish to remake their homelands green. Friends of Nature was established in 1994 and is China's first mass organized civic environmentalist organization. Its principal founder Liang Congjie, member of the Chinese National Political Consultative Conference, and his colleagues advocate a green civilization through mass environmentalist education. They have striven to establish and spread a green culture with Chinese characteristics.[16] These two civic organizations, Friends of Nature and Longwanggou, co-organized tree-planting and mutual learning activities in Longwanggou from the first to the third of May 1998. At the same time about seventy students and teachers of the Beijing Municipal Eighth Secondary School exchanged ideas with teachers and students of the Longwanggou Primary School and experienced many aspects of village life in Shaanbei. In the end they organized a Be-Happy-Together evening gala and both hosts and guests had a lot of fun in Longwanggou.

We erect this stele to commemorate this event.

Hope all will work hard together for the greening of Shaanbei and of the whole of China!

Underneath this text were carved two lines, one in Japanese and one in English[17]:

Friends of Nature and Longwanggou hand in hand working for the environment (in Japanese)

Friends of Nature and Longwanggou co-organized this tree-planting event on May 1–3, 1998 (in English)

The ceremony of revealing the stele itself was very brief and simple, taking place right before the Beijingers were scheduled to depart in the early morning of May 3. The temple officers and the key Beijing organizers took pictures together standing around the stele. After many handshakes and mutual promises of see-you-again, the Beijing tree-planters left in their rented buses.

The tree-planting event was an immense success. The stele too was a big success. It sat beautifully on its custom-made stone base in a strategic location at the center of the temple ground. Many visitors to the temple lingered around the stele to read the texts, both front and back; some even took pictures in front of it. For years to come, the stele would provide a crucial textual service for Longwanggou and Lao Wang.[18] Traditional in physical appearance, the stele blended perfectly with the other temple stelae and the overall temple ground; yet both the form and the content of the stele texts (Dr. Liang's and mine) revealed entirely new sensibilities formed only during the reform era. Quite a number of expressions used in the stele text I wrote would appear very strange to an average semiliterate Shaanbei person, e.g., *huanbao* (environmental protection), *shengtai* (ecosystem), *lüse wenming* (green civilization). They might appear as mystical words, words that were suffused with a new power that had only begun to make itself felt locally. And why the two lines in Japanese and English? So as to "borrow" some power from strange foreign symbols! Maybe Lao Wang's enemies would think twice now before attacking him, for Lao Wang might even have powerful *international* protectors. Recall the concept of text act that I introduced in Chapter 5: A text act is an act of writing or inscribing that conveys its power through its physical presence as much as, or more than, the specific contents in the text. The Friends of Nature commemorative stele joined the other text acts at the temple site to exude and display legitimacy and power.

A Ceremony to Commemorate the Bestowal
of the Longwanggou Daoist Shrine
Management Committee Status

Every year the Heilongdawang Temple stages its annual temple festival in honor of the deity's birthday in the middle of the sixth month of the lunar calendar. The festival usually lasts for six days and culminates on Sixth Month Thirteenth, Heilongdawang's birthday. According to the lunar calendar, the Year of the Tiger had two fifth months (*run wuyue*), which pushed the Longwanggou annual temple festival to the very end of July 1998. Just a month earlier the temple had received the Daoist Shrine Management Committee status. To celebrate this important moment in the history of the temple, Lao Wang decided to hold a ceremony. He commissioned Liangr, the master carpenter from Chenjiapo, to make a beautiful, six-foot-long wooden plaque and on it the carved inscription "Longwanggou Daoist Shrine Management Committee" (*Longwanggou daoguan guanli weiyuanhui*). The ceremony was going to be called the "plaque-hanging ceremony" (*guapai yishi*). Organizational plaques like this are crucial material markers of an institution's legitimacy in Chinese political culture.[19] So, yet again we witness the creation of a text act that symbolically displays and broadcasts Longwanggou's legality and legitimacy.

Lao Wang invited the relevant officials and leaders of some other important temples in the area to come, and the ceremony was to be held at noon on Sixth Month Thirteenth (which was August 4 in 1998), i.e., Heilongdawang's birthday. Noontime of the thirteenth had traditionally been the most valued time of the entire temple festival; it had been the time when the opera troupe had to play "Bao Wenzheng Chopping off Chen Shimei's Head" (*Zhameian*), Heilongdawang's favorite opera piece.[20] The fact that Lao Wang chose to hold the ceremony at this particular time indicated how serious he was about the event. By holding the ceremony he had literally arranged a meeting between Heilongdawang, himself the temple boss, the guests he invited (especially the official representatives of the local state), and the festival-going masses. The ceremony would infuse the secular authority of the state into the popular religious space and time of Longwanggou to ritually bolster Longwanggou's and Lao Wang's legitimacy. At this ceremony the politics of legitimation was given a ritual form, and a popular religious festival was impregnated with political significance.

The opera performances began on sixth month ninth and would last until sixth month fourteenth. This year three opera troupes were invited, including one from Kaifeng, Henan Province, one from Xi'an, the provincial capital of Shaanxi Province, and one from Yulin City. As had been the case in the past decade or so, it was by far the best and the most expensive set of opera performances in Shaanbei. By rough estimate a few hundred thousand visitors and pilgrims came to Longwanggou during the six days of the temple festival. The entire valley was jam-packed with people, food stalls, watermelon sheds, game circles, pool tables, circus and performing troupe tents (even some with freak shows), incense and firecracker stands, makeshift convenience stores, all kinds of small, mobile peddling devices, and even little gambling dens strewn here and there in the crowd.

It was almost noon. The yellow dust stirred up by yangge dancers and drummers during the offering-presenting procession (*yinggong*) earlier in the morning had already settled, and the Henan opera troupe had just finished their performance. It was decided that Heilongdawang's favorite opera would be performed by the famous troupe from Xi'an after the plaque-hanging ceremony. Tables and chairs were set up on the opera stage facing Heilongdawang and the audience. The entire valley was one big chaos and packed to the rim, though the space in front of the stage and on the stepped stone audience stand was relatively more orderly, with a few thousand people in the audience. Everywhere one heard a drone of confused noise. The loudspeakers announced that there was going to be a ceremony at noon and after that the opera performance would resume. More people pushed near the stage to see what was happening.

The guests and speakers came on the stage from backstage and were seated. The usual polite negotiations ensued about who would sit where. The head priest of the White Cloud Mountain Daoist Shrine ended up sitting in the middle, the seat of honor, apparently because he was the oldest in the group. The chief of the prefectural Religious Affairs Bureau and the assistant chief of the prefectural Civil Affairs Bureau sat on the left of the priest. Lao Wang himself chose to sit at the corner, perhaps as a gesture of modesty. Other guests included three temple bosses from other temples, two officials from the township government, and one former Longwanggou temple association officer. They sat in one row behind the adjoining long tables covered with ceremonial red cloth. A microphone stood in the middle and was passed to Lao Wang, the first speaker. In a deliberate, slightly nervous tone, Lao Wang read from a piece of paper the text of his speech:

Every leader (*lingdao*), every honorable guest, ladies and gentlemen:
Today is the occasion of the founding of the Longwanggou Daoist Shrine
Management Committee. Representing the people (*qunzhong*) of the nine villages around Longwanggou as well as all the members of the shrine committee, I sincerely express my warm welcome to you for coming here; and my
heartfelt thanks for your help and support of our work. Thank you!

It has been 18 years now since the initial preparation for the reconstruction
of the temple in 1981. In these 18 years it was only because of the warm support and great sponsorship by people with insights (*youshizhishi*) from all
quarters that the temple could be built to this stage. I would like to borrow
this opportunity to express ten thousand thanks to you.

Since its inception in 1988, it took only four years for the Longwanggou
Hilly Land Arboretum to turn into a hilly land forest park occupying 1,200
mu of land and with about 820 species of trees and other plants. In 1991, we
were invited to attend "The Eighth Academic Conference of the Botanical
Garden Association of the Chinese National Botanical Academy" that took
place in Yinchuan[21]. On the 13th of September of the same year the Chinese
Flowers Newspaper[22] had a story on the arboretum; it was positioned as the
first article on the first page (*touban toutiao*) and was entitled "Utilizing the
temple festival to collect funds for the beautification of the environment of a
famous site: The Longwanggou Hilly Land Arboretum has been established in
Yulin." Ever since, the Longwanggou Hilly Land Arboretum has been getting
attention and acclaim both from within China and from the world outside
China. Specialists and scholars (*zhuanjia xuezhe*) from more than a dozen
countries have since visited the arboretum. In 1992, the China News Agency
released to the world the story: "The only civic managed hilly land arboretum
in China has been established in Yulin." In the same year, we participated in
"The Second Conference on the Co-Operation of Chinese and International
Civic Organizations (NGOs)" that took place in Ji'nan, Shandong. From the
17th to the 20th of August in 1996, Longwanggou hosted "The Twelfth
Academic Conference of the Botanical Garden Association of the Chinese
National Botanical Academy." Ninety-seven specialists and scholars from
twenty-seven provinces, cities, and autonomous regions and relevant leaders
(*youguanlingdao*) from the prefecture and county governments participated in
the conference. On the 23rd of September of the same year, the director of the
Longwanggou Hilly Land Arboretum was invited by the Japanese NGO Inter-
Asia to have a friendship tour to Daban [Osaka], Hegeshan [Wakayama], and
other places in Japan, and to attend "The Eighth International Forestry Conference."

From the first to the third of June this year, members of Friends of Nature,
a Chinese civic environmental protection organization, together with more
than seventy students and teachers of the Beijing Municipal Eighth Secondary
School, came to Longwanggou to plant trees. Reporters from China Central
Television (CCTV) followed the group and made a special report.

The process of rebuilding Longwanggou in the past 18 years has been an arduous journey with difficult steps along the way. It is not easy to have come this far. But there are still some problems that cannot be solved. For example: 1. The Hilly Land Arboretum and the problem of using farmers' arable hilly land; 2. It has been five years since we began the construction of the Longwanggou Primary School building, but it hasn't been finished and we don't know when it can be finished; 3. The problem of the road, i.e., the Thousand Dragon Road. We don't know when the construction project can start.

Anyway, if one wants to do well on something that benefits the people, one has to mobilize all the forces of society and have the support and help of relevant leaders. It is only when everyone cooperates and works together and when support comes from all sides that one can succeed in the endeavor. As a Daoist shrine we should seriously carry out the religious policies of the Party and make ourselves into a model in loving the country and the religion (*aiguo aijiao*) and in promoting our great traditions.

My speech is over; Thank you, everybody.

There was applause from the audience.[23] Then a long string of giant firecrackers was ignited next to the stage. This was the moment when the wooden plaque was lifted up from behind the guests and brought to the front to be shown to the audience. "I announce," now the chief of the Religious Affairs Bureau had the microphone, "that the Longwanggou Daoist Shrine Management Committee has officially been established!" More applause came from the audience. Lao Wang shook hands with the bureau chief and excused himself because he was too busy with all the work of the temple festival to even sit through the rest of the ceremony. The plaque was brought to the temple office and hung alongside the other plaques (of the Cultural Treasure Office and the Arboretum). The ritual proper of the plaque-hanging ceremony was apparently over. But a few more people made speeches after Lao Wang left. The head priest of the White Cloud Mountain Daoist Shrine talked about how happy he was that the Heilongdawang Temple had now become a "brother" Daoist shrine. The chief of the Religious Affairs Bureau explained the importance of gradually ridding Longwanggou of all superstitious elements and becoming an exemplary Daoist shrine.[24] The assistant chief of the Public Affairs Bureau used the opportunity to advertise the bureau's new charity program. One of the two township officials lauded Longwanggou's role in promoting the economy of the area. The whole ceremony lasted for approximately forty-five minutes. When it was over, the stage was quickly cleared and the opera performance "Bao Wenzheng Chopping off Chen Shimei's Head" began.

Lao Wang's speech seemed to have gone very well. He, however, did not write the speech himself. Lao Jiang wrote it for him. Lao Jiang was a recently retired member of the Yulin City "cultural station" (*wenhuazhan*). He had been coming to the Longwanggou temple festival every year. In exchange for free accommodation and free food he offered to help Lao Wang with things "cultural" during the temple festival, such as writing the opera posters and arranging the schedule for the performances. This year he had also been entrusted with the task of writing the speech for Lao Wang. In other words, he was Lao Wang's "ghost-writer" (see Schoenhals 1992, chapter three, for discussion on the prevalence of ghostwriting for high officials in China). This did not surprise me at all because I knew that Lao Wang, while extremely eloquent and sometimes even exuberant in small group settings, tended to be nervous, rigid, and at a loss for words when in front of a large audience. I had seen that happen a few times before, including the time when he made the opening speech on the night of the variety show with the Beijing tree-planting visitors in May. Lao Wang himself seemed to be aware of this shortcoming, and he most likely asked Lao Jiang to write the speech for him to avoid potential embarrassment on such a crucial occasion.

But had Lao Jiang sufficiently grasped Lao Wang's intentions and embodied them in the speech (see Schoenhals 1992: 55)? I think he had, just as I had grasped Lao Wang's intentions when I wrote the stele inscription. The genre of the speech was a kind of "making a work report" (*zuo gongzuo baogao*), a common yet important component of the repertoire of socialist Chinese bureaucratic (speech) behaviors. Every bureaucrat had to make work reports to his superior, colleagues, and constituency regularly so as to have his work performance evaluated. As a former bureaucrat (specifically, a local cultural work officer), Lao Jiang knew the ropes. Lao Wang of course was not a bureaucrat, but being the temple boss and presenting on an occasion as official as the plaque-hanging ceremony, he picked his genre well. A brief analysis of Lao Wang's work report suffices. It conveyed three major messages:

First, that it was only because of "you" (i.e., the officials, the masses) that Longwanggou could have achieved so much in so little time; here Lao Wang was showing a gesture of humility.

Second, that Longwanggou had gained a lot of recognition, not just in China but also internationally; here Lao Wang was more than implicitly hinting at the importance of his leadership in harnessing outside supporters.

And third, that Longwanggou still faced some challenges, but you (i.e., the officials and the masses) would help us overcome these problems; here Lao Wang wanted to say: My enemies, beware; I have powerful friends and protectors and I am determined to overcome all difficulties.

The brevity of the remark at the end of the speech concerning religion is curious. Why so brief? Why was the speech so much about the arboretum and so little about the temple? Here again, it seemed that Lao Wang was playing his trump card: the Longwanggou Hilly Land Arboretum. After all, it was the arboretum that had made Longwanggou and Lao Wang so famous. Therefore, it seemed that the "plaque-hanging ceremony" was used as a pretext for staging something bigger, not just the Heilongdawang Temple's now officially sanctioned legal status as a Daoist temple (hence its being protected by law), but more importantly the legitimacy of the entire Longwanggou *complex* (including the Heilongdawang Temple, the arboretum, the Longwanggou Primary School, and *especially temple boss Lao Wang himself*). In other words, Lao Wang used a *specific* occasion to assert a *general* point about power and legitimacy.

Michael Schoenhals once asked, "Why is it that the art of doing things with words so dear to China's *homo politicus* has not received the same attention as, for instance, the "art of *guanxi*"" (Schoenhals 1992: 7)?[25] I share with him a similar concern, and Lao Wang's speech at the plaque-hanging ceremony demonstrates the importance of "doing things with words" not only for top party-state leaders, as studied by Schoenhals, but also for the *homo politicus* at lower levels of society and at the margin of formal political structures.

Legitimation Rituals: The Interpenetration of Religion and Politics

By definition, all legitimation rituals are at once specific and general. A cremation procession for a Rajah in nineteenth-century Bali was simultaneously a specific political event and a general statement of Balinese political theory (Geertz 1980). The seasonal grand sacrifices of the Qianlong Emperor can be seen in a similar light (Zito 1997). The material and symbolic resources available to Lao Wang to stage the plaque-hanging ceremony-*cum*-legitimation ritual would certainly pale in comparison to those available to the Qianlong Emperor to stage the imperial sacrifices or those available to the Chinese party-state to stage an October First

National Day Ceremony (e.g., the 1999 fiftieth anniversary of the founding of the PRC). But the financial and symbolic resources Lao Wang
could mobilize were nevertheless considerable. As the temple boss, he not
only had Heilongdawang on his side, so to speak, but also commanded
Heilongdawang's large pool of donation money.[26] For example, this year
he spent about 250,000 yuan on inviting the opera troupes to perform at
the temple festival. The plaque-hanging ceremony itself might have been
short and simple, but when looked at in the larger context, the ceremony
became a condensed moment in the greater temple festival spectacle. As I
have mentioned earlier, the timing of the ceremony corresponded to the
moment when the Heilongdawang was supposed to be the most present.
The *personal-charismatic presence* of Lao Wang was made to coincide
with the *magical presence* of the Heilongdawang and the *political presence* of the local state. The ceremony *presupposed* as well as *further generated* the powers of Lao Wang's leadership.[27]

The plaque-hanging ceremony thus illustrates poignantly the "sym-
bology of power" in Longwanggou (Geertz 1980: 98; see also Fujitani
1996). The legitimacy, not to mention legality, of the Longwanggou
Complex (including Lao Wang's leadership) was ritually evoked and confirmed by the co-presence of all the participants at the temple festival: the
Heilongdawang (looking down from his throne, receiving offerings, and
listening to prayers and requests), Lao Wang (receiving guests, making
the speech, hanging the plaque, busying himself with matters big and
small), representatives of the local state (being hosted and entertained,
making speeches, shaking hands with old friends and colleagues), leaders
of neighboring religious organizations and communities (chatting with
one another, making speeches), and, most important of all, the festival-
going masses (paying respect to Heilongdawang, burning incense, setting
off firecrackers, watching the opera, listening to the speeches, playing
games, selling and buying food and other things, or just being there and
enjoying themselves). The whole ambiance was one of abundance, great
fun (*honghuo*), and "shared well-being" (Abélès 1988: 396). Much "ritual labor" (ibid: 398) had been expended by Lao Wang and Longwanggou, and to good effect. Though not a religious specialist, Lao Wang was
certainly a master of the ritual orchestration of power and authority.

The plaque-hanging ceremony at the temple festival also illustrates the
coming together of many interests: the political ambition of Lao Wang,
the regulatory and increasingly people-friendly assertion of the local
state, and the collective religiosity and fun-seeking desire of the festival-

going masses. Ritual form is only a medium into which different social actors infuse their different meanings and agendas. Out of political considerations, and with his rivals in mind, Lao Wang enlisted the help of the local state to protect the temple and to confirm his leadership position. On the other hand, Lao Wang was also demonstrating to representatives of the local state that the Heilongdawang Temple is truly a popular temple and that it would only be in their best interest to protect this local institution and not to meddle in its affairs. The local state officials were willing accomplices in Lao Wang's agenda because they had much to gain from promoting the reputation of a local pilgrimage site. Increasingly seen as corrupt and uncaring, the officials were only too happy to show their presence as benevolent figures among the masses, paternalistically endorsing these folksy, and perhaps in their eyes foolish, activities.

And what about the masses witnessing the ceremony? Did they feel that there was a deliberate intrusion of the political into sacred space and sacred time (if in fact they conceived of the temple festival as sacred space and sacred time)? Or, what is perhaps the more likely case, in their minds the ceremony was just one more piece in the entire temple festival's staging of red-hot sociality? Besides receiving the messages Lao Wang and the officials wanted to project, the masses seemed as entertained by the ceremony as by the opera performances (remember the long string of giant firecrackers). Political drama, though perhaps less exciting than real drama, is interesting to watch nonetheless. After all, many if not most of the festivalgoers had only heard of but never seen the famous temple boss Lao Wang, and most had never had the privilege of listening to officials talk, except on television.

The interpenetration of religious and political power/authority connotations in this legitimation ritual points to the conclusion that, quoting the political theorist Lefort, "it is impossible to separate what belongs to the elaboration of a political form . . . from what belongs to the elaboration of a religious form" (Lefort 1986, quoted in Abélès 1988). Many ritual forms and religious connotations exist in today's political acts, e.g., those "political dramas" engaged in by the former French president François Mitterand studied by Abélès (1988), or the U.S. presidential "sociodramas" studied by McLeod (1999). In the context of contemporary rural China, the resurgence of religious symbolism at all in political life and the conscious presence of the secular state in the midst of folk religion indicate a shift away from the Communist party-state's former, purely political ritualism (see Apter and Saich 1994; Bennett 1976;

Whyte 1974) toward a more complex amalgam of expressions and assertions of sociopolitical power and authority feeding on different sources within an increasingly pluralizing society.

The "Channeling Zone" between the Local State and Local Society

The concept of *"minjian"* (civic, nongovernmental) has gained currency in reform-era China, as the state is increasingly tolerant of, and often even encourages, the springing forth of mass initiatives and self-organization in different social sectors (e.g., business, education, leisure) (see Yang 1994). Lao Wang and his associates have capitalized on the high appeal of the fact that the Longwanggou Hilly Land Arboretum was the first minjian hilly land arboretum in China. In fact, the twin features of minjian-ness and folk environmentalism exemplify two of the most important ideological emphases of the reform era: privatization and environmental protection. This has lent Longwanggou an aura of legitimacy and savvy that other temples are rightfully jealous of. Yet the example of legitimation ritual involving local state agents also shows that the expansion of the minjian realm in rural China is often accompanied by the subtle insinuation and occasionally not–so-subtle intrusion of the state into this realm. The local state definitely has a place in the agrarian public sphere.

One metaphor that may appropriately characterize (local-) state-society interactions in China today is "channeling." As the Longwanggou case study has shown, the temple association interacts with not the local state per se but rather the separate local state agencies that are relatively autonomous from one another. Different "channels" (which can be even more concretely imagined as tubes, pipes, ducts, conduits) of linkage and articulation were established by the temple with each individual local state agency. And each local state agency likewise establishes channels with multiple local-organizational (i.e., minjian) supplicants. Through these channels the local state agencies siphon "upward" money and gifts while bestowing "downward" official institutional statuses and protection. From the perspective of the local-organizational supplicants (e.g., temple associations), they pay "upward" tributes and deference to the local state agencies and capture "downward" official recognition and legitimacy. The reemergence of the importance of the locale (as mentioned earlier) and the increasing compartmentalization of the local state further facilitate the multiplication of these channels.

We may call the space that is traversed by these channels the "channeling zone." I have borrowed this expression from the title of the anthropologist Michael Brown's book on New Age channeling communities in the U.S. In fact, the channels established between local state agencies and local minjian organizations in China are very similar in nature to the New Age channelers Brown describes. The channelers are vessels through which spirits of different entities (e.g., Buddha, Jesus, aliens, "ascended masters," etc.) speak and interact with the audience. Likewise, the local state agencies or agents do not generate legitimacy or legal protection themselves; they merely channel them to those who need these precious "cargoes" for a price. And the temple associations or temple bosses do not produce the gifts and money they pay to the local state; rather, they channel "upward" these resources from the local communities and the masses. Applying Deleuze and Guattari's metaphor of the rhizome (tubers that grow in an uncentered, unhierarchical, unpredictable, and meandering way), Mayfair Yang (1994) has aptly characterized the *guanxi-*based social relations in China as rhizomatic networks that are capable of subverting the state, which is rigid, mono-organizational, and "arborescent" (i.e., tree-like, with a central trunk; also Deleuze and Guattari's expression). The Longwanggou case suggests that sometimes this rhizomatic growth does depend on guiding structures (like vines growing on trellis): As local elites like Lao Wang reach out and up to different local state agents through guanxi-pulling, it is a case of rhizomes growing inside or alongside the channels of linkage forming between local state agencies and minjian organizations.

CHAPTER TWELVE

Conclusion

This book is an ethnography and cultural analysis of the Black Dragon King Complex of Longwanggou. I have attempted to show how Longwanggou is not just a place of purely religious activities; more important, it is a site of interaction between elements of popular religion, the socialist state, and agrarian society in reform-era China. By revealing the process of *how* the Black Dragon King Temple is revived and run, I have hoped to answer, however partially, the question of *how it is possible* that popular religion has revived in the past twenty or so years. I have tried to provide a more nuanced understanding of the sociocultural processes of "doing religion" in today's China, and for that matter, "doing religion" in any other historical or cultural context. The many different facets of Shaanbei popular religion I have described and analyzed show how intimately embedded religious activities are in their social and political milieus, and how "religious beliefs" are but a small part of what religion is all about.

I have also hoped that the book would provide an antidote to the prevailing trend in Western interpretations to view religious revival in China as some kind of spiritual movement or a grassroots resistance against the Communist party-state. These simplistic and overly enthusiastic interpretations tell us more about Western observers' desires than Chinese realities; they impute "spirituality" and political intentions to a social landscape where things are in reality much more complicated and therefore much more interesting. My study reveals how Chinese rural society has changed to make doing popular religion "materially feasible, or politically practical, or morally powerful, or personally exciting—or all of these at once" (Ortner 1989: 195) for Shaanbei people.

A number of important conclusions emerged from this study pertaining to (1) the nature of popular religion and popular religious institutions in rural China; (2) the shifting character of the local elite and local political dynamics; and (3) the shifting character of the state and state-society relations at the local level.

The Nature of Popular Religion and Popular Religious Institutions in Rural China

Unlike the Judeo-Christian tradition (except for the worship of local saints in popular Catholicism), in which only one or a very limited number of deities are worshiped, Shaanbei popular religion is filled with a wide variety of deities. Because each village or community of some size has its own deity and the identity of this deity is never predetermined, every deity at least has a guaranteed local base of support and worship. Even if many of the deities worshiped at village temples are well known and widely worshiped figures in the Chinese popular religious pantheon such as Guandi and the Monkey King, the village temples themselves often remain local and obscure. On the other hand, a local deity such as the Black Dragon King can sometimes achieve regional fame and broad appeal.

The believed-in degree of efficacy (*ling*) or "efficacious response" (*lingying*) is the most important determinant of a deity's ranking in the local world of spiritual power. Stories of divine efficacy for the devout and divine retribution against blasphemers spread by word of mouth (and occasionally through devotional literature, e.g., Baiyunshan daojiao xiaozu n.d.) within and across communities of worshipers and pilgrims. Each person has his or her own "meaningful god set" (Roberts, Chiao, and Pandey 1975); the number and type of deities within this set can, and usually do, change over time, and so does the person's relationship to each deity within the set. A young person's religious habitus is bound to be different from, and usually less developed than, that of an adult because the latter is likely to have experienced many more of life's troubles, heard about and witnessed many more cases of divine efficacy, and sought divine assistance on many more occasions.

As one observes the worshipers in action at the Heilongdawang Temple or at other temples in Shaanbei, one cannot doubt the sincerity of their trust and their emotional investment in the deities' power to cure an illness, illuminate a problem, bring good fortune to the family and the community, and keep misfortune at bay. Shaanbei people's religiosity exemplifies what scholars of Chinese popular religion have always observed: an inclination toward beseeching for practical benefits, especially in times of trouble, and a lack of interest in theologizing and systematization (see Weller 1987a).

However, popular religion is about much more than just people's religiosity and religious habitus; popular religion is enabled by a central folk social institution, the temple association. Made up of a group of locally respected and experienced men, the temple association oversees the building and maintenance of the temple, manages the incense money donated by worshipers, stages the biannual temple festivals in honor of the deity (one on the deity's birthday and the second during the first month of the lunar calendar), and negotiates with other village organizations (e.g., the villagers' committee), other temple associations, and the local state. Most of the popular religious expressions would not be possible without the organizational efforts of the temple association. Temple associations are what Timothy Brook calls auto-organizations (Brook 1997), and they have played an important role in expanding folk cultural space and the agrarian public sphere in contemporary China.[1] Because so many of the revived folk cultural traditions are associated with the temples (e.g., opera performances, storytelling, temple festivals, folk dances), temples and the temple associations behind them are really the motor of folk cultural revivalism in contemporary Shaanbei.

Popular religion also provides a space for the production and consumption of desired social co-presence (what I have called red-hot sociality), especially during event productions such as funerals and temple festivals. Shaanbei peasants use the idiom of hosting to stage these important event productions, and they derive satisfaction from participating in these activities. Different modalities of "doing religion" inform the ways in which they engage in popular religious life, and participating and helping out at temple festivals is no less important than praying to receive divine help from the deities. The relationship established between deities and worshipers also provides the context for the building of relationships and sociality among the worshipers.

One theme that has been implied here and there but not explicitly addressed in this book is the question of identity and subjectivity. Anthro-

pologists studying Taiwanese popular religion have long noted the important role popular cults around deities play in helping to constitute
sub-ethnic identities (e.g., people of Zhangzhou origin against people of
Quanzhou origin) or later, a Taiwanese identity against the oppressive
Nationalist regime that was dominated by mainlanders (e.g., Ahern
1981b; Rohsenow 1973; Sangren 2003; Weller 1987b). Expressions of
folk religiosity served also as expressions of contrastive identity formation, and temples and temple festivals sometimes became sites for not-
too-subtle political mobilization. In China, popular religion has also
served as a vehicle for identity formation; in the case of Shaanbei and
other predominantly rural areas, this identity bears a strong peasant sensibility. As more cosmopolitan and translocal forces enter into the lives of
peasants via television, the market, and rural-urban migration, the contrast between revived peasant traditions and urban-based cultural practices will undoubtedly become more and more stark. How a new generation of temple bosses and popular religious worshipers respond to this
contrast will be an interesting issue to pursue.

Besides being a site of both individual and communal worship, a temple is also a political, economic, and symbolic resource and resource-gen-
erator. A beautifully built temple and a well-attended temple festival attest not only to the efficacy of the deity but also to the organizational
ability of the temple association and the community. Though most temples have a modest donation income and can only break even financially,
some temples such as Longwanggou can harness a large surplus income
for the local community. With the increase of fame and financial strength
comes the possibility of political influence in a local society, not to mention better roads, irrigation systems, and a better school for the village.

On a personal level, to be elected as an officer of the temple association can bring a person extra income (in the form of salary or graft), prestige, respect, power to manage temple finances and influence local affairs,
occasions to work and interact with other prominent local figures and to
use the connection with the temple to further personal gains (legally or il-
legally). Through the cultural idiom of "serving the god," being a temple
officer is often emotionally satisfying for the officer and members of his
family. However, not everyone can or wants to become a temple officer.
Most villagers in fact shy away from direct involvement with temple affairs because, after all, temple office is public office, and decision making
inevitably means stepping on some people's toes and creating enemies. In-

dividuals most inclined to want to become temple officers are ambitious local activists who enjoy public life.

Even though Shaanbei and many other rural locales in China are physically far away from metropolitan centers or international borders, transnational and translocal forces do impact local society and the development of local religion. One of the consequences of the increasing contact between the PRC and Taiwan is an increased flow of religious ideas and persons between the two polities. Popular religious groups are often at the forefront of cross-Strait relations, pushing the limit of the restrictions of contact between the PRC and Taiwan. For example, in the 1990s different Mazu temples in Taiwan began to organize pilgrimages to their ancestral temple on the island of Meizhou off the Fujian coast. The leading theoretician of the Republic of China Association of Spirit Mediums, Lai Zongxian, went to study at a university in Sichuan Province for a doctoral degree in Daoist studies (Paper 1996: 126). The same association also organized group pilgrimages to the "ancestral" Mazu temple in Fujian Province, Mount Tai in Shandong Province, and even a tomb-sweeping pilgrimage of 15,000 people to the tomb of the Yellow Emperor in Huangling County of Shaanbei (Yan'an Prefecture) (Paper 1996: 115–16).

The academicization of popular religion has also spread to the PRC, most noticeably in Fujian, where connections to Taiwan have been renewed in the past two decades. Kenneth Dean (1993, 1998b) has reported on the "conferences of the gods" in Fujian, where academics, popular religious practitioners, local officials, and worshipers gathered at public stagings of academic conferences on local deities and local religious traditions. The France-based Daoism scholar John Lagerwey cooperated with Chinese local scholars in producing a series of volumes, in Chinese, on traditional Hakka society and culture, especially Hakka religious practices (e.g., Luo and Lagerwey 1997). These scholarly discourses have the effect of raising the status of popular religion and legitimizing it (as had occurred in Taiwan). It is not inconceivable that sometime in the future a scholarly conference on popular religion in Shaanbei will take place, perhaps even in Longwanggou, and temple boss Lao Wang or his successor will most likely welcome this opportunity to host a new kind of event production, one that produces not only red-hot sociality but also scholarly discourse.

The Shifting Character of the Local Elite and Local Political Dynamics

The nature of political life in the reform era is decidedly different from that of the Maoist era. At the national level, the reform era saw the replacement of the older generation of revolutionary leaders by a new generation of technocrats. At the local state level, economic development has largely replaced political performance as the main criterion for judging an official's worth. At the grassroots, local-society level, village elections have been introduced in recent years. What has not changed in the political culture, however, is the importance of *guanxi* in the complex webs of patron-client relations stretching from as low as the village to as high as the central party-state leadership.

This study has highlighted the career of temple boss Lao Wang to illustrate the changing character of the local elite in rural China. Energetic, enterprising, and extremely capable, Lao Wang has capitalized on the changing policies over the past two decades to emerge in his own village as well as in the Zhenchuan township area as a member of the new local elite. China scholars have long recognized the crucial role local elites play in mediating the larger polity (imperial state or modern state) and the local peasant communities (e.g., Duara 1988a; Esherick and Rankin 1990; Friedman, Pickowicz, and Selden 1991; Hsiao 1960; Huang 1998; Rankin 1986). Local elites occupy positions of prominence in local society because of their wealth, formal political position, political influence, social connections, moral authority, education, ritual knowledge, experience, leadership abilities, or a combination of these qualities. They tend to desire to occupy local leadership positions especially when these positions yield tangible or intangible dividends (e.g., extra income, prestige, opportunities to network with other local elites). Their strategies for maintaining an elite status across generations involve the conversion between symbolic capital (e.g., education, imperial degree titles) and other forms of capital (e.g., land, business, political connections, etc.) (see Bourdieu 1984). It has been argued that relative insecurity was a fundamental factor shaping the strategies of local elites in traditional Chinese society (Rankin and Esherick 1990: 306); hence they are usually the most sensitive and responsive to outside forces. The same can be said about the local elite in contemporary rural China. Only a few avenues of social advancement are open for too many contenders.

In Shaanbei, becoming an official in the local state is still the most desired route to local elite status, so much so that many are rumored to have paid tens of thousands of yuan to buy a position such as a county's vice mayorship. That is why, I was told, there are so many vice mayors in each county. Official positions are understood to be lucrative because officials can take bribes (the same is true of managerial elites in state-owned enterprises such as coal mines and factories). On the other hand, village official positions (e.g., village head, village Party secretary) are often no longer eagerly sought after because the trouble is perceived by many to outweigh the benefits.

The reform era has created two more routes to local elite status that were not available during the Maoist era. The first new route to local elite status is to become rich through private commercial activities and enterprises because money denotes status and can buy influence. Members of what can be called the New Rich are individuals who have reaped financial benefit from the economic reform through a combination of hard work, connections, and political savvy. The famous Yu Zuomin of Daqiuzhuang belongs to this type (Gilley 2001; Lin and Chen 1999).

The second new route to local elite status is to become a leader in a local folk social institution such as the temple association. This type of local elite tends to be the moral leader, i.e., individuals who wield authority and influence because of their moral rectitude and advocacy for traditional social values. The Confucian Temple vow-takers studied by Jun Jing and the village leaders studied by Wang Mingming and Stephan Feuchtwang belong to this type (Jing 1996, 2002; Wang 1996; Feuchtwang and Wang 2001). It is significant that the temple association has emerged in rural Shaanbei as the most prominent folk civic (nongovernmental) organization. As mentioned above, the temple and the temple association are both resources and resource-generators for the local community and the temple officers. Helping to revive a temple and becoming a temple officer are culturally sanctioned means of harnessing local power (magical as well as secular-political). Because of the traditional cultural conservatism of social values embodied in temple legends and divination messages, temple officers are willy-nilly aligned with traditional idioms of authority and community. Of course, many men want to become temple officers precisely because they are interested in reviving or maintaining traditional values in what they perceive as a society in moral decline. These tend to be older villagers who have a vested interest in reviving a folk cultural space in which they can exercise moral authority and where their knowledge of traditional lore is valued. However, being involved in reviving local cultural traditions often entails considerable innovation and creativity, as Lao Wang's reforestation and other projects can attest. The New Rich and the Moral Leader are of course ideal types, and often individuals, such as Lao Wang, embody characteristics of both types. The two types of new local elite have a symbiotic relationship with the conventional local elite, i.e., village-level cadres and local state officials, and sometimes they simply merge into each other (e.g., through marriage and kinship ties).

When there is village factionalism, members of opposing factions vie for control of the temple association the way they would compete for control of the Villagers' Committee. The example of Lao Wang and his enemies amply illustrates the way in which the temple serves as yet another battleground for local political maneuvers and intrigues. Because temple offices are public, the cultural ideal for a temple officer is caring for the common good with impartiality. In reality, however, all recognize the inevitability of temple officers' serving their particularistic interests. Given the internal divisions of every community, a temple officer is bound to be perceived as a benefactor and ally by some people and as a bully and enemy by others; hence the importance of legitimation politics. With or without the temple association, micro-politics is endemic in village communities. The political aspect of popular religion has long been noticed by anthropologists who studied Taiwanese local societies (e.g. Rohsenow 1973; Seaman 1978); in the context of reform-era rural China, however, we witness the reemergence of a site of local political contest and negotiation that had been completely suppressed during the Maoist era (see Jing 1996). One wonders if the political possibilities promised by the realm of popular religion were not sufficient reason for it to have been revived by local activists such as Lao Wang.

The Shifting Character of the State and State-Society Relations at the Local Level

The Chinese state has changed its priorities in the past twenty years from political campaigns to promoting economic growth. The party-state not only gave up socialist planned economy to a considerable extent but also abandoned socialism as a cultural project. Except for the occasional rhetoric on "building socialist spiritual civilization," the state has retreated from sponsoring cultural work aimed at transforming supposedly old, traditional culture into new, socialist culture. The entire official cultural work apparatus in rural China has collapsed, and most of the former socialist propaganda workers (e.g., opera performers, musicians, choreographers) find themselves performing at folk event productions such as temple festivals in place of socialist event productions such as production drives and political campaigns. It seems that the state has already accepted the revival of popular religion as a reality and a relatively harmless expression of folk culture and is willing to assume a regulatory rather than suppressive role. This shift in attitude from radical anti-traditionalism to broad tolerance parallels the development of the state's relationship to popular religion in Taiwan in recent decades (see Katz 2003).

The local state in particular has shifted from demonstrating political loyalty to the central party-state by following its policies closely to adopting a laissez-faire stance toward local matters. The Longwanggou case shows that local state agencies are inclined to exchange protection of local temples for economic benefits even if it means protecting theoretically illegal "feudal superstitious" activities. The relaxed attitude of the local state toward popular religion is one of the most important factors in enabling the latter's revival in Shaanbei.

The rapid growth during the reform era of many diverse forms of qigong such as Falungong (Karmic Wheel Practice), Zhonggong (Chinese Magical Practice), Xianggong (Fragrance Practice), and Yuanjigong (Original Ultimate Practice) has posed threats, among many other things, to the Chinese regime's ability to control space (see Chen 1995, 2003).[2] Group qigong practices effectively turn public spaces into intensely private and communal domains, as private health and vitality concerns override any ideologically orchestrated uses of the same spaces (recall mass processions and public struggle campaigns during the high-socialist era). The state's paranoid reactions to these challenges speak volumes about how much importance the state still puts on these spaces.[3] On the other hand, the state is much more tolerant of unthreatening activities within people's private home space such as playing mah-jongg or the installation of domestic deity altars.

Popular religious institutions such as Longwanggou carve out spaces from the state in a much less confrontational manner. In a way, the state reacted strongly to group qigong practices because qigong practitioners use spaces originally created and still maintained by the state (e.g., urban spaces, public parks, squares). Similarly, the state cannot tolerate rural migrants' intrusion into urban spaces and often resorts to violent means to "clean up" squatter communities (see Zhang 2001). On the other hand, the state's presence in the valleys and on the hilltops of Shaanbei is momentary and only infrequently palpable insofar as religious control is concerned, its impact having been softened by local state agencies, deflected and channeled by local elites, and sometimes seemingly swallowed by the great ocean that is rural China.

Notes

Chapter 1

1. Even though some of the narratives in this book bring us back in time to the Republican and Maoist periods, the focus of the book is squarely on the reform era, which is already more than two decades old. Many China scholars have conducted extensive studies on state-peasant relationships during the Maoist high Socialist era through documentary research and oral history interviews, but fewer studies have focused on the reform era. A desire to tell the whole story of the Communist Revolution has often rendered the reform period a post-Mao epilogue. To redress this imbalance, I decided quite early in my fieldwork that I would focus more on the reform era. A more historical investigation of conditions of popular religion and state-society relations during the earlier eras (late imperial, Republican, and Maoist) in Shaanbei would have to wait for another occasion.

2. The official name for this place is Heilongtan (Black Dragon Pool); however, all locals refer to the place as Longwanggou. I follow the local usage for my book.

3. Scholars have used a variety of approaches to study Chinese popular religion. The intellectual labor has typically been divided amongst anthropologists, religious studies specialists, and historians. Even though there is occasional overlap in approach between these different specialists, they tend to choose their focus according to well-established discipline-specific concerns and consequently employ distinctive discipline-specific methodologies. Religious studies specialists are more concerned with aspects of popular religion that are closer to the systematized, elite traditions of Confucianism, Daoism, and Buddhism. They are more preoccupied with written texts, religious ideas, doctrines, hagiography, iconography, ritual sequence and their meanings. They are usually as interested in the history and transformation of religious ideas and symbols as they are in studying these ideas and symbols as constituting a religious system. Anthropologists, on the other hand, tend to study the practices of popular religion in their so-

cial settings through interviews and participant observation. Some scholars in recent years have broken this division of intellectual labor by combining insights from anthropology with those from social history and religious studies (e.g., Bruun 2003; Dean 1993, 1998b; DuBois 2005; Feuchtwang 1992; Hymes 2002; Jordan and Overmyer 1986; Katz 1995; Sangren 1987; Sutton 2003; Weller 1987a).

4. Early examples include Raymond Firth (1950), George Foster (1953), Robert Redfield (1956), Sidney Mintz (1960), Clifford Geertz (1963), and Eric Wolf (1957, 1966).

Chapter 2

1. Qin culture is a cultural area named after the Qin State of early China. The Chinese indigenous discourse on these regional "cultures," based on climate, ecology, history, dialect, cuisine, expressive culture (e.g., opera), character, etc., is well worth study.

2. Jin culture is also a cultural area named after a state in early China, the Jin State.

3. The place name Yulin or Yan'an can refer to the prefecture, the county, or the city depending on context. To avoid confusion, throughout this book I will specify which level of government or geographical unit to which I am referring (i.e., Yulin Prefecture, Yulin County, Yulin City). In fact, during the period of my fieldwork there was no such official appellation as Yulin County or Yan'an County because these two counties were called *shi* (cities), i.e., county-equivalent cities—Yulin County, for example, was converted to Yulinshi in 1988. In other words, Yulinshi comprised both the city of Yulin as well as the rural townships. I retain the use of Yulin County to refer to the entire county while using Yulin or Yulin City to refer to the urban areas of Yulinshi exclusively. The situation for Yan'an is even more confusing. From January 1, 1997, Yan'an Prefecture officially became the prefecture-equivalent Yan'an Municipality (Yan'anshi), whose jurisdiction includes all the original counties under the prefecture. At the same time the urban area of Yan'an City was renamed Baota District. I will use Yan'an Prefecture, Yan'an County, and Yan'an City (or simply Yan'an) respectively to refer to the three different administrative levels. Similarly, county names are the same as county seat names. For clarity's sake, for example, I use Mizhi County when I refer to the entire county and Mizhi or Mizhi Town to refer to the county seat.

4. At the end of the 17th century the Qing state abolished military contract land development in Shaanbei in favor of purely civilian-based land development (YLDQZ:18).

5. The most infamous of these mission-related conflicts was the Sanbian Mission Case (*sanbian jiaoan*). See Litzinger 1996 and Thompson 1996 for mission-related conflicts in rural Zhili (Hebei) and Shanxi, which illustrate similar processes at work.

6. These of course were the terms used by the Communists. When the Nationalists were fighting the Communists they called the areas occupied by the Communists "bandit areas" (*feiqu*) and the areas under Nationalist control "Nationalist-controlled areas" (*guotongqu*).

7. But see Pauline Keating's book on how the land reforms and the cooperative movement differed in the Yanshu and Suide areas under the Communists because of two distinct preexisting eco-social formations (Keating 1997). Many scholars have studied the Yan'an period of Chinese Communism; see especially Apter and Saich 1994; Esherick 1994, 1998; Holm 1984; Judd 1986, 1990; Keating 1994a, 1994b, 1997; Selden 1971; see also Holm 1994; Myrdal 1965; and Rawski 1986.

8. Zhenchuan Town (the seat of the Zhenchuan township) had a population of approximately 25,000 in 1998.

9. For detailed anthropological-historical accounts of these processes in different local, village communities, see Chan, Madsen, and Unger 1992 (Guangdong), Gao 1999 (Jiangxi), Jing 1996 (Gansu), Friedman, Pickowicz, and Selden 1991 and forthcoming (Hebei), Madsen 1984 (Guangdong), Shu-min Huang 1998 (Fujian), Liu 2000 (northern Shaanxi), Potter and Potter 1990 (Guangdong), Ruf 1998 (Sichuan), Seybolt 1996 (Henan), Siu 1989a (Guangdong), and Wang Mingming 1996 (Fujian). Driven by an intellectual desire to know what had really happened in rural China during the Maoist era, most of these scholars have focused their attention on pre-Reform years at the expense of ethnographic descriptions of contemporary situations. As I have mentioned in Chapter 1, in this study I try to focus on the reform era.

10. For example, in 1989, about two-thirds of the financial income of Yulin Prefecture came from the central government in the form of subsidies (YLDQZ: 340–41).

11. In 1986 the agricultural population of Yulin Prefecture was 91% of the total population (YLDQZ: 127).

12. The coal reserve in Shaanbei, especially that in Shenmu and Fugu counties, is estimated to be one of the world's largest. The natural gas reserve is estimated to be one of China's largest. In the late 1990s the natural gas from Jingbian County was already supplying Beijing through direct pipelines.

13. The private ownership of sedan cars during the Maoist era was nonexistent. Even today, very few people in Shaanbei own cars for private use. The two overwhelmingly large categories of sedan cars in Shaanbei are taxicabs (a very recent phenomenon, mostly in urban areas) and chauffeured cars for officials.

14. Each of the following areas of administration has its own bureau or office: county general affairs, civic affairs, labor and personnel, cadre affairs, county gazetteer, county archive, jurisprudence, public security (police), planning, statistics, finance, grain, industry, commerce, provisions, construction, economics, transportation, science, education, sports and cultural affairs, hygiene and health care, family planning, broadcasting, agriculture, irrigation and water conservancy, forestry, animal husbandry and herding, village and township enterprises, land administration, public morality advocacy, tobacco sales, environmental protection, mining, foreign trade, structural reform, etc. See Shue 1995 on the phenomenon of "state sprawl" in post-Mao China. See also Blecher and Shue 1996 for description and analysis of the expansion of a county-level local state in Hebei Province.

15. According to YLDQZ (454), in 1986 there were a total of 40,845 offi-

cials in Yulin Prefecture, among whom 6 were chief and deputy prefecture com-missioners, 538 were prefecture-level chief and deputy bureau heads, 59 were chief and deputy county head administrators, 1,538 were county-level chief and deputy bureau heads, 620 were chief and deputy township and xiang head administrators. The number of ordinary officials in Yulin Prefecture in 1986 was thus 38,084. The total working population in Yulin Prefecture in 1986 was 1,069,090 (YLDQZ 127).

16. See Bian (1994) for a detailed sociological analysis of state sector em-ployment in urban China and the hierarchy within it.

17. In Yulin Prefecture at the end of 1986, 103,709 people worked for state-owned danweis; 25,747 people worked for city and township collective danweis (YLDQZ 127).

18. This percentage of course varies depending on which county or prefecture is in question. The percentage is much higher when one looks at Yulin County and Yan'an County because of the concentration of state enterprises and admin-istrative units in the prefectural seats. For example, the "state folks" in Yan'an County comprised close to 30% of the total working population in that county in 1990 (calculated from figures in Yan'an juan: 440–52).

19. Peasant is a broad category that includes farmers, forestry workers, pas-toralists, and fishery workers. Since the overwhelming majority of Shaanbei peas-ants are farmers, I will equate the two terms and ignore the other subcategories in my discussion, unless specified otherwise. And in this study when I use "Shaan-bei people" I refer mostly to peasants.

20. The springing up of these roadside businesses-cum-residence has con-tributed to town sprawl and village sprawl along major highways, often eating up valuable irrigated agricultural land.

21. As the other side of the same coin, the parents of back-valley brides fur-nish very small dowries while those of town brides invariably furnish elaborate and expensive dowries so as not to lose face.

22. This amount, which has not changed following the inflation rate in the past two or three decades, seems to have been based on a pre-Liberation tradi-tional practice of paying 24 silver dollars as the standard brideprice. However, 24 silver dollars back then was worth much more than 240 yuan today.

23. See Liu (2000: 51–57) for a poignant account of marriage crisis in a re-mote Shaanxi rural community.

24. Ming, fate, is more long-term and permanent. Yun, fortune, refers to short-term changes in one's life. See Harrell 1987 for a discussion of the concept of fate in Chinese folk ideology.

25. According to the survey, 183 villages had a population lower than 50 per-sons, and there were 288 villages with 50–99 persons, 345 villages with 100–199 persons, 168 villages with 200–299 persons, 99 villages with 300–399 persons, 59 villages with 400–499 persons, and 80 villages with over 500 persons (ibid. 110–11).

26. See Kevin J. O'Brien 1994 for an account of the origins and the imple-mentation of the Organic Law of Villagers' Committees.

27. Perhaps due to language usage inertia, when some township or rural dis-

trict officials are coming to visit, many villagers still say "Somebody is coming from the *commune*" (*gongshe lai ren la*).

28. For a participant-observer's scathing critique of "squatting" officials, see Pan 1997.

29. The Cultural Revolution in Shaanbei was particularly violent compared to many other places in China.

30. Yan (1996b: 197) did not mention directly that the budding off of the new household usually involves the division of the most important family property, the family house.

31. Susan Greenhalgh (1993: 233 and 235) observed that in 1983 the government had new regulations calling for concentration of wedding ceremonies during three annual holiday periods (May 1 International Labor Day, October 1 National Day, and Spring Festival, i.e., Lunar New Year). As she discovered that 78% of all weddings in her sample from the rural Guanzhong area of Shaanxi Province took place during the Spring Festival holidays (and 4% each during the other two major holidays), she concluded that the state must have a lot of power to determine when people wed in rural China. However, traditionally, in Shaanbei at least, most weddings would have taken place around Spring Festival anyway. One main reason why this is so is that according to the traditional handbook for selecting auspicious and inauspicious days (for a wedding, traveling, construction, etc.), all the days in the twelfth month in the lunar year are auspicious for all purposes (*bai wu jinji*, i.e., no taboo on anything). Other reasons include, for example, that food prepared for the wedding feast will not spoil easily in winter, and that people who have traveled away will come back during Spring Festival time so more people can attend the wedding ceremony.

32. See Luo (2000) for a detailed analysis of village reciprocity arrangements.

33. The simple dirt yao, dirt yao with rock face, and rock yao are called *tuyao*, *jiekouyao*, and *shiyao* respectively. Rock yaos usually have their backside touching the chipped vertical end of a slope, or they can be entirely freestanding.

34. This row-style village home construction resembles those in the North China Plain and other areas in rural China where one-story houses (*pingfang*) made of bricks or mud bricks are common. I suspect that it was only during the collective era that peasants in different parts of China began the straight, parallel row-style house construction. For example, in rural Mizhi County in the 1970s some villages collectively began constructing row-style yaos in an attempt to build socialist "New Villages" (*xin nongcun*) (MZXZ: 257). Xiajia Village, studied by Yan Yunxiang, has a typical row-style spatial organization, complete with parallel streets, which I assume took shape in the Maoist era (Yan 1996b: 23 Map 1). The villagers might simply be copying urban layouts, as is the case in rural Taiwan (Hill Gates, personal communication).

35. There is a taboo against building yao in even numbers, so the typical combinations are in threes and fives.

36. The most basic, thin, cheap version of a woolen rug is called *zhan*. In recent years many peasant families can afford to appoint their kang with a thick, decorated, high quality rug called *tan*.

Chapter 3

1. For discussions on Chinese researchers' attitudes toward popular religion, see Feuchtwang 1989a, 1989b; Feuchtwang and Wang 1991.

2. For example, most of the volumes in the Traditional Hakka Society Series edited by the Daoism scholar John Lagerwey cover popular religious activities (e.g., Luo and Lagerwey 1997). The Min-su ch'ü-i Series edited by Wang ch'iu-kuei is a large collection of primary research on popular religious activities, especially relating to drama and ritual, done by Chinese local researchers.

3. Various foreign observers had provided excellent descriptions of North China temples and temple organizations before the Communist victory, e.g., Gamble 1954, 1963; Goodrich 1964; Grootaers 1952, 1995; Grootaers, Li, and Wang 1951; and the Japanese Mantetsu Group. C. K. Yang's Religion in Chinese Society also utilized data from North China. For recent historical studies on North China popular religion, see Duara 1988b (based on Mantetsu materials); DuBois 2005; Johnson 1994, 1997; Naquin 1988, 1992, 2000; and Zhao 1992.

4. In the late 19th century and the early 20th century some Catholic and Protestant missions established footholds in parts of Shaanbei and began attacking local popular religion, even though the effects were very limited.

5. For example, during Sun Fa Hsu's tenure as the magistrate of Ding (Ting) County in Hebei Province between 1914 and 1917, 68% of the existing temples were discontinued, many of which were converted to schools (Gamble 1954: 404).

6. It was estimated that there were more than two thousand spirit mediums in the Shaan-Gan-Ning Border Region in the 1930s and 1940s (population 1,500,000) when the Central Red Army was stationed in Shaanbei (from Mao's speech of 1944, quoted in Selden 1971: 273). I suspect that the actual number was much higher.

7. It was common practice that 10 percent of the proceeds from these operations went to the sponsoring of the opera performances. In Yulin County at least, the resident Nationalist army often set up their own gambling and opium sheds at temple festivals.

8. In the North China Plain, religious life seemed to have prospered until the Great Leap Forward Campaign of 1958 (Friedman et al. 1991: 171, 205–6, 210, 230). Shaanbei, being farther away from central government control, enjoyed a freer political and cultural climate compared to the North China Plain. This is still true today, as popular religion in Shaanbei has revived at a much faster pace than in the North China Plain.

9. The biggest irony is that the descendants of rich landlords and merchants were actually the most modern and reformist-minded, whereas the poor peasants were often the most "superstitious." So the Communist victory might have worked in popular religion's favor in terms of granting more people the resources to sponsor and consume popular religion.

10. Of course, this statistic on the temples as physical structures does not reveal to us how actively they were used. Based on what my informants in different parts of Shaanbei told me, it seems that regular worship and periodic temple fes-

tivals continued up to the Socialist Education period (1963) and the beginning of the Cultural Revolution (1966). Other parts of China might have seen harsher repression earlier.

11. Religious life during the so-called "hard times" (*kunnan shiqi*) warrants a detailed study. It suffices to note here that Shaanbei was not as hard-hit by the Great Leap as many other places in China (see Friedman et al. 1991; Mueggler 2001).

12. Whether a yinyang master or spirit medium had to be jailed and reeducated depended on the relationship he (usually he) had with local officials. One 84-year-old medium in Shenmu County boasted to me that, while 9 out of 10 "practitioners of superstition" had to go to jail, he did not because he had cured the relatives of many of the top officials so they protected him. Also, very poor (thus of good class background) yinyang masters and mediums were not bothered too much by the campaigns.

13. This practice with cigarettes resembles, by coincidence I believe, the cigarette-burning practice in the amoral-cultic worship of the Eighteen Kings in Taiwan described by Weller, where it has a definite flavor of the immoral (Weller 1994a).

14. The White Cloud Mountain is linked to the Daoist abbey in Beijing, also named White Cloud, even though I did not investigate their exact relationship. The Beijing White Cloud Abbey is the headquarters of the Complete Perfection (Quanzhen) Daoist sect. The main deity of the Jia County White Cloud Mountain is the Perfected Warrior Zhenwu zushi (see Grootaers 1952 for a hagiography of Zhenwu zushi; and Seaman 1987 for an annotated translation and analysis of the folk novel *Journey to the North*, which is an elaborate hagiography of Zhenwu zushi).

15. This practice of identifying famous religious sites not by the names of the temples or shrines but by the names of the places is apparently common in other parts of China, e.g., Foguangshan, Nankunshen, Beigang in Taiwan, Miaofengshan near Beijing, all the famous Daoist and Buddhist mountains, as well as in Korea and Japan.

16. For a comparison between the popular religious landscape in Shaanbei and that in Taiwan, see Chau (2003: 47–50).

17. These are occasions for descendants to visit the graves of ancestors.

18. See Stevan Harrell 1974b on similar practices in Taiwan.

19. This is indicative of the reluctance of the state to allow organized religions to expand their spheres of influence.

20. But I was told that in Yan'an City a female medium's possessing deity is General Zhu De and that she was very powerful and popular.

21. See Goossaert (2000) for a study that treats Chinese temples as the most fundamental feature of Chinese religious life. See Hur (2000) for a historical study of the mixture of religiosity, commerce, and entertainment at a famous Japanese temple.

22. When a deity speaks through the mouth of a possessed person it is said that the deity has "spoken out" (*chukou*) about his request.

23. See Wu (1988) for a study of temple festivals in late imperial China.

24. Yangge is a traditional north China village group entertainment and activity. Village men, some cross-dressed as women, form troupes in sizes ranging from a dozen people to over a hundred, and they dance with drums and gongs and other instruments.

25. The first congregation is in Yulin County, the second in Suide County, the third in Mizhi County, the fourth in neighboring Shanxi counties (mostly Lin County and Lishi Town across the Yellow River), the fifth in Wupu County and all counties in Yan'an Prefecture, and the sixth in Hengshan, Jingbian, Dingbian and Baoan (now Zhidan) counties. I did not record which communities constituted the other two congregations (perhaps Inner Mongolia and Guanzhong?).

26. Because my research focus was not on mediumism, and because I did not want to attract unwanted attention from the local government by doing research on activities that are clearly labeled as superstitious, I did not do any research on mediums until toward the end of my stay in Shaanbei.

27. For an analysis of similar beliefs and ritual in Minnan (southern Fujian) culture, see Baptandier-Berthier 1994 and Chang 1993.

28. This is similar to the Taiwanese practice of hiring performance troupes to conduct Buddhist funeral rituals.

29. Of course, the "legitimate" clergy (monks and priests) are supposed to help suppress or reform, not revive, popular religious rituals, as they share a similar elitist contempt for popular practices.

Chapter 4

1. Boas was arguing in particular against the then prevalent evolutionary and diffusionist paradigms in the nascent science of anthropology.

2. For detailed treatments of ling in the Taiwanese popular religious context, see Sangren 1987 and 2000. Unlike those in southern Fujian and Taiwan, Shaanbei popular religious cults are not territorial cults. The sense of boundary maintenance prominent in southeastern Chinese religious tradition is very weak in Shaanbei, perhaps due to the historical pattern of settlement. As I mentioned in Chapter 2, the settlement of Shaanbei was not characterized by violent confrontations between Han and non-Han peoples or between different Han sub-ethnic groups, such as those found during the settlement of Taiwan. Sangren (1987, 2000) argues that the deities' ling in Taiwan is constructed upon the perceived role the deities played in protecting the communities against enemies and rival communities or in mediating order and disorder. My Shaanbei data do not support such an interpretation of ling. Because popular religion is so embedded in its socio-historical milieu, it is not surprising to find such a discrepancy in the different manifestations of ling. But as the community-protection role of different deities in Taiwan has slowly receded to the background, the more personal problem-solving role would inevitably come to the fore.

3. Helen Siu found that the young people she talked to in her field site in the Canton Delta in the early 1980s did not know much about the gods they prayed to or the meanings of ritual activities (Siu 1989a: xxi). I suspect their lack of knowledge is partly due to their youth and hence a not yet well-developed religious habitus. On the other hand, even many adults would not have been able to

explain the meanings behind various ritual actions because interpretation is often not as important as ritual action, i.e., orthopraxy (see Watson 1988b).

4. I borrow this phrase from Mallon (1995), who used this Gramsci-inspired idea to characterize the nature of community involvement in agrarian politics in rural Mexico and Peru. See also Gates and Weller (1987).

5. This principle of correspondence (homeopathy) is very common in these divine retribution stories. Another story related to me was about a Party secretary in another community who said, during the Cultural Revolution, that he "didn't piss" (*buniao*, Shaanbei dialect expression for "not being afraid of") the local god. He subsequently died of urine poisoning because he couldn't urinate.

6. See Hymes (2002) for a cogent historical analysis of the Daoist co-optation of the bureaucratic metaphor. See Dean (1993) for a discussion on the role of the "Daoist liturgical framework" in enlisting and enframing local cults into a symbolic imperium. See Sangren (2000) for an analysis of the implications of the figure of the patricidal Nezha. See Shahar and Weller (1996) for studies on deities that do not fit the bureaucratic image of Chinese deities.

7. Note that this debate rests on premises that already transcended the earlier view that in China there were Buddhism, Daoism, Confucianism, and lastly popular religion. The "many" in "many religions" does not refer to these reified categories. Weller 1987a remains one of the most systematic reflections on the issue of unity and diversity in Chinese religious interpretations and practices.

Chapter 5

1. This section is based on oral history collected from older villagers in Longwanggou, especially from Zhang Xuexian of Batawan Village, who was 74 years old in 1998. I have chosen to present this material in the present tense so that readers can try to transport themselves to 1938 and view the temple festival through the eyes of the festivalgoers.

2. See Duara (1988a, based on the Mantetsu survey); Gamble (1954, based on the Ting County survey), (1963); and Grootaers, Li, and Wang (1951). See Jing (2002) for a historical study of a dragon king temple in southern Shanxi.

3. Nowadays these rituals of rain-begging (*qiyu*) occur less and less frequently in Shaanbei. See the last scene of the movie *The Yellow Earth* (*Huangtudi*) for a dramatized version of the rain-begging ritual. The Yangjiagou Research Group made a video of a recent rain-begging ritual in Yangjiagou village which took place in 1995 (Luo Hongguang, personal communication).

4. The Daoist White Cloud Mountain in a nearby county remains the most famous and most visited religious site in Shaanbei, but it is completely under the county government's control.

5. This is a creative and modified version of a more common Chinese saying *di ling ren jie*, which means the place (*di*) is blessed and [therefore] the people are brilliant.

6. The nine villages together constitute the "southern spread" (*nanpian*) of the Zhenchuan Township.

7. These other six villages all had their own temples in the past but they were also destroyed during the Cultural Revolution. Their initial willingness to join

forces with the three Longwanggou villages to rebuild the Heilongdawang Temple was primarily a gesture of submission to the power of Heilongdawang because in the past they had begged for rain at the Heilongdawang Temple. All six villages subsequently rebuilt their village temples as well, all with some financial support from Longwanggou.

8. This story can be interpreted as a justification of the usurpation of the deity and his power by the Chenjiapo villagers.

9. It is also possible that the older foundation belonged to a temple dedicated to another deity but was "eaten" by the Heilongdawang Temple. However, I did not encounter traces of a displaced deity in local folklore.

10. See Luo (1999: 272–78) for an analysis of the relationship between the two temples.

11. The only better mural I myself have seen in Shaanbei is the surviving old mural in the main hall dedicated to Zhenwu zushi on the White Cloud Mountain in Jia County. And the Heilongdawang mural is the only one I have seen in Shaanbei that has freestanding figurines. On temple murals as ritual paraphernalia, see Katz 1999.

12. On the practice of granting titles to deities during imperial times, see Watson 1985 and Duara 1988a.

13. There was a certain General Zhang Yao in Zuo Zongtang's army during its military expedition in the Northwest to suppress the Muslim rebels of the mid-19th century (Fields 1978), which might have served as a historical source for the legend.

14. In their capacities to shed light on the understanding of each other, they are also each other's "co(n)-texts" (see Silverstein and Urban 1996).

15. Important exceptions in recent scholarship that focuses on the role writing plays in politics and empire-building, and the relationship between writing and materiality are Connery (1998), Kern (2000), Kraus (1991), Lewis (1999), Zeitlin and Liu (2003), and Zito (1997).

16. The expression is obviously inspired by J. L. Austin's concept of speech acts (Austin 1962).

17. Recent major exceptions are Messick (1993) and Shryock (1997), both dealing with textual authority and domination in Islamic societies.

Chapter 6

1. I use the present tense for most of this and other ethnographic chapters, but it should be made clear that the present is the "ethnographic present" of 1997 and 1998, the period of my fieldwork, unless otherwise specified.

2. Shaanbei people often distinguish fierce gods from benevolent gods (*shanshen*) who are always good-tempered, e.g., the fertility goddesses. See Duara (1988a: 32) for similar fierce depictions of dragon kings in the North China Plain.

3. The set is called the Black Dragon King Miraculous Divination Set (*Heilongdawang shenqian*).

4. More and more worshipers bring their fertility-related problems to the

Dragon mother (*Longmu niangniang*) ever since the worship of her began in Longwanggou in 1996.

5. Unlike the divination sticks, the gua, to my knowledge, is only popular in North China, just as the *pue* has only a regional spread in Southeast China, mostly in Fujian and Taiwan. See Jordan 1982 for an analysis of pue divination.

6. Heilongdawang's mother, the Longmu Niangniang, has her own oracle roller. The eight messages on the *niangnianggua* are:

—One son will become famous (*yizi chengming*);

—One pair of sons and one pair of daughters (*nanshuang nüdui*);

—Give thanks when you get a son (*dezi huanyuan*);

—Will get well after taking the magical medicine (*fuyao nenghao*);

—Extremely auspicious (*shangshang daji*);

—Not clear how you would thank me for the help (*kouyuan buming*);

—Not in accordance with god's ways (*buhe shendao*);

—Pray with a sincere heart (*qianxin qidao*).

7. On more detailed studies of popular religious temple oracles, see Banck 1985; Ding 1996; Morgan 1998; and Pas 1984.

8. It was Baolin who showed me my room and gave me the padlock room key when I first got settled in Longwanggou; it was also he who on occasions brought me great watermelons from storage in the summer.

9. For the better part of the year people at the temple eat two meals a day at the temple canteen. The brunch is at about 11 a.m. and the dinner is at about 5 p.m. In the morning it is almost invariably the simple yet delicious pressed noodle, with hot and sour soup serving as condiment. It is called "sour soup pressed noodle" (*suantang helao*), a ubiquitous dish in Shaanbei.

10. Fake money had been a perennial problem in Shaanbei as well as in other parts of China. Many restaurants, stores, and other businesses had equipped themselves with bill-verification devices.

11. The market in Zhenchuan Town meets on the fourths and ninths of every lunar month (i.e., 4th, 9th, 14th, 19th, 24th, 29th).

12. This is a term traditionally used for the owner of a business. The cabinet (*gui*) of course refers to the money cabinet.

13. The Chinese state, on the other hand, is no less adept at corporatist organizations. Hill Gates (1996) provides in-depth analysis of what she calls the tributary mode of production, with ample illustrations of state-controlled corporations (see especially chapter 11). Similarly, some other scholars have noticed that, with the advent of reform-era rural industrialization, many local states in China engage in corporate behaviors, and they characterize these behaviors as local state corporatism (e.g., Oi 1988, 1999; Oi and Walder 1999).

14. I did not find out how people at Gejiagelao, the Dragon Mother's native village and original place of worship, felt about Lao Wang's usurpation of the Dragon Mother. As far as I know, worship continued at the original temple and it continued to be a very local temple.

Chapter 7

1. See Dean (1998b, especially chapter 1) for an inspiring exposition on the concept of "ritual-events."

2. Note that I am speaking of hosting in terms of receiving guests who are known to the host. This concept of hosting is related to but very different from what is commonly understood in the West as "hospitality" (receiving and being kind mostly to strangers) (see, for example, Derrida and Dufourmantelle 2000 and Rosello 2001).

3. The marrying off of a daughter typically involves a relatively small banquet and ceremony compared to the other two types of major hosting occasions. The groom's family hosts the big wedding banquet in his village.

4. Ortner calls these life scripts "cultural schemas" (Ortner 1989).

5. The deaths of the wife's parents are not major events in the household, as it is the wife's brothers' responsibility to bury their parents.

6. When there is more than one son, all of the sons assume responsibility for sponsoring the funerals for their parents. However, the eldest son typically is the chief host, and the funeral usually takes place in his courtyard. And aging parents typically live with their eldest son's family. The kind of meal rotation in which parents live in each son's family in turn, as is found in Taiwan, is not common in Shaanbei.

7. In fact, one could argue that fulfilling one's ritual obligation (e.g., providing a proper funeral for a dead parent) is ultimately to fulfill one's social obligation (e.g., the son's filial obligation to his parents).

8. Ortner (1978) writes about the use of aggressive hosting among the Sherpas: because the host (giver of food and drinks) is morally superior, he or she can ask favors of the guest, who becomes indebted. One is tempted to interpret in a Lévi-Straussian structuralist manner the position of the host vis-à-vis that of the guest in the following list of contrasting qualities: active vs passive; mobilizer vs mobilized; inside vs outside; center vs periphery; one vs many; giver vs receiver; provider vs consumer; superior vs inferior.

9. Just as points of contrast: in 1998, an unskilled laborer made between 20 and 30 yuan a day (e.g., as a member of a construction crew); the total yearly cash income of an average peasant household not engaged in any sidelines in the Longwanggou area was estimated to be between 1,000 and 2,000 yuan. Compared to most other areas of rural Shaanbei, the Longwanggou area is relatively well-off, thanks to its proximity to a main road and a major market town, Zhenchuan.

10. A cynical Shaanbei saying goes: If you have money, you bury money [while burying the person]; if you don't have money, you just bury the person (*youqian maiqian, meiqian mairen*).

11. In fact, one can argue that more popular religious elements (though not related to deities) are condensed and mobilized in a funeral compared to those religious elements at temple festivals. In Shaanbei at least, funerals are liturgically more complex than temple festivals. But popular religious temple festivals in Fujian and Taiwan tend to have complex liturgical components as a result of the

symbiotic relationship temples have developed with Daoist ritualists (see Dean 1993).

12. When a person dies at an advanced age and after having had male descendants (especially grandsons), he or she is considered to have had a good life. Therefore his or her death is seen as a joyous event, which is why there is the expression "red and white joyous events" (*hongbai xishi*), which is used to refer to both funerals and weddings as major life events.

13. See Kipnis (1997), Liu (2000), Luo (1999), and Yan (1996b) for detailed descriptions of weddings in North China village communities.

14. See Watson and Rawski 1988 for a benchmark collection of essays on Chinese funerary rituals. Naquin's piece on funerals in late-Qing and Republican North China (Hebei area) provides useful descriptions of late imperial and early modern North China funeral practices that are very similar to those described in local gazetteers of the same period for Shaanbei, testifying to the force of ritual standardization in traditional China. Chapter ten of Jankowiak (1993) describes a complete funeral ritual in the Inner Mongolian city of Huhhot staged by ethnic Han residents originally from Shanxi Province (bordering Shaanxi).

15. Ordinarily Shaanbei peasant households have only two meals a day. Only during agricultural busy times do they eat three meals a day because of the demands of heavier labor.

16. Shaanbei funerary practices largely conform to what is described by Watson (1988b) and Naquin (1988), testifying to the force of standardization of proper ritual procedures concerning funerals in late imperial China.

17. One most clear example of the shortening and simplification of traditional ritual procedure is found in the practice of "revisiting the grave on the third day after burial" (*fusan*) on the same day as the burial. Some do it in the afternoon, and some do it in the same morning. The mourners descend the hill and rest a little at some distance away from, and not in the line of sight of, the grave (symbolic of absence), and then return to the grave to conduct the "third day" offering.

18. I draw inspiration for this section from Naquin's analysis of the different roles played by the yinyang master, the Confucian master of ceremony, and the Buddhist and/or Daoist clergy at the funeral (Naquin 1988: 53–66). Naquin, however, does not discuss the guest-catering aspect of funerals.

19. Because of the layers of many traditions, the Chinese have a quite confused conception of what exactly happens to the soul after one dies. See Cohen (1988).

20. Sometimes Daoist priests were hired to do similar rituals.

21. The night before the burial, all the mourners and guests go on a procession after dusk. The dozen or so young men who help out catering the guests now make up the firecracker squad, leading the procession by throwing lit firecrackers into the air. A dozen other male helpers carry fire bundles (made of corn husks soaked in tar) and spread small clusters of fire along the procession route (hence the name of the procession ritual: spreading road lamps, or *sa ludeng*).

22. The yinyang master rings a small, high-pitched bell while mumbling some chants. The three assistants follow him into each house and make a quick round

in the main room: the one with a small, wooden, mock bow and arrow makes a gesture of shooting the arrow into the air; the one with a bowl of water (standing for vinegar or clear liquor?) and a brush sprinkles some water in the air; and the one with a bowl of five grains sprinkles some grains around.

23. As descendants of the deceased, women married to the descendants, or as agnatic kin, the mourners who are not members of the zhujia are of course partly hosts in relation to those who come to the funeral only to pay respect to the deceased. See Appadurai (1981) for an interesting analysis of the politics of playing partial host and partial guest in wedding ceremonies in a South Asian context.

24. For a detailed study of Chinese mourning clothes and how they encode social relationships, see Wolf (1970).

25. In his study of revived ritual activities in a Confucian temple in Gansu, Jun Jing noted the contrast between the relative chaos surrounding ritual actions and symbolic understandings and the relative clear-headedness surrounding banquet seating arrangements among festivalgoers. He aptly characterized the contrast as "ritual disarray" versus "dietary rationality" (Jing 1996: 157).

26. See Sangren (1987: 55–60) for an analysis of the Taiwanese practice of rotating among respected male household heads the responsibility of being the "*host* of the incense burner" (*luzhu*) and chief organizer of the temple festival or community ritual (see also Harrell 1982: 183–94). See Younger 2001 for a study of hosting in south Indian religious culture.

27. In southeastern China, the role of hosting a temple festival is often relegated to the professional Daoist priest, who, on behalf of the community that hires him, invites the Daoist high gods to partake in the festivities as well. See Stafford (2000: 74–77) for an analysis of receiving gods as guests.

28. A standard temple festival lasts for three days.

29. The relationship between the two temples was built upon the friendship between the two temple bosses as well as the evolving devotion of the Yan'an pilgrims toward the Black Dragon King. Significantly, the people of Longwanggou do not reciprocate by helping out at the temple festivals at the Zhenwu zushi temple in Ansai, thus demonstrating Longwanggou's higher status in the relationship.

Chapter 8

1. See Nasaw (1993) and Ozouf (1988) for examples of studies on Western modes of sociality.

2. One is tempted to speculate that the Communist victory in China was in no small measure thanks to the adoption of the color red for all aspects of the Communist movement (e.g., the Red Army, the red flag, the red star on the hat, etc.). For the Chinese peasants, red did not so much stand for blood and revolution as for happiness and good fortune.

3. Fire can signify very different things in different cultural traditions. In the West, fire can connote anger ("And every day, the proletarian heart burns with a sense of deprivation and injustice") (Lüdtke 1995: 199); danger and destruction ("hell, the terrors of the damned, and the destruction of the world at the Second

Coming") (Danforth 1989: 127); an ardent faith in God (ibid.: 191); the Holy Spirit (Winston 1999: 11); sexual excitement (Danforth 1989: 130), etc.

4. See Ellen Hertz (1998) on the stock fever; Jing Wang (1996) for the high culture fever; Brownell (1995) for "old people's disco dancing" fever; Graezer (1998, 1999) on yangge fever in urban Beijing.

5. Markets (including periodic markets) are favorite social spaces because of their honghuo qualities. For an analysis of the transformations of Taiwanese night markets (*yeshi*), see Yu (2004).

6. See Beck 1969 for a symbolic analysis of the conceptions of colors and changes in temperature in South Indian rituals and religion.

7. See Harrell (1981) for an analysis of normal drinking and deviant drinking in Taiwan.

8. Hostesses and prostitutes have to drink because of their professions.

9. Shaanbei people have not yet taken up wine drinking, which is a new practice confined to the cosmopolitan elite.

10. Liquor is usually more expensive than cigarettes (depending on the brands of the liquor and the cigarette of course), and serving liquor requires more work than serving cigarettes. Shaanbei men exchange cigarettes with or pass cigarettes to strangers on a regular basis, but never drink with strangers except when seated together at a banquet (but some sort of relationship is assumed on these occasions, e.g., all are related to the hosting family in one way or another).

11. See Kipnis 1997 for a cogent analysis of Chinese banqueting etiquette. See Farquhar 2002 for the relational effects of banqueting.

12. See Liu (2002) for the prevailing phenomenon of using hostesses and sometimes prostitutes in entertaining guests.

13. See Harrell 1981 for a description of virtually the same drinking game in rural Taiwan. Apparently the format of this drinking game has a wide geographical spread and is perhaps quite old.

14. Often better fist-swingers utter idiomatic expressions to go with the numbers, which makes watching the game a genuine pleasure.

15. Similarly, playing mah-jongg is a honghuo activity mainly because of the noise from shuffling and throwing the mah-jongg tiles and the bantering around the mah-jongg table. It is not fun to play on a table that is covered with cloth that muffles the tile noise.

16. As in most rural areas, in Shaanbei a peasant couple can have a second child if the first one is a girl. But even two children cannot make a household adequately honghuo.

17. As in most rural areas, women in Shaanbei are almost universally married unless they have extremely debilitating mental or physical handicaps. Many men, on the other hand, remain single because they cannot afford the brideprice.

18. The juxtaposition of the acknowledged misery of the shepherd and the happiness of occasions such as a wedding or a temple festival did not seem jarring at all to Shaanbei people. Similarly beggars are welcome and feasted as well at wedding and funeral banquets as well as temple festivals. Presumably they add to the honghuo and feasting them shows the host's generosity and abundance.

19. My use of "social heat" is obviously different from the journalistic usage, which refers to media attention (usually negative), as in: This scandal has been generating a lot of social heat.

20. This is what anthropologists call the domestic cycle.

21. It is interesting to note that in the U.S. young people consider their favorite places "cool" places, in contradistinction to "hot" places in Shaanbei.

22. Because there are no temple festivals in the Euro-American cultural tradition, it is tempting for a Westerner to think of the Chinese temple festival as a carnival (e.g., Zhao 1996; see also Gao 1992). A temple festival is like a carnival in many ways: special time marked off from ordinary time; people doing things that they ordinarily wouldn't do (e.g., gambling, getting drunk). But some typical carnival elements are not found at temple festivals: the pervasive use of masks, open sexuality, large-scale parades and pageantry, and pervasive revelry.

23. I understand affect as a diffused, embodied feeling (as opposed to the more specific and immediate emotional responses) such as excitement, boredom, languidness, moodiness, fondness, sensuality, spirituality, blessedness, security, nostalgia, bonding, aloofness, generalized fear, resentment, powerlessness, despair, happiness, euphoria, exhilaration, etc.

24. There has been a call in recent years among anthropologists for more sensory-oriented studies of other cultures (e.g., Chuengsatiansup 1999; Classen 1993; Classen, Howes, and Synnott 1994; Desjarlais 2003; Farquhar 1995; Geurts 2003; Howes 1990, 1991; Stoller 1989).

25. Needless to say, the festival crowd does not generate a "soul," as Le Bon would argue (1920).

26. How long people can stay also depends on how far they live from the temple site. Those who live nearby often come more than once during the festival (most often three days). Those who live far away tend to stay for more than one day, spending the nights at the temple ground or with relatives in nearby villages and towns.

27. See Apter and Saich (1994) on the institutionalization of Maoist political rituals during the Yan'an period; see Apter (1994) on how stories were textualized and "writ-ualized" in Chinese Communist political culture; see Whyte (1974) on the prevalent use of small groups in Maoist political rituals; see Madsen (1984) on analysis of Maoist study rituals and "rituals of struggle."

28. See Binns (1979–80) on the "Soviet ceremonial system" in the former USSR.

29. See Klima (2002) and Rafael (2003) for studies of the politics of "crowds" in urban southeast Asia (Thailand and the Philippines).

Chapter 9

1. *Ganlur* (literally "dry stove") or *youganlur* ("oil dry stove") is an English-muffin-shaped, common Shaanbei staple food made from wheat dough.

2. One of the temples was a fertility goddess temple (*niangniangmiao*) while the other was for the "Three Divine Officials" (*sanguanmiao*). *Huiyao* are *yao* specifically constructed for the purpose of holding temple association meetings, storing temple properties, accommodating temple watchmen if there are any, and

putting up guests (e.g., opera troupe performers or the storyteller during the temple festival).

3. The boundaries between villages in today's China are fixed, a legacy of the Revolution.

4. More humiliation for Chenjiapo followed, as Lao Wang repeatedly refused Chenjiapo village leaders' request to merge Chenjiapo Primary School with Longwanggou Primary School to take advantage of the latter's better funding and better teaching staff.

5. Shaanbei people always count their age using the traditional Chinese way, which counts a baby at birth as already one year old. In this book a person's age is always given in the traditional Chinese count unless otherwise noted.

6. Lao Wang's not being a member of the Communist Party came in handy when the temple applied to be recognized as an official Daoist shrine in 1998. According to Party regulations, no Party member can join any religion because a Communist is by definition an atheist. Lao Wang had to change two names on the temple association officer list because they were Party members.

7. Like many people in Shaanbei, they believe that their ancestors came from the "big locust tree" in Shanxi (*Shanxi dahuaishu*). See Chapter 2 for the "big locust tree" legend.

8. My account of Lao Wang's life is based on interviews with Lao Wang and other villagers in Longwanggou as well as Luo Hongguang's account (Luo 1999: 179–80).

9. Among the eight brothers, only the second died as a child. The others were all alive in 1998 and each had his own household. During my fieldwork I met three of Lao Wang's six brothers.

10. Shaanbei peasants traditionally dug caves on cliffs or in isolated corners of valleys to hide from bandits, rebels, and marauding armies. Rebels were called *fande* and the cry "*fande laile*" (The rebels are coming!) used to send everybody fleeing to these caves.

11. During the Maoist era the Chenjiapo Primary School was the only primary school for the three villages surrounding Longwanggou.

12. The per diem wage of a small laborer was lower than 1 yuan while that of a skilled laborer could reach 2 yuan.

13. During the collective period a member of the brigade who sought work outside had to take a leave of absence and pay the brigade collective to compensate for his absence (unfulfilled labor).

14. This military airport was never in active use, and in the 1990s the Yulin prefectural government negotiated with the military to turn the airport into a civilian one. Before I left my fieldsite at the end of the summer of 1998, rumor had it that the request had finally been approved and the conversion might be realized in the near future. The presence of a civilian airport in Zhenchuan would undoubtedly speed up changes in the area.

15. Because Lao Wang was one of the first people who began running private businesses in Zhenchuan at the beginning of the reform period, he had amassed a personal fortune that was beyond the wildest dreams of most of his co-villagers who remained farmers.

16. The older folks who were instrumental in initiating the revival of the temple willingly receded to the background. They were often close relatives of the new association members. As new leaders of a new era, Lao Wang and his cohort mates would presumably continue to assume leadership positions until their retirement, not unlike Mao and the Long Marchers' generation's prolonged dominance in post-Liberation national politics.

17. The wool trade crashed soon afterwards because of severe problems of adulteration (with bricks, rocks, and sand!) and a subsequent plunge in the number of orders. Shijiazhuang is the provincial capital of Hebei and serves as a major entrepôt between the Northwest and northern port cities such as Tianjin.

18. The People's Political Consultative Conference (*renmin zhengzhi xieshang dahui* or more commonly known as *zhengxie*, its shortened form) is a non-Party political organization with the usual national-provincial-prefecture-county hierarchical structure. Its county branch is one of the five governing organs of local government. The other four are the county government, the county Party branch, the county branch of the National People's Congress, and the county court.

19. Lao Wang had acquired a passport for the purpose of going to Japan in 1996 for an international conference and study tour. On the policy of hukou, see Cheng 1991 and Cheng and Selden 1994.

20. In 1998 this gate was less than half-finished. It would take quite a few years to build, and, according to Lao Wang, would eventually cost close to two million yuan. A teacher in Longwanggou told me that Lao Wang, just like some emperors in Chinese history, "took a liking to embarking on big projects and obtaining fame and glory" (*haoda xigong*).

21. The Renaissance label for such multitalented master artisans was *artifex polytechnes* (the artisan with many skills).

22. Even though they knew I was a doctoral student Shaanbei people occasionally address me as either a university student (*daxuesheng*) or a doctor (*boshi*), both polite terms of address, when they want to emphasize the fact that I am a highly educated person.

23. I say theoretically because some Chinese also bluff with fake or inflated titles.

24. See Chapter 2 for a description of the hierarchy of ranks in Shaanbei officialdom.

25. Huang (1989: 42–44) tells the story of the ironic rise to power of a poor peasant opportunist following this route of upward mobility.

26. One account of a son succeeding his father as village leader, in this case as Party secretary, can be found in Seybolt (1996: 101), even though the time was 1984, thus already in the post-Maoist era. The practice of "inheriting" (*dingti*) one's parent's job was of course common in state danweis (see Bian 1994).

27. He would not have been able to be the leader of a religious organization had he been a Party member.

28. In the case of Lao Wang's second son I happened to know who helped him in the process of switching from an undesirable teaching job to a promising bureaucratic job: a senior female performer and leader of a famous Xi'an qin-

qiang opera troupe who became a good friend of Lao Wang's. In 1998 the troupe was invited to perform in Longwanggou for the third time.

29. *Gong* refers to *gong'an*, the Public Security Bureau (i.e., the Police); *jian* refers to *jianchayuan*, the Prosecutors' Bureau; *fa* refers to *fayuan*, the Court, all powerful organs of the local state.

30. Even though geographic mobility in job-seeking has increased tremendously in China in the past decade or so, most rural-hukou college or specialized academy graduates are still assigned jobs in their hometown or county. The policy is called "go back to where you came from" (*cong nali lai, hui nali qu*).

31. Examples of scholarship of the "big" elite include Donald Gillin's (1967) study of the warlord Yen Hsi-shan (Yan Xishan), Thomas Robinson's (1972) study of Lin Biao, William Rowe's (1998) study of the Qing Dynasty Governor Chen Hongmou, and James Sheridan's (1966) study of the warlord Feng Yü-hsiang (Feng Yuxiang).

32. It is worth noting that most of the "translocal" elite began their careers as the local elite, and only history will tell whether Lao Wang will stay a local elite or rise in influence and become a translocal elite.

33. Examples include a Polynesian "aristocrat" by Raymond Firth (1960), a tribal chief by Thomas Gladwin (1960), a Navaho politician by Clyde Kluckhohn (1960), an Overseas Chinese entrepreneur by Ellen Oxfeld (1993), and a female shaman by Anna Tsing (1993).

34. However, I would like to caution against the deployment of the facile binary opposition between "tradition" and "socialist anti-tradition."

Chapter 10

1. This is even more true in the case of ancestral hall as village temple, found in single-lineage villages (e.g., in the Pearl River Delta). For such an example in North China, see Jing (1996).

2. As is common in this kind of village office, a huge chart is hung on the wall, listing the names of all the married women and their reproductive history. There are also markers for those women who have been granted permission to have children that particular year.

3. Jun Jing (1996) studied conflicts between villagers and the state as well as among villagers, revealing much that would otherwise have been hidden. Conflict studies has also been popular among cultural historians, not least because many conflicts led to elaborate records that survived in the archives, e.g., religious persecutions such as the Inquisition. For an example related to rural China and folk religion, see Litzinger 1996.

4. Lao Wang was jailed in a detention center (*juliusuo*) in Yulin City, not a formal prison.

5. Lawyers came back to the Chinese legal realm in the 1980s. For analysis of the penetration of "law" into contemporary village China, see select articles in Wang and Wang 1997.

6. The text of the "curse," reproduced by Wer and posted in public as well, together with the denunciation poster, is included as an appendix to this chapter.

Chapter 11

1. During my fieldwork I had also gone to another plaque-hanging ceremony near Longwanggou. The temple was called the Huashiyan Temple and it was granted the status of a "place for Buddhist religious activities" (*fojiao huodong changsuo*).

2. Recent studies on the behaviors of the local state include Blecher and Shue 1996; Esherick 1994; Oi 1989, 1999; Shue 1995; Wank 1995, 1999.

3. Unlike the Civil Affairs Bureau, the Religious Affairs Bureau in Shaanbei does not have county-level branches and operates only at the prefectural level.

4. The local state is still alarmed by, and occasionally cracks down on, potentially subversive religious activities such as the revival of sectarian movements (e.g., Yiguandao) and clandestine Christian proselytizing.

5. As I understand it, even though the Religious Affairs Bureau collects applications from temples and grants official status to qualified temples, the decision has to be approved by the prefectural government, the prefectural Communist Party committee, the prefectural People's Congress, and the prefectural court. Unfortunately I did not investigate the details of this internal process.

6. The Republic of China government on Taiwan has always made temple registration an important task. Similar to what is happening in the PRC, all popular religious temples in Taiwan that are not obviously Christian, Muslim, or Buddhist are identified as Daoist in the official classifications (Jordan and Overmyer 1986: 243).

7. C. K. Yang (1961: 188) has noted that in the early Qing Dynasty 84% of the registered temples and monasteries in China were built without official approval, which suggests a rather weak form of government control over temple building similar to Shaanbei's situation today. And there must have been many more temples that were not even registered.

8. To a considerable extent, scholarly attention to folk traditions legitimizes the latter. The academicization and scholarly legitimation of popular religion have gone on in Taiwan and Hong Kong for quite some time (more on this in the concluding chapter).

9. Even though temples are not local-state-operated enterprises, they can still be viewed as "backyard profit centers" (Lin and Zhang 1999) for some local state agencies (see Chau forthcoming).

10. For example, the temple association head of the Gushui (Hengshan county) Temple of Eastern Peak was a veteran village Party secretary. He was the one who initiated the construction of the temple-like building dedicated to Mao Zedong, Zhou Enlai, and Zhu De on the temple ground mentioned in Chapter 3.

11. Most of these other eight villages also have their own village temples, which had been revived in recent years. However, these are all minor temples compared to the Heilongdawang Temple despite the fact that some of the deities enshrined in them are much higher ranked than Heilongdawang in the divine hierarchy (e.g., the Jade Emperor).

12. This instrumentalist reading of the temple association's maneuvers should not detract from the fact that the villagers also genuinely wished to have a better

school or a reforestation project for their own sake.

13. I present the details of their visit to Longwanggou in Chau n.d. Here I will present only the context surrounding the production of the stele inscription commemorating the tree-planting event.

14. The effect would be similar to taking pictures with important party-state leaders and prominently displaying these pictures, a legitimation strategy often used in China.

15. Though feeling apprehensive at first about my involvement in local cultural production, I did not feel I unnecessarily or inappropriately intervened in local affairs. Longwanggou is not a sealed community, and mobilizing outside assistance is part of what locals do. In fact, I saw Lao Wang's invitation to write the stele text as a sign of the local people's acceptance of me. By studying Longwanggou I was already implicated in local politics whether I liked it or not.

16. These expressions (e.g., green civilization and green culture with Chinese characteristics) were gleaned from Friends of Nature's organizational mission statement.

17. Dr. Luo Hongguang was doing fieldwork in nearby Yangjiagou (Mizhi County). He came to Longwanggou during the Friends of Nature visit. He wrote the Japanese line and I wrote the one in English.

18. After I had assisted with the Friends of Nature tree-planting commemoration stele, Lao Wang approached me with requests for another two temple stelae. I had to decline because I thought they should be written in classical prose and I thought Lao Ren, Lao Wang's "court literatus," would be more competent to write them.

19. Only Communist Party organs are allowed to use red for the characters on these organizational plaques.

20. Heilongdawang is thought to love this opera piece because it is about the legendary Song Dynasty Kaifeng City magistrate Bao Zheng (popularly known as Bao Gong), and Heilongdawang himself is believed to be also a god of justice. Older people say that this particular piece has been played at noon on the thirteenth for as long as they can remember.

21. Yinchuan is the provincial capital of the Ningxia Hui Autonomous Region.

22. A national paper on flowers and plants for specialists and laypeople.

23. Shaanbei people normally don't applaud during or after an opera performance at temple festivals. Yet they do applaud after the performance if they are in a theater hall and the performance is officially organized. They have also learned to applaud after a speech, which is almost always on an official occasion.

24. As far as I know Longwanggou did not become any more Daoist after this ceremony than it had been before. The Religious Affairs Bureau cadre told me that Daoist music and rituals should be introduced to Longwanggou, but I suspect Lao Wang would have laughed at the idea. I think Lao Wang would not easily submit Longwanggou to the authority of Daoist priests.

25. The expression "doing things with words" had obviously been inspired by J. Austin.

26. This year the donation money during the temple festival topped 600,000

yuan, a 50,000 yuan increase from last year's. The yearly donation income for 1998 is estimated at 1.3 million yuan.

27. This ceremony can be fruitfully compared and contrasted with the role Daoist priests play in legitimating local elites at temple festivals in Fujian and Taiwan under the "Daoist liturgical framework" (Dean 1993: 181).

Chapter 12

1. Luo Hongguang has suggested that all temple associations are really NGOs (personal communication). However, it is perhaps important to maintain an analytical distinction between NGOs (mostly urban-based and translocal) and folk social organizations such as temple associations, which are mostly local and modeled on traditional organizational patterns.

2. See Palmer 2003 and forthcoming for detailed sociohistorical accounts of the rise of qigong in the PRC and Fan 2000 for a study on urban religiosity (in Shenzhen) that is heavily influenced by qigong practices.

3. For analyses of uses of the same urban spaces by neighborhood, voluntary yangge dance troupes (without religious overtones), see Graezer 1998, 1999.

References Cited

Shaanbei Gazetteers Consulted

Hengshan xianzhi or HSXZ (Hengshan County Gazetteer). 1993. Xi'an: Shaanxi renmin chubanshe.

Jingbian xianzhi or JBXZ (Jingbian County Gazetteer). 1993. Xi'an: Shaanxi renmin chubanshe.

Mizhi xianzhi or MZXZ (Mizhi County Gazetteer). 1993. Xi'an: Shaanxi renmin chubanshe.

Shenmu xianzhi or SMXZ (Shenmu County Gazetteer). 1990. Beijing: Jingji ribao chubanshe.

Wupu xianzhi or WPXZ (Wupu County Gazetteer). 1995. Xi'an: Shaanxi renmin chubanshe.

Yan'an diquzhi or YADQZ (Yan'an Prefecture Gazetteer). 2000. Xi'an: Xi'an chubanshe.

Yan'an juan. Zhongguo guoqing congshu: bai xianshi jingji shehui diaocha (The Yan'an Volume of the China's Current Condition Series: Investigations of Economy and Society of One Hundred Counties and Cities). 1994. Beijing: Zhongguo dabaikequanshu chubanshe.

Yanchang xianzhi or YCXZ (Yanchang County Gazetteer). 1991. Xi'an: Shaanxi renmin chubanshe.

Yulin diquzhi or YLDQZ (Yulin Prefecture Gazetteer). 1994. Xi'an: Xibei daxue chubanshe.

Yulin fuzhi or YLFZ (Yulin Prefecture Gazetteer). 1968 (1841, 21st year of Daoguang of Qing Dynasty). Li Xiling, ed. Reprinted by Xuesheng shuju in four volumes.

Yulin shizhi or YLSZ (Yulin City Gazetteer). 1996. Xi'an: Sanqin chubanshe.

Zichang xianzhi or ZCXZ (Zichang County Gazetteer). 1993. Xi'an: Shaanxi renmin chubanshe.

Zizhou xianzhi or ZZXZ (Zizhou County Gazetteer). 1993. Xi'an: Shaanxi renmin jiaoyu chubanshe.

Other Sources

Abélès, Marc. 1988. "Modern Political Ritual: Ethnography of an Inauguration and a Pilgrimage by President Mitterand." *Current Anthropology* 29(3): 391–404.

Ahern, Emily Martin. 1981a. *Chinese Ritual and Politics*. Cambridge: Cambridge University Press.

———. 1981b. "The Thai Ti Kong Festival." In Emily Martin Ahern and Hill Gates, eds., *The Anthropology of Taiwanese Society*, pp. 397–425. Stanford: Stanford University Press.

Ames, Roger T. 1994. *The Art of Rulership: A Study of Ancient Chinese Political Thought*. Albany: State University of New York Press.

Anagnost, Ann S. 1987. "Politics and Magic in Contemporary China." *Modern China* 13(1): 40–61.

———. 1994. "The Politics of Ritual Displacement." In Charles F. Keyes, Laurel Kendall, and Helen Hardacre, eds., *Asian Visions of Authority: Religion and the Modern States of East and Southeast Asia*, pp. 221–54. Honolulu: University of Hawaii Press.

Anderson, Benedict. 1991. *Imagined Communities*. Revised edition. New York: Verso.

Appadurai, Arjun. 1981. "Gastro-Politics in Hindu South Asia." *American Ethnologist* 8(3): 494–511.

Apter, David E. 1994. "Yan'an and the Narrative Reconstruction of Reality." In Tu Wei-Ming, ed., *China in Transformation*, pp. 207–32. Cambridge, MA: Harvard University Press.

Apter, David E., and Tony Saich. 1994. *Revolutionary Discourse in Mao's Republic*. Cambridge, MA: Harvard University Press.

Austin, John. 1962. *How to Do Things with Words*. Cambridge, MA: Harvard University Press.

Baity, Philip Chesley. 1975. *Religion in a Chinese Town*. Asian Folklore and Social Life Monographs, Vol. 64. Taipei: The Orient Cultural Service.

Baiyunshan daojiao xiaozu (Daoist Small Group of White Cloud Mountain), compilers. n.d. *Baiyunshan shenhua chuanshuo* (Legends and Miracles of White Cloud Mountain). Pamphlet for Internal Circulation.

Bakhtin, Mikhail M. 1984. *Rabelais and His World*. Translated by Helene Iswolsky. Bloomington: Indiana University Press.

Banck, Werner. 1985. *Das chinesische Tempelorakel*. Asiatische Forschungen 90. Wiesbaden: Otto Harrassowitz.

Baptandier-Berthier, Brigitte. 1994. "The *Kaiguan* Ritual and the Construction of the Child's Identity." In Hanxue yanjiu zhongxin 1994: 523–86.

Beck, Brenda E. F. 1969. "Color and Heat in South Indian Ritual." *Man* 4(4): 553–72.

Bennett, Gordon. 1976. *Yundong: Mass Campaigns in Chinese Communist Leadership*. China Research Monographs, 12. Berkeley, CA: Center for Chinese Studies.

Bian, Yanjie. 1994. *Work and Inequality in Urban China*. Albany: State University of New York Press.

Binns, Christopher A. P. 1979–80. "The Changing Face of Power: Revolution and Accommodation in the Development of the Soviet Ceremonial System. Parts I and II." *Man* 14: 585–606; 15: 170–87.

Blecher, Marc, and Vivienne Shue. 1996. *Tethered Deer: Government and Economy in a Chinese County.* Stanford: Stanford University Press.

Boas, Franz. 1974. *The Shaping of American Anthropology, 1883–1911: A Franz Boas Reader.* Edited by George Stocking Jr. New York: Basic Books.

Bosco, Joseph. 1994. "Yiguan Dao: 'Heterodoxy' and Popular Religion in Taiwan." In Murray A. Rubinstein, ed., *The Other Taiwan, 1945 to the Present,* pp. 423–44. Armonk, NY: M. E. Sharpe.

Bourdieu, Pierre. 1977. *Outline of a Theory of Practice.* Translated by Richard Nice. Cambridge: Cambridge University Press.

———. 1984. *Distinction: A Social Critique of the Judgement of Taste.* Cambridge, MA: Harvard University Press.

———. 1991. *Language and Symbolic Power.* Cambridge, MA: Harvard University Press.

Brook, Timothy. 1993. *Praying for Power: Buddhism and the Formation of Gentry Society in Late-Imperial China.* Cambridge, MA: Harvard University Press.

———. 1997. "Auto-Organization in Chinese Society." In Brook and Frolic, eds., pp. 19–45.

Brook, Timothy, and B. Michael Frolic, eds. 1997. *Civil Society in China.* Armonk, NY: M. E. Sharpe.

Brownell, Susan. 1995. *Training the Body for China: Sports in the Moral Order of the People's Republic.* Chicago: University of Chicago Press.

Bruun, Ole. 1996. "The *Fengshui* Resurgence in China: Conflicting Cosmologies Between State and Peasantry." *The China Journal* 36: 47–65.

———. 2003. *Fengshui in China: Geomantic Divination Between State Orthodoxy and Popular Religion.* Honolulu: University of Hawaii Press.

Casagrande, Joseph B. 1960. *In the Company of Man: Twenty Portraits by Anthropologists.* New York: Harper & Brothers.

The Catholic Encyclopaedic Dictionary. 1951. Second edition. Edited by Donald Attwater. London: Cassell.

Chamberlain, Heath B. "On the Search for Civil Society in China." *Modern China* 19(2): 199–215.

Chan, Anita, Richard Madsen, and Jonathan Unger. 1992. *Chen Village Under Mao and Deng.* Berkeley: University of California Press.

Chang Hsun. 1993. "Taiwan hanren shoujing yishi yu hunpoguan" (Rituals of Fright-Soothing Among Han Chinese in Taiwan and Conceptions of *Hun* and *Po*). In Huang Ying-kuei, ed., pp. 207–31.

Chao, Emily. 1999. "The Maoist Shaman and the Madman: Ritual Bricolage, Failed Ritual, and Failed Ritual Theory." *Cultural Anthropology* 14(4): 505–34.

Chastel, André. 1991 (1988). "The Artist." In Eugenio Garin, ed., *Renaissance Characters,* pp. 180–206. Chicago: University of Chicago Press.

Chau, Adam Yuet. 2003. "Popular Religion in Shaanbei, North-Central China." *Journal of Chinese Religions* 31: 39–79.

————. 2004. "Hosting Funerals and Temple Festivals: Folk Event Productions in Rural China." *Asian Anthropology* 3: 39–70.

————. 2005. "The Politics of Legitimation and the Revival of Popular Religion in Shaanbei, North-Central China." *Modern China* 31(2): 236–78.

————. forthcoming. "Expanding the Space of Popular Religion: Local Temple Activism and the Politics of Legitimation in Contemporary Rural China." In Yoshiko Ashiwa and David Wank, eds. *The Politics of Religion in China*. (Under Contract with Stanford University Press)

————. n.d. "Of Temples and Trees: Articulating Environmentalisms in Contemporary China." (Article Manuscript)

Chen, Nancy N. 1995. "Urban Spaces and the Experiences of *Qigong*." In Davis, Kraus, Naughton, and Perry, eds., pp. 347–61.

————. 2003. *Breathing Spaces: Qigong, Psychiatry, and Healing in China*. New York: Columbia University Press.

Cheng, Tiejun. 1991. "Dialectics of Control—the Household Registration (*hukou*) System in Contemporary China." PhD diss., State University of New York at Binghamton.

Cheng, Tiejun, and Mark Selden. 1994. "The Origins and Social Consequences of China's *Hukou* System." *The China Quarterly* 139: 644–68.

Chu, Wen-Djang. 1966. *The Moslem Rebellion in Northwest China 1862–1878: A Study of Government Minority Policy*. Central Asiatic Studies Series. The Hague and Paris: Mouton & Co.

Chuengsatiansup, Komatra. 1999. "Sense, Symbol, and Soma: Illness Experience in the Soundscape of Everyday Life." *Culture, Medicine, and Psychiatry* 23: 273–301.

Classen, Constance. 1993. *Worlds of Sense: Exploring the Senses in History and Across Cultures*. London and New York: Routledge.

Classen, Constance, David Howes, and Anthony Synnott. 1994. *Aroma: The Cultural History of Smell*. London and New York: Routledge.

Cohen, Myron L. 1988. "Souls and Salvation: Conflicting Themes in Chinese Popular Religion." In James L. Watson and Evelyn S. Rawski, eds., *Death Ritual in Late Imperial and Modern China*, pp. 180–202. Berkeley: University of California Press.

————. 1990. "Lineage Organization in North China." *Journal of Asian Studies* 49(3): 509–34.

————. 1992. "Family Management and Family Division in Contemporary Rural China." *The China Quarterly* 130: 357–77.

Cole, Alan. 1998. *Mothers and Sons in Chinese Buddhism*. Stanford: Stanford University Press.

Connery, Christopher Leigh. 1998. *The Empire of the Text: Writing and Authority in Early Imperial China*. Lanham, MD: Rowman and Littlefield.

Danforth, Loring M. 1989. *Firewalking and Religious Healing: The Anastenaria of Greece and the American Firewalking Movement*. Princeton, NJ: Princeton University Press.

Davis, Deborah S., Richard Kraus, Barry Naughton, and Elizabeth J. Perry, eds. 1995. *Urban Spaces in Contemporary China: The Potential for Autonomy and Community in Post-Mao China*. New York: Cambridge University Press.

Dean, Kenneth. 1993. *Taoist Ritual and Popular Cults of Southeast China*. Princeton, NJ: Princeton University Press.

———. 1994. "Comic Inversion and Cosmic Renewal: The God of Theater in the Ritual Traditions of Putian." In Hanxue yanjiu zhongxin 1994: 683–731.

———. 1997 "Ritual and Space: Civil Society or Popular Religion?" In Brook and Frolic, eds., pp. 172–92.

———. 1998a. "Despotic Empire/Nation-State: Local Responses to Chinese Nationalism in an Age of Global Capitalism." In Kuan-Hsing Chen, ed., *Trajectories: Inter-Asia Cultural Studies*, pp. 153–85. New York: Routledge.

———. 1998b. *Lord of the Three in One: The Spread of a Cult in Southeast China*. Princeton, NJ: Princeton University Press.

———. 2003. "Local Communal Religion in Contemporary South-east China." *The China Quarterly* 174: 338–58.

Derrida, Jacques, and Anne Dufourmantelle. 2000. *Of Hospitality: Anne Dufourmantelle Invites Jacques Derrida to Respond*. Translated by Rachel Bowlby. Stanford: Stanford University Press.

Desjarlais, Robert. 2003. *Sensory Biographies: Lives and Deaths Among Nepal's Yolmo Buddhists*. Berkeley: University of California Press.

Ding, Huang. 1996. "Tainan jiumiao yunqian de chubu yanjiu" (A Preliminary Analysis of the Divination Sets of Tainan's Old Temples). In Li Fengmao and Zhu Ronggui, eds., *Yishi, miaohui yu shequ: daojiao, minjian xinyang yu minjian wenhua* (Ritual, Temple Festival, and Community: Daoism, Folk Beliefs, and Folk Culture), pp. 375–425. Institute of Literature and Philosophy, Academia Sinica.

Duara, Prasenjit. 1988a. *Culture, Power, and the State: Rural North China, 1900–1942*. Stanford: Stanford University Press.

———. 1988b. "Superscribing Symbols: The Myth of Guandi, Chinese God of War." *Journal of Asian Studies* 47(4): 778–95.

———. 1991. "Knowledge and Power in the Discourse of Modernity: The Campaigns against Popular Religion in Early Twentieth-Century China." *The Journal of Asian Studies* 50(1): 67–84.

DuBois, Thomas David. 2005. *The Sacred Village: Social Change and Religious Life in Rural North China*. Honolulu: University of Hawaii Press.

Durkheim, Emile. 1965 [1915]. *The Elementary Forms of the Religious Life*. New York: Free Press.

Esherick, Joseph W. 1994. "Deconstructing the Construction of the Party-State: Gulin County in the Shaan-Gan-Ning Border Region." *China Quarterly* 140: 1052–79.

———. 1998. "Revolution in a Feudal Fortress: Yangjiagou, Mizhi County, Shaanxi, 1937–1948." *Modern China* 24(4): 339–77.

Esherick, Joseph W., and Mary Backus Rankin, eds. 1990. *Chinese Local Elites and Patterns of Dominance*. Berkeley: University of California Press.

Fan Guangchun. 1997. "Dangdai Shaanbei miaohui kaocha yu toushi" (An Investigation of Contemporary Shaanbei Temple Fairs). *Journal of Yanan University Social Science Edition* 1 (19): 97–100.

Fan Lizhu. 2000. "Study of Religious Beliefs and Practices in Contemporary China: Case Study of Popular Religion in Shenzhen." Doctoral Dissertation, Sociology, the Chinese University of Hong Kong.

Farquhar, Judith. 1995. "Eating Chinese Medicine." *Cultural Anthropologist* 9(4): 471–97.

———. 2002. *Appetites: Food and Sex in Postsocialist China*. Durham, NC: Duke University Press.

Faure, Bernard. 1987. "Space and Place in Chinese Religious Traditions." *History of Religions* 26(4): 337–56.

Feierman, Steven. 1990. *Peasant Intellectuals: Anthropology and History in Tanzania*. Madison: University of Wisconsin Press.

Fernandez, James W. 1986. "Convivial Attitudes: A Northern Spanish Kayak Festival in Its Historical Moment." In *Persuasions and Performances: The Play of Tropes in Culture*. Bloomington: Indiana University Press.

Feuchtwang, Stephan. 1989a. "The Problem of 'Superstition' in the People's Republic of China." In G. Benavides and M. W. Daly, eds., *Religion and Political Power*, pp. 43–68. Albany: State University of New York Press.

———. 1989b. "The Study of Chinese Popular Religion." *Revue Européenne des Sciences Sociales* 27(84): 69–86.

———. 1991. "A Chinese Religion Exists." In H. Baker and S. Feuchtwang, eds., *An Old State in New Settings: Studies in the Social Anthropology of China in Memory of Maurice Freedman*, pp. 139–61. Oxford: JASO.

———. 1992. *The Imperial Metaphor: Popular Religion in China*. London: Routledge.

———. 1993. "Historical Metaphor: A Study of Religious Representation and the Recognition of Authority." *Man*, 28(1): 35–49.

———. 2000. "Religion as Resistance." In Elizabeth J. Perry and Mark Selden, eds., pp. 161–77. London: Routledge.

Feuchtwang, Stephan, and Wang Mingming. 1991. "The Politics of Culture or a Contest of Histories: Representations of Chinese Popular Religion." *Dialectical Anthropology* 16: 251–72.

———. 2001. *Grassroots Charisma: Four Local Leaders in China*. London: Routledge.

Fields, Lanny. 1978. *Tso Tsung-T'ang and the Muslims: Statecraft in Northwest China, 1868–1880*. Kingston, ON: Limestone Press.

Firth, Raymond. 1950. "The Peasantry of Southeast Asia." *International Affairs* 26(4): 503–14.

———. 1960. "A Polynesian Aristocrat (Tikopia)." In J. B. Casagrande, pp. 1–40.

———. 1967 [1940]. "An Analysis of Mana: An Empirical Approach." In *Tikopia Ritual and Belief*, pp. 174–94. Boston: Beacon Press.

Freedman, Maurice. 1974. "On the Sociological Study of Chinese Religion." In Arthur P. Wolf, ed., *Religion and Ritual in Chinese Society*, pp. 19–41. Stanford, California: Stanford University Press.

Friedman, Edward, Paul G. Pickowicz, and Mark Selden (with Kay Ann Johnson). 1991. *Chinese Village, Socialist State*. New Haven, CT: Yale University Press.

———. forthcoming. *Revolution, Resistance, and Reform in Village China.* New Haven, CT: Yale University Press.

Friedrick, Paul. 1986. *The Princes of Naranja: An Essay in Anthropological Method.* Austin: University of Texas Press.

Fukao Yoko. 1998. "Chugoku seihokubu kodokogen ni okeru "miaohui" o meguru shakai kokan to jiritsu teki gishu" ("Miaohui" as Self-organization in Northwestern China in the Post-Mao Era). National Museum of Ethnology (Osaka, Japan) Research Report Vol. 2, No. 23.

Fujitani, T. 1996. *Splendid Monarchy: Power and Pageantry in Modern Japan.* Berkeley: University of California Press.

Gamble, Sydney D. 1954. *Ting Hsien: A North China Rural Community.* New York: Institute of Pacific Relations.

———. 1963. *North China Villages: Social, Political and Economic Activities Before 1933.* Berkeley: University of California Press.

Gao, Mobo C. F. 1999. *Gao Village: Rural Life in Modern China.* Honolulu: University of Hawaii Press.

Gao Zhanxiang. 1992. *Lun miaohui wenhua* (On Temple Festival Culture). Beijing: Wenhua yishu chubanshe.

Gates, Hill. 1987. "Money for the Gods." *Modern China* 13(3): 259–77.

———. 1991. "Eating for Revenge: Consumption and Corruption Under Economic De-Reform." *Dialectical Anthropology* 16: 233–49.

———. 1993. "Cultural Support for Birth Limitation among Urban Capital-owning Women." In Deborah Davis and Stevan Harrell, eds., *Chinese Families in the Post-Mao Era*, pp. 251–74. Berkeley: University of California Press.

———. 1996. *China's Motor: A Thousand Years of Petty Capitalism.* Ithaca, NY: Cornell University Press.

———. 2000. "Religious Real Estate as Indigenous Civil Space." *Bulletin of the Institute of Ethnology, Academia Sinica.* Special Issue in Honor of Professor Li Yih-yuan's Retirement (I). Pp. 313–33.

Gates, Hill, and Robert P. Weller, eds. 1987. "Hegemony and Chinese Folk Ideologies." *Modern China* 13(1): 3–16.

Geertz, Clifford. 1963. *Agricultural Involution: The Processes of Ecological Change in Indonesia.* Berkeley: University of California Press.

———. 1973. "Deep Play: Notes on the Balinese Cockfight." In *The Interpretation of Cultures.* New York: Basic Books.

———. 1980. *Negara: The Theatre State in Nineteenth-Century Bali.* Princeton, NJ: Princeton University Press.

Geurts, Kathryn Linn. 2003. *Culture and the Senses: Embodiment, Identity, and Well-Being in an African Community.* Berkeley: University of California Press.

Gilley, Bruce. 2001. *Model Rebels: The Rise and Fall of China's Richest Village.* Berkeley: University of California Press.

Gillin, Donald G. 1967. *Warlord: Yen Hsi-shan in Shansi Province, 1911–1949.* Princeton, NJ: Princeton University Press.

Gladwin, Thomas. 1960. "Petrus Mailo, Chief of Moen." In J. B. Casagrande, pp. 41–62.

Goodrich, Anne Swann. 1964. "The Peking Temple of the Eastern Peak: The Tung-yueh Miao in Peking and its Lore (With an Appended Description of the

Tung-yueh Miao of Peking in 1927 by Janet R. Ten Broeck)." Nagoya: Monumenta Serica.

Goossaert, Vincent. 2000. *Dans les Temples de la Chine: Histoire des Cultes, Vies des Communautés.* Paris: Albin Michel.

Gould-Martin, Katherine. 1975. "Medical Systems in a Taiwanese Village: Ong-ia-kong, the Plague God as Modern Physician." In Arthur Kleinman et al., eds., *Medicine in Chinese Cultures: Comparative Studies of Health Care in Chinese and Other Societies*, pp. 115–41. Washington, DC: U.S. Dept. of Health, Education and Welfare.

Graezer, Florence. 1998. "Le '*Yangge*' dans la Vie Associative à Chengfu, Quartier de Pékin. Monographie d'une Activité Populaire et Quotidienne" ("Yangge" in Associative Life in Chengfu, a Peking Neighborhood. Monograph concerning a Popular Daily Activity), M. Phil. Dissertation, Paris, EHESS.

———. 1999. "The *Yangge* in Contemporary China: Popular Daily Activity and Neighbourhood Community Life." *China Perspectives* 24: 31–43.

Gramsci, Antonio. 1971. *Selections from the Prison Notebooks.* New York: International.

Greenhalgh, Susan. 1993. "The Peasantization of the One-Child Policy in Shaanxi." In Deborah Davis and Stevan Harrell, eds., *Chinese Families in the Post-Mao Era*, pp. 219–50. Berkeley: University of California Press.

Grimes, Ronald L. 1976. *Symbol and Conquest: Public Ritual and Drama in Santa Fe.* Albuquerque: University of New Mexico Press.

Grootaers, Willem A. 1952. "The Hagiography of the Chinese God Chen-wu." *Folklore Studies* 11(2): 139–81.

———. 1995. "The Sanctuaries in a North-China City: A Complete Survey of the Cultic Buildings in the City of Hsuan-hua (Chahar)." Mélanges chinois et bouddhiques, vol. 26. Brussels: Institut Belge des Hautes Études Chinoises.

Grootaers, Willem A., with Li Shih-Yu and Wang Fu-Shih. 1951. "Rural Temples Around Hsuan-hua (South Chahar), Their Iconography and Their History." *Folklore Studies* Vol. X, 1.

Guldin, Gregory Eliyu. 1997a. "Desakotas and Beyond: Urbanization in Southern China." In Guldin 1997b, pp. 47–67.

———. 1997b. ed. *Farewell to Peasant China: Rural Urbanization and Social Change in the Late Twentieth Century.* Armonk, NY: M. E. Sharpe.

Hanxue yanjiu zhongxin. 1994. *Minjian xinyang yu zhongguo wenhua: guoji yantaohui lunwenji* (Proceedings of the International Conference on Folk Beliefs and Chinese Culture). Volumes One and Two. Taipei: Hanxue yanjiu zhongxin.

Hardacre, Helen. 1997. *Marketing the Menacing Fetus in Japan.* Berkeley: Berkeley: University of California Press.

Harrell, Stevan. 1974a. "Belief and Unbelief in a Taiwan Village." PhD diss., Department of Anthropology, Stanford University.

———. 1974b. "When a Ghost Becomes a God." In Arthur P. Wolf, ed., *Religion and Ritual in Chinese Society*, pp. 193–206. Stanford: Stanford University Press.

———. 1981. "Normal and Deviant Drinking in Rural Taiwan. In Arthur Kleinman and Tsung-Yi Lin, eds. *Normal and Abnormal Behavior in Chinese Society*, pp. 49–59. Dordrecht, Holland: D. Reidel Publishing Company.

———. 1982. *Ploughshare Village: Culture and Context in Taiwan*. Seattle: University of Washington Press.

———. 1987. "The Concept of Fate in Chinese Folk Ideology." *Modern China* 13(1): 90–109.

Hayes, James. 1985. "Specialists and Written Materials in the Village World." In David Johnson, Andrew J. Nathan, and Evelyn S. Rawski, eds., *Popular Culture in Late Imperial China*, pp. 75–111. Berkeley: University of California Press.

He Guojian, ed. 1998. *Mizhi wenshi huicui* (A Selection of Mizhi County Literary and Historical Works). Mizhi, Shaanxi: Mizhixian danganguan.

Hershkovitz, Linda. 1993. "Political Ecology and Environmental Management in the Loess Plateau, China." *Human Ecology* 21(4): 327–53.

Hertz, Ellen. 1998. *The Trading Crowd: An Ethnography of the Shanghai Stock Market*. Cambridge: Cambridge University Press.

Hevia, James L. 1995. *Cherishing Men From Afar: Qing Guest Ritual and the Macartney Embassy of 1793*. Durham, NC: Duke University Press.

Hobsbawm, E. J., and Terence Ranger, eds. 1983. *The Invention of Tradition*. Cambridge: Cambridge University Press.

Holm, David L. 1984. "Folk Art as Propaganda: The *Yangge* Movement in Yan'an." In Bonnie S. McDougall, ed., *Popular Chinese Literature and Performing Arts in the People's Republic of China 1949–1979*, pp. 3–35. Berkeley: University of California Press.

———. 1994. "The Labyrinth of Lanterns: Taoism and Popular Religion in Northwest China." In Hanxue yanjiu zhongxin 1994: 797–852.

Howes, David. 1990. "Controlling Textuality: A Call for a Return to the Senses." *Anthropologica* 32(1): 55–73.

———, ed. 1991. *The Varieties of Sensory Experience: A Sourcebook in the Anthropology of the Senses*. Toronto: University of Toronto Press.

Hsiao Kung-chuan. 1960. *Rural China: Imperial Control in the Nineteenth Century*. Seattle: University of Washington Press.

Hsieh Jin-chang and Chuang Ying-chang, eds. 1985. *The Chinese Family and Its Ritual Behavior*. Monograph Series B, No. 15. Taibei: Institute of Ethnology, Academia Sinica.

Huang Meiying. 1994. *Taiwan Mazu de xianghuo yu yishi* (Incense and Rituals of Mazu in Taiwan). Taipei: Zili wanbao wenhua chubanshe.

Huang, Philip C. C. 1993. " 'Public Sphere'/'Civil Society' in China? The Third Realm Between State and Society." *Modern China* 19(2): 216–40.

Huang, Shu-min. 1998. *The Spiral Road: Change in a Chinese Village through the Eyes of a Communist Party Leader*. Second edition (first edition 1989). Boulder, CO: Westview Press.

Huang Ying-kuei, ed. 1993. *Renguan yiyi yu shehui* (The Concept of the Person, Meaning, and Society). Institute of Ethnology, Academia Sinica.

Huang Youquan, Gao Shengen, & Chu Ren. 1993. *Hongtong dahuaishu yimin* (Migration and the Big Locust Tree of Hongtong). Taiyuan: Shanxi guji chubanshe.

Huo Shichun, ed. 1996. *Heilongtan* (The Black Dragon Pool). Famous Sites in Yulin Series. Yulinshizhi bangongshi.

Hur, Nam-lin. 2000. *Prayer and Play in Late Tokugawa Japan: Asakusa Sensōji and Edo Society.* Cambridge, MA: Harvard University Asia Center.

Hymes, Robert P. 1986. *Statesmen and Gentlemen: The Elite of Fu-chou, Chiang-hsi, in Northern and Southern Sung.* Cambridge: Cambridge University Press.

———. 2002. *Way and Byway: Taoism, Local Religion, and Models of Divinity in Sung and Modern China.* Berkeley: University of California Press.

Jacobs, J. Bruce. 1980. *Local Politics in a Rural Chinese Cultural Setting: A Field Study of Mazu Township, Taiwan.* Canberra: Contemporary China Centre, Australian National University.

Jankowiak, William. 1993. *Sex, Death and Hierarchy in a Chinese City: An Anthropological Account.* New York: Columbia University Press.

Jing, Anning. 2002. *The Water God's Temple of the Guangsheng Monastery: Cosmic Function of Art, Ritual, and Theatre.* Leiden: Brill.

Jing, Jun. 1996. *The Temple of Memories: History, Power, and Morality in a Chinese Village.* Stanford: Stanford University Press.

———. 2000. "Environmental Protests in Rural China." In Elizabeth J. Perry and Mark Selden, eds., pp. 143–60. London: Routledge.

———. 2002. "Knowledge, Organization, and Symbolic Capital: Two Temples to Confucius in Gansu." In Thomas A. Wilson, ed., *On Sacred Grounds: Culture, Society, Politics, and the Formation of the Cult of Confucius*, pp. 335–75. Cambridge, MA: Harvard University Asia Center.

Jochim, Christian. 1990. "Flowers, Fruit, and Incense Only: Elite Versus Popular in Taiwan's Religion of the Yellow Emperor." *Modern China* 16(1): 3–38.

Johnson, David, ed. 1989. *Ritual Opera, Operatic Ritual: "Mu-lien Rescues His Mother" in Chinese Popular Culture.* Berkeley: Institute of East Asian Studies.

———. 1994. "Temple Festivals in Southeastern Shansi: The *Sai* of Nan-she and Big West Gate." *Min-su ch'ü-i* 91: 641–734.

———. 1997. "'Confucian' Elements in the Great Temple Festivals of Southeastern Shansi in Late Imperial Times." *T'oung Pao* 83(1–3): 126–61.

Johnson, David, Andrew J. Nathan, and Evelyn S. Rawski, eds. 1985. *Popular Culture in Late Imperial China.* Berkeley: University of California Press.

Jordan, David. 1982. "Taiwanese *Poe* Divination: Statistical Awareness and Religious Belief." *Journal for the Scientific Study of Religion* 21: 114–18.

———. 1994. "Changes in Postwar Taiwan and Their Impact on the Popular Practice of Religion." In C. Stevan Harrell and Huang Chun-chieh, eds., *Cultural Changes in Postwar Taiwan*, pp. 137–60. Boulder, CO: Westview.

Jordan, David K. and Daniel L. Overmyer. 1986. *The Flying Phoenix: Aspects of Chinese Sectarianism in Taiwan.* Princeton, NJ: Princeton University Press.

Judd, Ellen R. 1986. "Cultural Redefinition in Yan'an, China." *Ethnos* 51(1–2): 29–51. Stockholm.

———. 1990. "Cultural Articulation in the Chinese Countryside." *Modern China* 16(3): 269–308.

———. 1994. "Mulian Saves His Mother in 1989." In Rubie S. Watson, ed., pp. 105–26.

Just, Peter. 2001. *Dou Donggo Justice: Conflict and Morality in an Indonesian Society*. Lanham, MD: Rowman and Littlefield Publishers, Inc.

Kang, Xiaofei. 2002. "In the Name of the Buddha: the Cult of the Fox at a Sacred Site in Contemporary Northern Shaanxi." *Min-su ch'ü-i* 138: 67–110.

Katz, Paul R. 1995. *Demon Hordes and Burning Boats: The Cult of Marshal Wen in Late Imperial China*. Albany: State University of New York Press.

———. 1999. *Images of the Immortal: The Cult of Lü Dongbin at the Palace of Eternal Joy*. Honolulu: University of Hawaii Press.

———. 2003. "Religion and the State in Postwar Taiwan." *The China Quarterly* 174: 395–412.

———. 2004. "Divine Justice in Late Imperial China: A Preliminary Study of Indictment Rituals." In John Lagerwey, ed., *Religion and Chinese Society*, volume II: *Taoism and Local Religion in Modern China*, pp. 869–901. Hong Kong: The Chinese University Press and École Française d'Extrême-Orient.

Katz, Paul R., and Murray A. Rubinstein, eds. 2003. *Religion and the Formation of Taiwanese Identities*. New York: Palgrave Macmillan.

Keane, John. 1998. *Civil Society: Old Images, New Visions*. Stanford: Stanford University Press.

Keating, Pauline B. 1994a. "The Ecological Origins of the Yan'an Way." *The Australian Journal of Chinese Affairs* 32: 123–53.

———. 1994b. "The Yan'an Way of Co-operativization." *The China Quarterly* 140: 1025–51.

———. 1997. *Two Revolutions: Village Reconstruction and the Cooperative Movement in Northern Shaanxi, 1934–1945*. Stanford: Stanford University Press.

Kern, Martin. 2000. *The Stele Inscriptions of Ch'in Shih-huang: Text and Ritual in Early Chinese Imperial Representation*. New Haven, CT: American Oriental Society.

Kipnis, Andrew. 1997. *Producing Guanxi: Sentiment, Self, and Subculture in a North China Village*. Durham, NC: Duke University Press.

Klima, Alan. 2002. "Bloodless Power: The Moral Economy of the Thai Crowd." In *The Funeral Casino: Meditation, Massacre, and Exchange with the Dead in Thailand*. Princeton, NJ: Princeton University Press.

Kluckhohn, Clyde. 1960. "A Navaho Politician." In J. B. Casagrande, pp. 439–65.

Knapp, Ronald. 1989. *China's Vernacular Architecture: House Form and Culture*. Honolulu: University of Hawaii Press.

Kraus, Richard Curt. 1991. *Brushes With Power: Modern Politics and the Chinese Art of Calligraphy*. Berkeley: University of California Press.

Kuhn, Philip A. 1984. "Chinese Views of Social Stratification." In James L. Watson, ed., *Class and Social Stratification in Post-Revolution China*, pp. 16–28. Cambridge: Cambridge University Press.

Lagerwey, John. 1987. *Taoist Ritual in Chinese Society and History*. New York: Macmillan Publishing Company.

Lamley, Harry J. 1981. "Sub-Ethnic Rivalry in the Ch'ing Period." In Emily Martin Ahern and Hill Gates, eds., *The Anthropology of Taiwanese Society*, pp. 282–319. Stanford: Stanford University Press.

———. 1990. "Lineage and Surname Feuds in Southern Fukien and Eastern Kwangtung Under the Ch'ing." In Kwang-Ching Liu, ed., *Orthodoxy in Late Imperial China*, pp. 255–78. Berkeley: University of California Press.

Le Bon, Gustave. 1920 [1895]. *The Crowd: A Study of the Popular Mind*. New York.

Lefort, Claude. 1986. *Essais sur le Politique (XIXe–XXe Siècle)*. Paris: Le Seuil.

Lewis, Mark Edward. 1999. *Writing and Authority in Early China*. Albany: State University of New York Press.

Li Peilin, ed. 1995. *Zhongguo xinshiqi jieji jieceng baogao* (Social Stratification in the Market Transition in China). Shenyang: Liaoning renmin chubanshe.

Lin, Nan, and Chih-jou Jay Chen. 1999. "Local Elites as Officials and Owners: Shareholding and Property Rights in Daqiuzhuang." In Oi and Walder, eds., pp. 145–70.

Lin, Yi-min, and Zhanxin Zhang. 1999. "Backyard Profit Centers: The Private Assets of Public Agencies." In Oi and Walder, eds., pp. 203–25.

Litzinger, Charles A. 1996. "Rural Religion and Village Organization in North China: The Catholic Challenge in the Late Nineteenth Century." In Daniel H. Bays, ed., *Christianity in China: From the Eighteenth Century to the Present*, pp. 41–52. Stanford: Stanford University Press.

Liu Tieliang. 1996. "Cunluo—minsu chuancheng de shenghuo kongjian" (The Village—The Living Space for the Perpetuation of Folk Traditions). *Beijing shifan daxue xuebao* (shehui kexue ban), 6: 42–48.

Liu, Xin. 1998. "Yao: The Practice of Everyday Space in Northern Rural Shaanxi." In Wen-Hsin Yeh, ed., *Landscape, Culture, and Power in Chinese Society*, pp. 129–52. Institute of East Asian Studies, University of California, Berkeley. China Research Monograph 49.

———. 2000. *In One's Own Shadow: An Ethnographic Account of the Condition of Post-Reform Rural China*. Berkeley: University of California Press.

———. 2002. *The Otherness of Self: A Genealogy of Self in Contemporary China*. Ann Arbor: University of Michigan Press.

Lüdtke, Alf. ed. 1995 [1989]. *The History of Everyday Life: Reconstructing Historical Experiences and Ways of Life*. Translated by William Templer. Princeton: Princeton University Press.

Luo Hongguang. 1995. "Shaanbei mizhixian yangjiagoucun jieceng xingcheng de baogao" (A Report on the Formation of Social Stratification in Yangjiagou Village of Mizhi County in Shaanbei). In Li Peilin, ed., pp. 434–96.

———. 1997. "Quanli yu quanwei: heilongtan de fuhao tixi yu zhengzhi pinglun" (Power and Authority: Symbolic System and Political Critique at Heilongtan). In Wang and Wang, eds., pp. 333–88.

———. 1998. *Heilongtanren de lishiguan* (Historical Consciousness of People of the Black Dragon Pool). Working Papers and Translations in Anthropology, vol. 1, issue 7, Oct. 1998. Institute of Sociology and Anthropology, Beijing University.

———. 1999. *Kokuryuutan: chyuugoku hokubu nooson ni okeru zai wo meguru gireiteki katei no kenkyuu* (The Black Dragon Pool: A Study on the Ritual Process of Property in Northern Rural China). Kyoto: Koroosha.

———. 2000. *Budengjia jiaohuan: weirao caifu de laodong yu xiaofei* (Exchanges of Unequal Value: Work and Consumption Around Wealth). Hangzhou: Zhejiang renmin chubanshe.

Luo Yong, and John Lagerwey, eds. 1997. *Gannan diqu de miaohui yu zongzu* (Temple Festivals and Lineages in Gannan). Traditional Hakka Society Series, No. 3. HK: International Hakka Studies Association, Overseas Chinese Archives, and l'Ecole Française d'Extrême-Orient.

Madsen, Richard. 1984. *Morality and Power in a Chinese Village*. Berkeley: University of California Press.

Mallon, Florencia E. 1995. *Peasant and Nation: The Making of Postcolonial Mexico and Peru*. Berkeley: University of California Press.

McFarland, Horace Neill. 1967. *The Rush Hour of the Gods: A Study of New Religious Movements in Japan*. New York: Macmillan.

McLeod, James R. 1999. "The Sociodrama of Presidential Politics: Rhetoric, Ritual, and Power in the Era of Teledemocracy." *American Anthropologist* 101(2): 359–73.

Meskill, Johanna Menzel. 1979. *A Chinese Pioneer Family: The Lins of Wu-feng, Taiwan 1729–1895*. Princeton, NJ: Princeton University Press.

Messick, Brinkley. 1993. *The Calligraphic State: Textual Domination and History in a Muslim Society*. Berkeley: University of California Press.

Mintz, Sidney W. 1974 [1960]. *Worker in the Cane: A Puerto Rican Life History*. New York: The Norton Library.

Morgan, Carole. 1998. "Old Wine in a New Bottle: A New Set of Oracle Slips from China." *Journal of Chinese Religions* 26: 1–20.

Moskowitz, Marc L. 2001. *The Haunting Fetus: Abortion, Sexuality, and the Spirit World in Taiwan*. Honolulu: University of Hawaii Press.

Mueggler, Eric. 2001. *The Age of Wild Ghosts: Memory, Violence, and Place in Southwest China*. Berkeley: University of California Press.

Murray, Julia K. 2002. "Varied Views of the Sage: Illustrated Narratives of the Life of Confucius." In Thomas A. Wilson, ed., *On Sacred Grounds: Culture, Society, Politics, and the Formation of the Cult of Confucius*, pp. 222–64. Cambridge, MA: Harvard University Asia Center.

Myrdal, Jan. 1965. *Report from a Chinese Village* (translated from the Swedish by Maurice Michael). New York: Pantheon Books.

Naquin, Susan. 1988. "Funerals in North China: Uniformity and Variation." In Watson and Rawski, eds., pp. 37–70.

———. 1992. "The Peking Pilgrimage to Miao-feng Shan: Religious Organizations and Sacred Site." In Susan Naquin and Chun-Fang Yü, eds., *Pilgrims and Sacred Sites in China*, pp. 333–77. Berkeley: University of California Press.

———. 2000. *Peking: Temples and City Life, 1400–1900*. Berkeley: University of California Press.

Nasaw, David. 1993. *Going Out: The Rise and Fall of Public Amusements*. Cambridge, MA: Harvard University Press.

Nee, Victor. 1985. "Peasant Household Individualism." *International Journal of Sociology* 14(4): 50–76.

Needham, Rodney. 1972. *Belief, Language, and Experience*. Oxford: Blackwell.

O'Brien, Kevin J. 1994. "Villagers' Committees: Implementing Political Reform in China's Villages." *The Australian Journal of Chinese Affairs* 32: 33–59.

Oi, Jean C. 1988. "The Chinese Village, Inc." In Bruce L. Reynolds, ed., *Chinese Economic Reform: How Far, How Fast?* pp. 67–87. Boston, MA: Academic Press.

———. 1989. *State and Peasant in Contemporary China: The Political Economy of Village Government*. Berkeley: University of California Press.

———. 1999. *Rural China Takes Off: Institutional Foundations of Economic Reform*. Berkeley: University of California Press.

Oi, Jean C., and Andrew G. Walder, eds. 1999. *Property Rights and Economic Reform in China*. Stanford: Stanford University Press.

Ortner, Sherry B. 1978. *Sherpas Through Their Rituals*. Cambridge: Cambridge University Press.

———. 1989. *High Religion: A Cultural and Political History of Sherpa Buddhism*. Princeton, NJ: Princeton University Press.

Oxfeld, Ellen. 1993. *Blood, Sweat, and Mahjong: Family and Enterprise in an Overseas Chinese Community*. Ithaca, NY: Cornell University Press.

Ozouf, Mona. 1988. *Festivals and the French Revolution*. Translated by Alan Sheridan. Cambridge, MA: Harvard University Press.

Palmer, David. 2003. "Modernity and Millenialism in China: Qigong and the Birth of Falun Gong." *Asian Anthropology* 2: 79–110.

———. forthcoming. *Qigong Fever: Body, Science, and the Politics of Religion in China, 1949–1999*. London: Hurst.

Pan Nianying. 1997. *Fupin shouji* (Fieldnotes on My Poverty Relief Work). Shanghai: Shanghai wenyi chubanshe.

Paper, Jordan. 1996. "Mediums and Modernity: The Institutionalization of Ecstatic Religious Functionaries in Taiwan." *Journal of Chinese Religions* 24: 105–29.

Parsons, James Bunyan. 1970. *The Peasant Rebellions of the Late Ming Dynasty*. Tucson: University of Arizona Press.

Pas, Julian. 1984. "Temple Oracles in a Chinese City: A Study of the Use of Temple Oracles in Taichung, Central Taiwan." *Journal of the Hong Kong Branch of the Royal Asiatic Society* 24: 1–45.

———. 1996. "Religious Life in Present Day Taiwan; A Field Observations Report: 1994–95." *Journal of Chinese Religions* 24: 131–58.

Perry, Elizabeth J., and Mark Selden, eds. 2000. *Chinese Society: Change, Conflict and Resistance*. London: Routledge.

Pickowicz, Paul G. 1994. "Memories of Revolution and Collectivization in China: The Unauthorized Reminiscences of a Rural Intellectual." In Rubie S. Watson, ed., pp. 127–48.

Pieke, Frank N. 2004. "Contours of an Anthropology of the Chinese State: Political Structure, Agency and Economic Development in Rural China." *Journal of the Royal Anthropological Institute (N.S.)* 10: 517–38.

Potter, Sulamith Heins, and Jack M. Potter. 1990. *China's Peasants: The Anthropology of a Revolution.* Cambridge: Cambridge University Press.

Rafael, Vicente L. 2003. "The Cell Phone and the Crowd: Messianic Politics in the Contemporary Philippines." *Public Culture* 15(3): 399–425.

Rankin, Mary Backus. 1986. *Elite Activism and Political Transformation in China: Zhejiang Province, 1865–1911.* Stanford: Stanford University Press.

Rankin, Mary Backus, and Joseph W. Esherick. 1990. "Concluding Remarks." In Joseph W. Esherick and Mary Backus Rankin, eds., pp. 305–45.

Rawski, Evelyn S. 1986. "The Ma Landlords of Yang-chia-kou in Late Ch'ing and Republican China." In Patricia B. Ebrey and James L. Watson, eds., *Kinship Organization in Late Imperial China, 1000–1940,* pp. 245–73. Berkeley: University of California Press.

———. 1988. "A Historian's Approach to Chinese Death Ritual." In Watson and Rawski, eds., pp. 20–34.

Reader, Ian, and George J. Tanabe Jr. 1998. *Practically Religious: Worldly Benefits and the Common Religion of Japan.* Honolulu: University of Hawaii Press.

Redfield, Robert. 1956. "The Social Organization of Tradition." In *Peasant Society and Culture,* pp. 40–59. Chicago: University of Chicago Press.

Roberts, John M., Chien Chiao, and Triloki N. Pandey. 1975. "Meaningful God Sets From a Chinese Personal Pantheon and a Hindu Personal Pantheon." *Ethnology* 14(2): 121–48.

Roberts, John M., Saburo Morita, and L. Keith Brown. 1986. "Personal Categories for Japanese Sacred Places and Gods: Views Elicited from a Conjugal Pair." *American Anthropologist* 88(4): 807–24.

Robinson, Thomas W. 1972. "Lin Biao as an Elite Type." In Scalapino ed., pp. 149–95.

Rohsenow, Hill Gates. 1973. "Prosperity Settlement: The Politics of *Pai-pai* in Taipei, Taiwan." PhD diss., Department of Anthropology, University of Michigan.

Rosello, Mireille. 2001. *Postcolonial Hospitality: The Immigrant as Guest.* Stanford: Stanford University Press.

Rowe, William T. 1998. "Ancestral Rites and Political Authority in Late Imperial China: Chen Hongmou in Jiangxi." *Modern China* 24(4): 378–407.

Ruf, Gregory A. 1998. *Cadres and Kin: Making a Socialist Village in West China, 1921–1991.* Stanford: Stanford University Press.

Sangren, P. Steven. 1984a. "Traditional Chinese Corporations: Beyond Kinship." *Journal of Asian Studies* 43(3): 391–415.

———. 1984b. "Great Tradition and Little Traditions Reconsidered: The Question of Cultural Integration in China." *Journal of Chinese Studies* 1: 1–24.

———. 1987. *History and Magical Power in a Chinese Community.* Stanford: Stanford University Press.

———. 2000. *Chinese Sociologics: An Anthropological Account of the Role of Alienation in Social Reproduction.* London: Athlone Press.

———. 2003. "Anthropology and Identity Politics in Taiwan: The Relevance of Local Religion." In Paul R. Katz and Murray A. Rubinstein, eds., pp. 253–87.

Scalapino, Robert A., ed. 1972. *Elites in the People's Republic of China*. Seattle: University of Washington Press.

Schipper, Kristopher M. 1974. "The Written Memorial in Taoist Ceremonies." In Arthur P. Wolf, ed., *Religion and Ritual in Chinese Society*, pp. 309–24. Stanford: Stanford University Press.

Schoenhals, Michael. 1992. *Doing Things with Words in Chinese Politics: Five Studies*. Berkeley: University of California Press.

Scott, James. 1998. *Seeing Like a State: How Certain Schemes to Improve the Human Condition Have Failed*. New Haven, CT: Yale University Press.

Seaman, Gary. 1978. *Temple Organization in a Chinese Village*. Asian Folklore and Social Life Monographs, Vol. 101. Taipei: The Orient Cultural Service.

———. 1987. *Journey to the North: An Ethnohistorical Analysis and Annotated Translation of the Chinese Folk Novel "Pei-yu chi."* Berkeley: University of California Press.

Selden, Mark. 1971. *The Yenan Way in Revolutionary China*. Cambridge, MA: Harvard University Press.

———. 1993. "Family Strategies and Structures in Rural North China." In Deborah Davis and Stevan Harrell, eds., *Chinese Families in the Post-Mao Era*, pp. 139–64. Berkeley: University of California Press.

Seybolt, Peter J. 1996. *Throwing the Emperor from His Horse: Portrait of a Village Leader in China, 1923–1995*. Boulder, CO: Westview.

Shaanxi nianjian (Shaanxi Yearbook). 1998. Xi'an: Shaanxi nianjianshe.

Shahar, Meir, and Robert P. Weller, eds. 1996. *Unruly Gods: Divinity and Society in China*. Honolulu: University of Hawaii Press.

Sheridan, James E. 1966. *Chinese Warlord: The Career of Feng Yü-hsiang*. Stanford: Stanford University Press.

Shryock, Andrew. 1997. *Nationalism and the Genealogical Imagination: Oral History and Textual Authority in Tribal Jordan*. Berkeley: University of California Press.

Shu Hsin-yi. 1969. "The Cultural Ecology of the Locust Cult in Traditional China." *Annals of the Association of American Geographers* 59(4): 731–52.

Shue, Vivienne. 1995. "State Sprawl: The Regulatory State and Social Life in a Small Chinese City." In Davis, Kraus, Naughton, and Perry, eds., pp. 90–112.

Silverstein, Michael, and Greg Urban, eds. 1996. *Natural Histories of Discourse*. Chicago: University of Chicago Press.

Singer, Milton. 1972. *When a Great Tradition Modernizes: An Anthropological Approach to Indian Civilization*. New York: Praeger Publishers.

Siu, Helen F. 1989a. *Agents and Victims in South China: Accomplices in Rural Revolution*. New Haven, CT: Yale University Press.

———. 1989b. "Recycling Rituals: Politics and Popular Culture in Contemporary Rural China." In Richard Madsen, Perry Link, and Paul Pickowicz, eds., *Unofficial China: Essays in Popular Culture and Thought*. Boulder, CO: Westview.

———. 1990. "Recycling Tradition: Culture, History, and Political Economy in the Chrysanthemum Festivals of South China." *Comparative Study of Society and History* 32(4): 765–94.

Siu, Helen F., and David Faure, eds. 1995. *Down to Earth: The Territorial Bond in South China.* Stanford: Stanford University Press.

Skinner, G. William. 1964–65. "Marketing and Social Structure in Rural China." *Journal of Asian Studies* 24(1): 3–43; (2):195–228; (3):363–99.

———. 1971. "Chinese Peasants and the Closed Community: An Open and Shut Case." *Comparative Studies in Society and History* 13(3): 270–81.

———, ed. 1977. *The City in Late Imperial China.* Stanford: Stanford University Press.

Solomon, Richard H. 1971. *Mao's Revolution and the Chinese Political Culture.* Berkeley: University of California Press.

Stafford, Charles. 2000. *Separation and Reunion in Modern China.* Cambridge: Cambridge University Press.

Stoller, Paul. 1989. *The Taste of Ethnographic Things: The Senses in Anthropology.* Philadelphia: University of Pennsylvania Press.

Sutton, Donald. 2003. *Steps of Perfection: Exorcistic Performers and Chinese Religion in Twentieth-Century Taiwan.* Harvard University Asia Center. Cambridge, MA: Harvard University Press.

Teiser, Stephen F. 1988. *The Ghost Festival in Medieval China.* Princeton, NJ: Princeton University Press.

———. 1995. "Popular Religion." Chinese Religions—The State of the Field Part II. *The Journal of Asian Studies* 54(2): 378–95.

Thompson, Roger R. 1996. "Twilight of the Gods in the Chinese Countryside: Christians, Confucians, and the Modernizing State, 1861–1911." In Daniel H. Bays, ed., *Christianity in China: From the Eighteenth Century to the Present*, pp. 53–72. Stanford: Stanford University Press.

Tsing, Anna Lowenhaupt. 1993. *In the Realm of the Diamond Queen: Marginality in an Out-of-the-Way Place.* Princeton, NJ: Princeton University Press.

Turner, Victor. 1967. *The Forest of Symbols: Aspects of Ndembu Ritual.* Ithaca, NY: Cornell University Press.

———. 1969. *The Ritual Process: Structure and Anti-Structure.* Ithaca, NY: Cornell University Press.

Unger, Jonathan. 1984. "The Class System in Rural China: A Case Study." In James L. Watson, ed., *Class and Social Stratification in Post-Revolution China*, pp. 121–41. Cambridge: Cambridge University Press.

Van Gennep, Arnold. 1960 [1909]. *The Rites of Passage.* Chicago: University of Chicago Press.

Vermeer, Eduard B. 1991. *Chinese Local History: Stone Inscriptions from Fukien in the Sung to Ch'ing Periods.* Boulder, CO: Westview.

Volkman, Toby Alice. 1985. *Feast of Honor: Ritual and Change in the Toraja Highlands.* Urbana and Chicago: University of Illinois Press.

Walder, Andrew G., ed. 1995. *The Waning of the Communist State: Economic Origins of Political Decline in China and Hungary.* Berkeley: University of California Press.

Waldron, Arthur. 1990. *The Great Wall of China: From History to Myth.* Cambridge: Cambridge University Press.

Wang Chengyun and Ma Yongsheng, eds. 1990. *Yulinshi minjian wenxue jicheng jingxuan* (Best Selections of Folk Literature in Yulin City). Yulin City Cultural Bureau.

Wang, Jing. 1996. *High Culture Fever: Politics, Aesthetics, and Ideology in Deng's China.* Berkeley: University of California Press.

Wang Mingming. 1996. *Shequ de licheng: Xicun hanren jiazu de ge'an yanjiu* (A Community's Path: A Case Study of a Han Lineage in Xicun). Tianjin renmin chubanshe.

Wang Mingming and Wang Sifu (Stephan Feuchtwang), eds. 1997. *Xiangtu shehui de zhixu, gongzheng yu quanwei* (Order, Justice and Authority in Rural Society). Zhongguo zhengfa daxue chubanshe.

Wank, David L. 1995. "Bureaucratic Patronage and Private Business: Changing Networks of Power in Urban China." In Andrew G. Walder, ed., pp. 153–83. Berkeley: University of California Press.

———. 1999. *Commodifying Communism: Business, Trust, and Politics in a Chinese City.* Cambridge: Cambridge University Press.

Watson, James L. 1985. "Standardizing the Gods: The Promotion of T'ien Hou ('Empress of Heaven') Along the South China Coast, 960–1960." In Johnson, Nathan, and Rawski, eds., pp. 292–324.

———. 1988a. "Funeral Specialists in Cantonese Society: Pollution, Performance, and Social Hierarchy." In Watson and Rawski, eds., pp. 109–34.

———. 1988b. "The Structure of Chinese Funerary Rites: Elementary Forms, Ritual Sequence, and the Primacy of Performance." In Watson and Rawski, eds., pp. 3–19.

Watson, James L., and Evelyn S. Rawski, eds. 1988. *Death Ritual in Late Imperial and Modern China.* Berkeley: University of California Press.

Watson, Rubie S. 1988. "Remembering the Dead: Graves and Politics in Southeastern China." In James L. Watson and Evelyn S. Rawski, eds., pp. 203–27.

———. ed. 1994. *Memory, History, and Opposition Under State Socialism.* Santa Fe: School of American Research Press.

Weller, Robert P. 1985. "Bandits, Beggars, and Ghosts: The Failure of State Control Over Religious Interpretation in Taiwan." *American Ethnologist* 12(1): 46–61.

———. 1987a. *Unities and Diversities in Chinese Religion.* Seattle: University of Washington Press.

———. 1987b. "The Politics of Ritual Disguise: Repression and Response in Taiwanese Popular Religion." *Modern China* 13(1): 17–39.

———. 1994a. "Capitalism, Community, and the Rise of Amoral Cults in Taiwan." In Charles F. Keyes, Laurel Kendall, and Helen Hardacre, eds., *Asian Visions of Authority: Religion and the Modern States of East and Southeast Asia,* pp. 141–64. Honolulu: University of Hawaii Press.

———. 1994b. *Resistance, Chaos and Control in China: Taiping Rebels, Taiwanese Ghosts and Tiananmen.* Seattle: University of Washington Press.

———. 1999. *Alternate Civilities: Democracy and Culture in China and Taiwan.* Boulder, CO: Westview.

Wen Chung-i. 1991. "Guanmin jieji yu jieji yishi: zhongguo de jieji muoshi" (A Chinese Model of Class and Class Consciousness). *Bulletin of Institute of Ethnology* 72: 63–106.

Whyte, Martin K. 1974. *Small Groups and Political Rituals in China.* Berkeley: University of California Press.

Wilson, Scott. 1994. "About Face: Social Networks and Prestige Politics in Contemporary Shanghai Villages." PhD diss., Department of Government, Cornell University.

Winston, Diane. 1999. *Red-Hot and Righteous: The Urban Religion of the Salvation Army.* Cambridge, MA: Harvard University Press.

Wolf, Arthur P. 1970. "Chinese Kinship and Mourning Dress." In Maurice Freedman, ed., *Family and Kinship in Chinese Society*, pp. 189–207. Stanford: Stanford University Press.

———. 1974a. "Gods, Ghosts, and Ancestors." In Arthur P. Wolf, ed., *Religion and Ritual in Chinese Society*, pp. 131–82. Stanford: Stanford University Press.

———. 1974b. "Introduction." In Arthur P. Wolf, ed., *Religion and Ritual in Chinese Society*, pp. 1–18. Stanford: Stanford University Press.

———. 1974c. "Preface." In Arthur P. Wolf, ed., *Religion and Ritual in Chinese Society*, pp. v–vii. Stanford: Stanford University Press.

———. 1989. "Social Hierarchy and Cultural Diversity: A Critique of G. William Skinner's View of Chinese Peasant Culture." Proceedings of the Second International Conference on Sinology, Academia Sinica, pp. 311–18. Taibei.

———. 1996. "The 'New Feudalism': A Problem for Sinologists." In Leo Douw and Peter Post, eds., *South China: State, Culture and Social Change during the 20th century*, pp. 77–84. Amsterdam; New York: North-Holland.

Wolf, Eric. 1966. *Peasants.* Englewood Cliffs, NJ: Prentice-Hall.

———. 1967 [1957]. "Closed Corporate Peasant Communities in Mesoamerica and Central Java." In Jack M. Potter et al., eds., *Peasant Society: A Reader*, pp. 230–46. Boston, MA: Little, Brown and Company.

Wu Cheng-han. 1988. "The Temple Fairs in Late Imperial China." PhD diss., Princeton University.

Xu Hong (with comments by Liu Cuirong). 1982. "Ming hongwu nianjian de renkou yixi" (Migrations during the Hongwu Years of the Ming Dynasty). In *The First Conference on History and Social Change in China (Chinese Social History)*, Conference Publication Volume One, pp. 235–96. Taibei: Sanmin zhuyi Institute of Academia Sinica.

Yan, Yunxiang. 1992. "The Impact of Rural Reform on Economic and Social Stratification in a Chinese Village." *Australian Journal of Chinese Affairs* 27: 1–23.

———. 1996a. "The Culture of Guanxi in a North China Village." *The China Journal* 35: 1–25.

———. 1996b. *The Flow of Gifts: Reciprocity and Social Networks in a Chinese Village.* Stanford: Stanford University Press.

———. 2003. *Private Life Under Socialism: Love, Intimacy, and Family Change in a Chinese Village, 1949–1999.* Stanford: Stanford University Press.

Yang, C. K. 1961. *Religion in Chinese Society: A Study of Contemporary Social Functions of Religion and Some of Their Historical Factors.* Berkeley: University of California Press.

Yang, Mayfair Mei-hui. 1994. *Gifts, Favors, and Banquets: The Art of Social Relationships in China.* Ithaca, NY: Cornell University Press.

———. 2000. "Putting Global Capitalism in Its Place: Economic Hybridity, Bataille, and Ritual Expenditure." *Current Anthropology* 41(4): 477–509.

———. 2004. "Spatial Struggles: Postcolonial Complex, State Disenchantment, and Popular Reappropriation of Space in Rural Southeast China." *Journal of Asian Studies* 63(3): 719–55.

Younger, Paul. 2001. *Playing Host to Deity: Festival Religion in the South Indian Tradition.* Oxford University Press.

Yu, Shuenn-der. 2004. "Hot and Noisy: Taiwan's Night Market Culture." In David Jordan, Andrew Morris, and Marc L. Moskowitz, eds., *The Minor Arts of Daily Life: Popular Culture in Taiwan*, pp. 129–49. Honolulu: University of Hawaii Press.

Zeitlin, Judith T., and Lydia H. Liu, eds. 2003. *Writing and Materiality in China: Essays in Honor of Patrick Hanan.* Cambridge, MA: Harvard University Press.

Zeitlyn, David. 2001. "Finding Meaning in the Text: The Process of Interpretation in Text-Based Divination." *The Journal of the Royal Anthropological Institute* 7(2): 225–40.

Zhang Junyi. 1993. *Yulin fengqing lu* (Accounts of Yulin Culture and Customs). Xi'an: Shaanxi renmin jiaoyu chubanshe.

Zhang, Li. 2001. *Strangers in the City: Reconfigurations of Space, Power, and Social Networks Within China's Floating Population.* Stanford: Stanford University Press.

Zhao Shiyu. 1992. "Ming qing shiqi huabei miaohui yanjiu" (A Study on the Temple Fairs in Northern China during the Ming and Qing Dynasties). *Lishi yanjiu* (Historical Studies, Beijing) 5: 118–30.

———. 1995. "Mingqing shiqi Jiangnan miaohui yu Huabei miaohui de jidian bijiao" (Comparisons between Temple Fairs in Jiangnan and North China During the Ming and Qing Dynasties). In Zhou Tianyou, ed, *Diyu shehui yu chuantong Zhongguo* (Regional Societies and Traditional China), pp. 135–44. Xi'an: Xibei daxue chubanshe.

———. 1996. "Zhongguo chuantong miaohuizhong de kuanghuan jingshen" (The Carnival Spirit in Traditional Chinese Temple Fairs). *Zhongguo Shehui Kexue* 97(1): 183–96.

Zito, Angela. 1997. *Of Body and Brush: Grand Sacrifice as Text/Performance in Eighteenth-Century China.* Chicago: University of Chicago Press.

List of Chinese Characters

Note: Even though this ethnography is about a place in mainland China, where simplified characters have been used since the character reforms in the 1950s, I have elected to use traditional (non-simplified) characters for this character list. The main reason for this choice is considerations of historical continuity: most of the place names, deity names, and Shaanbei native terms are not creations of the socialist era. This list is not comprehensive.

The twelve counties of Yulin Prefecture

Dingbian 定邊
Fugu 府谷
Hengshan 橫山
Jiaxian 佳縣
Jingbian 靖邊
Mizhi 米脂

Qingjian 清澗
Shenmu 神木
Suide 綏德
Wupu 吳堡
Yulin 榆林
Zizhou 子洲

Other place names

Baiyunshan 白雲山
Baotou 包頭
Batawan 八塔灣
Chenjiapo 陳家坡
Guanzhong 關中
Hongliutan 紅柳灘
Longwanggou 龍王溝
Ningxia 寧夏
Shaanbei 陝北

Shaan-Gan-Ning 陝甘寧
Shanxi 山西
Taiheshan (in Yan'an City) 太和山
Taiyuan 太原
Wanfodong 万佛洞
Xi'an 西安
Yan'an 延安
Yinchuan 銀川
Yulin 榆林

Deities and spirits commonly found in Shaanbei:

Bazha 八蜡
Caishen 財神
chenghuang 城隍
daxian 大仙
Dongyue zushi 東嶽祖師
Guan laoye (Guandi) 關老爺
Guanyin 觀音
huxian 狐仙
Laofoye (Buddha) 老佛爺
lingguan 靈官
longwang 龍王
Lüzu (Lü Dongbin) 呂祖

Mawang 馬王
niangniang 娘娘
Qitian dasheng 齊天大聖
Sanguan 三官
Sanqing 三清
Sanxiao niangniang 三霄娘娘
Shanshen 山神
Wenchang 文昌
Yaowang 藥王
Yuhuang dadi 玉皇大帝
Zhenwu zushi 真武祖師

Four-character messages on the Heilongdawang medicine oracle roller:

shangshang daji 上上大吉
xiaxia zhongping 下下中平
kouyuan buming 口願不明
xingren zaohui 行人早回

buhe shendao 不合神道
qianxin qidao 虔心祈禱
quyao daishui 取藥帶水
fuyao nenghao 服藥能好

In the rain gua, the last two phrases are replaced by:

jiri youyu 即日有雨

sanri youyu 三日有雨

Four-character messages on the Longmu niangniang fertility/child rearing oracle roller:

yizi chengming 一子成名
nanshuang nüdui 男雙女對
dezi huanyuan 得子還願
fuyao nenghao 服藥能好

shangshang daji 上上大吉
kouyuan buming 口願不明
buhe shendao 不合神道
qianxin qidao 虔心祈禱

Roles at a funeral:

chipan (duanpan) 持盤 / 端盤
hunguo 葷鍋
hunguotou 葷鍋頭
jingzhuo 淨桌
kanchuishou 看吹手
kanke 看客
kanyinyang (daipingshi) 看陰陽 / 待平士
lingpeng (lingqian) 靈棚 / 靈前
qingke 請客

shaoshui 燒水
shuli 書禮
suguo 素鍋
suguotou 素鍋頭
tugong 土工
xiaozi 孝子
xiwan 洗碗
yanjiu 煙酒
zongling 總領

Other characters

aiguo aijiao 愛國愛教

badahui 八大會

bai wu jinji 百無禁忌

Baiqiuen shenshen (Norman
   Bethune) 白求恩神神

baiqu 白區

baishi 白事

bangongshi 辦公室

banshi 辦事

banxin banyi 半信半疑

baogongtou 包工頭

baoguan 保管

baohuang pai 保皇派

baojia 保甲

baoyou 保佑

beiwen 碑文

benshi 本事

bian 匾

biangong 變工

bianqiang 邊牆

bianshang 邊商

biao 表

bude renxin 不得人心

bu honghuo 不紅火

buke buxin buke quanxin
   不可不信，不可全信

buniao 不尿

bushi 布施

buxing 不行

caili 彩（財）禮

caiyun 財運

cangfan yaoyao 藏反窯窯

chaiqian 拆籤

changdifei 場地費

chaxu geju 差序格局

chengzhen hukou 城鎮戶口

chi fenhui 吃墳會

chouqian 抽籤

chu longgong fengtiao yushun;
   ruhai cang guotai minan
   出龍宮風調雨順 入海藏國泰民安

chuguore 出國熱

chuji 處級

chukou 出口

chuankou 川口

chuanli 川裡

chuantong wenhua 傳統文化

chuishou 吹手

chuke (S.) 出喀

churen (S.) 處人

cungan 村幹

cunmiao 村廟

cunmin gongyue 村民公約

cunmin weiyuanhui 村民委員會

cun shuji 村書記

cunzhang 村長

dabao shen'en 答報神恩

daguofan 大鍋飯

dahui 大會

dahuizhang 大會長

daji 打擊

danwei 單位

danwei lingdao 單位領導

dangguerde 當官兒的

dangjia zuozhu 當家作主

dangyuanhui 黨員會

daodiaolü 倒吊驢

daotale (S.) 倒塌了

daxian 大仙

dayantu 大煙土

diangui 點櫃

dianlaohu 電老虎

dianliju 電力局

dietan (S.) 跌壇

diejihua (S.) 跌計劃

diling renjie 地靈人傑

diqu 地區

diqu renshiju 地區人事局

dishiji 地師級

disikere 迪斯科熱

dizi 弟子

dongpao 冬跑

duigan 隊幹

dundiar 蹲點兒

erji gonglu 二級公路

erren (S.) 兒人

ersun mantang 兒孫滿堂

eryaoling guodao 二么零國道

Falungong 法輪功

fang 房

fen 份

fengjian jiazhang 封建家長

fengjian mixin 封建迷信

fengsu 風俗

fengsu xiguan 風俗習慣

fenhui 墳會

fenjia 分家

fensheng 分牲

fojiao huodong changsuo
    佛教活動場所

fudishiji 副地師級

futingji 副廳級

fugao 訃告

funü zhuren 婦女主任

fuyin 符印

gaili (S.) 街裡

gan honghuo (S.) 趕紅火

ganji 趕集

gao 糕

gao 高

gei Longwangye ta laorenjia
    banshi/xianghuo 給龍王
    爺他老人家辦事 / 相伙

gei renjia chi le 給人家吃了

Gelaohui 哥老會

geming junren 革命軍人

geming shengdi 革命聖地

getihu 個體戶

gongan 公安

gongbu weilin 功簿威霖

gongjia 公家

gongjiaren 公家人

gongjia xiaoche 公家小車

gongjianfa 公檢法

gongshangju 工商局

gongshe lairen la 公社來人啦

gongzuoren 工作人

gua 卦

guapai yishi 掛牌儀式

guan 關

guanche zongjiao zhengce
    貫徹宗教政策

Guanlaoye qian 關老爺籤

guansha 關煞

guanxi buhao 關係不好

guanxi hao 關係好

guanxi keyi 關係可以

guanzhi 官職

guiren 貴人

guoguan 過關

guotai 鍋台

gupiaore 股票熱

haiyan 海眼

hanshi 寒食

hao 好

haoda xigong 好大喜功

hao guanxi 好關係

haoting 好聽

hapi (S.) 黑皮

hehuo 合伙

heiparpar 黑牌兒牌兒

Heilongdawang 黑龍大王

Heilongdawang shenqian
    黑龍大王神籤

helao (S.) 河老?

hetao 河套

honghuo (S.) 紅火

hongparpar 紅牌兒牌兒

hongshi 紅事

hougou 後溝

huaquan 划拳

huaiyingge 懷英閣

huanbao 環保

Huangtudi 黃土地

huangtu gaoyuan 黃土高原

huansu 還俗

Hui 回

hui kande kan mentou jiadao,
　　buhui kande kan honghuo
　　renao 會看的看門頭家道，
　　不會看的看紅火熱鬧

hui niangjia 回娘家

huishou 會首

huiyao 會窯

huiyishi 會議室

huizhang 會長

hukou 戶口

hukouben 戶口本

hun 昏

hundongle me (S.) 婚動了麼

Hunyuanjiao 混元教

huodong 活動

huo zhe ne! 火著呢！

jia nüzi (S.) 嫁女子

jiali zuo 家裡坐

jiancha gongzuo 檢查工作

jiancha yuan 檢察院

jianchen 奸臣

jianggong 匠工

jiang mixin 講迷信

jiaohun 叫魂

jiaojing 交警

jiaojing dadui 交警大隊

jiaoyuju 教育局

jiawushi 家務事

jiebei yishi 揭碑儀式

jiefangqu 解放區

jiexiang 接箱

jieyue 解曰

jiguan danwei 機關單位

jihe 集合

jihua shengyu gongzuo
　　計劃生育工作

jiji 積極

Jin 晉

Jingdaren 井大人

jingjiuge 敬酒歌

jingshen 敬神

jingshen shenzai bujing buguai
　　敬神神在，不敬不怪

jinju 晉劇

jitong 乩童

jiubian zhongzhen 九邊重鎮

jiudi chuzhi 就地處置

jiuquer 酒曲兒

ju 局

jueren (S.) 撅人

juliusuo 拘留所

junchen gushi 君臣故事

kaiguang 開光

kaigui 開櫃

kandiande 看電的

kan honghuo 看紅火

kang 炕

kangshang zuo 炕上坐

keji 科級

kouwai 口外

kuaiji 會計

lajiu 辣酒

langan (S.) 爛稈

langong (S.) 攬工

lanyanghan (S.) 攔羊漢

lanyong zhiquan 濫用職權

laohuihui 老回回

laojiaqin (S.) 老家親

laoqu 老區

lauziat/lau-jiat (Minnan) 鬧熱

layue 臘月

lisheng 禮生

lizhang 禮帳

ling 靈

lingdao 領導

lingsheng 領牲

lingying 靈應

Lingyinghou 靈應侯

linyeju 林業局

liunian yunqi 流年運氣

Longmugong 龍母宮

Longmu niangniang 龍母娘娘

Longsheng dian 龍盛殿

longwang 龍王

Longwanggou daoguan guanli
    weiyuanhui 龍王溝道觀管
    理委員會

Longwanggou shandi shumuyuan
    龍王溝山地樹木園

Longwanggou wenwu guanlisuo
    龍王溝文物管理所

longwangye ta laorenjia
    龍王爺他老人家

longxue cangzhen 龍穴藏珍

lü ken bozi gong bian gong (S.)
    驢啃脖子工變工

luanjia 鑾架

luopan 羅盤

lüse wenming 綠色文明

mafan si le 麻煩死了

mai laoren (S.) 埋老人

maimairen 買賣人

mairen (S.) 埋人

maoguishen 毛鬼神

maomaoqian 毛毛錢

matong (S.) 馬童

mei benshi 沒本事

mei liuxia maming 沒留下罵名

menzi (mer) (S.) 門子（門兒）

mengdi 蒙地

mixin 迷信

mianzi 面子

miaohui 廟會

minban 民辦

minban jiaoshi 民辦教師

ming 命

minjian 民間

minzhengju 民政局

mo 饃

naochang 鬧場

naodai yire 腦袋一熱

naodongfang 鬧洞房

naofang 鬧房

naogeming 鬧革命

naohong 鬧紅

naoshi 鬧市

naoshi 鬧事

naotai 鬧台

nao yijian 鬧意見

neng gudong (S.) 能鼓動

niangniang qian 娘娘籤

pa gongjia menkar 爬公家門檻兒

pailou 牌樓

peng 碰

pi'ning (S.) 皮硬

pingshi 平士

poguansha 破關煞

qian 籤

qianbu 籤簿

qiantong 籤筒

qianzheryao 籤紙兒窯

qianzhi 籤紙

qifu ren 欺負人

qigong 氣功

qima 起馬

Qin 秦

qinqiang 秦腔

qinggongyan 慶功宴

Qinglongdawang 青龍大王

qingming 清明

qiu nilaorenjia baoyou zanmen daji
   dali pingpingan 求你老
   人家保佑咱們大吉大利平平安安

qixi 起戲

qiye danwei 企業單位

qiyu 乞雨

Quanzhenjiao 全真教

qunzhong 群眾

relie huanying 熱烈歡迎

relie qingzhu 熱烈慶祝

remer 熱門兒

renao 熱鬧

ren ping shen, shen ping ren
   人憑神，神憑人

renmin 人民

rensher 人市兒

run wuyue 閏五月

sa ludeng 撒路燈

sanguo 三國

san menzi 三門子

Shaanbei shige hao difang
   陝北是個好地方

Shaanbei xiao xianggang
   陝北小香港

shan gao huangdi yuan 山高皇帝遠

shandi 山地

shanli 山裡

Shanxi dahuaishu 山西大槐樹

shang xitian 上西天

shaozhi 燒紙

shehui liliang 社會力量

shenfen zheng 身份證

shengchandui 生產隊

shengjitu 聖蹟圖

shengtai 生態

shenguan 神官

shengyuan 生員

shenling ganying 神靈感應

shenling renjie 神靈人傑

shenshen 神神

shenshui 神水

shentuan 神團

shenweipai 神位牌

shifu 師傅

shijiang 石匠

shiyun 時運

shiye danwei 事業單位

shouchou (S.) 手稠

shouku 受苦

shoukuren 受苦人

shu 疏

shuji 書記

shuidi 水地

shuiwuju 稅務局

shuixiu 水秀

shuo guchao (S.) 說古朝

songxiang 送箱

suozhang 所長

suqu 蘇區

tandi 灘地

tanggua (S.) 趟卦

taohao 討好

te huo! 特火！

tengshe 騰蛇

tianshi, tili, renhe
   天時，地利，人和

tiaodashen 跳大神

tingji 廳級

tongji (tang-ki; Minnan) 童乩

touban toutiao 頭版頭條

tudifa 土地法

tuhuangdi 土皇帝

wanmin 萬民

weizhu dagou 餵豬打狗

wenhuaju 文化局

wenhuare 文化熱

wenhuazhan 文化站

wenzhong 穩重

wunü xingtang zhuan 五女興唐傳

wushen 巫神

wuyi laodong jie 五一勞動節

xiagang 下崗

xiama 下馬

xian 顯

xianghuo (S.) 相伙

xiangshi (S.) 相事

xianji wenwu 縣級文物

xianling 顯靈

xiantuanji 縣團級

xiaobaihuo menshi 小百貨門市

xiaoche 小車

xiaogong 小工

xiaomi lüdouzhou 小米綠豆粥

xiaozu 小組

xiaozuzhang 小組長

xiazhongnong 下中農

xiebing 邪病

xiexi 寫戲

xilu bianwai 西路邊外

xingle (S.) 行了

xingzhengcun 行政村

xinyongshe 信用社

xinshi 信士

xiongshen 兇神

xitong 系統

xiucai xue yinyang, yibo jiuzhuan
　　秀才學陰陽，一撥就轉

xukouyuan 許口願

xueyingyure 學英語熱

Yan'an shanglai de 延安上來的

yangge 秧歌

yanggere 秧歌熱

yangpigu 羊皮鼓

yangpiren 羊皮人

yangzhai 陽宅

yanmenzi (S.) 沿門子

yao 窰

Yaochidao 瑤池道

yaodong 窰洞

yaogua 藥卦

yeceng qingdi feng gaojue, wuguai
　　limin shuo weiming 也曾清帝封
　　高爵，無怪黎民說威名

yi mabao maomaoqian
　　一麻包毛毛錢

yiban ganbu 一般干部

Yiguandao 一貫道

yinggong 迎供

yinhunfan 引魂旛

yinxifu 引媳婦

yinyang (yinyang xiansheng)
　　陰陽（陰陽先生）

yinzhai 陰宅

you benshi 有本事

yougongzuode 有工作的

youguan lingdao 有關領導

youqian maiqian, meiqian mairen
　　有錢埋錢，沒錢埋人

youqiu biying 有求必應

youren 有人

youshizhishi 有識之士

youyue 又曰

Yuanxiao 元宵

yugua 雨卦

yun 運

zaofanpai 造反派

zaotai 灶台

Zhameian 鍘美案

zhangguide 掌櫃的

Zhangshenguan, Lishenguan,
　　yangqi bianzi qiu dongtan
　　張神官，李神官，揚起辮子屄
　　動彈

zhengdang zongjiao huodong
正當宗教活動
zhengdian 正殿
zhengrizi 正日子
zhengshen (zhengshishen)
正神（正式神）
zhengxie 政協
zhengyue shiwu 正月十五
zhengyue shiwu nao yangge
正月十五鬧秧歌
zhengzhi biaoxian 政治表現
zhigong 職工
zhiqian 紙錢
zhiquan 職權
zhongchen 忠臣
Zhonggong (Zhonghua shengong)
中功（中華神功）

zhongyuan 中原
zhuanguotaide 轉鍋台的
zhuanjia xuezhe 專家學者
zhuanzheng 轉正
zhuanghu 莊戶
zhujia 主家
zhuwang 主王
zirancun 自然村
Zongjiao huodong changsuo
宗教活動場所
zongjiaoju 宗教局
zungui 尊貴
zuo gongde 做功德
zuo gongzuo baogao 做工作
報告
zuoshengyide 做生意的

Index

In this index an "f" after a number indicates a separate reference on the next page, and an "ff" indicates separate references on the next two pages. A continuous discussion over two or more pages is indicated by a span of page numbers, e.g., "57–59." *Passim* is used for a cluster of references in close but not consecutive sequence.

affect, 163, 266n23; and belief, 61; and sociality, 148
agrarian public sphere, 9–12, 15, 18, 166–68, 212, 242; and local state, 238. *See also* peasants; political culture
agriculture, 21ff, 26, 40, 42; irrigation, 21–22, 37, 199, 220f, 243; and herding, 21; colonization of pastureland, 23; agricultural fairs, 48; leaving, 183
Ahern, Emily Martin, 65, 108
Anagnost, Ann S., 8, 211
ancestors, 38, 173, 201; worship, 50; ancestral halls, 1, 50; ancestral scrolls, 50; turned into deities, 50
Ansai County, 140
artisans: craftsmanship, 93, 180–81; stonemasons, 170, 175; Lao Wang as master artisan, 176, 178–81; stone carver, 226f; carpenter, 230
Austin, John, 260n16, 271n25
Australian aboriginals, 158, 163
authority, 13, 191, 246; structure of, 220, 238; and knowledge, 247. *See also* local elites; power

Baiyunshan, 49, 54, 57, 231, 233, 257n14, 259n4, 260n11; eight big congregations

(*badahui*), 54, 258n25; took over by local state, 219
Bali, 151, 235
banks, 208; and temple finance, 112, 114; and embezzlement charges, 199; and house building, 202
banquets, 10; and officials, 36, 216; at funerals, 134; at temple, 142; and *honghuo*, 149–56 *passim*, 163, 166
baojia (neighborhood surveillance system), 25
Baotou, 26, 34, 85
Bataille, Georges, 137
Batawan Village (Eight Tower Bay), 79, 85, 125, 130, 139, 200, 207, 223
Beijing, 212, 222, 227f
belief, 59–77 *passim*, 240; belief system, 6; vs. practice, 59; experienced vs. constructed, 59; and language, 59; as analytical category, 60; in Shaanbei, 60; types of believers, 67; and unbelief, 67; manifest in public discourse, 71, 84. *See also* communities of believers
Bethune, Norman, as deity, 47, 51
birth, 1, 218; and divination, 102
birth control work, 36, 73, 211; policy, 121, 153, 204; and local state, 218–19

304 Index

blasphemy, 66, 70–71, 241. *See also* legends
Boas, Franz, 60, 258n1
Bourdieu, Pierre, 67
bribes, 2, 29, 37, 204, 207, 246; bribing deities, 121
Brook, Timothy, 192, 242
Brown, Michael F., 239
Buddhism, 5, 6, 13, 39, 57, 75, 122, 145f, 158, 211, 216, 251n3; Buddhist monks, 13, 47, 57, 135, 179; as Great Tradition, 44; Daixing Monastery (Yulin City), 45; monasteries, 50; Buddhist Association, 57, 216; funeral service, 57; Tibetan, 62; Zen, 62; propaganda, 122; and places for religious activities, 217
bureaucratic model of divinity, 72–73, 100, 108, 123, 259n6. *See also* personal model of divinity
business, and divine assistance, 64, 83; and divination, 101. *See also* enterprises; entrepreneurs; petty capitalism
business model, and temples, 9, 115, 120

cabinet, incense money, 99f, 112; opening the cabinet, 112–13. *See also* incense donation money
cadres, 16, 185, 189; army man turned, 189. *See also* local state agents; officials
calligraphy, 95ff; emperor's, 91
Canton Delta, 24, 258n3
cars, and privilege, 27; as testimony of mediums' popularity, 56
channeling zone, between local society and local state, 238–39
Chao, Emily, 6
chaxu geju (patterns of differential relations), 69
Chenjiapo Village (Chen Family Slope), 79, 85, 87, 93, 104, 139, 169, 201ff, 230; Primary School, 174
children, 63, 78; soul loss, 50, 56, 63; ritual protection of, 56, 141; and religious habitus, 67; and fertility goddesses, 120; education of, 183, 223
Christianity, 13; Christian religiosity, 60–62; church, 62; congregation, 62. *See also* religions
cigarettes, 129ff, 137, 141, 170, 217, 265n10; as offering, 47, 51, 257n13
cities, 34, 190

City Gods, 72, 91
civil collectivities, 118
civil society, 11, 15
class, 10, 27, 189; struggle, 11; designation, 174, 189; poor-peasant class domination, 193
cogeneration and reverberation, of interpretations, 92
Cole, Alan, 122
collective effervescence, 149, 158, 163. See also *honghuo*
collectivization, 25, 70, 174; decollectivization, 9, 175; brigades, 35, 119, 174f, 189; commune, 70, 189, 254n27; production teams, 71, 119; brigade leaders, 174, 189; work-points, 175. *See also* Maoist period
commemoration, 92, 228; and Communist top leaders, 51; commemorative stele, 92, 97, 225–29; ceremony, 230–38
commerce, at temple festival, 53, 139ff, 160, 216, 231
Communism, 2, 24; Communists, 46, 78, 145; Godless Communist China, 62
Communist Party, 13, 28, 190, 204; membership, 28, 36, 71, 173f, 190, 219; Party secretaries, 12, 27, 36f, 71, 108, 174f, 179, 187, 193, 200, 205, 219, 246, 259n5, 270n10; county headquarters, 215 (figure). *See also* party-state; state
Communist Revolution, 9; guerrillas, 24; revolutionary holyland, 24; old regions, 26
communities, village, 7–13 *passim*, 68–69, 246f; resistance against the state, 7–14 *passim*, 69, 72, 212, 215, 240; disruptive communities, 10; reified, 14; blessedness, 51; and temple building, 52; communal solidarity, 68; as moral communities, 68; communal concerns and religiosity, 69; communal hegemony, 69–72, 219; as discourse community, 71; interpretive community, 97. *See also* villages
communities of believers, 10, 52, 69f, 241
computer, 183
conferences, 177, 183, 232; of the gods, 244
conflicts: intra-village, 37–38; between villagers and Christian converts, 68, 70;

also deities; religions; religious administration; religious specialists; social organization of traditions; temple festivals; temples; traditions
possession, spirit, 52, 54f, 257n22. *See also* spirit mediumism
poverty, 26, 32
power, 3, 12–13, 18, 27, 186, 191, 205, 229, 236, 238, 243; divine, 65, 84, 94, 98f, 120, 165f, 171, 209, 241f; and officials, 186; genealogy of, 189–90; powerlessness, 206; local, 246. *See also* efficacy
practice, religious, *see* religiosity
prayers, 62, 64, 93, 138; Christian, 62
processions, 140, 142, 165, 231; processional insignia, 90f, 94; funeral, 155, 263n21. *See also* temple festivals
propaganda, 36; temple, 89, 120, 232; socialist, 95, 248
prostitution, 212; prostitutes, 79, 141
public sphere: bourgeois, 10f; multiple, 10; and a political public, 11. *See also* agrarian public sphere; civil society

qigong, 7, 75, 105, 211; Falungong, 6, 75, 211, 248; Zhonggong, 211, 248; Xianggong, 248; Yuanjigong, 248; and space, 248
Qin (central Shaanxi) culture, 20, 252n1
Qingming (grave-sweeping day), 50, 173
Quanzhou, 243

rain, 21, 64, 68, 77, 79, 93, 121; rain-begging ritual, 77, 94, 214, 259n3; divination for, 104
rain gods, *see* dragon kings; Heilongdawang
reciprocity, 126, 131, 137, 143. *See also* mutual aid
Red Army, 24
red guards, 1, 70. *See also* Cultural Revolution
Redfield, Robert, 124
red-hot sociality, see *honghuo*
reductionism, 9
reforestation, 5, 176–77, 183, 202, 207, 247. *See also* Longwanggou; tree planting
reform era, 1–8 *passim*, 12, 15, 28, 121, 150, 217, 229, 245f; economic reforms,

1, 10; privatization, 29, 238; houses, 41; and local elites, 191, 193f; state relaxed toward popular religion, 218; environmentalism in, 222
relationships: among people, 137, 242; between deities and people, 2, 65, 75, 124, 165, 170, 242
religions: Three in One cult, 10; officially recognized, 13, 213; Japanese, 9; one or many Chinese religion debate, 73–76; religious system, 73; Hinduism, 124; diffused, 143; Protestantism, 211; Catholicism, 211, 241; Western bias in viewing religious revivalism, 240. *See also* religiosity; religious administration
religiosity, 2, 13, 17, 48, 61–68, 236, 242f; doing religion, 2, 123, 240; theological, 7, 75, 242; atheism, 13, 48, 62, 71, 219; modalities of doing religion, 17, 73–76, 124, 242; Christian, 60–62; ritualism vs. piety, 61; religious habitus, 61–68 *passim*, 241; pluralism, 62; crises and, 63; basic principles, 65–66; Hindu, 66; diversity of, 74; religious conceptions, vs. doing religion, 74–76; religious consumerism, 122–23; and *honghuo*, 164. *See also* worship
religious administration, 224, 249; temple registration, 213–18 *passim*; policies, 213–18 *passim*, 233; places for religious activities, 217, 270n1
religious specialists, 2, 13, 17, 45, 54–58, 61, 67, 74ff, 122–29 *passim*, 146, 236; as counterrevolutionaries, 47; as grassroots cultural brokers, 95; hiring of, 136, 143–45, 263n20. *See also* Buddhism; Daoism; spirit mediums; yinyang masters
ren ping shen, shen ping ren (people depend on gods, gods depend on people), 138, 169–71
renao, see *honghuo*
Republican period, 9, 23f, 45, 86f, 150, 165
resistance, *see under* communities
reunion: family reunion, 156; reunion imperative, 156
Rites of Passage, The, 157
rituals, 1–13 *passim*, 75, 125, 129, 157; bricolage, 6; expenditure, 8, 137; ritual systems, 10; ritual dramas, 44, 53; para-

phernalia, 54, 56, 131; at funerals, 56;
passing the obstacle (*guoguan*), 56, 141;
sacrifice, 68; zone of ritual interaction,
99–101; orthodoxy vs. orthopraxy, 127,
258n3; ritual handbooks, 136; ritual
process, 157; initiation, 157; rite of passage model, 157–58; and symbols, 158;
studies, 158; rite of convergence model,
158, 167; semiotic and hermeneutic
approaches, 163; actions, 164; ritual
economy, 196; ritual indictment, 203–8;
disguise, 224; manipulation, 224, 236;
timing of ritual action, 230, 236; and
politics of legitimation, 230–39; form
and contents, 230, 237; ritual labor,
236; political drama, 237. *See also* religious specialists
roads, 26, 42, 85, 220, 233, 243; and commerce, 31; and village settlement patterns, 41; National Highway 210, 85f,
141f
Roberts, Chiao, and Pandey, 66
Romance of the Three Kingdoms, 38
Ruf, Gregory, 12
rural China, 5, 10, 16, 240–43 *passim*,
249; images of rural life, 217

sacrifice, 3, 68f, 99–100
salaries, 29, 36, 114–17 *passim*, 206f
Sangren, Steven, 145, 165, 258n2
Schoenhals, Michael, 235
scholars, and politics of legitimation, 217,
232, 244
schools, 2, 5, 24, 45, 116, 139, 174, 205,
220f, 228, 243; school building, 199;
non-government-operated, 223. *See also*
under Longwanggou
Seaman, Gary, 192
Second United Front, 24
secret societies, 24
sectarianism, 8, 24, 46f, 75, 166; Hunyuanjiao, 24, 46f; Yiguandao, 46f;
Yaochidao, 46; leaders persecuted, 47
sensations, 159–64; sensoric, 162; sensorium, 162
separation constraint, 156
serving the god, 243
Shaanbei, 2, 4 (map), 5, 16, 20–43, 78,
175, 243; in north-central China, 5,
44; townships (*zhen*), 14; in northwest
macroregion, 21; landscape, 21–22

(fig.), 222, 228; history, 22–26, 258n2;
natural resources, 26, 32, 43, 253n12;
rural districts (*xiang*), 27, 34; market
towns, 34; topography, 35, 41, 228
Shaan-Gan-Ning Border Region, 24, 44,
46, 78, 256n6
Shaanxi Province, 4, 20–21, 85; population, 21
Shandong Province, 244; granite from,
226
Shanxi Province, 20–26 *passim*, 46, 53, 85,
142, 151, 226
Shen Tzu (Shenzi), 169, 194
Shenmu County, 33, 37, 154
shepherd, 154
Shijiazhuang, 176
Sichuan Province, 12, 193, 219, 244
Singer, Milton, 124
sites, sacred, 67
Siu, Helen F., 6, 258n3
Skinner, G. William, 21, 34, 35–36
small group (political study group), 167
snakes, 88, 169, 195
Snow, Edgar, 21
social actors, 2
social co-presence, *see* sociality
social organization of traditions, 9, 52,
124, 143, 145; rotation, 8; organizational simplicity, 143, 145–56. *See also*
popular religion; traditions
social stratification, 27–34 *passim*
social suffering, 32
socialism, 10, 167, 248; socialist culture, 1,
95, 247–48; socialist spiritual civilization, 247. *See also* Maoist period
sociality, 10, 147–68 *passim*; at cinema,
148; American, 148; religion-based,
168. See also *honghuo*
sociothermic affect, 163, 167. See also
honghuo
sorcery, Lao Wang accused of, 203–8
soul, 63; loss, 55f; soul-directing canopy
(*yinhunfan*), 56; soul-calling (*jiaohun*),
63
space, 8, 248; social, 147; as form, 167
speech, 204, 231–35; bureaucratic speech
genre, 234
speech acts, 260n16. *See also* text acts
spirit mediumism, 10, 214, 216; spirit
mediums, 13, 44–57 *passim*, 63, 75,
154, 179, 211, 256n6, 257n12; and